D1223458

LONDON RECORD SOCIETY
PUBLICATIONS

VOLUME VIII
FOR THE YEAR 1972

THE PORT AND TRADE OF
EARLY ELIZABETHAN LONDON
DOCUMENTS

EDITED BY

BRIAN DIETZ

LONDON RECORD SOCIETY

1972

© *London Record Society*

SBN 9009 5205 9

*Transcripts of Crown-copyright records in the Public
Record Office appear by permission of the Controller
of H.M. Stationery Office.*

THIS VOLUME IS PUBLISHED WITH THE HELP
OF A GRANT FROM THE LATE
MISS ISOBEL THORNLEY'S BEQUEST TO
THE UNIVERSITY OF LONDON

Printed in Great Britain by
W & J MACKAY LIMITED, CHATHAM, KENT

CONTENTS

PREFACE

The present volume contains a calendar of the London Port Book for 1567/8, recording native and Hanse imports, together with a number of other documents illustrating the port and trade of London in the early years of Elizabeth I's reign. Nearly all of these are preserved in the Public Record Office, and the London Record Society is indebted to the Keeper of Public Records for permission to publish them.

Dr. Dietz has asked me to express his indebtedness to the University of Glasgow for leave of absence, and a travel and maintenance grant which enabled him to complete the volume.

William Kellaway
Honorary General Editor

ABBREVIATIONS

Books and manuscripts

E.	Exchequer (Public Record Office)
Guildhall MSS	Guildhall Library, London
I.p.m. London	*Abstracts of Inquisitiones post mortem relating to the city of London . . . during the Tudor period*, i (1896) ed. G. S. Fry; ii (1901) ed. S. J. Madge; iii (1908) ed. E. A. Fry
Lans.	Lansdowne Manuscripts (British Museum)
PCC	Prerogative Court of Canterbury Will (Public Record Office, formerly Somerset House)
S.P.	State Papers (Public Record Office)
Stow, *Survey*	John Stow, *Survey of London*, ed. C. L. Kingsford, 2 vols (Oxford, 1908)
Willan, *Rates*	*Tudor Book of Rates*, ed. T. S. Willan (Manchester, 1962)

Weights and measures

brl	barrel
cwt	hundredweight of 112 lbs
doz.	dozen
grs	gross
hd	hundred (content unknown)
hhd	hogshead
lb	pound
pc.	piece
qr	quarter
thou.	thousand (as for pins etc.)
yds	yards

INTRODUCTION

The port and customs

The documents in this volume consist of a port book recording native imports into London in 1567/8 and certain other texts illustrative of the port's functions and topography in the early Elizabethan period. They were the product, however, of a systematic and thorough reform of the customs which was begun in the reign of Mary. Following the report of the commission on the king's courts of revenue in 1552 the lord treasurer, the marquis of Winchester, issued a revised Book of Rates in May 1558. His revision, the first for fifty years and the last of the century, was radical and comprehensive. Some 300 commodities were added to the Book of 1545 and valuations for the duty of 1s in the £ seem on average to have been slightly more than doubled. The specific duties were also raised.[1] Whether England became in consequence a high-tariff country is debatable, but one likely effect of the new rates was to make smuggling more profitable and the need for stricter administration more urgent. So for obvious reasons the lord treasurer did not stop with his revised Book. With London his first concern he extended his reforms and in the process the organisation of the port was radically altered.

In his treatise *De Portibus Maris* Sir Matthew Hale defines a port as '. . . *quid aggregatum*, consisting of somewhat that is natural, viz. an access of the sea whereby ships may conveniently come . . . something that is artificial, as keys and wharfs and cranes and wharehouses and houses of common receipt; and something that is civil, viz. priveleges and franchises. . . .'.[2] Of the three aspects, Winchester's reforms directly affected the artificial and the civil. His immediate concern throughout was with the latter, in the sense that the royal customs were among the chief 'priveleges and franchises' of the port, but in improving them he necessarily interested himself in the artificial. As his reforms show he was fully aware that the efficiency of the customs depended not only on its procedure and personnel but also on the organisation of the port through which the dutiable cargoes passed. Indeed, one of his first moves, preceding the issue of the Book of Rates, was the crown's purchase, on his advice, of the Custom House, the quay on which it stood, and the adjacent Old Wool Quay.[3] Thus, appa-

1. N. S. B. Gras, *Early English customs system* (Cambridge, Mass., 1918), 89–94, 123–9; Willan, *Rates*, pp. xxii–xxvi.
2. *Treatise in three parts*, pt. 2 in *Collection of tracts*, ed. Francis Hargrave, i (1787), 46. Chief Justice Hale (1609–76) wrote one of the earliest systematic accounts of ports and the customs. Cf. R. C. Jarvis, 'The appointment of ports', *Economic History Review*, 2nd series, xi (1958–9), 455–66.
3. Below, pp. 161–2.

rently for the first time, the crown owned the centre of its customs administration. What Winchester had in mind is not quite clear. He did, however,
want to rebuild these properties;[1] and apparently he contemplated con-
centrating most, if not all, of the overseas trade on them.[2] From the
administrative point of view the advantages were obvious. In the event
Winchester was dissuaded from confining the port so closely and, perhaps
for this reason, he did not rebuild.[3] The crown kept the house and quays
but abandoned any intention it might have had of creating a 'royal' port.
Instead, the properties were leased and the lord treasurer's acquisition
merely added to the complexity of ownership in the port.[4] Thus, not
untypically, the administrator's designs were compromised by the hedges
and obstacles to reform. Nevertheless, what did emerge was a notable
advance. This was the first statutory definition of the fiscal port of London.[5]
In accordance with the Act of 1559, which established general regulations
for the loading and discharging of cargoes, a commission was appointed to
survey the port and authorise quays for overseas trade.[6] The commissioners, including the lord treasurer, made their report on 24 August.[7]
With the exception of coal, beer and corn, overseas shipments were to be
limited to wharfs and quays on the north bank of the Thames between
Queenhithe and Tower Dock or Wharf. The total frontage of the 'legal'
quays, as they were later known, was about 2,000 feet.[8] This was the
Elizabethan Port of London for overseas trade.[9]

From the port Winchester turned his attention to the customs. After a
national survey of ports and creeks, on the model of that of London, he
completed his reforms in November 1564 with the issue of the Book of
Orders.[10] The aim was to improve administration and apply a uniform

1. His letter to the queen 30 July 1558, S.P. 11/13, f. 94.
2. Lans. 35, ff. 20–4.
3. This emerges from a memorandum addressed to Lord Burghley in Sept. 1573
which refers to a plan for rebuilding 'long since' drawn up but not carried through.
S.P. 12/151, ff. 20–30. The statement in the London County Council *Survey of London*,
xv (1934), 36 that the Custom House was rebuilt by Winchester appears to be based
solely on his letter to Mary, cited above, in which he merely recommends reconstruc-
tion.
4. For details of ownership etc. of the quays see below, Appendix IV.
5. It is not clear what the earlier fiscal limits were, if any. Until the 15th century the
customs officials' area of jurisdiction was defined in very general terms in their com-
missions of appointment; but the jurisdictional and fiscal limits were probably not the
same. Cf. E. M. Carus-Wilson and Olive Coleman, *England's export trade 1275–1547*
(Oxford, 1963), Appendix II.
6. 1 Eliz. I, c. 11.
7. Below, Appendix IV.
8. All the legal quays but the Steelyard Wharf were measured by the commissioners.
9. The port was redefined after the Great Fire of 1666 and all the legal quays were
then limited to the north bank east of London Bridge. They remained so until the end
of the 18th century, when the frontage was less than 1,500 feet. The port's great
expansion was accommodated by the appointment of 'sufferance wharfs'. T. F.
Reddaway, *Rebuilding of London after the Great Fire* (1940), ch. 8; E. E. Hoon,
Organisation of the English customs system 1696–1786 (New York & London, 1938),
125.
10. The orders were entered into the Exchequer Queen's Remembrancer, Memoranda
Roll 7 Eliz. I, Hilary Communia rot. 319. They are printed in B.Y., *Modern practice
of the court of exchequer* (1730).

system throughout the country.[1] It dealt first, however, with London, a further recognition of her commercial pre-eminence and of the size and complexity of the customs administration. The senior officials were the collectors and controllers, the head searcher, the surveyor and the tide-waiters.[2] These were the men to whom the exchequer sent the 'Queen's original' or port books, the main innovation of Winchester's final reform. The books, as opposed to enrolled accounts, were not in themselves new. In 1428 they had been introduced in a similar attempt at reform.[3] They had not, however, superseded the enrolled Particular Accounts. This was the effect of the Elizabethan orders. Henceforth all the customs accounts kept in the ports were entered in the special parchment books which are preserved in the Public Record Office in the series E. 190.

Since they became available to scholars earlier this century port books have been the subject of a growing number of studies and analyses.[4] It is not, therefore, necessary to explain them in detail. Essentially there were two kinds of book, varying according to the duties of the officials who kept them. The first was produced by those who were directly concerned with collecting revenue; the second by officials who reported the arrival and departure of ships and checked their cargoes. These subordinate officials were principally the waiters and the searchers who worked at the quays and on board ship. Incoming shipments were registered as follows. The waiters went on board as soon as the ship anchored and required from the master a certificate specifying the ship's name, its home-port ('of whence') and size, his own name and nationality, the port of departure ('from whence'), and a bill of lading for the whole cargo. From these the waiters made up ship-masters' or certificate books. Thus the officials who collected and accounted for the customs had detailed, first-hand information of shipments before they processed them themselves. They also knew that there was an independent record with which their own had to agree. Moreover, since two officials kept separate accounts of the subsidy on inward cargoes, there were further checks and counter-checks. This arose as follows. The merchant could enter his goods either 'at sight' or by bill. If he was uncertain as to the exact quantity and value of his shipment he could get a warrant *ad visum* to bring his goods, under the custody of two waiters, to the Custom House where they were viewed by the collector and the controller. A bill of content was then drawn up, on the basis of which entries were made by the two officials in their respective volumes. Alternatively, the owner could enter his shipment before unloading by presenting a bill in which he gave details of the ship and its voyage, as in the master's certifi-

1. For Winchester's reforms in the out-ports see *Chester customs accounts 1301–1566*, ed. K. P. Wilson, Lancs. and Cheshire Record Society, cxi (1969); W. R. B. Robinson, 'The establishment of royal customs in Glamorgan and Monmouthshire under Elizabeth I', Board of Celtic Studies *Bulletin*, xxiii pt. iv (May 1970).
2. The officials and their duties are explained by Gras, *op. cit.* 94–100. Cf. A. P. Newton, 'The establishment of the Great Farm of the English customs', Royal Historical Society *Trans.*, 4th series, i (1918), 129–55.
3. *Calendar of Close Rolls 1422–9*, i (1933), 428–9.
4. See D. M. Woodward, 'Short guide to records: Port Books', *History*, lv (June 1970), 207–10 (with a bibliography). The introduction to the Public Record Office *Descriptive list of Exchequer, Queen's Remembrancer, Port Books* is also valuable.

cate, and of his consignment. He was required to specify the number and type of containers, their contents and the merchant's mark. The bill went first to the collector who, after valuing the shipment, passed on the bill to the controller, with the valuation, for entry in his book. The bill was then returned to the collector who made up his own account. There were thus two separate records of the collection of tonnage and poundage on imports which should correspond exactly. In addition there were the waiters' record and the bills and certificates from which the books were compiled. These bills were filed in the order that they were entered in the books.

This system of multiple controls was intended to prevent fraud by the officials. To be undetected somewhere in the records fraud would require a considerable degree of collusion. The system did not, however, touch upon the problem of smuggling without the connivance of officials. This was dealt with elsewhere in the Book of Orders. Cargoes were not to be unloaded until two-thirds of the owners had presented their bills and a licence for bulk to be broken had been issued by the collector. The unloading itself was to be done by lighter, except for 'massy wares' which could only be raised by crane at the quay. All 'fine wares' and haberdashery had to come by lighter to the Custom House Quay.

These were the main orders of 1564 as they affected imports. The crucial question, which has an obvious bearing on the value of port books, is: how effective were Winchester's reforms in offsetting the greater inducement to smuggling and fraud after 1558? This is a problem that has received a good deal of attention in recent years.[1] Even so, there is no precise and satisfactory answer. The balance of evidence and arguments is complex but inconclusive. On the one hand, while it is clear that smuggling and fraud were serious problems after as well as before the mid-century reforms, the student of London port books can take some reassurance from the general consensus of contemporaries and historians that the provincial ports were more vulnerable than the metropolis. Yet it must be conceded that much of the evidence of evasion concerns London, where the sheer volume and value of trade presented the greatest opportunities to the smuggler and the fraudulent official. Charges of fraud and negligence against individual officers recur throughout Elizabeth's reign, and some were substantiated. More generalised criticisms were directed against lax senior officials who failed to supervise their unreliable assistants; and all ranks, it was claimed, were subject to pressures, familiar to any student of Tudor administration, which discouraged probity and efficiency. Legitimate rewards in wages and fees were said to be so low that employees, especially of the lower ranks, were open to bribery and corruption: the more so because, as the same informant observed, offices at all levels were commonly sold at prices which made conflict between private profit and service to the crown inevitable.[2] Moreover, as other critics argued, these faults in the administration throve in a port which was ill equipped, badly congested and difficult to control.

1. G. D. Ramsay, 'The smugglers' trade', Royal Hist. Soc. *Trans.*, 5th series, ii (1952), 131–57; N. J. Williams, *Contraband cargoes* (1959), especially ch. 2. For a discussion of smuggling and its effect on customs accounts before 1558 see Carus-Wilson and Coleman, *op. cit.*, 18–33.
2. S.P. 12/151, ff. 20–30.

The royal quays in particular were said to be inadequate. A timber structure, the Old Wool Quay was badly in need of repair, while the Custom
House Quay, although more soundly built of stone, lay so far back from
the low-water mark that access, even for lighters, was limited. Without
extensive rebuilding any attempt to limit the legal quays, as Winchester
may have planned, was impractical. Yet without some restriction, it was
claimed, there were too many 'blind' quays where proper supervision was
beyond the resources of the queen's customs.[1]

All these indictments of the London customs, and it is by no means a
comprehensive list,[2] suggest that Winchester's reforms fell well short of
their objective. The evidence does not, however, provide conclusive proof
of widespread smuggling by merchants or of endemic fraud by officials.
And where the latter did try to defraud the crown, they might well take
their cut in the revenue *after* compiling their accounts, which could still
therefore be an accurate record. This seems to be the lesson to be drawn
from the noted case of William Bird who defrauded the crown of revenue
from cloth exports on a scandalous scale in the fifteen-sixties. For the
student of port books what is significant and reassuring about Bird's
fraudulent practices is that they were detectable in his accounts, at least
until he so erased and altered them that they were quite illegible. Another
official who came under suspicion was driven to even more desperate
measures when he sent an accomplice through the window of the Custom
House to set fire to incriminating documents. In these cases at least, the
system of checks and counter-checks seems to have worked.[3]

Bird's case is firm, well-documented evidence of serious malpractices.
The same cannot necessarily be said of the more generalised charges against
the customs. Although cumulatively impressive they must be treated carefully. While exaggeration must be allowed for as a matter of course, close
inspection of particular cases can suggest special grounds for scepticism.
The example of George Needham, one of the most persistent critics of the
London customs in the fifteen-eighties, illustrates this point. Needham, who
acquired the lease of the Custom House Quay about 1578, offered as his
solution to smuggling and fraud the not unfamiliar proposal to limit the
fiscal port and close the 'blind' quays. He accompanied his suggestion with
an offer to buy the lease of the other royal quay. London's overseas trade,
or at least the greater part of it, should then be confined to the two quays.[4]
It is not difficult to see what Needham's personal interests were. As the
wharfingers who opposed him darkly implied, a monopolist would be
particularly well placed to profit not only from the wharfingers' legitimate
rewards but also from connivance at evasion of the customs.[5] The case does
indeed suggest that if the unreformed officials exploited office for private
gain their critics had much the same end in view; and this could well lead
to exaggeration. No doubt their charges had some substance: equally one

1. E. 163/14/4; Lans. 35, f. 119; Lans. 41, ff. 54–6.
2. See, for example, a list of 'craftie pollices' for evading the customs in Lans. 41,
ff. 50–3.
3. Williams, *Contraband cargoes*, 33–8.
4. Lans. 35, ff. 17–21, 119; E. 163/14/4.
5. Lans. 35, f. 117. Note that according to Hale the wharfingers occupying legal quays
were not free to raise their charges to an 'immoderate rate'. *Treatise*, pt. 2, ch. 6

may suspect that they magnified the evils for which their 'remedies' were offered.

If one accepts that customs officials were negligent, or, worse, dishonest, does it follow that merchants were willing and able to smuggle goods on a scale that would invalidate port books as commercial records? The smuggler's profits obviously had to be balanced against the risks, and while the new Book of Rates improved the profit margins Winchester's reforms presumably increased the chances of detection. In time, as the early impetus of reform declined, bureaucratic inertia was likely to set in. Against this probable decline in efficiency, however, must be set the fact that continuing inflation made the nominal valuations of 1558 less and less realistic, thus narrowing the smuggler's margin of profit.[1] And the ad valorem duty was at most only 5 per cent of the nominal value of the goods as compared with 35 per cent in the eighteenth century, the era of organised smuggling. The smuggler's profits would not therefore be so great as to tempt him into indiscriminate evasion, and in all probability he would choose goods of high value in proportion to bulk as offering the highest return at the least risk. Hence one would expect the port books to under-record imports like spices and silk but to give an accurate account of the trade in 'massy' wares like timber, canvas and fish. Altogether, the debate on smuggling and its share of the nation's trade is likely to be endless. Further research will produce more evidence of the former, but there can be no satisfactory way of quantifying the latter. As far as the port books are concerned, the most realistic attitude towards them is one which avoids, as the analyst of the Boston books[2] advises, the extremes either of uncritical acceptance or of complete distrust. With all their defects and limitations they remain the chief source for the study of English trade in the sixteenth and seventeenth centuries; 'no other country can boast such comprehensive records for its commerce during these centuries'.[3]

Trade and shipping

Such a claim for the London books in particular must be subjected to one important qualification. Because of their haphazard survival[4] they do not allow a study of long-term secular trends and the historian who requires from his sources continuity over a long period will inevitably be disappointed. For Elizabethan imports 1567/8 is one of only two years for which books survive—the other is 1587/8—and there is no record of the important aliens' trade.[5] For a detailed breakdown of imports at other times there are only occasional government surveys, compiled from the port books. Fortunately, William Cecil in particular was interested enough

1. Willan, *Rates*, pp. xliii–lv.
2. *Port Books of Boston 1601–40*, ed. R. W. K. Hinton, Lincoln Record Society, 1 (1956), pp. xxxii–xxxiii.
3. N. J. Williams, 'The London Port Books', London and Middlesex Archaeological Society *Trans.*, xviii, pt. 1 (1955), 13–26.
4. *ibid.*, 14.
5. E. 190/5/5 is the only book of alien imports in a full year, 1571–2, in the early part of Elizabeth's reign. Many of the entries, however, are incomplete so a detailed analysis of the alien trade does not seem possible.

in trade statistics to call for them frequently.[1] Those that survive, however, are mere fragments;[2] and it should be observed that they are not necessarily objective, accurate statements. Not uncommonly such surveys were designed to illustrate an argument or prove a case.

Because the historian falls so far short of his goal of continuity of sources it is especially important that his short-term data should be most carefully studied in their context. Is the period 'typical' or was trade then under exceptional influences which would produce 'untypical' trends and fluctuations? The point is obvious but it is perhaps of particular relevance in the middle decades of the sixteenth century when trade was unduly disturbed. From the late forties, when the Great Debasement sharply stimulated exports,[3] its course was highly erratic. In the fifties Antwerp, the barometer of European trade, achieved record 'highs' and exceptional 'lows'. As the Table printed below suggests, England shared in a general recovery about 1559, but the revaluation of the coinage in 1560 depressed exports, leading indirectly to an even more serious collapse in 1564. Because of their weakened position after revaluation the merchant adventurers sought compensation for falling markets at the expense of foreign traders. In the Low Countries the government retaliated with an embargo which lasted from November 1563 to December of the following year. The closure of Antwerp was a most serious blow to English merchants who found Emden a quite inadequate alternative for their staple. When the embargo was lifted they hurried back to the Netherlands, and 1565 proved to be a year of exceptional activity. Thereafter trade was more settled until the end of 1568 when a new and longer embargo was imposed in the Netherlands and in Spain. For over four years trade with both countries was suspended, and when the ban was lifted a full return to the status quo, as in 1565, was neither possible nor desirable. Although the Spanish trade was resumed the London–Antwerp axis was never restored. A distinctive phase of London's trade had ended and a new pattern or structure was to develop.

Against this background the port book for 1567/8 has a special significance. It records imports in a year which was relatively undisturbed, and was also the last of a particular phase in the distribution of metropolitan trade. Over a long period, concentration, above all on Antwerp, was the essential characteristic. This is observable in individual merchants like the Ishams, who seem to have had no knowledge of markets other than Antwerp;[4] and it is apparent also on a more general level. This does not mean that trade had been static. Apart from the periodic fluctuations and disturbances, there had been significant structural changes, particularly in the fifteen-fifties, when the founding of the Russia Company and the opening of markets in Morocco and Guinea had extended and diversified trade. At the same time native merchants had begun to return to the Baltic. In

1. L. Stone, 'Elizabethan overseas trade', *Economic History Review*, 2nd series, ii, no. 1 (1949), 30–58.
2. Surveys of imports in 1559/60 and 1565/6 are printed below in Appendix III.
3. But note J. D. Gould's criticism of the orthodox view of the effect of debasement on exports in *The Great Debasement* (1970), ch. 6.
4. *John Isham, mercer and merchant adventurer*, ed. G. D. Ramsay, Northampton Record Society, xxi (1962), p. lxxxiii.

their immediate impact, however, these developments were of small importance. As a proportion of the whole of London's trade, whether measured in terms of volume, value or transportation, these areas were peripheral economically as well as geographically. Even the most cursory survey of our record for 1567/8 will show how restricted were London's markets, with the great bulk and value of imports coming from ports on the Atlantic coastline, from Marbella in the south to the Zuiderzee.

Fluctuations in London's trade 1558–68

Year	Exports Petty Customs[1]	Imports[2] Valuations for poundage Native	Total	Wines: French	Rhenish	Spanish	Sweet
	£	£	£	*tuns*	*awms*	*tuns*	*tuns*
1558/9	30,951	—	—	—	—	—	—
1559/60	36,982	—	—	—	—	—	—
1560/1	27,605	—	258,781	1,883	1,721	2,147	533
1561/2	25,250	—	299,606	1,854	3,519	1,894	1,006
1562/3	18,146	115,765	194,742	—	—	—	—
1563/4	19,196	82,323	147,483	—	—	—	—
1564/5	45,439	206,095	324,674	—	—	—	—
1565/6	27,873	156,865	249,498	—	—	—	—
1566/7	23,320	141,072	238,753	2,300	2,417	1,871	636
1567/8	31,557	140,268	238,192	2,976	1,726	1,134	822

The year for exports is regnal, for imports from Michaelmas. Values to the nearest £.

In this relatively confined trading area Spain was more important than is sometimes allowed. So much emphasis may be placed on the political, religious and maritime antipathy between the two countries that the solid commercial links of peacetime are easily understated. It is worth noting that in the year of San Juan de Uloa, a battle which epitomises this mutual hostility, well over fifty laden ships passed up the Thames on peaceful voyages from Spain. They came from widely distributed ports. In contrast the French trade was centred on three. This at least was the pattern of native imports, which came mainly from Rouen, Bordeaux and La Rochelle. From Rouen were distributed the local linen and canvas manufactures. Bordeaux, of course, was the great wine port. The heavy impost of 1558 on wine apparently cut imports for a while.[3] Even so, wine—mostly French—still represented some 10 per cent of the value of imports in 1559/60; and the

1. E. 122/88/9. On the petty customs see F. C. Dietz, *English public finance 1558–1641* (1932), 310 n. They included 3*d* in the £ on all exports and discriminatory charges on cloth shipments.
2. From the Enrolled Customs Account [E. 356] 28 except 1560/1 from E. 122/88/13 and 1564/5 from E. 122/88/15. Figures for wine imports are incomplete because the Enrolled Account does not always distinguish between the different kinds.
3. This is suggested by a comparison of the figures in the table with those for the later years of Henry VIII (in G. Schanz, *Englische Handelspolitik*, ii (1881), 128–9) and with imports in the last five years of Elizabeth's reign when they averaged over 5,000 tuns a year. A. M. Millard, 'The import trade of London 1600–1640', unpublished London Ph.D. thesis (1956), appendices.

Bordeaux voyage held its importance in England's carrying trade.[1] La Rochelle was also important in employing native ships because in salt it supplied one of the few bulk cargoes which were carried over relatively long routes.

The French and Spanish trades involved the exchange of a comparatively small range of commodities. Trade with the Netherlands was quite different. Whereas cloth was overwhelmingly the most valuable export, the range of imports, especially from Antwerp, was considerable. Some, like drugs, spices, dyestuffs and metalware—from Germany—were constituents of Antwerp's transit trade, but others were products of the local industries which had been a key factor in the port's revival in the fifteen-thirties and 'forties. The 'triumph of the light drapery' is reflected in the import of says, bays and fustian. The products of the satin and drugget industry, located mainly in Antwerp itself and in Bruges, are well represented in the port book, as are embroidery, tapestry and damask-linen, with linen from Flanders and Brabant, ticks or bedding—especially from Turnhout—and metalware from Liège.[2]

Thus Antwerp's preeminence in London's import trade was based not only on her function as an entrepôt but also on the distribution of local manufactures. Both strands in this trade were soon to be broken. Even by 1560 the 'golden age' was over. Twenty years later there were few remnants of Antwerp's commercial greatness; and as the great port declined London's trade routes were diversified and extended. In the fifteen-seventies English ships and merchants entered the Mediterranean to trade with Italy and the Levant. Routes across the North Sea to Germany, Scandinavia and the Baltic developed rapidly. By the end of the century ships were regularly crossing the Atlantic, and in 1600 the East India Company was formed to compete with the Dutch and the Portuguese in India and South-East Asia. The mid-century pattern of trade had disappeared.

The Port Book of 1567/8 [E. 190/4/2]

The port book calendared below was the 'original book' of the controller of the subsidy of tonnage and poundage inwards. Although it is a record of native trade—alien imports were entered in separate books—it includes shipments by Hanse merchants, who paid native rates, and some alien consignments. The controller was William Temys or Temmes, who was appointed the previous year.[3] His volume has traces of an inscription on

1. A survey of English ships carrying the first vintage from Bordeaux in 1571 listed 71 for London, of 4,113 tons. Lans. 14, ff. 79–81.
2. On Antwerp cf. Oskar de Smedt, *De Engelse natie te Antwerpen in de 16e eeuw*, 2 vols (Antwerp, 1954) and H. van der Wee, *Growth of the Antwerp market and the European economy*, 3 vols (The Hague, 1963).
3. His letters patent of 26 Feb. 1566 are in P.R.O. Chancery Fine Roll C. 60/382, no. 50–1. The office is not named but this presumably was the controllership—for which he entered a recognisance of £200 in the Hilary term of 8 Eliz.I. At the same time he produced as sureties four London merchants: Thomas Brown and John Mylner, merchant taylors, Roger Sadler, draper, and John Best, haberdasher, E. 122/196/2. Temys himself has left few other traces. Probably he was William Temys who was apprenticed as a draper in 1540, *Roll of the Drapers' company of London*, ed. P. Boyd (1934), 181.

the cover. This was presumably the customary statement, written in the exchequer before the books were issued, as to their size—how many leaves or folios—the port and official to whom they were sent, and the period they were intended to cover. This information is reproduced in Temys' book at the head of the first folio and in a note at the end of the volume. The heading is as follows:

> London William Temys generosus contrarollatur contrarotulamentum sub-
> sidii inductorum pro indigenis. Post Festum sancti Michaelis
> Archangeli anno regni domine Elizabeth dei gracia Anglie, Francie
> et Hiberni regni fidei defensor nono vsque idem festum ex tunc
> proxime sequentum scilicet per spacum vnum annum integro.

The note on the last folio, dated 17 November 1568, states that the book had contained 300 folios, of which 258 'plenarum scribunt'. The remaining blank leaves have been removed.

Temys' book follows the conventional port book format and the 1564 Orders in all but two respects. First, there is no other single volume in the Public Record Office which covers a whole year of the subsidy in Elizabeth's reign; and in doing so this book departs from the official instruction that one should be used for each exchequer term. Probably it was issued for only the Michaelmas term but was extended to the end of the year because so much space remained.[1] Secondly, it is clear that the book was not foliated before it left the exchequer. The original folio numbers are placed in such a way as to suggest that they were added to each page after the controller had made his entries. This was another departure from the Book of Orders which had repeated the instruction of 1428 that the port books should be foliated by the exchequer before their issue. Apart from these two discrepancies the book adheres to the orders and practices of the customs. Although the handwriting appears to be the same throughout it varies somewhat in its neatness and regularity. This would suggest that the record was kept, as the Orders allowed, at convenient intervals and not necessarily day by day. Consequently, despite some signs of hasty composition, Temys' volume impresses by its clarity and the general care with which the account was kept. Corrections and alterations are few and they are made neatly, as the Orders required, without obscuring the original error. Most in any case occur in those parts of the record that were not essential to the account. For example, ships were entered 'ut postea' when in fact they were being registered for the first time. There are more crucial errors which pass uncorrected; but the overall impression of the record, given its size and complexity, is one of careful and conscientious preparation, albeit in the awkward 'dog latin' used by the customs.

While the book inspires some confidence it does pose the problems of use and interpretation that are common to the series. Most of these arise from the conflict of interest between the historian and the recorder. Our concern is mainly with the record of trade and shipping; his was to keep an account of revenue, not of trade. Consequently, the account has many limitations as a commercial record. Most obviously, the port books only

---

1. This interpretation is supported by the fact that in the statement as to the period covered by the book the words 'vsque' onwards were clearly entered later.

register customable, i.e. laden ships. Those in ballast were of no concern. Nor do the main accounts enter duty-free goods: this ambiguous category had a separate record which rarely survives.[1] What is entered can also be affected, adversely from our point of view, by this preoccupation with revenue rather than commerce. Where the data have no direct fiscal relevance, the record can be cryptic, casual and even positively misleading. By following the entries item by item we can indicate some of the difficulties and frustrations that arise. First, however, it should be noted that one of the worst results of this negligence is incompleteness in recording those details that had no direct relevance to the accounts. Thus details of the ship and its voyage are often omitted. At worst only its name and home-port might be entered.

In entering a shipment the controller or his clerk recorded first, under the appropriate date, the name of the ship carrying it. Some problems of identification can arise here, as elsewhere, through the vagaries of phonetic spelling. This particularly applies to foreign vessels. Nor is the record always consistent. The *Black Falcon* may, for example, be entered elsewhere as simply the *Falcon*; and with Dutch ships particular confusion can arise over the fact that *Eagle* and *Spredeagle*—or *Spledegle*—were both common and interchangeable names. Next was entered the home-port. Apart from some problems of identification[2] there is the larger question of what this designation means. The most reasonable assumption is that it denotes the place where the ship would usually be found when not at sea; and this, in all probability, would be the domicile of the master or owner, who might well be the same person.[3] To complete the ship's description on its first entry the book should record its tonnage, the master and his domicile, and the port of departure. As to tonnage, which is often left out, accuracy should not be expected; only a rough impression of size or carrying capacity can be gained. The master's name and that of his domicile do not present any particular problem beyond those of spelling and identification. Lastly is entered the port of departure. This is in fact often omitted, which leads one to be suspicious of the frequent use of the term 'ab ibidem' to denote that 'from whence' was the same as 'of whence'. This could well be correct, particularly in the case of foreign ships; but there may be some suspicion that the controller, who was not consistently interested in recording the port of departure, was merely resorting to a convenient shorthand in preference to an awkward place-name. If the nature of the cargo does cast doubt on the designated port of departure,[4] it could well be that our accountant had preferred the economy of 'ab ibidem' to the labour of accuracy. The port of departure might be misleading for another reason. The naming of only one port, which is almost always the case, could be a serious oversimplification of the voyage. We know from such records as

1. Willan, *Rates*, p. x.
2. Particularly helpful in identifying place-names is H. J. Smit, *Bronnen tot de Geschiedenis van den Handel met Engeland, Schotland en Ierland 1485–1585*, Rijks Geschiedkundige Publicatiën, 86, 91 (The Hague, 1942, 1950).
3. Cf. T. S. Willan, *English coasting trade 1600–1750* (1938), Appendix 6.
4. For example, the *Morian* of Hamburg (**180**) which was described as entering 'ab ibidem' with bay salt. There must be a strong suspicion that she came directly from Bourgneuf Bay or Brouage.

charter parties that ships often put into more than one port in the course of a voyage. This will not emerge from the port book, so the existence of multilateral, port-to-port traffic is completely obscured.

Under the heading of the ship's name etc. are entered the merchants' goods as they were declared and attested to the customs. This was the essential fiscal record so there are fewer errors and omissions. There remain, however, some problems of interpretation. Was the merchant named the 'very owner'? This was required by law,[1] but according to Hale—though writing about a century later—'the practice by indulgence and connivance both run contrary'.[2] The 'owner' might, in fact, be an agent, possibly acting illegally for an alien; or the representative of a partnership—although this can be indicated in the book—or a merchant who bought on board ship and not overseas.[3] He was still, however, required to give his trade, domicile or nationality. Thereafter the book details his consignment. There can be some difficulties in identifying commodities, as the Descriptive List[4] will illustrate; and some of the weights and measures pose problems.[5] Finally, the controller entered the valuation and the amount of duty as assessed by the collector. His record was now complete.

1. 1 Eliz.I, c. 77.
2. *Treatise*, pt. 3, ch. 22.
3. *Port Books of Boston 1601–40*, pp. xxiii–xxiv.
4. Below, Appendix II.
5. These are discussed below, p. xxii.

NOTES ON EDITORIAL METHOD

Method and form of the calendar

Although the port book's size precluded a full transcription the calendar aims to reproduce all the significant material in a simplified and systematic form. Only two categories of information in the original have been excluded from the calendar, while a third—the way the merchants or owners of cargoes are described—has been concentrated in the Index. Details of containers (e.g. bolts, fardels) were judged to be of little importance in relation to the space they occupy in the port book; and more space was saved, with rather more reluctance, by omitting the figures for poundage. The problem here is that although there is a fixed relationship of 1s in the £ between valuation and poundage, it is not always possible to calculate the latter from the former. In most cases it is: but where the valuation involved units of less than one pound the collector might be forced to round up or down his charge for poundage. For example, John Clint, who imported paper worth £14 2s 6d on the *Mary George*, the second ship in the calendar, paid 14s 1d duty. His was, however, the only consignment in the *Mary George* that did not allow an exact charge of one-twentieth of the valuation to be made. The Book of Rates naturally valued commodities so that the officials could work out the duty easily and exactly. A very close approximation of the poundage can, therefore, be reached from the valuations, which are recorded in the calendar, as are the tonnages for wine. Lastly, much space was saved by transferring the details of the merchants' trades, domicile or nationality to the Index.

The calendar also departs from the form of the original by consolidating shipments under the heading of each ship, and in the order that they were entered by the controller. This arrangement has clear advantages over the form of the port book, where a ship's cargo can be dispersed over many pages; and by dating the individual merchants' entries nothing serious is lost through this reorganisation. Appendix I, which lists the total daily entry of shipments, provides the only significant information that could be gained from the port book but not from the calendar.

The heading under which the cargo appears is made up as follows. First is the ship's name, followed by its home-port and tonnage. Next is the master's name and, in those rare instances when it differed from the home-port, his domicile; e.g. Richard Cornish of Ratcliff. The full heading is then completed by the port of departure, which is marked off from the preceding item by a semi-colon. Beneath this heading, which is often incomplete, the cargo is detailed as follows. After the folio reference to the first entry appears the merchant's name, followed by details of his shipment. As has been explained, the valuation is given but not the poundage. The day the shipment was entered is then recorded. This is also the date of subsequent entries until it is changed; and so on through the cargo. The last entry is preceded by its folio reference if it does not appear on the same page as the first.

Weights and measures

These have been converted where possible into meaningful and recognisable units. Fortunately, the Book of Rates, which has been made widely available through Willan's invaluable edition, explains the content of most of the original weights and measures, including the troublesome 'hundred' or 'c'. This can be a measure of weight—either metric or of 112 lbs—or of volume, with the quantity again varying; for example a hundred of stock-fish contained 120. In a few instances the Book of Rates values commodities by units of measurement other than those in the port book. Thus spices like pepper and ginger, though valued by the pound, were also imported by the hundred and quarter. The valuation establishes that the hundred was, as one would surmise, metric, giving a quarter of 25 lbs. Similarly, the valuations prevented a possible error in converting bales of fustian into yards. According to the Book a bale containing 22½ pieces was valued at £15. A half-piece of 15 yards was worth 7s 6d, a full piece 15s. At these valuations it cannot be assumed that the bale contained, by calculation, 675 yards since that number valued by the piece was worth more than £15. For this reason it was decided to retain the original measure. A similar problem arose with flax, which was measured and valued by the pack, the dozen lbs, or the cwt. A pack contained 20 cwt, so it would have been consistent with the general practice in the calendar to convert the pack into this more meaningful unit. This was not done, however, because the valuations by the pack and by the cwt are unequal. The 'thousand' or 'M' also presents some difficulties. Normally it means ten hundredweight of 112 lbs; but this measure is hardly appropriate for commodities like pins and teazles, which seem to have been measured by number and not by weight. These and similar articles were presumably packed in standard-size containers, as were glass—by the case or chest as well as by the wey—and nails, which were shipped by the barrel. Cloth measures varied. Some were valued by the piece of so many yards or ells; in such cases the latter measures are given in the calendar. Other cloths were actually valued by these units. But there remain some cloths valued by the piece for which no measurement is given in the Book of Rates. As this is the basis and guide for all our conversions those cloths are recorded by the piece. And, generally, where the Book offers no guidance or leaves room for doubt the original measure is retained.

Spelling, transcription and dates

Spelling in the calendar has been modernised except for the names of ships and persons and in cases where the modern form was either unknown or clearly in doubt. This applies to some place-names and to commodities which escaped identification. An original spelling is indicated by single quotation marks. In the appendices, unless otherwise stated, the original spelling is kept but the punctuation has been modernised and abbreviations extended. The year has been reckoned to begin on 1 January.

Index

In the interests of clarity, the index has been divided under the following heads:—

Masters. The master's domicile is given in round brackets.

Merchants. The description of their trade, domicile or nationality, is given when it appears in the document. It should be noted that a merchant may be given various designations or none at all.

Other persons. This includes persons mentioned in the introduction and appendices.

Places. Home-ports are distinguished from ports of departure by the phrases 'ship(s) of' and 'ship(s) from'.

Ships.

Subjects. For commodities see Appendix II where every commodity is listed with a reference to its first appearance in the text.

All references are to entries and not to pages unless preceded by the letter p. Only significant variations in spelling are noted.

LONDON PORT BOOK, 1567/8
(E. 190/4/2)
A CALENDAR

1. *Confidence* of London (50) Richard Cornish of Ratcliff; La Rochelle
[f. 1] William Bulley: 30 weys great salt £30 (30 Sept 1567). William Catcher: 4 hhds 1 pipe train oil, 9 pcs resin £9.

2. *Mary George* of London (45) Robert Osburn; Rouen
[f. 1] Robert Broke: 35 cwt prunes, 7 cwt rosalger £31 10s (30 Sept 1567). Humphrey Brown: 220 reams paper, 7 grs crewel chain-lace, 2 grs inkhorns, 3½ grs looking glasses, 2 cwt loose pack thread, 1 grs wicker bottles £40 10s. Richard Patrik: 30 grs playing cards, 30 doz. woolcards, 6 grs inkhorns, 10 grs combs, 3 grs woollen-lace at 3s the gross £53 10s. William Handford: 30 grs playing cards, 100 reams paper £43 6s 8d. Nicholas Warner: 1100 ells canvas £27 10s. Oliver Fisher: 9 cwt prunes, 4 doz. chafing dishes £5 3s 4d (1 Oct). John Bodleygh: 1300 ells canvas £32 10s. Wolston Dixi: 850 ells canvas £21 5s. John Newton: 23 grs playing cards £23. Hugh Offley: 180 reams paper £24. Thomas Starkey: 800 ells canvas £20. John Wanton: 40 doz. woolcards £20 (2 Oct). William Body: 140 reams paper, 21 grs playing cards £39 13s 4d. Henry Buxton: 450 ells canvas, 4 doz. chafing dishes £12 11s 8d (4 Oct). John Clint: 160 reams paper £14 2s 6d. Henry Hayward: 1200 ells canvas £16 (8 Oct). Edmund Anselm: 20 thou. teazles £6 13s 4d. [f. 7b] Anthony Gamask: 1200 ells packing canvas £16.

3. *Wildman* of Hamburg (60) Christian Becker; Hamburg
[f. 1] Court Ellers: 6 lasts titlings £40 (30 Sept 1567). Otte Frolik: 2400 ells middlegood, 2 lasts croplings £40. Matthew Hope: 5 lasts croplings £33 6s 8d. Edward van Crog: 45 cwt cables £30 (1 Oct). George Lubkin: 1500 ells Osnabrücks, 2 cwt estrige wool £21 13s 4d (2 Oct). [f. 3] Jerome Rice: 5½ lasts croplings, 240 lings £44 13s 4d.

4. *John* of London (30) John Sherwood; Rouen
[f. 1] Humphrey Brown: 7 grs crewel chain-lace, 4¼ grs rings, 2 grs inkhorns, 1 cwt pack thread, 3½ grs looking glasses, 100 reams paper, 1 grs wicker rattles £19 10s (30 Sept 1567). John Bingley: 10 cases glass £10. Robert Sadler: 160 reams paper £21 6s 8d (1 Oct). John Harding: 800 ells canvas £20. Anthony Cage: 1200 ells canvas £30. [f. 3] Richard Hodchet: 2 tuns vinegar, 8 cwt prunes, 6 cases glass, 10 doz. wicker bottles, 12 hour glasses, 6 compasses, 12 lanterns, 6 grs playing cards, 1½ grs mattriss cards £23 13s 4d (2 Oct).

5. *Unicorn* of St. Omer (14) Marin Potawin; St. Omer
[f. 1b] John Atkinson: 3500 bunches onions £12 11s 8d (30 Sept 1567).

1

6. *Star* of London John Podge
[f. 1*b*] John Clint: 96 reams paper, 6 doz. coarse heath brushes £13 10*s*
(30 Sept 1567).

7. *Swan* of Amsterdam (35) Jacob Tyser; Amsterdam
[f. 2] Edward van Crog: 550 wainscots £22 (1 Oct 1567).

8. *Cloverblade* of Hamburg (20) Cornilis Derikson; Hamburg
[f. 2] Edward van Crog: 650 wainscots £26 (1 Oct 1567).

9. *Saviour* of Aldeburgh (50) Thomas Beversam; La Rochelle
[f. 2] Thomas Beversam: 31 weys bay salt £31 (1 Oct 1567).

10. *Falcon* of Bergen-op-Zoom Adrian Williamson; Bergen-op-Zoom
[f. 2] Joan Bower: 2 lasts rape oil £32 (1 Oct 1567). George Stockmed: 11
cwt flax, 2 lasts rape oil £43. Ancelm Becket: 6¼ cwt flax £6 5*s* (2 Oct).
William Hobs: 1 last rape oil, 21 cwt flax £37. John Boylson: 10 cwt flax
£10 (4 Oct). Reynold Starkey: 14 cwt oakum £3 10*s*. [f. 6] William Hewet:
6 cwt flax £6 (6 Oct).

11. *Samson* of Bruges (45) Marten Fryse; Bruges
[f. 2] Richard Renolds: 26 lbs Paris silk, 2 doz. purse rings £8 15*s* (1 Oct
1567).

12. *James* of Rouen (20) Cornilis Cok; Rouen
[f. 2] John Bodleygh: 1500 ells canvas £37 10*s* (1 Oct 1567). William Bond:
34 cwt prunes £17 (2 Oct). [f. 3] John Bingley: 10 cases glass £10 (3 Oct).

13. *Seahen* of Amsterdam (80) Gortik de Frise; Danzig
[f. 2*b*] William Cokin: 5 lasts pitch £10 (2 Oct 1567). Richard Gourney:
6 packs flax £48 (4 Oct). [f. 6*b*] William James: 10 lasts pitch £20 (6 Oct).

14. *Bonadventure* of Antwerp (18) Anthony Joyson; Antwerp
[f. 2*b*] John Jackman: 6 cwt hops £3 (2 Oct 1567). Edward Jackman:
10 cwt hops £5. William Coles: 34 cwt hops £17. [f. 3*b*] John Colmer:
16 cwt hops £8 (3 Oct).

15. *Anne* of Antwerp (46) Barthel Paules; Antwerp
[f. 2*b*] John Jackman: 30 cwt hops £15 (2 Oct 1567). William Coles: 12 cwt
hops £6. John Spencer: 10 cwt hops £5 (3 Oct). Humphrey Fairfax: 60 cwt
hops £30. Richard Howlet: 7 brls rape oil £9 6*s* 8*d*. William Cokin: 18
timber untawed mink £36 (4 Oct). Thomas Thorp: 6 cwt hops £3. [f. 7]
Robert Taylor: 4 cwt hops £2 (7 Oct).

16. *Spledegle* of Antwerp (40) Barnard Peters
[f. 2*b*] George Lubkin: 1500 ells Osnabrücks £20 (2 Oct 1567).

17. *Saviour* of Aldeburgh (50) Thomas Leverson; Aldeburgh [*sic*][1]
[f. 3] Francis Wight: 40 doz. goatskins £40 (2 Oct 1567).

1. This could be Thomas Beversham's *Saviour*, 9.

18. *Lion* of Lee (60) John Boner; Antwerp

[f. 3] William Hewet: 14 cwt estrige wool £11 13s 4d (3 Oct 1567). John Spencer: 220 lbs pepper £18 6s 8d. George Breame: 10 cwt battery £20. Edward Jackman: 650 lbs pepper £54 3s 4d. Edmund Burton: 3 half-brls head nails, 5 cwt frying pans, 24 doz. coarse sword blades, 7 cwt white plates, 12 hd 'stass' steel, 3 cwt pack thread, 60 lbs clavichord wire, 2 grs carving tools, 1 grs horse bells, 4 doz. dog chains, 6 grs paper buckles £34 3s 4d. Anthony Warffild: 36 cwt liquorice, 150 lbs ginger £29 5s. Roger Warfild: 400 lbs matches, 150 lbs ginger £14 11s. John Alden: 15½ cwt galls £20 13s 4d (4 Oct). Alexander Sherington: 100 yds taffeta £33 6s 8d. Charles Bond: 6 cwt woad £4. George Collimore: 30 doz. lbs Bruges thread, 12 doz. lbs worsted yarn, 15 doz. lbs bottom thread £33. John Eliots: 16 doz. lbs Oudenaarde thread, 7 doz. lbs crewel, 3 doz. lbs inkle, 4 doz. crewel pieces, 6 doz. lbs bottom thread, 200 thimbles £21 16s 8d. Wolston Dixi: 25 pcs Ghentish cloth, 100 ells Bar canvas £32. John Car: 12 cwt latten wire, 36 doz. small candle plates at 6s 8d the doz., 2 doz. bed pans at 20s the doz. £39. Thomas Thorp: 6 cwt corn powder, 3 cwt hops £11 10s. Edward Bright: 36 cwt steel, 1 ton 13 cwt small square iron, 1 half-brl head nails, 1 half-brl small nails, 12 pair iron andirons, 12 pair tongs, 12 pair fireshovels £44 11s 8d. William Salkins: 17 cwt Cologne hemp £17. Roland Erlington: 35 doz. lbs Bruges thread, 6 doz. lbs bottom pack thread £24 10s. Thomas Gardyner: 18 cwt hops, 80 doz. hemp £19. John Boorne: 3 doz. crewel pieces, 1 doz. lbs coarse crewel, 2 grs thread points, 2 doz. lbs Bruges thread, 20 doz. yds Cyprus cotton, 10 doz. thou. pins £10 6s 8d (6 Oct). William Laire: 1 brl painter's oil, 2½ cwt brimstone £2 3s 4d. Edmund Smith: 2 bales Ulm fustian, 8 pcs say £38. John Isham: 28 pcs broad worsted £28. William Sherington: 56 cwt flax £37 6s 4d. Sir William Garet: 7 cwt latten basnets, 15 grs coarse knives, 1 cwt glass beads £37 10s. Henry Smith: 12 cwt latten wire £24. William Towerson: 190 ells wool tapestry, 320 ells hair tapestry £20 3s 4d. Gerson Hills: 7¾ cwt hemp £7 15s. Thomas Longston: 8 cwt rice, 500 lbs pepper £48. William Elkin: 1100 ells Osnabrücks, 330 ells white Hazebroucks, 200 stone pots £23 18s 4d. Thomas Aldersey: 250 ells sarcenet, 70 yds satin, 35 yds damask £84 8s 4d. John Gardner: 600 lbs pepper, 12 cwt red lead, 4 half-brls 4 firkins litmus, honey cost 10s, 6 cwt aniseed, 4 cwt starch £73 16s 8d. Ancelm Becket: 28 cwt madder £18 13s 4d. Thomas Gawdbie: 930 yds harnesdale cloth £37 5s. William Dauntzie: 44½ pcs Holland cloth £53 8s 4d (7 Oct). Robert Broune: 75 yds velvet £56 5s. Roger Warfilde: 150 lbs ginger £11 5s. Thomas Randall: 47 doz. yds Cyprus cotton £9 8s 4d. Richard Billam: 90 Turnhout ticks, 7 cwt hops £33 10s. William Gifford: 3 pcs stammel £30. Robert Taylor: 7½ cwt argol £8 11s 8d. Robert Turvill: 3 doz. pcs cap ribands £4 (8 Oct). Alice Lambert: 7 cwt rice £5 16s 8d. William Coles: 5 cwt sumach, 3 cwt litmus £4 16s 8d. John Jackman: 6 cwt sumach £4. Thomas Parker: 10 half-pcs broad dornick, 2 pcs colombet at 8s the pc, 6 doz. neckerchief bands at 3s the doz., 7 doz. coarse ruffs, 2 doz. 'hedlands', 26 lbs thread, 11 doz. lbs crewel £12 3s 4d. Edmund Hugin: 160 ells sarcenet £26 13s 4d. John Sutton: 1½ thou. dudgeon £7 10s (10 Oct). Robert Skarborrow: 40 pcs mockado £26 13s 4d (22 Oct). [f. 14b] Roger Warfilde: 1½ cwt gunpowder £2 10s.

19. *Asse* of Antwerp (40) Francis Peters; Antwerp
[f. 3*b*] John Jackman: 19 cwt hops £9 10*s* (3 Oct 1567). John Spencer: 13 cwt hops £6 10*s*. Humphrey Fairfax: 56 cwt hops £28. Richard Howlet: 2½ cwt saltpetre, 6 brls rape oil £12 3*s* 4*d*. William Coles: 10 cwt hops £5. Edward Jackman: 17 cwt hops £8 10*s* (4 Oct). John Colmer: 12 cwt hops £6. Thomas Longston: 6 cwt hops £3 (6 Oct). [f. 6*b*] Richard Grange: 50 fans £1 5*s*.

20. *Fortune* of Antwerp (50) John Dorne
[f. 3*b*] Humphrey Fairfax: 46 cwt hops £23 (3 Oct 1567). William Coles: 42 cwt hops £21. Hartik van Spreckleman: 2 packs flax £16. John Smith: 4 chests Rhenish glass £8 (4 Oct). [f. 6*b*] George Lubkin: 1500 ells Osnabrücks £20 (7 Oct).

21. *Angell* of Hamburg (60) Harman Bondman; Hamburg
[f. 4] Paul Tornull: 3 goshawks, 3 tercel-goshawks, 1 falcon, 3 tercel-gentle £7 13*s* 4*d* (3 Oct 1567). Alard Bartrinck: 1560 ells hinderlands £19 10*s* (6 Oct). Otte Frolik: 2640 ells middlegood, 3½ lasts croplings, 1 vat [*sic*] white Hamburg cloth £70 3*s* 4*d*. Matthew Hope: 4 lasts croplings £26 13*s* 4*d*. Court Ellers: 2160 ells hinderlands, 4 lasts titlings £40 6*s* 8*d*. Daniel van Eitson: 5 lasts croplings, 1 last titlings, 2160 ells hinderlands £63 13*s* 4*d*. George Lubkin: 1500 ells Osnabrücks £20 (7 Oct). John Miller: 480 ells middlegood £5 6*s* 8*d*. John Rainckin: 6 cwt feathers £9 (8 Oct). [f. 8*b*] George Gees: 2 packs flax £16 (9 Oct).

22. *Nightingale* of Amsterdam (30) John Garetson; Amsterdam
[f. 4] Richard Mouse: 3 lasts fish £18 (3 Oct 1567).

23. *Jerusalem* of Amsterdam (30) Jacob Garetson; Amsterdam
[f. 4] Richard Mouse: 5 lasts fish, 240 lings, 400 staplefish £44 (3 Oct 1567). [f. 5*b*] John Violet: 1200 lings, 2 lasts fish £52 (6 Oct).

24. *Sea Ridder* of Amsterdam (30) Lorance Balle
[f. 4] Richard Lee: 2 packs flax, 2 lasts pitch £20 (4 Oct 1567). [f. 8] Matthew Colcloth: 10 lasts pitch, 135 bundles flax £27 17*s* (8 Oct).

25. *Spledegle* of Amsterdam (30) Peter Huick
[f. 4*b*] John Smyth: 4 weys Rhenish glass £10 (4 Oct 1567).

26. *Abram* of London (40) Peter Marram; Southampton
[f. 4*b*] Stephen Borrogh: 1 last fish £6 (4 Oct 1567).

27. *Falcon* of Amsterdam (28) Simon Alardson
[f. 5*b*] John Violet: 4 lasts fish £24 (6 Oct 1567).

28. *Abraham* of Hamburg Hans Bowart; Danzig
[f. 6*b*] George Milner: 26 cwt cables, 1 pack flax £25 6*s* 4*d* (7 Oct 1567). William Jeames: 4 packs flax £32. Edmund Bolder: 5 lasts fish, 1 pack flax £18 (8 Oct). Thomas Allen: 8 packs flax, 10 lasts fish, 6 shocks deals, 100

wainscots, 4000 clapholt, 3½ hd rasters for oars¹ £157. Richard Gourney: 70 cwt small cables and hawsers £46 13*s* 4*d*. Hartik van Spreckleson: 9 packs flax £72. William Cockin: 10 lasts pitch, 8 half-packs flax, 52 cwt cordage £87. Maurice Tymbreman: 5 packs flax £40 (9 Oct). Robert Hillson: 8 packs flax £64. Robert Barker: 7 packs flax £56 (10 Oct). [f. 9] Roger Alabaster: 48 cwt wax £144 (13 Oct).

1. Oars were entered by the hd, containing 120.

29. *Michell* of Amsterdam (30) Cleys Peter Moone; Amsterdam
[f. 6*b*] Hartik van Sprecleman: 2 packs flax £16 (7 Oct 1567). [f. 7] Thomas Sanford: 600 lings, 500 staplefish £27 10*s*.

30. *Mearman* of Hamburg (20) Garret Thomas; Hamburg
[f. 7] Edward van Krog: 750 wainscots £30 (7 Oct 1567).

31. *Spledegle* of Akersloot (30) Peter Hugin; Amsterdam
[f. 7] John Lence: 12 pcs Holland cloth £14 8*s* 4*d* (7 Oct 1567).

32. *Falcon* of Amsterdam Alard Alardson
[f. 7] Thomas Sanford: 120 lings, 1 last fish £10 10*s* (7 Oct 1567).

33. *Spledegle* of Dordrecht Godfrey Dirikson
[f. 8] Reynold Thirling: 1200 bowstaves £20 (8 Oct 1567).

34. *Mychell* of Amsterdam (40) Henrik Johnson; Amsterdam
[f. 8] Robert King: 24 half-packs flax £96 (8 Oct 1567). John Edmunds: 3 lasts fish, 400 staplefish £24 (9 Oct). [f. 8*b*] John Haines: 5 lasts fish £30 (13 Oct).

35. *Catt* of Haarlem (40) John Jurianson; Haarlem
[f. 8*b*] George Jenens: 2160 lings, 2000 staplefish, 6 brls fish £105 (10 Oct 1567).

36. *Sea woolf* of Amsterdam (30) William Robe; Amsterdam
[f. 9] William Cokin: 6 packs flax £48 (13 Oct 1567). Maurice Tymberman: 4½ packs flax £36. Thomas Allen: 35 cwt cables, 5 packs flax £63 8*s* 4*d*. Dunstan Walton: 6 lasts pitch, 4 packs flax £44 (14 Oct). Thomas Russell: 15 cwt tarred rope, 12 doz. playing tables £109. Hartik van Spreckleson: 1 pack flax £8 (15 Oct). William Vaghen: 4 lasts pitch £8. [f. 9*b*] Robert Barker: 9½ packs flax £76.

37. *Thomas* of London (40) Robert Smyth; Rouen
[f. 9] Richard Patrick: 15 grs playing cards £15 (15 Oct 1567). Thomas Cambell: 32 cwt prunes £16. John Allot: 1500 ells canvas £37 10*s*. Richard Morris: 1000 ells canvas, 50 cwt prunes £50. William Thwaytes: 500 ells canvas £12 10*s*. John Harding: 400 ells canvas £10 (16 Oct). William Handford: 14 grs playing cards, 24 lbs wrought crewel £15 13*s* 4*d*. John Bodleigh: 1000 ells canvas £25. John Savell: 750 ells canvas £18 15*s*. John

Oliff: 1200 ells canvas £30. Robert Sadler: 1200 ells canvas, 24 cwt prunes £42 (17 Oct). [f. 18] Anthony Cage: 1600 ells canvas £40 (27 Oct).

38. *Grace of God* of Lee (30) John Stephen; Rouen
[f. 9] Richard Patrick: 20 doz. lbs thread, 30 grs combs, 10 doz. woolcards £25 16s 8d (15 Oct 1567). Richard Morris: 1400 ells canvas £35. John Harding: 800 ells canvas £20 (16 Oct). Richard Hills: 1000 ells canvas £25. John Newton: 150 reams paper £20. John Milner: 800 ells canvas £20 (17 Oct). William Salter: 17½ cwt prunes, 3½ cwt raisins of the sun £11 13s 4d. John Marshall: 800 ells canvas, 20 doz. woolcards £30. Robert Sadler: 600 ells canvas £15. Henry Waite: [ ][1] playing cards, 4 cwt prunes, 60 lbs nutmegs £22. Anthony Gamage: 1400 ells canvas £35. Lucas Harison: 41 reams unbound books £4 13s 4d (20 Oct). John Marshall: 24 doz woolcards £12. Wolston Dixi: 1200 ells canvas £30. John Byngley: 14 cwt prunes £7. John Bodleygh: 1400 ells canvas £35. Oliver Fisher: 9 cwt prunes £4 10s (21 Oct). Thomas Starkey: 1700 ells canvas £42 10s. William Salter: 95 butts Lyons thread £9 10s (22 Oct). [f. 16] Thomas Carter: 26 reams printing paper, 5 grs playing cards £8 1s 4d.

    1. Blank; by calculation 10 grs.

39. *Swallow* of London (120) Stephen Aborro; Russia
[f. 10] Stephen Twerdico and Theodore Pogorell 'of Russia merchants':[1] 322 cwt wax, 140 cwt tallow[2] (16 Oct 1567).

    1. Twerdico and Pogorell were Russian merchants. Their cargoes belonged to the Tsar, who asked Elizabeth to allow them in free of duty. Her only concession was to exempt their exports from the aliens' duty. T. S. Willan, *Early history of the Russia Company*, 80–1.
    2. The valuation and subsidy are illegible. Tallow is not listed in the Book of Rates.

40. *Charity* of London (130) Richard Gybbes; Russia
[f. 10] Stephen Twerdico and Theodore Pogorell: 189 cwt wax, 119 cwt tallow[1] (16 Oct 1567).

    1. The valuation is illegible; the duty paid was £33 2s 6d.

41. *Popingaye* of Haarlem (30) Marten Johnson
[f. 10b] James Heath: 30 cwt hops £15 (17 Oct 1567).

42. *Unicorn* of Haarlem (30) Cleys Roverson; Arnemuiden
[f. 10b] Robert Wilkinson: 20 weys great salt £20 (17 Oct 1567). John Freman: 350 stone cruses £1 15s.

43. *Pellican* of Amsterdam (30) Naninck Johnson; Amsterdam
[f. 10b] Hartik van Sprecleson: 4 packs flax £32 (17 Oct 1567).

44. *Robert* of Aldeburgh (70) William Huggans; The Bay
[f. 10b] William Huggans: 54 weys great salt £54 (20 Oct 1567).

45. *Prym Rose* of Milton (80) Harry Church; Antwerp
[f. 11] Lucas Harryson: 40 reams unbound books, 40 reams paper with

certain parchment ad valorem 40*s* £11 6*s* 8*d* (20 Oct 1567). George Stockmed: 45 cwt unwrought flax £30. Richard Cotton: 36 doz. yds Cyprus cotton £7 3*s* 4*d*. George Bisshop: 60 reams unbound books £6. Humphrey Whitelok: 5 doz. Turnhout ticks £20. George Colimor: 80 doz. thou. pins, 70 pins, 6 doz. lbs bottom thread £26 5*s*. John Jackman: 32 cwt madder, 50 lbs ginger, 3 qrs 7 lbs cloves, 214 lbs pepper £63 8*s* 4*d*. Richard Billam: 140 Turnhout ticks £46 13*s* 4*d* (21 Oct). John Eliots: 8 doz. lbs crewel, 12 doz. lbs thread, 30 doz. thou. pins, 3 grs coarse looking glasses, 8 grs minikins, 4 grs coarse hat bands, 4 doz. thou. needles, 4 doz. crewel pieces, 2 thou. thimbles, 3 cwt black plates £36 18*s* 4*d*. Thomas Longston: 300 lbs pepper £25. William Coles and John Newman: 44½ cwt madder £29 13*s* 4*d*. Lawrence Wythers: ½ brl nails, ¼ brl small nails £4. Edward Jackman: 650 lbs pepper, 12 brls rape oil £70 3*s* 4*d*. Lucas Lane: 450 lbs pepper £37 10*s*. Roland Erlington: 6 thou. balls £6. Thomas Gardener: 90 doz. hemp, 400 lbs pepper, 6¾ cwt aniseed, 2 cwt coriander seed £54 18*s* 4*d*. William Loddington: 12 cwt madder, 25 lbs mace, 3½ cwt rice, 1½ cwt brown candy, 4½ cwt dates, 170 lbs ginger, 1¾ cwt aniseed £47 16*s* 8*d*. Robert Brook: 1350 lbs pepper £112 10*s*. Roger Warfyld: 400 lbs ginger, 600 lbs pepper, 4 cwt litmus, 200 lbs crossbow thread, 1 cwt orpiment, 150 lbs marmalade, 2 cwt lignum vitae £67 13*s* 4*d*. Thomas Brassy: 2 bales Ulm fustian £30. Thomas Eaton: 10 grs halfpennyware looking glasses, 30 doz. thou. pins, 2½ grs 'almaines' knives, 1 doz. thou. needles, 16 doz. yds Cyprus cotton, 18 cwt madder, 5 cwt black plates £30 6*s* 8*d*. John Carr: 36 cwt iron pans, 15 cwt 'ames' iron, 3½ cwt varnish, 4 hd iron plates, 150 iron doubles, 6 cwt fireshovel plates £41 15*s*. Thomas Thorp: 2 brls painter's oil £2 13*s* 4*d*. Thomas Hale: 5 cwt rosalger, 3 cwt galls £14. William Bond: 10 sacks coarse hat wool[1] £14 13*s* 4*d* (22 Oct). Robert Broune: 61 yds velvet, 53 ells sarcenet £54 11*s* 8*d*. John Boorne: 10 doz. lbs thread, 20 grs harp strings, 3 thou. thimbles, 10 doz. thou. needles, 20 grs lute strings, 2 grs comb brushes, 5 thou. awl blades, 3 doz. files, 3 grs trenchers, 1 doz. compasses, ½ grs hour glasses, 10 grs halfpennyware looking glasses, 3 doz. lbs counters, 4 grs coarse hat bands, 2 doz. crewel pieces, 1 doz. lbs clavichord wire £41 10*s*. William Hewet: 2 bales Ulm fustian £30. John Rivers: 450 lbs ginger, 400 lbs pepper £67. Nicholas Luddington: 16 cwt madder £10 13*s* 4*d*. Henry Hungat: 8 lbs half-silk fringe £8. Robert Scarborugh: 13 cwt madder £8 13*s* 4*d*. William Salkins: 1600 ells Dutch packing canvas £21 6*s* 8*d*. Thomas Blank: 20 pcs Hondschoote say £20. Ancelm Becket: 5¾ cwt flax £5 15*s*. John Sutton: 153 Turnhout ticks, 13 counterfeit Turnhout ticks £55 6*s* 8*d*. Humphrey Fayrefax: 220 lbs ginger £16 10*s*. John Taylor: 120 doz. thou. pins £20. Robert Bladwell: 350 lbs pepper £29 3*s* 4*d*. John Wanton: 36 cwt German madder £24. Richard Goddard: 16 cwt mull-madder £2. Stephen Slany: 41 pcs Holland cloth, 300 ells 'clincent' canvas £53 13*s* 4*d*. John Fytzwilliams: 14 cwt madder £9 6*s* 8*d* (23 Oct). Nicholas Spering: 10 lbs combs, 3 grs knives £7. Francis Keightley: 140 yds velvet, 100 ells sarcenet £121 13*s* 4*d*. John Gardner: 100 lbs cloves, 50 lbs cinnamon, 125 lbs nutmegs, drugs ad valorem 60*s* £58 16*s* 8*d*. Edmund Hills: 140 lbs cloves £35. George Southak: 225 lbs ginger £16 16*s* 8*d*. Thomas Hale: 50 lbs cloves, 30 lbs ginger £14 15*s*. Robert Marres: 300 lbs ginger £22 10*s*. William Smith: 30 pcs broad worsted £30. John Isham:

102 yds velvet, 60 yds satin, 60 pcs mockado £143 10*s*. Abraham Smith: 3 doz. crystal glasses £6 (24 Oct). Roger Warfilde: 400 lbs pepper £33 6*s* 8*d*. Thomas Randall: 66 yds velvet £49 10*s*. William Tench: 132 lbs ferret silk £55. Thomas Gryme: 30 pcs Holland cloth £36. Thomas Parker: 48 pcs mockado, 54 half-pcs 4 pcs bustian £52 13*s* 4*d*. John Alden: 3 cwt white lead, 3 cwt starch, drugs ad valorem 133*s* 4*d* £10 18*s* 4*d* (25 Oct). John Spencer: 400 lbs matches £3 6*s* 8*d*. John Johnson: 20 pcs mockado, 8 grs copper hat bands, 80 lbs nutmegs, 20 lbs ginger, 5 thou. awl blades, 120 yds Naples fustian, 30 doz. crewel pieces, 40 papers ferret silk £91 10*s*. John Colmer: 4 cwt sumach, 4 thou. balls £6 13*s* 4*d* (27 Oct). Wolston Dixi: 17 pcs Holland cloth, 400 ells 'clincent' canvas £26 8*s* 4*d*. William Smith: 20 pcs camlet £20 (31 Oct). Thomas Eaton: 200 ells Levant taffeta £16 13*s* 4*d* (3 Nov). Henry Smith: 25 lbs fringes, 30 lbs Spanish silk, 12 doz. yds passement lace £71. William Hobs: 300 ells hair tapestry, 100 ells caddis tapestry, 3 doz. coarse cushions, 12 pair blankets, 28 pcs carpet, 3 doz. Ghentish or sealed carpets, 32 Turnhout ticks £43 8*s* 4*d* (7 Nov). [f. 22] Henry Beecher: 10 doz. thou. pins, 10 doz. lbs worsted checks, 10 reams unbound books £7 13*s* 4*d*.

1. The sacks contained 11 hd lbs. Hat wool is identified as Spanish wool which was rated by the hd lbs; this was probably a cwt: see **46**.

46. *John* of Lee (60) Richard Higham; Antwerp

[f. 11] George Stockmed: 15 cwt unwrought flax £10 (20 Oct 1567). George Colimor: 8 thou. balls £8. John Eliots: 6 doz. lbs thread, 3 thou. awl blades, 80 lbs counters, 10 lbs clavichord wire, 5 grs coarse looking glasses, 5 doz. lbs crewel, 6 doz. thou. pins, 2 doz. crewel pieces £17 1*s* 8*d* (21 Oct). Thomas Longston: 250 lbs pepper £20 16*s* 8*d*. George Breme: 10 cwt battery £20. William Coles: 21½ cwt madder, 3 qrs 6 lbs cloves, 62 lbs mace £55 18*s* 4*d*. Thomas Aldersay: 325 yds sarcenet, 40 yds velvet £84 3*s* 4*d*. William Bower: 5 half-brls head nails, 8 cwt estrige wool £16 13*s* 4*d*. Wolston Dixi: 900 ells Newcastle canvas, 700 ells Bar canvas, 3 pcs 'brissels' £30. Edward Jackman: 425 lbs, [*sic*] 250 lbs ginger, 12 brls rape oil £70 3*s* 4*d*. Lucas Lane: 180 lbs cloves £45. Roland Erlington: 110 doz. thou. pins, 4 doz. lbs bottom thread £18 6*s* 8*d*. John Spencer: 4½ cwt aniseed, 200 lbs ginger, 200 lbs pepper, 3 qrs candy £40 3*s* 4*d*. Thomas Gardener: 5 brls painter's oil, 2¾ cwt gunpowder, 3 qrs nutmegs, 30 lbs long pepper, 125 lbs ginger, 1 cwt coriander seed, 100 lbs turnsole £44 11*s* 8*d*. William Luddington: 12 cwt madder, 212 lbs pepper, 200 lbs ginger, 2 cwt aniseed £43 6*s* 8*d*. Thomas Brassy: 2 bales Ulm fustian £30. John Alden: 3 brls painter's oil, 710 lbs pepper £63 3*s* 4*d*. Thomas Starkey: 7 hd 'plaine barrs',[1] 200 ells 'clincent' canvas £17. John Carr: ironmongery ad valorem £30, 'locke persers of wood', 2 grs horse bells, 3 doz. cooper's tools cost 20*s*, 2 doz. short hand-saws at 5*s*, 1 doz. iron chafing dishes cost 6*s* 8*d*, 4 cwt iron plates £36 16*s* 8*d*. Thomas Hale: 450 lbs pepper, 356 lbs aniseed, 2 cwt coriander seed, 30 lbs senna, 3 cwt red lead, 1 bag nigella, 40 lbs capers £50 6*s* 4*d*. Robert Exton: 18 brls rape oil £24. William Bond: 10 sacks hat or Spanish wool £14 13*s* 4*d* (22 Oct). Edmund Burton: 4 doz. whip-saws, 6 doz. two-hand-saws, 12 doz. hand-saws, 150 doubles, 5½ cwt wrought flax, 325 lbs bottom thread, 18 doz. locks, 1 grs horse bells, 20 doz.

8

coarse snuffers £29 5s. Edmund Smith: 3 bales Ulm fustian £45. William Sherington: 10 lbs Bruges silk, 6 lbs fringe £16. Alexander Sherington: 150 yds taffeta £50. John Borne: 10 doz. lbs thread, 2 doz. lbs crewel, 50 doz. thou. pins, 20 doz. lbs pack thread, 3 doz. crewel pieces £22 13s 4d. Robert Scarborugh: 13 cwt madder, 8 doz. yds Cyprus cotton £10 6s 8d. William Salkins: 700 ells Dutch packing canvas £9 6s 8d. Humphrey Fayrefax: 220 lbs ginger £16 10s. John Wanton: 54 cwt German madder £36. Richard Goddard: 14 cwt mull-madder £1 15s. Stephen Slany: 700 ells 'clincent' canvas, 300 ells Bar canvas £16 10s. John Fytzwilliams: 12 cwt madder £8 (23 Oct). Francis Keightley: 40 yds velvet, 180 ells sarcenet £60. John Gardner: 110 lbs ginger, 75 lbs nutmeg, 50 lbs long pepper, 400 lbs pepper £53 6s 8d. Edmund Hills: 300 lbs ginger £22 10s. George Southak: 225 lbs ginger £16 6s 8d. Thomas Gardner: 275 lbs ginger, 75 lbs mace, 75 lbs cinnamon, 30 lbs nutmeg, 25 lbs long pepper £71 16s 8d. John Isham: 80 yds velvet, 100 yds damask £100. Thomas Randell: 250 yds Levant taffeta, 20 doz. yds Cyprus cotton £24 16s 8d (24 Oct). Thomas Gryme: 25 pcs Holland cloth £30. John Eliots: 3 doz. lbs thread, 3 thou. awl blades, 20 lbs counters, 10 lbs clavichord wire, 5 doz. crewel pieces, 2 doz. 'knit cotten' petticoats £10 5s. Thomas Parker: 8 half-pcs dornick with thread, 13 pcs crewel dornick, 4 pcs Naples fustian, 6 Venice carpets £18 6s 8d. Humphrey Marbury: 13 pcs fustian, 150 ells sarcenet £38 (25 Oct). John Colmer: 4 cwt bay berries, 80 lbs candy, 5 brls rape oil £12 (27 Oct). John Boorne: 10 papers silk, 50 doz. thou. pins £28 6s 8d (31 Oct). William Smith: 20 pcs camlet £20. John Lambert: 6 cwt frying pans, 17 cwt flax £21 (3 Nov). Henry Smith: 20 pcs mockado £13 16s 8d. [f. 22] Henry Beacher: 20 reams unbound books, 4 doz. lbs wrought inkle, 3 doz. lbs thread £6 13s 4d (7 Nov).

1. Probably Bar canvas.

47. *Spledegle* of Bruges (60) Francis Bauwins; Bruges
[f. 11] Thomas Bressy: 165 pcs buckram £33 6s 8d (20 Oct 1567).

48. *Andrew* of Antwerp (40) Cornilis Johnson Sprite
[f. 12] John Lambert: 950 lbs pepper £79 3s 4d (21 Oct 1567). Thomas Aldersay: 110 yds satin, 30 yds damask £61 10s. [f. 14b] John Reinkin: 1 pack flax £8 (22 Oct).

49. *Seahorse* of Hamburg (40) Harman Crite; Hamburg
[f. 12b] Otte Frolick: 2160 ells middlegood,[1] 6 lasts croplings £55 13s 4d (21 Oct 1567). Court Ellers: 16 cwt estrige wool, 1080 ells soultwich[2] £31 6s 8d. George Lubkin: 1500 ells Osnabrücks £20. Daniel van Eytson: 7 lasts croplings, 2 lasts titlings £53 6s 8d. John Rainkin: 10 lasts croplings, 2040 ells middlegood £76 (22 Oct). Sir John White: 25 lbs nutmegs, 175 lbs ungarbled mace £62 10s. Edward van Crog: 4½ cwt estrige wool, 150 wainscots £9 15s. George Geys: 1 pack flax £8. [f. 16] Alard Bartrinck: 5 lasts stockfish £33 6s 8d (23 Oct).

1. Entered as 18 hd lbs. In the Book of Rates middlegood is valued by the C = 120 ells.
2. Also entered by the hd lbs and not, as in the Book of Rates, by the C = 120 ells.

50. *Falcon* of Dordrecht (30) Adrian Dottell; Dordrecht
[f. 13*b*] Richard Robertson: 275 bundles rods £4 11*s* 8*d* (21 Oct 1567).

51. *Mary James* of Aldeburgh (60) Robert Perce; La Rochelle
[f. 13*b*] Robert Perce: 50 weys bay salt £50 (21 Oct 1567).

52. *Unicorn* of London (45) Jacob Cornilison
[f. 14] Gawen van Alden: 85 awms Rhenish wine 85*s*, 50 pcs mockado
£33 6*s* 8*d* (22 Oct 1567).

53. *Santa Maria de Gracia*[1] of Venice (350) Manolly Chatity;[2] Venice
[f. 14] Innocento Luocatelly: 268 butts 30 caroteel malmsey and muscatel[3]
net 186 butts 286*s* 6*d* (22 Oct 1567). Anthony Donato: 147 butts malmsey
and muscatel, 6 caroteel muscatel *net* 103 butts 154*s* 6*d* (27 Oct). Baptist
de John: 54 butts 6 caroteel sweet wines *net* 38 butts 57*s*. Giles Flood:
375 lbs cinnamon, 900 lbs pepper, 64 lbs marmalade, 16 lbs green ginger,
16 lbs nutmeg £93 16*s* 8*d* (4 Nov). William Cooper: 6 Venice lutes £6
(5 Nov). [f. 28*b*] Innocento Lacatellye: 66 butts sweet wine *net* 45 butts
67*s* 6*d* (14 Nov).

> 1. Also the *Cross*.
> 2. Also Lucas Chatity or Lucas de Manolli.
> 3. All the sweet wines from Venice were entered under the licence of Benedict
> Spinola, the Italian merchant and financier. His current licence was granted 2 July
> 1566. *Calendar of Patent Rolls 1563–6*, 473.

54. *Goldowe* of Hamburg (130) Henryk Milner; Brouage
[f. 15] Humphrey Keel: 100 weys bay salt £100 (22 Oct 1567). [f. 18*b*]
Nicolas Nells: 3 tuns Rochelle wine *net* 2 tuns 6*s* (27 Oct).

55. *Peter* of Flushing (15) Anthony Antonison; Flushing
[f. 15*b*] Robert Wilkinson: 3 weys bay salt £3 (22 Oct 1567).

56. *Nightingale* of Haarlem Derick Alardson
[f. 16] John Lence: 26 pcs Holland cloth £31 3*s* 4*d* (23 Oct 1567).

57. *Merman* of Amsterdam (30) Peter Garetson
[f. 16*b*] John Violet: 1200 lings, 2000 staplefish £70 (23 Oct 1567). John
Haynes: 5 lasts fish £30.

58. *Grace* of Rye (33) William Haman; Nantes
[f. 17] William Allen, Thomas Starkey and Oliver Fisher: 67 pipes 16 hhds
prunes[1] £162 10*s* (24 Oct 1567).

> 1. Containing 325 quintals.

59. *Reall* of Oléron (46) Maturin Toning; Oléron
[f. 17*b*] André Jerrard: 44 tuns Oléron wine *net* 37 tuns 111*s* (25 Oct 1567).

60. *Hearn* of London (36) John Davis; Nantes
[f. 17*b*] William Allen, Thomas Starkey and Oliver Fisher: 3 pipes prunes[1]

£7 10*s* (25 Oct 1567). [f. 18] Hugh Offley: 36 pipes 66 hhds prunes[2] £172 10*s* (27 Oct).

1. Containing 15 cwt.
2. 345 cwt.

61. *Host Pery* of Dunwich (44) Thomas Coper; Bordeaux
[f. 18] Thomas Pen: 13½ tuns Gascony wine *net* 12 tuns 36*s* (27 Oct 1567).
[f. 18*b*] Nicholas Culverwell: 26 tuns 2 hhds Gascony wine *net* 25 tuns 75*s*.

62. *Marigold* of Lee (45) Thomas Andros; Rouen
[f. 18] Richard Hill: 600 ells canvas £15 (27 Oct 1567). John Allot: 1400 ells canvas £35. John Oliff: 2200 ells canvas, 10 cwt prunes £60 (30 Oct). Richard Moris: 1200 ells canvas £30. William Handford: 400 butts Lyons thread £40. John Harding: 700 ells canvas £17 10*s* (31 Oct). Richard Carmardin: 40 reams unbound books £4. John Wanton: 30 doz. woolcards £15. Robert Sadler: 18 grs coarse combs, 250 ells canvas £15 5*s*. John White: 43¾ cwt woad £35. [f. 20*b*] William Body: 200 reams paper, 13 pcs remnants, 130 yds taffeta, 75 yds grogram silk £73 6*s* 8*d*.

63. *Falcon* of Lee (50) John Boner; Bilbao
[f. 18] Richard May: 5 tons iron, 5 hd lbs wool £24 3*s* 4*d* (27 Oct 1567). Anthony Pilboro: 5 tons iron £20. Richard Renolds: 16 hd lbs Spanish wool £13 6*s* 8*d*. William Hewet: 10 tons Spanish iron, 5½ hd lbs Spanish wool £47 6*s* 8*d*. Francis Bowyer: 10 tons iron £40 (30 Oct). Thomas Hewet: 9 tons iron £36. Edward Boys: 3 tons iron £12. Robert Car: 3 tons iron £12. [f. 20] Richard Folkes: 10 tons iron £40 (31 Oct).

64. *Edward* of London (40) Andrew Luce; Rouen
[f. 18] Wolston Dixi: 1600 ells canvas £40 (27 Oct 1567). Harry Waite: 10 cwt prunes £5. John Bingley: 7 cases Normandy glass £7 (30 Oct). John Bodleygh: 3000 ells canvas £75. John Oliff: 800 ells canvas £20. John Marshall: 1400 ells canvas £35. Richard Patrick: 20 grs combs, 4 grs inkhorns, 12 grs lead tablets, 12 doz. ounce balances, 40 doz. woolcards £30. Hugh Offley: 200 reams paper, 32 doz. woolcards, 3 grs pennyware combs, 4 grs points, 10 grs girdling, 6 grs crewel lace £55 16*s* 8*d*. Humphrey Broune: 40 grs combs, 4 cwt pack thread, 4 grs inkhorns, 3 grs pennyware combs, 48 reams paper, 20 grs combs £35 3*s* 4*d*. William Bond: 96 cwt prunes £48 (31 Oct). John White: 52½ cwt woad £35. [f. 20*b*] John Mylner: 700 ells canvas £17 10*s*.

65. *Claydon* of Audierne (40) John Regale; Bordeaux
[f. 18*b*] Remond Jerard: 34 tuns Gascony wine *net* 27 tuns 81*s* (27 Oct 1567).

66. *Mary and John* of London (55) John Diet; Bordeaux
[f. 18*b*] Thomas Robbley: 48 tuns Gascony wine *net* 40 tuns 120*s*, 2 tuns vinegar £4 13*s* 4*d* (27 Oct 1567). [f. 20] John Lendall: 4 tuns Gascony wine *net* 2 tuns 6*s* (30 Oct).

67. *Young Eagle* of Antwerp Anthony Cornish the younger
[f. 18*b*] John Lambert: 1000 ells Vitré canvas £16 13*s* 4*d* (27 Oct 1567).
Thomas Brasy: 3 bales Ulm fustian £45. Gervais Simons: 20 doz. lbs pack
thread, 400 fox backs, 40 doz. foin backs, 9 mantles foin wombs £35 3*s* 4*d*
(30 Oct). [f. 19*b*] Francis Wootton: 80 ells sarcenet £13 6*s* 8*d*.

68. *Prymrose* of Brightlingsea (50) William Hickson; Bordeaux
[f. 19] Steven Skidmore and coy: 46 tuns Gascony wine *net* 40½ tuns
121*s* 6*d* (30 Oct 1567).

69. *Red Hart* of Amsterdam Cleyse Derickson; Danzig
[f. 19] George Milner: 4 packs flax £32 (30 Oct 1567). Robert Hilson:
13½ packs flax £52. Edmund Boldero: 1 pack flax, 3 lasts 1 brl pitch £14.
William James: 4 packs flax £32. Thomas Allen: 4 packs flax, 2 packs [*sic*]¹
hemp, 3 lasts 5 brls pitch, 30 pcs poldavis £108 16*s* 8*d*. Dunstan Walton:
20 cwt cables £13 6*s* 8*d* (31 Oct). [f. 21*b*] Thomas Russell: 20 cwt cables
£13 6*s* 8*d* (4 Nov).

    1. Hemp is rated by the sack = 3 cwt.

70. *Falcon* of Flushing (12) Francis Johnson; Flushing
[f. 19] Robert Wilkinson: 7 weys bay salt £7 (30 Oct 1567).

71. *Catharin* of Dieppe (20) Thomas Swinet
[f. 20*b*] William Body: 10 pcs poldavis, 3 tuns vinegar £17 (31 Oct 1567).
[f. 21] John Rogers: 18 cwt woad £12 (3 Nov).

72. *Angell* of Amsterdam (50) Tylman Cornilis; Amsterdam
[f. 20*b*] Walter Lin: 56 awms Rhenish wine 56*s* (31 Oct 1567). [f. 21*b*]
Edward Hardandnoght: 18 cwt argol, 650 ells soultwich £31 15*s* (4 Nov).

73. *Owl* of Dordrecht (40) Jacob Florisson; Dordrecht
[f. 21] Gawen van Alden: 135 awms Rhenish wine 135*s* (3 Nov 1567).

74. *Mary Edward* of Brightlingsea (38) John Warald
[f. 21] Steven Skidmore and coy: 34 tuns Gascony wine *net* 30 tuns 90*s*
(3 Nov 1567).

75. *Mary Thomas* of Brightlingsea (28) John Davis; Bordeaux
[f. 21] Richard Whitelock: 23 tuns Gascony wine *net* 18 tuns 54*s*, 2 tuns
vinegar £4 13*s* 4*d* (3 Nov 1567).

76. *Bark* of Brightlingsea (90) Stephen Upchurch; La Rochelle
[f. 21*b*] Stephen Upchurch: 60 weys great salt £60 (4 Nov 1567). [f. 22*b*]
Stephen Upchurch: 8 weys great salt £8 (7 Nov).

77. *Lion* of London (80) Richard Bebell; La Rochelle
[f. 21*b*] John Broke 'cum sociis': 60 weys great salt £60 (4 Nov 1567).

78. *Bark Allen* of London (80) Lawrence Hayward of Ratcliff; Malaga
[f. 21*b*] Simon Brooke: 250 pcs raisins[1] £62 10*s* (5 Nov 1567). Edward
Jackman: 250 pcs raisins £62 10*s*. John Spencer: 250 pcs raisins £62 10*s*.
John Gill and John Jackson: 40 cwt raisins of the sun, 28 hd capers, 70 pcs
great raisins £96 16*s* 8*d* (6 Nov). [f. 23*b*] William Allen: 300 pcs raisins,
10 cwt almonds, 20 cwt raisins of the sun £111 13*s* 4*d* (10 Nov).

    1. According to this entry 25 pcs = 1 ton.

79. *Mary Fortune* of Aldeburgh (30) Thomas Baker; The Bay
[f. 22] Thomas Baker: 20 weys great salt £20 (5 Nov 1567).

80. *James* of Cherbourg (50) Michel Body; La Rochelle
[f. 22] John Perote: 22 tuns corrupt wine *net* 19½ tuns £58 10*s*, 8 tuns
Gascony wine *net* 7½ tuns 22*s* 6*d* (6 Nov 1567).

81. *Elizabeth* of London (80) Robert Burrell; Andalusia
[f. 22] John Bird: 120 pcs raisins £30 (7 Nov 1567). George Saunders:
250 pcs raisins £62 10*s*. [f. 24] John Hawes: 600 pcs raisins £150 (10 Nov).

82. *Mary* of Olonne (60) Francis Tasserons; La Rochelle
[f. 22*b*] Jacques de Quester: 22 tuns Rochelle wine *net* 20 tuns 60*s*, 33 tuns
corrupt wine £99 (7 Nov 1567).

83. *Mawdlin* of Cherbourg (48) Harry Marry; La Rochelle
[f. 22*b*] Michael Lion: 24 weys great salt £24 (7 Nov 1567). John Lion:
8 tuns Rochelle wine *net* 6 tuns 18*s*, 6 tuns corrupt wine £18.

84. *Margaret* of Le Croisic (48) John Le Rouse; Le Croisic
[f. 22*b*] Christopher Wilford: 38 weys bay salt £38 (7 Nov 1567).

85. *Jaquet* of Jard (56) Charles Evernoy; La Rochelle
[f. 22*b*] Elie Papie: 40 tuns Gascony wine *net* 35 tuns 105*s* (7 Nov 1567).

86. *Henry* of 'Marvers' (75) John Bayed; Bordeaux
[f. 22*b*] Robert Fryer: 70 pcs resin £11 13*s* 4*d* (7 Nov 1567).

87. *Mary fortune* of Harwich (66) John Pearson; Spain
[f. 23] Thomas Altham: 375 pcs Marbella raisins £93 15*s* (8 Nov 1567).
Thomas Hewet: 250 pcs raisins £62 10*s*. [f. 24] Richard Staper: 370 pcs
raisins £94 15*s* (10 Nov).

88. *Beniamin* of London (70) John Dunton; Marbella
[f. 23] Thomas Turnebull and Henry Wallis: 275 pcs Marbella raisins
£68 15*s* (8 Nov 1567). Anthony Pilborro: 275 pcs raisins £68 15*s*. John
Bird: 160 pcs raisins £40. William Wignall: 200 pcs raisins £50. Robert
Phillips: 250 pcs raisins £62 10*s*. Simon Broke: 275 pcs raisins £68 15*s*
(10 Nov). John Mun: 125 pcs raisins £31 5*s*. [f. 24] Reynold Barker: 275 pcs
raisins, 22 pcs raisins 'de lixa', 13 cwt raisins of the sun £86 1*s* 8*d*.

89. *Pelican* of Amsterdam (35)[1]
[f. 23] Richard Mouse: 6 brls dole-eels £14 (8 Nov 1567).

> 1. Entered 'ut postea', which is in error unless this is **43** and the dates make this unlikely.

90. *Red Lion* of Amsterdam (30) Simon Alardson; Amsterdam
[f. 23] John Violet: 3 lasts middle stockfish £20 (8 Nov 1567).

91. *Pelican* of Amsterdam Adrian Cornilis[1]
[f. 23] Hartik van Sprecle: 2 packs flax £16 (8 Nov 1567). John Rainkin: 6 packs flax £48 (10 Nov). Otte Frolik: 960 ells middlegood £10 13s 4d.
[f. 24] Court Ellers: 3 half-packs flax £12.

> 1. This could be **89**.

92. *Mary Anne* of Brightlingsea (36) John Chandler; Bordeaux
[f. 23] Thomas Pen: 25 tuns Rochelle wine *net* 22 tuns 66s, 4 tuns corrupt wine £12 (10 Nov 1567).

93. *Anne Gallant* of Brightlingsea (40) Thomas Gallway; Bordeaux
[f. 23b] Nicholas Culverwell: 23 tuns Gascony wine *net* 19 tuns 57s, 15 tuns corrupt wine £45 (10 Nov 1567).

94. *Michell* of Flushing (14) Peter Cleison; Flushing
[f. 23b] Robert Wilkinson: 5 weys great salt £5 (10 Nov 1567).

95. *Clement* of London (70) Thomas Rickman; Spain
[f. 23b] Reynold Holingworth: 120 pcs raisins £30 (10 Nov 1567). Robert How: 50 pcs raisins £12 10s. Richard Venables: 125 pcs raisins £31 5s. Richard Hill: 125 pcs raisins £31 5s. John Mun: 250 pcs raisins £62 10s. John Highlord: 125 pcs raisins £31 5s (11 Nov). [f. 27b] William Salter: 425 pcs raisins £106 5s (14 Nov).

96. *Marygold* of Harwich Thomas Twyde
[f. 23b] Edmund Flick: 100 pcs raisins £25 (10 Nov 1567). [f. 24] William Bond: 60 cwt and 1300 pcs raisins, 26 cwt almonds £407.

97. *Minion* of Harwich (65) Percival Wright; Marbella
[f. 24] William Bond: 1000 pcs raisins £250 (10 Nov 1567).

98. *Lady* of Arnemuiden (30) Jope Peters; Arnemuiden
[f. 24] Robert Wilkinson: 20 weys great salt £20 (10 Nov 1567).

99. *Flower de luce* of Haarlem (30) Naning Peters; Amsterdam
[f. 24] John Smith: 3 weys Rhenish glass £7 10s (11 Nov 1567).

100. *Nicolas* of Flushing (12) Martin Michellson; Flushing
[f. 24b] Robert Wilkinson: 4 weys great salt £4 (11 Nov 1567).

101. *Jacob* of Arnemuiden (30) Peter Johnson
[f. 24*b*] Richard Grange: 100 small bundles white rods £1 13*s* 4*d* (11 Nov 1567). Robert Wilkinson: 15 weys bay salt, 7 weys white salt £24 6*s* 8*d*.

102. *Pellican* of London (40) Harry Wright of Ratcliff; Spain
[f. 24*b*] Robert Dow: 800 pcs raisins £200 (11 Nov 1567). [f. 27] William Clark: 180 pcs raisins £45 (13 Nov).

103. *Unicorn* of Amsterdam (30) Peter Cleison
[f. 24*b*] Ralph King: 3 lasts pitch, 6 half-pcs Holland cloth £9 11*s* 8*d* (12 Nov 1567). John Violet: 1000 staplefish £15. William Plaisden: 3 packs flax, 30 cwt loose flax £44. Otte Frolik: 960 ells middlegood £10 13*s* 4*d* (14 Nov). Court Ellers: 8 half-packs flax £32. [f. 54*b*] John Lence: 11 pcs Holland cloth £13 3*s* 4*d* (12 Dec).

104. *Blak Raven* of Purmerend (40) Adrian Jacobson; Amsterdam
[f. 24*b*] John Broke 'et socio': 60 cwt hemp £60 (12 Nov 1567). [f. 27*b*] Court Ellers: 8 half-packs flax £32 (14 Nov).

105. *Pelican* of Amsterdam (30) Alert Allertson; Amsterdam
[f. 24*b*] Thomas Sanford: 600 lings £20 (12 Nov 1567).

106. *Meg* of Colchester (50) John Cok; Bordeaux
[f. 24*b*] Nicholas Culverwell: 44 tuns Gascony wine *net* 40 tuns 120*s*, 2 tuns vinegar £4 13*s* 4*d* (12 Nov 1567).

107. *Mary Jemes* of Brightlingsea (38) John Meyd; Bordeaux
[f. 25] Edmund Bird: 37 tuns Gascony wine *net* 32 tuns 96*s* (12 Nov 1567).

108. *Primrose* of Rye (46) John Chestell; Bordeaux
[f. 25] Henry Waite: 34 tuns Gascony wine *net* 27 tuns 81*s*, 1 tun vinegar £2 6*s* 8*d* (12 Nov 1567). John Hunwick: 5 tuns Gascony wine *net* 5 tuns 15*s* (14 Nov). [f. 29] Henry Waite: 7 tuns Gascony wine *net* 6 tuns 18*s* (17 Nov).

109. *Mearman* of Haarlem (30) Walter Simonson; Haarlem
[f. 25] John Edmunds: 2 lasts fish £12 (12 Nov 1567). George Gees: 3¼ packs flax £26. [f. 27] George Henens: 2 lasts barrelled fish £12 (13 Nov).

110. *Unicorn* of St. Omer (20) Gilliam Mercie; St. Omer
[f. 25] Thomas Kelley: 4 cwt Holland cheese, 2 brls apples £1 8*s* 4*d* (12 Nov 1567).

111. *Mary fortune* of Lee (75) John Mors; Bordeaux
[f. 25] Robert Fryer: 65 tuns Gascony wine *net* 56 tuns 168*s* (12 Nov 1567).

112. *Awdry Joanes* of London (70) John Burwell; Spain
[f. 25] William Allen: 250 pcs Malaga raisins £62 10*s* (12 Nov 1567). John Rivers: 400 pcs raisins £100 (14 Nov). [f. 28] John Barne: 350 pcs raisins £87 10*s*.

113. *Diamond* of Lee (50) Richard Hadock; Spain
[f. 25] Robert King: 3600 lbs figs-dode, 2400 lbs figs-merchant[1] £16 13s 4d
(12 Nov 1567). John Highlord: 270 pcs figs-merchant, 33600 lbs figs-dode,
36 lbs cinnamon, 40 lbs cloves, 500 lbs pepper, 20 doz. cork £192 10s.
[f. 27] John Bird: 7500 lbs 50 pcs figs £27 10s (13 Nov).

1. Figs are either given by the pc. or by the topnet of 30 lbs.

114. *Mary flower* of Lee (65) John North; Bordeaux
[f. 25] Thomas Searle: 56 tuns Gascony wine *net* 50½ tuns 152s 6d, 4 tuns
vinegar £9 6s 8d (12 Nov 1567). [f. 28] Davy Gittons: 3 tuns Gascony wine
net 2½ tuns 7s 6d (14 Nov).

115. *Star* of Haarlem (50) Albart Peterson; Haarlem
[f. 25b] George Gees: 1¾ packs flax £14 (12 Nov 1567).

116. *Mary Flower* of Lee (75) Robert Pope; Bordeaux
[f. 25b] Robert Fryer: 65 tuns Gascony wine *net* 56 tuns 168s (12 Nov 1567).

117. *Falcon* of Dordrecht (30) Anthony Williamson; Dordrecht
[f. 25b] Richard Grange: 300 small bundles white rods £5 (12 Nov 1567).

118. *Peter* of Lee (40) John Tylor; Bordeaux
[f. 25b] Thomas Loan: 38 tuns Gascony wine *net* 33 tuns 99s (12 Nov 1567).

119. *Greyhound* of Lee (60) William Mote; Bordeaux
[f. 25b] Edward Osburne: 17 tuns Gascony wine *net* 14 tuns 42s, 10 tuns
corrupt wine £30 (12 Nov 1567). Lawrence Mello: 13 tuns Gascony wine
net 12 tuns 36s, 10 tuns corrupt wine £30.

120. *Margaret* of Lee (45) Thomas Barret
[f. 26] Thomas Searle: 40 tuns Gascony wine *net* 36 tuns 108s, 3 tuns vinegar
£7 (13 Nov 1567).

121. *Fortune* of Newcastle (60) Edward Johnson; Bordeaux
[f. 26] Thomas Searle: 56 tuns Gascony wine *net* 50½ tuns 151s 6d (13 Nov
1567).

122. *Barsaby* of Lee (40) William Sims; Bordeaux
[f. 26] Richard Whitlok and John Lendall: 33 tuns Gascony wine *net* 28
tuns 84s, 2 tuns vinegar £4 13s 4d (13 Nov 1567).

123. *Julian* of Brightlingsea (40) Richard Broune; Bordeaux
[f. 26] Henry Pranell and Cuthbert Bucle: 38 tuns Gascony wine *net* 33 tuns
99s, 1 tun vinegar £2 6s 8d (13 Nov 1567).

124. *Trinetie* of London (55) John Dryver; Bordeaux
[f. 26] George Lucas: 48 tuns 1 hhd 1 tierce Gascony wine *net* 43 tuns 129s
(13 Nov 1567).

125. *Mary Flower* of Brightlingsea (66) Francis Harvey; Bordeaux
[f. 26] Steven Skidmore 'cum sociis': 43½ tuns Gascony wine *net* 38 tuns 114s, 4 tuns vinegar £9 6s 8d (13 Nov 1567). [f. 32] George Durber: 8 ballets woad £10 13s 4d (19 Nov).

126. *Barbary* of Brightlingsea (40) John Smally; Bordeaux
[f. 26] Steven Skidmore 'cum sociis': 28 tuns Gascony wine *net* 24 tuns 72s (13 Nov 1567). [f. 33b] Ralph Ridley: 2½ tuns Gascony wine *net* 2 tuns 1 hhd 6s 9d (19 Nov).

127. *Peter* of London (55) Randolph Goodwyn; Bordeaux
[f. 26] Michael Blake: 6 tuns Gascony wine *net* 5 tuns 15s (13 Nov 1567). Jacques Fisher 'cum socio': 24 tuns Gascony wine *net* 22 tuns 66s. [f. 29] Henry Sackford: 7 tuns Gascony wine *net* 6 tuns 18s (17 Nov).

128. *Mary Gallant* of 'St. Ousses'[1] (40) Stephen Williamson; Bordeaux
[f. 26b] Edmund Bird: 36 tuns Gascony wine *net* 32 tuns 96s, 2 tuns vinegar £4 13s 4d (13 Nov 1567).

    1. Perhaps St. Osyth or St. Ives.

129. *Swypstake* of Dover (30) Germaine Dove; Bordeaux
[f. 26b] Nicholas Culverwell: 28 tuns Gascony wine *net* 25 tuns 75s (13 Nov 1567).

130. *Jonas* of Aldeburgh (40) Thomas Wright; Bordeaux
[f. 26b] John Mesenger: 14 tuns Gascony wine *net* 12 tuns 36s (13 Nov 1567). Steven Skidmore: 11 tierce Gascony wine *net* ½ tun 4s 6d. Henry Sakford: 12 tuns Gascony wine *net* 10 tuns 30s. [f. 35] John Messenger: 3 tuns Gascony wine *net* 2 tuns 3 hhd 8s 3d (20 Nov).

131. *John Bonadventure*[1] (60) Richard Sayre; Bordeaux
[f. 26b] Anthony Radcliff: 48 tuns Gascony wine *net* 44 tuns 132s, 7 tuns Gascony wine[2] £16 6s 8d (13 Nov 1567).

    1. No home-port is given but see **522.**
    2. Presumably in error for vinegar.

132. *Mary grace* of Lee (48) John Pett; Bordeaux
[f. 26b] Robert Fryer: 37 tuns Gascony wine *net* 33 tuns 99s (13 Nov 1567). [f. 28] Gerard and Thomas Gore: 3 tuns Gascony wine *net* 3 tuns 9s (14 Nov).

133. *Anne Gallant* of Milton (36) William Morecock; Bordeaux
[f. 26b] William Lucas: 34 tuns Gascony wine *net* 29 tuns 87s, 2 tuns vinegar £4 13s 4d (13 Nov 1567).

134. *Jesus* of Aldeburgh (64) John Smyth; Marbella
[f. 27] Richard Renold: 100 pcs Malaga raisins £25 (13 Nov 1567). George Saunders: 250 pcs raisins £62 10s. John Baker: 120 pcs raisins £30. Nicholas

Atkins: 25 pcs raisins £6 5s (14 Nov). John Spencer: 625 pcs raisins £156 5s.
[f. 28] Thomas Blank: 225 pcs raisins £56 5s.

135. *Mary Jermaine* of London (50) William Crag; Bordeaux
[f. 27] Richard Whytlock: 41½ tuns Gascony wine *net* 33 tuns 99s, 2 tuns
vinegar £4 13s 4d (13 Nov 1567).

136. *Mary Fortune* of Brightlingsea (45) Michael Pode; Bordeaux
[f. 27] William Ketcher: 40 tuns Gascony wine *net* 33 tuns 99s, 3 tuns
vinegar £7 (13 Nov 1567).

137. *George Bewick* of Newcastle (85) Lionel Reveley; Spain
[f. 27b] Henry Callers 'cum socio': 112 butts sack *net* 101 butts 151s 6d
(14 Nov 1567). Henry Richards: 14 butts sack *net* 13 butts 19s 6d. Robert
Howe: 20 butts sack *net* 18 butts 27s. John Spencer: 10 butts sack *net*
9 butts 13s 6d. [f. 28b] George Sanders: 10 butts sack *net* 9 butts 13s 6d
(15 Nov).

138. *Mary James* of Newcastle (60) John Tynmouth; Bordeaux
[f. 27b] George Bond: 26 tuns Gascony wine *net* 23½ tuns 69s (14 Nov 1567).
William Bond: 23 tuns Gascony wine *net* 20½ tuns 61s 8d.

139. *Marygrace* of Brightlingsea (50) Thomas Page; Bordeaux
[f. 27b] William Bond: 10 tuns Gascony wine *net* 9 tuns 27s, 120 quintals
prunes £60 (14 Nov 1567). George Bond: 11 tuns Gascony wine *net* 10 tuns
30s, 120 quintals prunes £60.

140. *Margaret* of Amsterdam (30) Raire Cornilis; Amsterdam
[f. 28] Jacob Heath: 10 lasts oats £25 (14 Nov 1567).

141. *Mary An* of London (60) Thomas Dale; Bordeaux
[f. 28] Davy Gittons: 3 tuns Gascony wine *net* 2½ tuns 7s 6d (14 Nov 1567).
Christopher Edwards 'cum sociis': 58 tuns Gascony wine *net* 36¼ tuns
108s 9d (22 Nov). [f. 39] John Marten[1]: 2 tuns Gascony wine *net* 1½ tuns
4s 6d.

    1. Entered under the *Cat* of Newcastle, master Thomas Dale.

142. *Black Egle* of Antwerp Peter Johnson
[f. 28b] Jacob Dewes: 2½ cwt flax £1 13s 4d (14 Nov 1567).

143. *Mary Anne* of London (80) John Bonner; Bordeaux
[f. 28b] Cuthbert Bucle: 50 tuns Gascony wine *net* 45 tuns 135s, 4 tuns
vinegar £9 6s 8d (14 Nov 1567). Hugh Offley: 6 tuns Gascony wine *net*
5 tuns 15s (15 Nov). Randal Hankin: 3½ tuns Gascony wine *net* 3 tuns 1 hhd
9s 9d, ½ tun vinegar, 1 tun turpentine, 40 cwt brazil, 20 pcs resin £81 3s 4d.

144. *John* of Dartmouth (50) Patrick Stafford; Bordeaux
[f. 28b] Francis Anstry: 10 tuns Gascony wine *net* 9 tuns 27s, 1 tun vinegar,
12 pcs resin £4 6s 8d (15 Nov 1567). Edward Sheffell: 16 tuns Gascony wine

net 15 tuns 45*s*. John Elmes: 6 tuns corrupt wine *net* 5 tuns £15 (18 Nov). [f. 41] Patrick Stafford: 3 hhds Gascony wine *net* 3 hhds 2*s* 3*d* (25 Nov).

145. *Nightingale* of Newcastle (100) Richard Gybbes; Danzig
[f. 29] Thomas Russell: 9 packs flax, 5 lasts pitch £82 (15 Nov 1567). Thomas Allen: 45 cwt coarse madder, 18 cwt hemp £48 (18 Nov). Robert Best: 3 packs flax £24 (19 Nov). Robert Barker: 1½ packs flax £12. Thomas Cambell: 2 packs flax £16 (20 Nov). William James: 100 clapholt, 8 packs flax £64 5*s*. William Watts: 3 half-packs flax, 240 yds poldavis £20. [f. 44*b*] Alard Bartrinck: 1 cwt 'spruce' iron, 7 firkins sturgeon £6 (1 Dec).

146. *Christopher* of Antwerp (50) Christian Cornilis
[f. 29] Hartik van Sprecleson: 2 packs flax £16 (17 Nov 1567). John Smith: 4 chests Burgundy glass £8. Thomas Bower: 1 half-brl head nails, 7 cwt iron pans, 10 hd iron plates, 1 doz. bedpans, 1 grs candlesticks at 6*s* 8*d* the doz. £17 6*s* 8*d* (18 Nov). Thomas Bressie: 3 bales Ulm fustian £45. John Car: 1 half-brl small nails, 1 half-brl head nails, 50 pair andirons with creepers, fireshovels and tongs, 10 cwt iron plates, 20 lbs copper pans cost 10*s* £32 10*s*. William Sherington: 120 yds taffeta £40 (19 Nov). [f. 41*b*] Thomas Prat: 200 yds camlet, 30 lbs Spanish silk £50 (26 Nov).

147. *Christopher* of Dordrecht (60) Cleise Johnson
[f. 29] Reynold Thirling: 110 awms Rhenish wine 110*s*, 5 thou. bowstaves £100 (17 Nov 1567).

148. *Margaret* of Dover (34) Stephen Anderson; Bordeaux
[f. 29] Thomas Prowse: 7 tuns Gascony wine *net* 6½ tuns 19*s* 6*d* (17 Nov 1567). Robert Good: 5 tuns Gascony wine *net* 4½ tuns 13*s* 6*d*. [f. 30] Cuthbert Bucle: 2½ tuns Gascony wine *net* 2 tuns 1 hhd 6*s* 9*d* (18 Nov).

149. *Grene Cloverblade* of Amsterdam (32) Garet Isbrant; Amsterdam
[f. 29] Otte Frolik: 960 ells middlegood £10 13*s* 4*d* (17 Nov 1567). Alard Bartrinck: 8 cwt estrige wool £6 13*s* 4*d*. Court Ellers: 8 cwt estrige wool £6 13*s* 4*d*. George Jenens: 1300 staplefish, 840 lings £47 10*s* (18 Nov). Edward van Crog: 1080 ells middlegood £12 (19 Nov). [f. 35*b*] Richard Mouse: 4 lasts fish, 720 lings, 1300 staplefish £67 10*s* (20 Nov).

150. *Black Dragon* of Amsterdam (36) Lucas Garetson; Amsterdam
[f. 29*b*] Court Ellers: 16 cwt estrige wool £13 6*s* 8*d* (17 Nov 1567). Thomas Sanford: 200 staplefish, 240 lings £11. [f. 31*b*] Anthony Bevredge: 2 brls fish £3 (18 Nov).

151. *Longbow* of Amsterdam (40) Jacob Tyson; Amsterdam
[f. 29*b*] Thomas Sanford: 3 lasts fish, 240 lings £26 (17 Nov 1568). John Violet: 1000 staplefish, 15 brls fish £22 10*s* (18 Nov). Nicholas Spencer: 50 wainscot £2 (20 Nov). [f. 41] William Plaisden: 3 half-packs flax £12 (25 Nov).

152. *Mary George* of Brightlingsea (42) Thomas Catchpoll; Bordeaux
[f. 29*b*] Thomas Searle and Cuthbert Brand: 16 tuns Gascony wine *net*

14½ tuns 43*s* 6*d*, 6 tuns vinegar £14 (18 Nov 1567). Thomas Searle: 8 tuns Gascony wine *net* 7 tuns 21*s* (9 Dec). [f. 59*b*] John Lane: 6 tuns Gascony wine *net* 5 tuns 15*s* (19 Dec).

153. *Jesus* of Dartmouth (52) Thomas Tucker; Bordeaux
[f. 29*b*] Thomas Searle and Cuthbert Brand: 33 tuns Gascony wine *net* 30 tuns 90*s*, 6 tuns vinegar £14 (18 Nov 1567). Thomas Bates: 6 tuns Gascony wine *net* 5 tuns 15*s*.

154. *Peter* of Lee (60) Robert Cockerell; Antwerp
[f. 30] William Coles: 914 lbs pepper, 62 lbs nutmegs £76 1*s* 8*d* (18 Nov 1567). John Jackman: 150 lbs mace £50. Henry Becher: 222 doz. thou. paper-pins, 80 lbs cloves £57. Edward Jackman: 414 lbs ginger, 70 lbs cloves, 70 lbs nutmegs, 600 lbs pepper, 74 lbs mace, 24 cwt madder £150 18*s* 4*d*. Thomas Bressie: 39 pcs Genoa fustian £26. Lucas Lane: 345 lbs ginger, 90 lbs nutmegs £39. Leonard Holiday: 10 pcs Holland cloth £12. William Bower: 10 cwt frying pans, 7 cwt dripping pans £11 6*s* 8*d*. John Car: 1 half-brl small nails, 1 half-brl head nails, 18 cwt iron pans £18. Nicholas Spering: 2 grs painted boxes, 10 doz. lbs pack thread, 2 doz. wooden standishes, 12 doz. coarse gold weights, 1½ grs razors, 4 doz. basil leather, 6 doz. coarse knives £9 10*s* (19 Nov). George Stockmed: 200 lbs pepper, 175 lbs cloves £54 3*s* 4*d*. George Collimore: 120 doz. thou. pins, 30 grs harp strings, 10 doz. checks, 4 doz. gartering says, 10 doz. lbs bottom thread £31. John Boorne: 3 hd lbs unwrought inkle £10. John Eliots: 16 doz. yds Cyprus cotton, 20 grs coarse hat bands, 2 thou. thimbles, 50 doz. thou. pins, 20 coarse looking glasses, 3 doz. lbs crewel, 10 doz. lbs bottom thread, 8 doz. pcs thread riband £34. John Colimer: 11 cwt sugar £36 13*s* 4*d*. Thomas Aldersay: 60 yds velvet £45. Edward Best: 2 bales Ulm fustian £30. James Harvie: 2 brls head nails £8. John Spencer: 5¼ cwt sugar, 3 qrs cloves, 3 qrs nuts £49 11*s* 8*d*. John Lambert: 10 cwt iron pans, 46 cwt mull-madder £12 8*s* 4*d* (20 Nov). Thomas Longston: 3 cwt rice, 350 lbs pepper £31 13*s* 4*d*. Edmund Burton: 30 cwt mull-madder, 50 doz. straw hats £5 8*s* 4*d*. Thomas Heton: 210 yds satin, 60 yds damask £118 10*s*. Alexander Sherington: 80 yds taffeta £26 13*s* 4*d*. Robert Shaw: 72 yds frizado £18. William Gifford: 16 cwt madder £10 13*s* 4*d*. William Sherington: 40 pcs boultel £8. Anthony Warfilde: 150 lbs Genoa treacle, 160 lbs cloves, 150 lbs senna £58 5*s*. William Hewett: 5 cwt flax, 12 cwt mull-madder £6 10*s*. Robert Morris: 300 lbs pepper, 40 lbs senna, 40 lbs mace, 4 brls painter's oil, 1 brl Flemish treacle £49 13*s* 4*d*. Anthony Fitton: 300 lbs pepper, 40 lbs senna £29. Thomas Starkey: 1500 ells Bar canvas £30. Roger Warfild: 6 cwt onion seed, 80 lbs candy, 4 cwt ireos, 150 lbs senna £27 18*s* 4*d*. Humphrey Fayrefax: 85 lbs cloves £21 5*s*. Thomas Hale: 300 lbs pepper, 63 lbs cloves, 150 lbs ginger, 60 lbs nutmegs, 4 cwt saltpetre £76 10*s* (21 Nov). Thomas Rose: 72 yds frizado, 2 bales Ulm fustian £48. Thomas Gardner: 11 cwt onion seed, 4 chests Burgundy glass £22 13*s* 4*d*. William Hobbs: 836 ells hair tapestry, 45 pcs sealed carpets, 21 pcs white blankets, 4½ doz. Ghentish beds, 80 pcs lince, 1 last oil £73 5*s*. William Loddington: 30 lbs pepper £25. Thomas Gardner: 25 cwt madder £16 13*s* 4*d*. Thomas Parker: 1 bale Ulm fustian £15. Francis Warren: 16 cwt

madder £10 13s 4d. Thomas Barker: 11 cwt battery £22. John Wanton: 8 cwt madder £5 6s 8d. Robert Broune: 70 half-pcs Genoa fustian £23 6s 8d (22 Nov). Robert Smith: 18 cwt madder £12. William Allen: 950 lbs Eastland wool £7 18s 4d. Bartholomew Dod: 70 pcs Genoa fustian £46 13s 4d (24 Nov). [f. 40] John Gardner: 4 cases glass, 15 cwt matches, 50 doz. empty barrels £21 10s (25 Nov).

155. *Edward* of Milton (60) William Harris; Antwerp
[f. 30] William Coles: 48 cwt madder £32 (18 Nov 1567). Henry Becher: 110 doz. thou. pins, 40 doz. lbs Oudenaarde thread, 8 doz. lbs piecing thread, 82 lbs cloves, 140 lbs nuts £94. Edmund Smith: 40 pcs mockado £26 13s 4d. John Fitzwilliams: 32 cwt madder £21 6s 8d. Robert Brook: 32 cwt madder £21 6s 8d. William Bower: 2 bales Ulm fustian £30. John Car: 18 cwt iron pans, 8 cwt latten wire £28. Robert Turvile: 4 pcs loose sackcloth £10 (19 Nov). Wolston Dixi: 1 double-roll minsters £33 6s 8d. Ancelm Becket: 6 cwt flax, 25 pcs Genoa fustian £22 13s 4d. Nicholas Spering: 35 doz. crystal glasses, 3 doz. cotton petticoats, 15 grs copper bands, 10 doz. thou. pins, 6 doz. crewel girdlings, 6 doz. small writing tables, 3 grs halfpennyware glasses, 10 doz. lbs pack thread, 2 grs coarse knives, 6 doz. furred stomachers, 5 doz. drinking glasses £53 3s 4d. Richard Hills: 2 bales Ulm fustian £30. Edward Bright: 27 cwt iron pans, 120 double iron plates, 6 hd iron plates, 2 doz. spades cost 3s 4d £26 6s 8d. Henry Smith: 10 doz. thou. pins, 10 doz. lbs inkle £8 6s 8d. John Pasfilde: 2 half-brls head nails £4. George Collimore: 100 doz. thou. pins, 5 doz. lbs bottom thread, 8 thou. balls £25 13s 4d. John Boorne: 2 hd lbs unwrought inkle, 1 doz. pcs Rennes boultel, 1½ grs thread points, 6 doz. lbs crewel, 40 doz. thou. pins, 5 doz. crewel pieces, 5 doz. lbs thread, 2 doz. lbs clavichord wire £29 13s 4d. John Collimer: 6 cwt sugar, 160 lbs ginger £32. George Stockmed: 650 lbs pepper £54 3s 4d. Thomas Aldersey: 40 pcs grogram £53 13s 4d. Edward Best: 2 bales Ulm fustian £30. James Harvie: 2 brls head nails £8. Lady Lion: 650 lbs pepper £54 3s 4d. John Spencer: 175 lbs ginger, 40 lbs argentum vivum, 40 lbs white copperas, 25 lbs wormseed, 40 lbs senna £21 11s 8d. John Lambert: 34 cwt battery, 3¼ cwt [ ]¹, 150 lbs cinnamon £179 5s. Thomas Heton: 150 yds taffeta, 60 yds velvet £95 (20 Nov). John Sutton: 6 doz. Ghentish carpets £9. William Harding: 180 yds woollen dornick £6. Edward Jackman: 12 cwt flax, 15 cwt mullmadder £9 16s 8d. Edmund Burton: 1¾ tons iron, 2 half-brls head nails, 20 doz. heath brushes, 60 doz. straw hats £7 5s. Thomas Longston: 3 cwt rice, 350 lbs pepper £31 13s 4d. Henry Billingsley: 50 doz. thou. pins £8 6s 8d. John Alden: 5 cwt starch, 15 cwt copperas £10 16s 8d. Alexander Sherington: 80 yds taffeta £26 13s 4d. Thomas Cranfilde: 5 cwt flax £5. Anthony Warfilde: 5 cwt wormseed, 4 cwt saltpetre £14 6s 8d. William Sherington: 8 cwt flax £8. William Towerson: 27 ells silk tapestry, 150 ells caddis tapestry, 900 ells hair tapestry, 6 doz. Ghentish carpets £58 10s. Robert Moris: 450 lbs pepper, 80 lbs cloves, 40 lbs nuts, 30 lbs cinnamon £70 3s 4d. Anthony Fitton: 150 lbs pepper, 40 lbs cloves, 30 lbs nuts, 250 lbs ginger £46 5s. Thomas Starkey: 1600 ells plain Bar canvas £32. Roger Warfild: 300 lbs ginger, 4 hd lbs Flemish treacle, 16 cwt rice, 6 cwt red lead, 2 cwt white lead £31 6s 8d. William Hewet: 4 cwt unwrought flax, 1 brl

great nails, 13 cwt mull-madder £6 5s. John Colmer: 35 doz. lbs flax £4 13s 4d. Thomas Hale: 4 cwt sumach, 3 lbs cloves, 4 brls linseed oil, 64 lbs nutmegs, 70 lbs cinnamon £25 8s 4d (21 Nov). William Loddington: 125 lbs ginger, 50 lbs cloves, 30 lbs nutmegs £26 16s 8d. Thomas Parker: 2 bales Ulm fustian £30. Thomas Barker: 11 cwt battery £22. Robert Scarbrough: 60 pcs mockado, 6 chamber stools £40 15s. Thomas Danser: 100 doz. thou. pins, 4 doz. lbs inkle £19 6s 8d. William Smith: 60 yds velvet £45. Randal Maning: 20 pcs Holland cloth £24. Lucas Harrison: 2 small rolls of maps ad valorem 40s £2 (22 Nov). Thomas Parker: 1 bale Ulm fustian £15. Robert Broune: 70 half-pcs Genoa fustian £23 6s 8d. William Cokin: 6 furs foin potes, 5 pane 'vents' foin tails £7 10s. Robert Smith: 24 cwt madder £16. Bartholomew Dod: 5 cwt wrought flax £5 (25 Nov). John Gardner: 60 cwt mull-madder £7 10s. William Hobs: 16 brls rape oil, 8 doz. blue lince £27 6s 8d. Thomas Randall: 20 doz. yds Cyprus cotton £4 (28 Nov). [f. 50b] Stephen Slany: 800 ells 'clincent' canvas £12 (6 Dec).

1. Blank.

156. *Mary Catharin* of Lee Robert Parnell; Antwerp
[f. 30] Wolston Dixi: 42 pcs Holland cloth, 100 ells canvas £56 8s 4d (18 Nov 1567). John Alden and Edmund Pigot: 3¾ cwt red lead, 1110 lbs pepper, 1425 lbs ginger, 50 lbs mace £218 10s. Thomas Bower: 2 half-brls head nails £4. Henry Becher: 220 doz. thou. paper-pins, 6 doz. lbs piecing thread £44 13s 4d. Edmund Smith: 37 pcs Genoa fustian £24 13s 4d. William Hewet:[1] 269 half-pcs Genoa fustian, 1¼ tons iron, 10 cwt frying pans, 110 double iron plates £106 5s. William Bower: 3 half-brls head nails, 24 pair iron andirons with tongs and fireshovels, 6 cwt flax £21 6s 8d. John Car: 4 half-brls head nails £8. Roger Knott: 10 cwt battery £20. Ancelm Becket: 2 lasts rape oil £34 13s 4d (19 Nov). William Sherington: 138 yds taffeta £46. Lawrence Wethers: 12 brls rape oil £16. Henry Smith: 40 doz. yds Cyprus cotton, 36 yds Tours taffeta £14. George Collimore: 15 pcs mockado, 3 doz. coarse checks, 25 doz. lbs bottom thread £16 10s. Henry Billingsley: 10 doz. lbs Bruges thread, 20 doz. thou. pins, 10 doz. lbs bottom thread £12. Nicholas Ludington: 64 cwt madder £42 13s 4d. John Boorne: 10 doz. thou. pins, 2 thou. thimbles, 10 doz. lbs wrought inkle, 15 doz. crewel pieces, 4 doz. lbs crewel, 5 doz. lbs pack thread £21 10s. John Eliots: 6 doz. lbs wrought inkle, 2¼ cwt shaven latten, 3 grs halfpennyware glasses, 6 doz. weaver's brushes, 6 doz. shuttles, 4 doz. lbs crewel, 60 doz. thou. pins, 1 doz. lbs pack thread, 6 doz. lbs Bruges thread £28 5s. John Collmer: 600 lbs pepper, 85 lbs mace, 1 last rape oil, 12 cwt aniseed, 3½ thou. tennis balls £113 16s 8d. Thomas Aldersay: 115 yds damask, 56 yds taffeta, 46 yds velvet £63 13s 4d. James Harvie: 13½ cwt battery, 4 doz. whip-saws £33. William Lodington: 3 cwt rice £2 8s 4d. John Spencer: 450 lbs pepper £37 10s. John Lambert: 17 cwt flax, 18 cwt battery £47 6s 8d. Robert Taylor: 2 dyed kerseys, 90 yds sackcloth £2 10s (20 Nov). Randal Maneryng: 870 ells harnesdale cloth, 207 lbs pepper £52 1s 8d. Thomas Longston: 120 lbs cloves, 20 lbs mace £36 13s 4d. Humphrey Fairfax: 650 lbs ginger, 15 cwt madder £58 15s. John Sutton: 8 doz. lince £6. Alexander Sherington: 80 yds taffeta £26 13s 4d. William Gifford: 24 cwt madder £16. Thomas

22

Starkey: 800 ells Vitré canvas, 500 ells canvas £25 16s 8d. Richard Pipe: 82 yds black velvet £61 10s. Thomas Rose: 54 pcs mockado £36 (21 Nov). Thomas Gardner: 150 lbs cloves, 30 lbs mace, 125 lbs ginger, 2 cwt gunpowder £60 3s 4d. Thomas Barker: 10 cwt frying pans £6 13s 4d. Robert Scarbrough: 50 pcs mockado £33 6s 8d. John Woordes: 500 yds camlet £50. Sir William Chester: 1200 lbs pepper, 800 lbs ginger £160. Richard Holiman: 20 ungilt halberts £1 13s 4d (22 Nov). Robert Smith: 8 pcs linen cloth £9 11s 8d. William Bond: 11 hd lbs Spanish wool £9 3s 4d. Thomas Eaton: 40 grs halfpennyware glasses, 10 thou. tennis balls £20 (25 Nov). John Brond: 50 pcs Genoa fustian £33 6s 8d. William Hobs: 20 Turnhout ticks, 6 doz. Ghentish carpets, 7 doz. lince £11 18s 4d. William Towerson: 8 doz. Ghentish carpets, 4 doz. lince £15. Thomas Randall: 32 lbs ferret silk £13 6s 8d (26 Nov). [f. 50b] Hugh Bradley: 6 pcs striped canvas £2 (6 Dec).

1. This shipment is entered under the *Peter* of Robert Parnell. It is assigned here because the commodities are more consistent with this ship's cargo.

157. *Samson* of Bruges (60) Martin Frise
[f. 30b] Thomas Bressie: 162 pcs buckram £36 (18 Nov 1567). Matthew Colcloghe: 225 doz. hemp £28 2s 7d (19 Nov). William Gelders: 90 pcs buckram, 25 doz. lbs thread £36 (20 Nov). [f. 36] Gilbert Gager: 600 ells Hazebroucks, 200 ells white Eeklo cloth £17.

158. *Lion* of 'Seden'[1] (70) George or Joris Martin; Hamburg
[f. 30b] John Mun: 84 lbs cloves £21 (18 Nov 1567). Phillip Joanes 'cum socio': 28 lasts small stockfish £93 6s 8d (19 Nov). Court Ellers: 32 cwt estrige wool, 3000 titlings £43 6s 8d. Edward van Crog: 17½ cwt estrige wool £14 11s 8d. Daniel van Eitson: 24 cwt estrige wool £20. Alard Bartrinck: 8 cwt estrige wool £6 13s 4d. [f. 41] Jerome Rise: 20 cwt estrige wool £16 13s 4d (25 Nov).

1. Also called the *Black Lion* or *Bear*.

159. *Owl* of Haarlem (30) Simon Derickson; Amsterdam
[f. 31b] John Violet: 4 lasts fish, 480 lings £40 (18 Nov 1567).

160. *Ships Coy* of Amsterdam (36) Garet Bart; Amsterdam
[f. 31b] John Violet: 1000 staplefish, 18 brls fish £24 (18 Nov 1567).

161. *Mary* of Fécamp (70) Peter Mark; Bordeaux
[f. 31b] Simon de Starkey: 60 tuns Gascony wine *net* 48 tuns 134s (18 Nov 1567).

162. *Mary* of Fécamp (70) John Mun; Fécamp
[f. 31b] Simon de Starkey: 60 tuns Gascony wine *net* 34 tuns 102s (18 Nov 1567).

163. *Fortune* of Bruges (50) Cornilis Albright; Bruges
[f. 31b] Matthew Colcloghe: 180 doz. hemp £22 10s (19 Nov 1567). Thomas Sound: 600 ells Hazebroucks £15. William Gelders: 20 doz. lbs thread,

180 yds fustian, 4 pcs bustian £20 (20 Nov). Gilbert Gager: 600 ells white Hazebroucks £15. [f. 46*b*] Walter Garraway: 160 lbs short silk £40 (3 Dec).

164. *Mary fortune* of Newcastle (65) Thomas Johnson; Bordeaux
[f. 32] George Durber: 20 cwt woad £13 6*s* 8*d* (19 Nov 1567).

165. *Spedegell* of Dordrecht (40) John Leonard; Dordrecht
[f. 32] George Wrast: 150 bundles white rods £2 10*s* (19 Nov 1567). [f. 35] Thomas Hecker: 51 cwt hops £25 10*s* (20 Nov).

166. *Falcon* of Antwerp Christian Johnson
[f. 32] Hartik van Sprecleson: 1 last 1180 croplings £12 13*s* 4*d* (19 Nov 1567).

167. *John* of Fécamp (65) John Jaques; Bordeaux
[f. 33] Barnard Sere: 23 tuns Gascony wine *net* 20 tuns 60*s* (19 Nov 1567).

168. *James* of Antwerp (40) Jacob Lawrance; Antwerp
[f. 33] William Sherington: 16 lbs fringe, 50 lbs silk £66 (19 Nov 1567).

169. *George* of Amsterdam (40) Christian Cornilis; Amsterdam
[f. 34] John Rainkin: 1 pack flax £8 (19 Nov 1567). Henry Bukston: 1¼ packs flax £10 (24 Nov). John Haines: 720 lings, 3 lasts fish £42. [f. 40*b*] Robert King: 16 half-packs loose flax £64 (25 Nov).

170. *Egle*[1] of Dordrecht (50) Godfrey Derikson; Dordrecht
[f. 34*b*] Walter Lyn: 62 awms Rhenish wine 62*s* (20 Nov 1567). Melchior van Aldenek: 37 awms Rhenish wine 37*s*. [f. 36*b*] Barthelmew Broer: 30 awms Rhenish wine 30*s*.

    1. Also the *Spledegle*.

171. *Peter* of Antwerp Vincent Johnson[1]
[f. 35*b*] John Alden: 531 lbs pepper, 81 lbs nutmegs, 37 lbs mace, 26 lbs ginger £71 18*s* 4*d* (20 Nov 1567).

    1. Antwerp is a correction for Lee and Johnson for Robert Cockerell.

172. *Cat* of Amsterdam (40) John Garetson; Amsterdam
[f. 36] George Gees: 5½ packs flax £44 (20 Nov 1567).

173. *Claverblade* [*sic*] Cornilis Derikson
[f. 37*b*] Daniel van Eitson: 40 cwt estrige wool £33 6*s* 8*d* (21 Nov 1567). George Gees: 4 half-packs flax £16 (22 Nov). Court Ellers: 16 cwt estrige wool £13 6*s* 8*d* (24 Nov). Jerome Rise: 24 cwt estrige wool £20 (25 Nov). Luder van Dorne: 2 packs flax £16 (26 Nov). [f. 42] Edward van Crog: 480 ells middlegood £5 6*s* 8*d*.

174. *Sea Rider* of Bruges (28) Nicholas Fleming; Bruges
[f. 38] Matthew Colcloghe: 1300 ells white Hazebroucks, 400 ells green Hazebroucks £40 10*s* (21 Nov 1567).

175. *Catt* of Amsterdam Isbrandt Cornilis
[f. 38] Richard Candler: 55 cwt flax £38 6s 8d (21 Nov 1567).

176. *World* of Amsterdam Peter Engle
[f. 38b] John Lence: 30 pcs Holland cloth £36 (22 Nov 1567). Adam Cooper:
11 pcs Holland cloth £13 3s 4d (25 Nov). [f. 42b] Anthony Johnson: 7 pcs
Holland cloth £8 6s 8d (27 Nov).

177. *George* of Antwerp (15) William Peterson; Antwerp
[f. 38b] Thomas Brasie: 30 pcs broad worsteds £30 (22 Nov 1567).

178. *Jacob* of Antwerp (30) Jacob Lawrance; Antwerp
[f. 38b] Thomas Bowyer: 1 half-brl small nails, 1 half-brl head nails, 25 lbs
varnish, 4 doz. trunks, 2 doz. wooden beams, 1 doz. iron chimney rakes,
1 doz. gridirons, 4 grs padlocks, 2 doz. cooper's tools, ½ grs ladles, 2 sum
nails, 6 grs horse bells, 1½ grs dog chains, 7 grs joiner's tools, 6 doz. shears,
12 lbs iron wire, 20 pair andirons with creepers £23 16s 8d (22 Nov 1567).

179. *Falcon* of Antwerp (40) Vincent Johnson; Antwerp
[f. 39] John Gardener: 600 lbs pepper, 200 lbs crossbow thread £53 6s 8d
(22 Nov 1567).

180. *Morian* of Hamburg (100) Richard Hier; Hamburg
[f. 39] Richard Hier: 130 weys bay salt £130 (24 Nov 1567).

181. *Joll Owl* of Harlingen (40) Andrew Lynes; Harlingen
[f. 39] John Miller: 7 cwt estrige wool £5 16s 8d (24 Nov 1567). John
Reinkin: 16 cwt estrige wool £13 6s 8d. Daniel van Eitson: 78 cwt estrige
wool, 800 ells hinderlands £99. Hartik van Sprecleson: 48 cwt estrige wool
£40. Jerome Rise: 6 lasts croplings, 24 cwt estrige wool £60 (25 Nov).
[f. 41b] Edward van Crog: 17½ cwt estrige wool £14 3s 4d (26 Nov).

182. *Sea Rider* of Antwerp Jacob Lawrance; Antwerp
[f. 39] George Stockmed: 24 cwt madder £16 (24 Nov 1567). Hartik van
Sprecleson: 2 packs flax £16. Thomas Longston: 30 cwt madder £20.
Francis Nosley: 100 pcs Genoa fustian £66 13s 4d. John Gardener: 26 brls
rape oil £34 13s 4d (25 Nov). Robert Taylor: 16 cwt madder £10 13s 4d.
Richard Violet: 6 cwt hops £3. James Dowes: 4½ cwt flax £3. Richard
Dowler: 10 cwt rice £8 6s 8d (27 Nov). Christopher Jewkes: 3 cwt hops
£1 10s. [f. 42b] Edward Hardinrack: 3 half-brls steel £18.

183. *George* of Purmerend (40) Sebrant Cornilis; Purmerend
[f. 39] George Gees: 2 half-packs flax £8 (24 Nov 1567). Court Ellers: 8 hd
ells Hamburg cloth £20.

184. *Mearman* of Hamburg (36) Peter Hewkin; Hamburg
[f. 39b] Court Ellers: 32 cwt estrige wool £26 13s 4d (24 Nov 1567). Matthew
Hope: 2 lasts croplings £13 6s 8d. Hartik van Sprecleson: 16 cwt estrige
wool £13 6s 8d. Jerome Rise: 2½ lasts croplings, 1200 ells middlegood,

12 cwt estrige wool, 1 half-pack flax £44 (25 Nov). Luder van Dorne: 4 packs flax £32 (26 Nov). [f. 42] Edward van Crog: 38 cwt estrige wool £31 13s 4d.

185. *Morrian* of Hamburg (40) Otto Bare; Hamburg
[f. 39b] Matthew Hope: 400 qrs oats £100 (24 Nov 1567).

186. *Grey falcon* of Hamburg (60) Peter Alverman; Hamburg
[f. 39b] John Renikin: 16 cwt estrige wool, 840 ells soultwich £27 6s 8d (24 Nov 1567). Alard Bartrinck: 6 cwt estrige wool, 60 lbs bristles £7 10s (25 Nov). Hartik van Sprecleson: 48 cwt estrige wool, 1440 ells middlegood £56. Otte Frolik: 4½ lasts croplings £30. Court Ellers: 8 cwt estrige wool £13 6s 8d. Luder van Dorne: 1 pack flax £8 (26 Nov). Otte Frolik: 16 cwt estrige wool, 840 ells middlegood £22 13s 4d. Edward van Crog: 31 cwt estrige wool £25 16s. [f. 46] Peter Alverman: 7 tercel-falcons, 3 tercel-hawks, 10 falcons, 2 hawks £26 13s 4d (2 Dec).

187. *Bonadventure* of Antwerp (18) Anthony Joyson; Antwerp
[f. 40] John Eliots: 16 doz. lbs wrought inkle, 4 doz. lbs thread riband, 1 cwt unwrought inkle, 2 doz. lbs crewel £17 (24 Nov 1567). John Gardner: 100 lbs cloves, 26 lbs mace £33 13s 4d (25 Nov). John Alden: 33½ cwt rice £27 18s 4d. Mark Gryme: 100 yds taffeta £33 6s 8d. Christopher Jewkes: 3 cwt hops £1 10s (27 Nov). [f. 42b] Edward Hardinrack: 3 half-brls steel £18.

188. *Swan* of Flushing John Peterson
[f. 40b] Richard Violet: 3 cwt hops £1 10s (25 Nov 1567).

189. *Angell* of Bergen-op-Zoom (30) Cornilis Adrianson; Bergen-op-Zoom
[f. 40b] Ancelm Becket: 5½ cwt flax £5 10s (25 Nov 1567). Thomas Eaton: 7 cwt flax £7 (26 Nov). Richard Cotton: 6½ cwt flax £6 10s. John Colmer: 25 doz. lbs flax £3 13s 4d. Robert Exton: 13½ cwt flax £13 10s. Lawrence Wyther: 13 brls rape oil £17 6s 8d. John Boylston: 12 cwt flax £12. Robert Scarborogh: 7 cwt flax £7. William Gyfford: 10 cwt flax £10. William Bower: 2 lasts rape oil £34 13s 4d (27 Nov). William Hobbs: 2 lasts rape oil £32 (28 Nov). George Keightley: 15 cwt oakum £3 15s. [f. 42b] William Bower: 6 cwt wrought flax £6 (29 Nov).

190. *Spledegle* of Amsterdam (30) Floris Jacobsen; Amsterdam
[f. 41] Jerome Rise: 24 cwt estrige wool £20 (25 Nov 1567). Daniel van Eytson: 12 cwt estrige wool £10. Nicholas Spencer: 1 pc 4 half-pcs Holland cloth £3 11s 8d (27 Nov). George Lubkin: 1500 ells Osnabrücks £20. [f. 45] William Bond: 1 pack flax £8 (1 Dec).

191. *Grace of God* of London (45) Jacob Steward; Antwerp
[f. 42] Robert Broke: 63 cwt madder £42 (27 Nov 1567). George Stockmed: 32 cwt madder £21 6s 8d. John Pasfilde: 60 iron doubles, 1 cwt iron pans, 3 qrs latten andirons, 1 doz. warming pans, 20 doz. middle and small candlesticks £9. Robert Scarborough: 7 cwt madder £4 13s 4d. James

26

Harvie: 14 pair great andirons, 14 tongs and 14 fireshovels, 15 pair small andirons, 12 pair small creepers £9 3*s* 4*d*. Sir John York: 600 lbs pepper, 320 lbs ginger, 75 lbs cloves, 75 lbs nutmegs, 44 lbs cinnamon, 20 lbs mace £120 13*s* 4*d*. William Griffin: 20 pcs Hondschoote say £20. Thomas Brassie: 3 bales Ulm fustian £45. Richard Byllam: 7 cwt battery £14 (28 Nov). Robert Bladwell: 20 doz. lbs Oudenaarde thread £13 13*s* 4*d*. William Gyfford: 72 yds frizado £18. John Borne: 2½ doz. pcs Rennes boultel, 5 doz. thou. coarse needles, 2 grs pennyware glasses, 5 grs coarse knives, 2 doz. lbs latten counters, 2 thou. thimbles, 3 doz. lbs Bruges thread, 2 doz. lbs wrought inkle, 2 doz. crewel pieces, 5 doz. lbs bottom thread £27 12*s*. Henry Billingsley: 50 lbs short silk £12 10*s*. John Alden: 4¼ cwt saltpetre, 3 brls painter's oil £9 7*s* 6*d*. William Coles: 16 cwt madder £10 13*s* 4*d*. Lucas Lane: 88 lbs nutmegs £14 13*s* 4*d*. William Cokin: 54 cwt madder £36. Henry Smith: 16 doz. lbs coarse inkle, 5 lbs Bruges silk £15. Alexander Sherington: 80 ells sarcenet £13 6*s* 8*d*. George Colmer: 10 thou. large tennis balls £10. Thomas Walker: 45 cwt madder £30 6*s* 8*d*. William Laire: 6 cwt copperas, 30 lbs gum arabic, 4 brls painter's oil £7 6*s* 8*d* (29 Nov). William Tench: 24 doz. lbs pack thread £4 10*s*. Anthony Warfild: 6 cwt onion seed, 600 lbs pepper £60. Henry Hungatt: 7 lbs silk fringe £7. Christopher Jewkes: 6 cwt hops £3. Thomas Gryme: 16 pcs Holland cloth £19 3*s* 4*d* (1 Dec). Robert Scarborogh: 7 cwt madder £4 13*s* 4*d*. Francis Warren: 14 cwt madder £9 6*s* 8*d* (2 Dec). Thomas Parker: 9 pcs crewel dornick, 8 pcs 'turney'[1] carpet £8 10*s*. John Isham: 36 pcs narrow worsted £18. Thomas Heton: 150 ells sarcenet £25 (3 Dec). Richard Dowler: 10 cwt liquorice £5. Richard Hollyman: 35 lbs nutmegs £5 16*s* 8*d*. [f. 47*b*] Roger Ramsdon: 32 cwt mull-madder £4.

    1. ? Tournai or Turnhout.

192. *Blak Falcon* of Dordrecht (30) Adrian Frances; Dordrecht
[f. 42] Barthelmew Bore: 26 awms Rhenish wine 26*s* (27 Nov 1567). [f. 45*b*] Melchior van Aldeneck: 60 awms Rhenish wine 60*s* (2 Dec).

193. *Greyhound* of Lee (28) Henry Rawlins; Nantes
[f. 43*b*] William Bond: 24 tons prunes £120 (28 Nov 1567).

194. *Sacre* of Lee (28) Richard Harrys; Nantes
[f. 43*b*] William Allen, Thomas Starkey and Oliver Fysher: 20 tons prunes £80 (28 Nov 1567).

195. *Golden World* of Emden John Gowsen; Emden
[f. 43*b*] Henry Beecher: 12 doz. lbs Oudenaarde thread £8 (29 Nov 1567).

196. *John* of Flushing (40) John White; Flushing
[f. 44] Robert Wilkenson: 25 weys bay salt £25 (29 Nov 1567).

197. *Bark Gray* of London (70) Robert Gray; Danzig
[f. 44] George Miller and John Collet: 2 half-packs flax, 1 last pitch £22 (1 Dec 1567). William Watts: 1 pack flax £8. Alard Bartrinck: 1 half-pack

flax, 5 firkins sturgeon £7 6s 8d. Thomas Carter: 1 last pitch £2. William Cowper: 2 half-packs flax £8. Robert Carr: 1 half-pack flax £4. Richard Goddard: 20 cwt madder £13 6s 8d. Thomas Allen: 7 brls pitch, 1100 yds poldavis, 10 cwt hemp £48 3s 4d. Jerome Beale: 2 packs flax £16 (2 Dec). Robert Best: 1 pack hemp £20. Robert Barker: 20 cwt hemp £20 (3 Dec). [f. 51] Thomas Russhell: 35 cwt wax £105 (8 Dec).

198. *Pellican* of London (50) Richard Guydy; Spain
[f. 44] Reynold Holingworth: 5 tun bastards *net* 4½ tuns 13s 6d (1 Dec 1567). Anthony Pylborough: 25 tuns 1 pipe bastards and cuit *net* 23 tuns 69s. Edmund Flick: 9½ tuns bastards and cuit *net* 8½ tuns 25s 6d. John Bird: 5 tuns bastards *net* 4½ tuns 13s 6d (2 Dec). [f. 45b] John Mun: 10 pipes bastards *net* 4½ tuns 13s 6d.

199. *Sea dog* of Amsterdam (30) Cornilis Claison; Amsterdam
[f. 44b] John Violet: 6 lasts fish, 300 staplefish £40 10s (1 Dec 1567).

200. *Crab* of Amsterdam (30) John Reid; Amsterdam
[f. 44b] Alard Bartrinck: 16 cwt estrige wool £13 6s 8d (1 Dec 1567).

201. *Fortune* of Amsterdam (50) Giles de Wick; Hamburg
[f. 44b] John Reinold: 16 cwt estrige wool, 240 ells middlegood £16 (1 Dec 1567). Daniel van Eitson: 48 cwt estrige wool £40 (2 Dec). John Myller: 12 cwt estrige wool £10. Court Ellers: 8 cwt estrige wool £6 13s 4d. Edward van Crog: 11½ cwt estrige wool £9 6s 8d. [f. 46] Christopher Hargrave: 4 lasts croplings £26 13s 4d.

202. *William* of London (60) Thomas Foster; Andalusia
[f. 45] John Bird: 16 tuns bastards *net* 14½ tuns 43s 6d (1 Dec 1567). Anthony Pillborrow: 10 tuns bastards *net* 9 tuns 27s. John Chaplin: 16 tuns bastards *net* 14½ tuns 43s 6d. John Marshall: 6 tuns bastards *net* 5½ tuns 16s 6d. [f. 45] William Maynerd: 6 tuns bastards *net* 5½ tuns 16s 6d.

203. *Grace of God* of London (50) Thomas Wilson; Ayamonte
[f. 45] Richard May: 90 pipes bastards *net* 40 tuns 120s (1 Dec 1567). [f. 48b] Thomas May: 8 pipes bastards *net* 7 pipes £10 10s[1] (4 Dec).

    1. This shipment paid poundage; the figure is its valuation.

204. *Bark Bond* of London (70) John Benet; Ayamonte
[f. 45] William Bond: 65 tuns bastards and cuit *net* 59 tuns 177s (1 Dec 1567).

205. *George* of Amsterdam (40) Peter Jacobson; Amsterdam
[f. 45b] Daniel van Eitson: 16 cwt estrige wool £6 13s 4d (2 Dec 1567).

206. *Mearman* of Amsterdam (40) Peter Omes; Amsterdam
[f. 45b] Thomas Jenens: 2 brls stub-eels, 2 brls dole-eels, 20 brls fish, 480

lings, 800 staplefish £45 13s 4d (2 Dec 1567). [f. 46] John Edmunds: 600 staplefish, 240 lings £17.

207. *John Baptist* of London (50) Thomas Wright; Portugal
[f. 46] Thomas Blanck: 102 pcs figs-merchant, 8280 lbs figs-dode £42 18s 8d (2 Dec 1567). Richard Lyster: 7200 figs-dode £20. Gerard Gore: 85 pcs figs-merchant, 6900 lbs figs-dode £30 10s. [f. 52] Richard May: 260 pcs figs-merchant, 6000 lbs figs-dode, 30 cwt figs-dode, 5 cwt Algarve figs £74 13s 4d (9 Dec).

208. *Margereta* of Arvert (27) Jacques Erydall; Bordeaux
[f. 46] William Ricksman: 16 tuns Gascony wine *net* 14½ tuns 43s 6d, 4 tuns vinegar £9 6s 8d (2 Dec 1567). [f. 52b] William Rixsman: 5 tuns Gascony wine *net* 4½ tuns 13s 6d (10 Dec).

209. *Bonadventure* of Flushing (16) Giles Adrian; Flushing
[f. 46b] Humphrey Keill: 500 bunches onions £3 6s 8d (3 Dec 1567).

210. *Sampson* of Antwerp Adrian Williamson
[f. 46b] John Lambert: 18 cwt battery £36 (3 Dec 1567). Edmund Burton: 2 half-brls head nails £4. Richard Dowler: 3 brls painter's oil £4. George Stockmed: 4 cwt flax £4. Hartik van Sprecleson: 4 half-packs flax £16. William Salkins: 22 cwt onion seed £36 13s 4d. John Elietts: 10 doz. pcs thread riband, 70 lbs unwrought inkle, 4 doz. thou. needles, 120 lbs counters, 8 grs minikins, 16 lbs clavichord wire, 25 lbs coarse pack thread, 4¾ cwt shaven latten £30 18s 4d. Thomas Eaton: 2 doz. lbs crewel, 5 doz. crewel pieces, 8 doz. lbs wrought inkle, 35 lbs unwrought inkle, 6 cwt latten wire £22 13s 4d (4 Dec). Robert Bladwell: 450 lbs pepper £37 10s. Richard Hills: 25½ cwt onion seed £42 10s. Gerson Hills: 6 cwt onion seed £10. William Hobbs: 517 lbs flax £5 5s. William Cokin: 42 cwt madder £28. Hartik van Sprecleson: 2 packs flax £16. John Alden: 6½ cwt white lead, 7½ cwt red lead, 1¾ cwt senna £28. John Haydon: 60 pcs Genoa fustian £40. William Smith: 80 doz. lbs inkle £53 6s 8d (5 Dec). Robert Exton: 4 cwt prunes £2. Thomas Hale: 425 lbs pepper £35 8s 4d. Edward Bright: 2 half-brls small nails, 16 cwt estrige wool £13 3s 4d. Robert Skarbrough: 13 cwt madder £8 13s 4d. Thomas Parker: 16 pcs Milan fustian £16 (6 Dec). John Wanton: 42 cwt madder £28. Edward van Crog: 10½ awms Rhenish wine 10s 6d (9 Dec). [f. 52b] Thomas Randall: 30 lbs satin silk £30 (10 Dec).

211. *Owl* of Antwerp Arnold Popenduck; Antwerp
[f. 46b] Edmund Burton: 3 doz. whip-saws, 4 doz. tenon-saws, 6 doz. hand-saws, 6 cwt frying pans, 20 doz. coarse sword blades. 9½ grs small hanging locks, 48 lbs curtain rings, 20 lbs clavichord wire, 10 thou. awl blades £39 12s (3 Dec 1567). James Harvie: 4 doz. whip-saws £6. John Gardyner: 12 cwt red lead, 4 cwt white lead, 3 qrs white copperas, 2 hd[1] brown paper £21 3s 6d. Thomas Starkey: 600 ells Normandy canvas £15 (4 Dec). William Cokin: 49½ cwt madder £33. John Boorne: 6 cwt shaven latten, 26 cwt black and white plates £29 6s 8d. John Merest: 2¼ cwt onion

29

seed £3 14*s*. Thomas Hale: 2 cwt lapis calaminaris £1 (5 Dec). Edward Bright: 2 half-brls small nails, 6 pair andirons, 24 pair creepers, 2 doz. pair tongs, 2 doz. fireshovels, 7 cwt estrige wool £19 6*s* 8*d*. [f. 50*b*] William Wood: 13 doz. Flanders skins £39 (6 Dec).

1. Presumably bundles.

212. *James* of Antwerp (50) Simon Joyce; Antwerp
[f. 46*b*] Richard Dowler: 50 lbs quicksilver, 35 lbs mace £15 (3 Dec 1567). John White: 9 doz. lbs worsted yarn £7 10*s*. John Spencer: 200 lbs pepper, ½ cwt mace, 7 cwt onion seed £45. Hartik van Sprecleson: 4 half-packs flax £16. William Gyfford: 72 yds frizado £18. Ralph Conyers: 72 yds frizado £18. John Eliets: 4 hd 30 lbs wrought inkle, 4 doz. lbs crewel, 14 doz. crewel pieces, 5 grs half points £27 8*s* 4*d*. William Luddington: 150 lbs marmalade £5. Henry Hungat: 7 lbs silk fringe £7. Thomas Towerson: 25 ells silk tapestry, 50 ells wool tapestry £6 13*s* 4*d* (4 Dec). Thomas Eaton: 3 hd 50 lbs unwrought inkle, 6 grs minikins, 30 doz. thou. pins £19 13*s* 4*d*. William Laire: 175 lbs pepper, 50 lbs cloves £27 1*s* 8*d*. Robert Bladwell: 300 lbs pepper £25. William Hobbs: 57 Turnhout ticks, 7 small cradle rugs £22 10*s*. Roger Warfilde: 70 lbs cinnamon £14. William Hewet: 6 cwt flax, 1 bale Ulm fustian, 18 pairs andirons, 4 doz. tongs, 4 doz. fireshovels £29 13*s* 4*d*. William Cockin: 53½ cwt madder £35 13*s* 4*d*. Francis Warren: 24 cwt madder £16. John Haydon: 60 pcs Genoa fustian £40. Edmund Smith: 37 pcs Genoa fustian, 30 pcs mockado £44 13*s* 4*d* (5 Dec). William Sherington: 30 lbs ferret silk £12 10*s*. Anthony Warfilde: 275 lbs ginger, 5 cwt hops £23 2*s*. Thomas Eaton: 315 ells sarcenet £52 10*s*. Richard Cotton: 400 ells sarcenet £66 13*s* 4*d*. Edmund Hill: 450 lbs pepper £37 10*s*. William Laire: 40 lbs pepper, 12 lbs cloves £6 6*s* 8*d* (6 Dec).¹ Christopher Jewkes: 3 cwt hops £1 10*s*. Thomas Randall: 300 ells Levant taffeta £25. Thomas Parker: 32 pcs Milan fustian £32. Reynold Thirling: 4 cwt onion seed £6 13*s* 4*d* (8 Dec). John Muns: 36 doz. Cologne knives £10. John Gardner: 500 lbs matches £3 3*s* 4*d*. Thomas Hale: 9 cwt liquorice, 800 lbs crossbow thread £16 10*s*. Thomas Daunster: 5 hd lbs unwrought inkle £16 13*s* 4*d*. John Colmer: 2 cwt onion seed, 2 cwt rice, 6 cwt sumach £9. [f. 52] Edmund Burton: 50 cwt mull-madder, 15 cwt iron pans £16 5*s* (9 Dec).

1. 'That was misentred' is written after this item.

213. *Cock* of Antwerp (40) Andrew Adrianson; Antwerp
[f. 47*b*] John Elietts: 5 cwt shaven latten £10 (3 Dec 1567). Richard Billam: 32 cwt madder £21 6*s* 8*d* (5 Dec). Humphrey Marbury: 2 bales fustian, 60 lbs satin silk £90. John Lambert: 18 cwt battery £36. John Boorne: 30 cwt iron plates, 10 doz. lbs coarse pack thread, 3 grs coarse hat bands, 20 doz. crewel pieces, 1 grs coarse hour glasses, 4 doz. lbs counters, 5 grs coarse bells, 2 doz. lbs wrought inkle £36 5*s*. Thomas Eaton: 40 inkle [*sic*], 5 doz. lbs crewel, 24 thou. pins, 15 grs thread points, 15 thou. awl blades, 12 grs minikins, 2 doz. thou. needles, 150 lbs counters, 36 lbs clavichord wire, 4 doz. lbs bottom thread £38 18*s* 4*d*. Christopher Jewkes: 2 cwt hops £1 (6 Dec). John Pasfilde: 10 cwt iron wire, 12 doz. latten

candlesticks, 2 doz. bed pans £21 13s 4d. John Eliets: 19 doz. crewel pieces, 12 doz. lbs narrow inkle, 2½ doz. pcs thread riband, 1 grs single knives £20 5s. John Daniell: 5¾ cwt wrought flax £5 15s. William Coles: 50 lbs mace £16 13s 4d. Thomas Starkey: 150 reams paper, 150 ells Bar canvas, 150 ells Vitré canvas, 2 pcs Olonne cloth £26 16s 8d. Robert Skarbrough: 50 pcs mockado £33 6s 8d (8 Dec). John Boorne: 10 pcs Naples fustian, 4 doz. lbs counters £17 3s 4d. Robert Bladwell: 45 yds velvet £33 15s (10 Dec). Thomas Randall: 40 lbs cochineal £6 13s 4d (11 Dec). Stephen Slany: 12 cwt flax £12 (16 Dec). [f. 66b] John Colmer: 34 doz. lbs bottom thread £6 16s 8d (2 Jan).

214. *Mary* of Fécamp (32) Allen Fellon; Bordeaux
[f. 47b] Andrew de Loa: 8 tuns Gascony wine *net* 7 tuns 21s (4 Dec 1567).

215. *Browne* of Haarlem (30) John Marson; Haarlem
[f. 47b] Andrew de Loa: 8 tuns corrupt Gascony wine £24 (4 Dec 1567).

216. *Mearman* of Amsterdam (40) Peter Messe; Amsterdam
[f. 48] Richard Mouse: 480 lings, 600 staplefish, 1 last fish, 2 brls stub-eels, 2 brls pimper-eels £37 13s 4d (4 Dec 1567).

217. *Buckett* of Flushing (6) Davie Johnson; Flushing
[f. 48b] Humphrey Keil: 20 brls fish, 6 brls Scotch salmon £19 (4 Dec 1567). [f. 51] Humphrey Keil: 6 brls fish, 2 brls salmon £6 (8 Dec).

218. *Nicolas* of Flushing Martin Mychelson
[f. 48b] Humphrey Keil: 18 brls fish £9 (4 Dec 1567).

219. *Morian* of Flushing Henrick[1]; Flushing
[f. 49] Humphrey Keil: 18 brls fish £9 (5 Dec 1567).
    1. Surname illegible.

220. *Phenex* of Hull (50) Walter Haull; Bordeaux
[f. 49b] William Notshaw: 35 tuns Gascony wine *net* 30 tuns 90s (5 Dec 1567). [f. 53] Walter Hall: 2 hhds Gascony wine *net* 2 hhds 1s 6d (10 Dec).

221. *Nightingale* of London (30) John Thorneborrow; Nantes
[f. 49b] William Bond: 30 tuns prunes £150 (5 Dec 1567).

222. *Pellican* of St. Omer (30) Cornelis Keizer; St. Omer
[f. 50] Thomas Hecker: 48 doz. hemp £6 (6 Dec 1567).

223. *Pellican* of St. Omer (40) Nicholas Bullart; St. Omer
[f. 50b] John Atkinson: 600 bushels apples £10 (6 Dec 1567).

224. *Saviour* of Aldeburgh (50) Thomas Beversham; La Rochelle
[f. 50b] Thomas Beversham: 30 weys bay salt £30 (6 Dec 1567). [f. 55] Thomas Beversham 'cum sociis': 6 tuns corrupt wine of St. Martin *net* 5 tuns £15 (13 Dec).

225. *Elizabeth* of Ipswich (50) George Payne; Spain
[f. 51] Godfrey Wylson: 250 pcs Malaga raisins £62 10s (8 Dec 1567).

226. *Mary Thomas* of London (50) William Dixson of Brightlingsea;
Bordeaux
[f. 51] George Lucas: 38 tuns Gascony wine *net* 30 tuns 90s, 2 tuns vinegar
£4 13s 4d (8 Dec 1567).

227. *Cloverblade* of Amsterdam (40) John Rede; Amsterdam
[f. 51] Thomas Hanford: 18 brls fish £9 (8 Dec 1567).

228. *Romaine* of Antwerp Paul Lympet
[f. 51b] Henry Dunham: 3 cwt printer's ink, ½ cwt printing letters, 25 pair
'pumping stocks' ad valorem 3s 4d £3 3s 4d (8 Dec 1567).

229. *Yong Egle* of Antwerp (25) Anthony Cornilis; Antwerp
[f. 51b] John Car: 9 cwt iron wire, 9 cwt iron pans £21 (9 Dec 1567).
William Coles: 80 lbs nutmegs £13 6s 8d. Thomas and Edmund Brasy:
71 pcs Genoa fustian £47 6s 8d. John Alden: 650 lbs ginger £48 15s.
Anthony Warfilde: 200 lbs ginger £15 (10 Dec). Henry Hungat: 8 lbs silk
fringe £8. Christopher Jewkes: 6 cwt hops £3. Thomas Randall: 80 yds
velvet £60 (11 Dec). Thomas Longston: 8 cwt estrige wool £6 13s 4d
(12 Dec). Thomas Hooker: 4 cwt liquorice £2. [f. 56b] Jerome Rice: 48 cwt
estrige wool £38 6s 8d (15 Dec).

230. *Bonadventure* of London (70) Thomas Lawson; Bordeaux
[f. 51b] Thomas Bates: 3 tuns Gascony wine *net* 3 tuns 9s, 1 tun vinegar
£2 6s 8d (9 Dec 1567). Michael Blake: 6 tuns Gascony wine *net* 5½ tuns
16s 6d. Robert Fryer: 100 quintals damask prunes[1] £50. Robert Fryer:
10 tuns Gascony wine *net* 9 tuns 27s. Giles Rag: 3 tuns 1 tierce Gascony
wine *net* 3 tuns 9s (10 Dec). [f. 52b] Christopher Edwards and company:
12 tuns Gascony wine *net* 10½ tuns 31s 6d.

   1. 29 pcs.

231. *Slake* of Flushing (16) Peter Critor; Flushing
[f. 52b] Humphrey Keil: 2 lasts fish, 8 brls salmon £24 (10 Dec 1567).

232. *Angel* of Hamburg (60) Henrik Alverman; Hamburg
[f. 52b] Hartik van Sprecleson: 24 cwt estrige wool, 1560 ells soultwich,
32 cwt copperas £62 (10 Dec 1567). John Miller: 12 cwt estrige wool,
4 qrs hemp seed £11 6s 8d. Matthew Hope: 10 cwt estrige wool £8 6s 8d
(11 Dec). Luder van Dorne: 2 packs flax £16. John Reinkin: 16 cwt estrige
wool £13 6s 8d (13 Dec). Court Ellers: 24 cwt estrige wool £20. Edward
van Crog: 29 cwt estrige wool £24 3s 4d. [f. 57] Daniel van Eitson: 11
lasts titlings, 8 cwt estrige wool £43 6s 8d (16 Dec).

233. *Mary Fortune* of London (80) John Morecoks; Malaga
[f. 53] Robert Phillipson: 125 pcs raisins £31 5s (11 Dec 1567). Edward
Boyes: 50 pcs raisins £12 10s. Henry Callis 'cum sociis': 225 pcs raisins

£56 5s. Godfrey Wilson: 250 pcs Malaga raisins, 4 cwt raisins of the sun £67 13s 4d. Reynold Barker: 22 cwt almonds £44. Robert Kocks: 245 pcs Malaga raisins £61 5s. Henry Smyth: 125 pcs raisins £31 5s. William Crompton: 250 pcs raisins £62 10s. Thomas Candler: 100 pcs raisins, 20 cwt raisins of the sun £38 6s 8d (12 Dec). John Gyll: 120 pcs Malaga raisins £30 (13 Dec). [f. 56] William Wilkes: 20 pcs Malaga raisins, 14 cwt raisins of the sun £14 6s 8d (15 Dec).

234. *Barsaby* of Lee (35) William Syms; Antwerp
[f. 53] William Salkins: 14 cwt onion seed £23 6s 8d (11 Dec 1567). John Haydon: 50 pcs Genoa fustian £33 6s 8d. George Breme: 8 cwt frying pans, 80 yds copper hangings £15 6s 8d. Anthony Warfilde: 5 cwt hops, 3 cwt saltpetre, 1½ cwt gunpowder, 100 lbs ginger, 3¼ cwt starch £19 6s 8d. Ancelm Becket: 2 lasts rape oil, 6 cwt flax £40 6s 8d. John Fitzwilliams: 60 cwt madder £40. Robert Broke: 32 cwt madder £21 6s 8d. George Stockmed: 5½ cwt wrought flax £5 10s. George Colmer: 80 doz. thou. pins, 20 grs harp strings, 5 doz. lbs Bruges thread, 5 doz. lbs bottom pack thread £19. Thomas Hale: 4 cwt hops, 2 cwt gum arabic, 1½ cwt verdigris, 9 cwt rice, 2½ cwt starch, 60 lbs capers £19 6s 8d. John Pasfyld: 1 brl ½ hhd head nails, 20 iron backs £9 6s 8d. Thomas Longston: 300 lbs cotton wool, 4 cwt estrige wool, 80 lbs ginger, 4 cwt rice £22 13s 4d (12 Dec). John Alden: 26 cwt argol, 7 cwt bay berries, 4½ cwt starch, 3½ tons white lead £41 10s. Thomas Aldersay: 38 yds velvet £28 10s. John Sturtivant: 30 cwt woad £20. Thomas Barker: 11 cwt battery £22. John Car: iron-made ware £40. William Laire: 212 lbs pepper £17 13s 4d. Christopher Jewkes: 10 cwt copperas £5. Thomas Starkey: 1500 ells Osnabrücks £20. Richard Douler: 150 lbs ginger £11 5s. John Rivers: 914 lbs pepper £75. Thomas Davie: 5½ cwt latten wire £11 (13 Dec). Anthony Scoloker: 90 doz. dials, 280 razors ad valorem £13 6s 8d. John Gardener: 600 lbs pepper £50. Thomas Daunser: 280 doz. thou. pins £46 13s 4d. Thomas Eaton: 3 thou. thimbles, 7 thou. needles, 4 thou. pack needles, 14 thou. awl blades, 80 lbs counters, 6 doz. lbs crewel, 30 thou. pins, 1½ grs coarse pinpillows, 3 doz. lbs unwrought inkle £31 3s 4d. Henry Becher: 100 doz. thou. pins, 4 doz. lbs bottom pack thread, 10 doz. lbs Oudenaarde thread £25 6s 8d. Roger Owton: 600 lbs pepper £50. Richard Hills: 3 pcs stammel £30. Robert Skarbrough: 80 pcs mockado £53 6s 8d. John Gardener: 40 doz. empty barrels £4. Geoffrey Walkeden: 20 pcs Holland cloth, 200 ells Bar canvas, 4 pcs tartarines £30 13s 4d (15 Dec). Wolston Dixi: 1500 ells Osnabrücks £20. Steven White: 42 cwt madder £28. William Hewet: 8 cwt hops, 14 cwt estrige wool £15 13s 4d (17 Dec). Edmond Burton: 14 cwt flax £14. [f. 58b] Robert Broune: 570 yds dornick with thread £12 13s 4d.

235. *Hoy Wagon* of Amsterdam (40) Jacob Jacobson; Amsterdam
[f. 53] Roger James: 6000 clapholt £15 (11 Dec 1567).

236. *Barnaby* of London (45) Peter Hills; Rouen
[f. 55] Richard Northey: 32 doz. woolcards £16 (13 Dec 1567). Hugh Offley: 1500 ells canvas, 60 reams paper, 50 cwt prunes £70 10s. John Harding: 800 ells canvas £20. John Allot: 1600 ells canvas £40 (15 Dec).

Wolston Dixi: 1350 ells canvas £33 15s. Robert Sadler: 1000 ells canvas, 200 reams paper £51 13s 4d. John Olif: 2400 ells canvas £60. Anthony Gamage: 2000 ells canvas £50. Thomas Starkey: 2000 ells canvas £50 (16 Dec). Richard Morris: 2300 ells packing canvas £30 13s 4d. Anthony Cage: 2000 ells canvas £50. Edmund Anselm: 200 ells canvas, 3 pcs French dornick £12 10s. Richard Renolds: 2800 ells packing canvas, 27 cwt prunes, 60 cwt green woad £80 16s 8d. [f. 60] John Wanton: 16 cwt prunes £8 (19 Dec).

237. *Spled Egle* of Bruges (50) Francis Bowin; Bruges
[f. 55] Matthew Colclogh: 800 ells white 800 ells brown Hazebroucks £36 (13 Dec 1567). William Harris: 80 brls apples £4 (18 Dec). John Nicolson: 100 yds diaper towelling £7 10s (19 Dec). [f. 60b] Robert Langham: 10 pcs Holland cloth £12 (20 Dec).

238. *Falkon* of Dordrecht (35) Adrian Dudall;[1] Dordrecht
[f. 55b] Edward van Crog: 26 awms Rhenish wine 26s (13 Dec 1567).
[f. 56b] Melchior van Adinek: 4 awms Rhenish wine 4s (15 Dec).

    1. Or Dotell.

239. *Pellican* of Amsterdam (35) Tyman Cornilison; Amsterdam
[f. 56] Daniel van Eitson: 24 cwt estrige wool £33 6s 8d (15 Dec 1567). John Edmund: 5 lasts fish, 6 brls codsheads, 200 lings, 1 brl shaft-eels £41 6s 8d (16 Dec). Henry Keil: 3 brls shaft-eels £4 10s (17 Dec). [f. 58] John Smyth: 5 weys Rhenish glass £12 10s.

240. *Michell* of Amsterdam (30) Henrik Johnson; Amsterdam
[f. 56b] Daniel van Eitson: 16 cwt estrige wool £13 6s 8d (15 Dec 1567). Oliff Burr: 14 cwt hops £7. Court Ellers: 10 cwt estrige wool £8 6s 8d (16 Dec). John Edmund: 3 lasts fish £18. Thomas Sandford: 1200 lings, 2 lasts barrelled fish £52. [f. 57b] George Jenens: 480 lings, 300 staplefish, 420 coal-fish £24 (17 Dec).

241. *Half Mone* of Amsterdam (25) John Garedson; Amsterdam
[f. 56b] Jerome Rice: 14 cwt estrige wool £11 13s 4d (15 Dec 1567).

242. *Elizabeth* of London[1] (80) Thomas Sherland; Spain
[f. 57] William Wilkes: 3 hhds olives, 7 doz. Spanish skins, 1 hd lbs cork, 20 doz. hand baskets £31 3s 4d (16 Dec 1567). Christopher Edwards: 40 tuns sack *net* 36 tuns 108s. John Holanside: 25 tuns sack *net* 22½ tuns 67s 6d. [f. 59] Robert Dow: 20 butts sack *net* 18 butts 27s (18 Dec).

    1. Also described as of Newcastle.

243. *Andrew* of Ipswich (40) Thomas Swyte;[1] Bordeaux
[f. 57] Christopher Edwards: 15 tuns Gascony wine *net* 13½ tuns 40s 6d (16 Dec 1567). Anthony Ratclif: 22 tuns Gascony wine *net* 20 tuns 60s. [f. 58] John Marten: 2 tuns Gascony wine *net* 1½ tuns 4s 6d (17 Dec).

    1. Or Switman.

244. *Elizabeth Bonadventure* of London James Riddam; Malaga
[f. 57b] Richard May and Humphrey Fairfex: 235 pcs raisins £58 15s
(16 Dec 1567). John Spencer: 200 pcs raisins, 160 roves raisins of the sun
£76 13s 4d (17 Dec). Edward Jackman: 250 pcs raisins £62 10s (18 Dec).
Edward Osburne: 125 pcs raisins £31 5s. Edmund Huggan: 20 cwt raisins
of the sun, 7½ cwt almonds £30 13s 4d. Thomas Candler: 125 pcs raisins
£31 5s. John Baker: 360 pcs raisins £90. John Haule: 225 pcs raisins £56 5s
(19 Dec). John Barnes: 350 pcs raisins £87 10s. [f. 61] William Keeling:
350 ells Levant taffeta, 40 lbs satin £69 3s 4d (20 Dec).

245. *Julyan* of London (130) William Oxley; Spain
[f. 57b] Richard May and Humphrey Fairfex: 235 pcs raisins £58 15s
(16 Dec 1567). Robert How: 200 pcs raisins £50 (17 Dec). John Highlord:
125 pcs raisins £31 5s. William Wydnall: 125 pcs raisins £31 5s. George
and John Barne: 250 pcs raisins £62 10s. Emanuel Wolley: 250 pcs raisins
£62 10s. John Mon: 125 pcs raisins £37 10s. Thomas Turnebull: 200 pcs
Malaga raisins, 30 cwt raisins of the sun £70. Edward Jackman: 250 pcs
great raisins £62 10s. Thomas Altham: 250 pcs raisins £62 10s. Edward
Osburne: 250 pcs raisins £62 10s (18 Dec). Reynold Holingworth: 75 pcs
raisins, 7 cwt almonds, 10 cwt raisins of the sun £39 1s 8d (19 Dec).
[f. 60b] John Simcots: 80 pcs raisins, 14 cwt raisins of the sun, 5 cwt almonds
£39 6s 8d (20 Dec).

246. *Christ* of London (90) Bartholomew Storm; Andalusia
[f. 57b] Richard Venables: 125 pcs raisins £31 5s (17 Dec 1567). Arthur
Dawbeney: 250 pcs raisins £62 10s. Thomas Willford: 250 pcs raisins
£62 10s. Francis Wight: 200 pcs raisins, 15 cwt raisins of the sun £60.
Henry Becher: 125 pcs raisins £31 5s. Francis Benizen: 250 pcs raisins £62
10s. Robert Harding: 125 pcs raisins £31 5s (18 Dec). Richard Foster:
5 cwt almonds £10. John Branch: 13 cwt almonds £26 (19 Dec). William
Allen: 350 ells Levant taffeta £29 3s 4d (20 Dec). Thomas Walker: 300
pcs raisins £75. [f. 61] Thomas Altham: 70 pcs raisins, 17 cwt raisins of
the sun, 16 cwt almonds £60 16s 8d.

247. *Elizabeth* of London (40) Edward Smarley; Ayamonte
[f. 58] James Morley: 30 tuns bastards *net* 27 tuns 81s, 4500 lbs figs, 120 pcs
figs, 100 doz. cork £48 10s (17 Dec 1567).

248. *Edward* of London (40) William Holand
[f. 59] Mark Dingley: 50 lbs nuts, 150 lbs pepper, 2 cwt dates, 50 lbs cloves
£41 6s 8d (18 Dec 1567). [f. 61] James Hill: 20 lbs cloves, 20 lbs cinnamon,
20 lbs nuts, 10 lbs mace £15 13s 4d (20 Dec).

249. *Mary Catharin* of Ipswich (40) Thomas Lucas; Bordeaux
[f. 59] Arthur Jervaies: 26 tuns Gascony wine *net* 23½ tuns 90s 6d, 6 tuns
vinegar *net* 5½ tuns £12 16s 8d (18 Dec 1567).

250. *Mary George* of London (80) John Fryer; Andalusia
[f. 59b] Anthony Pilborro: 15 tuns sack *net* 13½ tuns 40s 6d (19 Dec 1567).

John Barker: 20 butts sack *net* 18 butts 27*s*. Thomas Turnebull: 20 butts sack *net* 18 butts 27*s*. John Spencer: 20 pipes oil *net* 17 pipes £68. George Sanders: 30 pipes train oil *net* 27 pipes £67 10*s*. George Sanders: 20 butts sack *net* 18 butts 27*s*. John Hawes: 14 hhds olives, 6 doz. Seville skins £55 6*s* 8*d* (20 Dec). [f. 61] Edward Osburne: 10 butts sack *net* 9 butts 13*s* 6*d*.

251. *Jesus* of Rye (35) William Skinner; Bordeaux
[f. 59*b*] John Lane: 6 tuns Gascony wine *net* 5 tuns 15*s* (19 Dec 1567). Thomas Busby: 4½ tuns Gascony wine *net* 4 tuns 12*s*. William Hamand: 2 tuns 1 hhd Gascony wine *net* 2 tuns 6*s*. James Beching: 5 tuns Gascony wine *net* 4½ tuns 13*s* 6*d*.

252. *Julian* of Millbrook (30) Pentecost Harris; Bordeaux
[f. 59*b*] Arthur Jervaies: 20 tuns Gascony wine *net* 18 tuns 54*s*, 6 tuns vinegar *net* 5½ tuns £12 6*s* 8*d* (19 Dec 1567). [f. 64*b*] Richard Bell: 3 hhds Gascony wine *net* 3 hhds 2*s* 3*d* (23 Dec).

253. *Jesus* of London (20) Thomas Clerk; Bordeaux
[f. 59*b*] Arthur Jervaies: 7 tuns Gascony wine *net* 6½ tuns,[1] 2 tuns vinegar £4 13*s* 4*d* (19 Dec 1567).

    1. No tonnage figure given.

254. *Mary An* of Orford (60) Robert Hart; Spain
[f. 60] Reynold Holingworth: 59 butts sack *net* 53 butts 79*s* (19 Dec 1567). John Watson: 39 butts sack *net* 35 butts 52*s* 6*d*, 5 pipes oil £20. John Mun: 6 butts sack *net* 6 butts 9*s* (20 Dec). [f. 61] William Dane: 10 butts sack *net* 9 butts 13*s* 6*d*.

255. *James* of London (30) Robert Fitzwilliams; Bordeaux
[f. 60] Thomas Busbie: 3 tuns Gascony wine *net* 2¾ tuns 5*s* 3*d* (19 Dec 1567). William Silvester: 55 cwt prunes £27 10*s*. [f. 60*b*] Lawrence Mellow: 11 tuns Gascony wine *net* 10 tuns 30*s*, 20 pcs resin, 30 cwt prunes £18 6*s* 8*d*.

256. *Confydence* of London (60) Erasmus Kedball; Bordeaux
[f. 60*b*] Robert Fryer: 33 tuns Gascony wine *net* 29 tuns 87*s*, 25 quintals prunes, 3 tons turpentine £27 10*s* (19 Dec 1567). [f. 61] William Bulley: 6½ cwt prunes £3 5*s*, 3 hhds Gascony wine 2*s* 3*d* (20 Dec).

257. *Prime Rose* of Dartmouth (38) Ellis Benet; Port St. Mary
[f. 60*b*] John Watson: 72 butts sack *net* 64 butts 96*s* (19 Dec 1567).

258. *Heare* of Lee (24) Peter Robson; Antwerp
[f. 61*b*] Thomas Eaton: 63 yds velvet £47 5*s* (22 Dec 1567). John Lambert: 13½ cwt battery, 225 lbs pepper £45 15*s*. William Coles: 41 cwt soap £30 15*s*. Thomas Barker: 9 cwt battery £18. John Pasfyld: 1½ cwt copper baking pans, 1 cwt iron wire £4 13*s* 4*d*. John Eliot: 140 doz. thou. pins, 5 doz. lbs crewel £27 10*s*. William Salkins: 7¼ cwt onion seed £12 1*s* 8*d*. Robert Taylor: 16 cwt madder £10 13*s* 4*d*. Robert Broke: 32 cwt madder

£21 6s 8d. John Fitzwilliams: 60 cwt madder £40. Roger Warfilde: 18 cwt soap, 400 lbs pepper, 150 lbs ginger £58 1s 8d. John Car: 18 cwt iron pans, 100 iron doubles, 43 iron backs £22 10s. Henry Billingsley: 1 hd lbs unwrought inkle, 12 pcs boultel, 6 doz. thou. pins, 10 doz. lbs bottom pack thread £8 14s 8d. Thomas Hale: 3 cwt saltpetre £4 10s. Thomas Parker: 180 yds dornick with thread, 4 great grs points, 3 doz. lbs checks £7 10s (23 Dec). John Sutton: 50 Turnhout ticks £16 13s 4d. Thomas Longston: 6 cwt rice, 8 cwt estrige wool £10. Christopher Jewkes: 10 cwt copperas £5. [f. 64] William Luddington: 15 cwt Castile soap £11 5s.

259. *Anne* of Antwerp (46) Bartholomew Paules: Antwerp
[f. 61b] John Lambert: 17 cwt battery £34 (22 Dec 1567). Edmund Burton: 3 cwt iron wire, 60 lbs clavichord wire, 9 thou. pack needles, 2 grs goldsmith's files, 7 grs horse bells, 4 doz. pincers £14 1s 8d. John Eliot: 50 doz. thou. pins, 4 doz. lbs crewel, 6 doz. lbs thread riband £13 13s 4d. Richard Hills: 12 cwt onion seed £20. Edward Bright: 3 half-brls head nails £6. William Hewet: 18 cwt estrige wool £15. Humphrey Fairfax: 14 cwt hops, 175 lbs cotton wool £12 16s 8d. William Hobs: 22 close stools £2 18s 4d. John Car: 10 cwt iron wire £16 13s 4d. Robert Skarbrogh: 7 cwt flax £7. Thomas Gardener: 50 lbs nuts, 40 lbs cinnamon £16 6s 8d. Robert Exton: 1 half-brl steel £6. Thomas Hale: 6 cwt hops £3. John Gardner: 150 lbs nutmegs, 1¼ cwt verdigris £16 13s 4d (23 Dec). William Gifford: 72 yds frizado, 3 pcs broad 'russels' £21. Thomas Eaton: 20 doz. crewel pieces, 1 doz. lbs crewel, 1 grs pinpillows, 6 thou. pack needles, 1 doz. thou. needles, 2 grs horse bells, 2 grs halfpennyware glasses, 3 doz. lbs wrought inkle, 2 thou. thimbles, 1 qr coarse pack thread £19 8s. John Mun: 3 grs coarse single knives, 2 grs coarse pairs of knives, 3 grs coarse cauls, 40 lbs fine inkle £16 (29 Dec). [f. 66] Anthony Warfield: 2½ cwt hops £1 5s (30 Dec).

260. *Pellican* of Antwerp (30) Leonard Johnson; Antwerp
[f. 61b] Thomas Barker: 8 cwt battery £16 (22 Dec 1567). Edward Bright: 3 half-brls head nails £6. William Hobs: 176 ells hair tapestry, 5½ doz. coarse cushions, 11 pcs Naples fustian, 4 doz. lince £31 5s. William Hewet: 8 cwt white plates, 5½ cwt flax £10 16s 8d. John Car: 8 cwt latten wire £16. Robert Brook: 48 cwt madder £32. Thomas Hale: 2 cwt hops, 3 cwt onion seed £5. Edmund Burton: 10 cwt white plates £6 13s 4d (23 Dec). Henry Barton: 8 brls rape oil £10 13s 4d. Christopher Jewkes: 6 cwt hops £3. Henry Hungat: 8 lbs silk fringe £8. William Megs: 6 brls rape oil £8 (24 Dec). Anthony Warffild: 2½ cwt hops £1 5s (30 Dec). [f. 66Ab] Steven White: 16 cwt madder £10 13s 4d (5 Jan).

261. *Leonard* of St. Omer (18) Leonard Johnson
[f. 61b] John Atkinson: 300 bushels apples £5 (22 Dec 1567).

262. *Elizabeth* of Dartford[1] (24) Peter Francis; Antwerp
[f. 61b] John Eliots: 10 doz. lbs crewel, 2½ cwt shaven latten, 30 thou. awl blades, 5 doz. crewel pieces, 5 doz. thou. pins, 3 hd thimbles £26 16s 8d (22 Dec 1567). Thomas Eaton: 3 cwt iron wire, 4 doz. pincers, 3 doz. lbs

Bruges thread £7 16s 8d (24 Dec). John Car: 8 cwt iron pans £5 6s 8d (13 Jan). William Hobs: 5 cwt flax £5. William Hewet: 20 cwt madder, 1 half-brl head nails £15 6s 8d. Robert Brook: 56 cwt madder £37 6s 8d. Richard Billam: 20 cwt soap £15. John Gardner: 400 lbs pepper £33 6s 8d. John Spencer: 5 cwt sugar £16 13s 4d. Roger Warfilde: 400 lbs pepper £33 6s 8d. Joan Bower: 5¼ cwt wrought flax £5. John Lambert: 900 lbs pepper £75. Anthony Warfilde: 18 cwt [ ],[2] 50 lbs cinnamon, 75 lbs nutmegs £34 6s 8d. Christopher Jewkes: 6 cwt estrige wool £5 (14 Jan). Thomas Barker: 9 cwt battery £18. Arthur Hall: 16 cwt madder £10 13s 4d. John Pasfyld: 18 pair iron andirons with shovels and tongs, 30 pair iron creepers £10 6s 8d. Thomas Eaton: 3 cwt iron wire, 6 doz. pincers, 3 doz. lbs Bruges thread £7 12s. William Ludington: 150 lbs pepper, 3 cwt bay berries £14 10s (16 Jan). Thomas Longston: 500 lbs pepper, 40 lbs nutmegs £45. John Sutton: 40 Turnhout ticks £13 6s 8d (17 Jan). Humphrey Fayrefax: 5 cwt wrought flax, 12 cwt Castile soap £14 (20 Jan). [f. 79b] Thomas Starkey: 1600 ells 'clincent' canvas £24.

   1. Or of Deptford.
   2. Blank.

263. *Fortune* of Amsterdam (50) Bartholomew de Wike; Hamburg
[f. 62] Henry Lessie: 2 lasts croplings £13 6s 8d (22 Dec 1567).

264. *Falcon* of Dordrecht (40) Job Peterson; Dordrecht
[f. 62b] Edward van Adena: 129 awms Rhenish wine 129s (22 Dec 1567).

265. *Julian* of Rochester (50) Thomas Usher; Rouen
[f. 63] Robert Sadler: 1800 ells canvas £45 (23 Dec 1567). John Nycolson: 750 ells canvas £18 15s. Robert Broke: 48 cwt prunes £24. Richard Patrik: 60 doz. woolcards, 300 reams paper £70. Robert Broke: 20 cwt brazil £33 6s 8d. Hugh Offley: 500 lbs guinea grains, 12 cwt prunes £22 13s 4d. John Bingley: 25 cwt prunes £12 10s. Humphrey Girdler: 13 cwt prunes, 40¼ grs combs £16 10s. John Olyf: 1400 ells canvas £35. John Thompson: 12 cwt prunes, 24 reams paper, 2 grs playing cards £11 13s 4d. John Savell: 1250 ells canvas £31 5s. John Myler: 1300 ells canvas £33 10s. Richard Billam: 7 doz. iron pots, 6 doz. iron chafing dishes £3 15s (24 Dec). Arthur Jervaies: 9 tuns Gascony wine *net* 8 tuns 24s. John Harding: 500 ells canvas £12 10s. Richard Morrys: 1200 ells canvas £30. John Wanton: 60 doz. woolcards £30. Thomas Starkey: 1000 ells canvas £25. John Clint: 132 reams paper £17 11s 8d (29 Dec). [f. 65b] Humphrey Marbury: 16 grs playing cards £16.

266. *Grehound* of Ipswich Miles Mason; Rouen
[f. 63] Anthony Gamage: 2300 ells [ ][1] £57 10s (23 Dec 1567). Thomas Cambell: 1300 ells canvas £32 10s. Richard Renolds: 140 reams paper £18 13s 4d. Robert Broke: 25 cwt brazil £41 13s 4d. Hugh Offley: 140 reams paper £18 13s 4d. Robert Sadler: 600 ells canvas £15. John Olyf: 2000 ells canvas £50. Edward Osborne: 1300 ells canvas £32 10s. Edmund Ansyll: 40 grs playing cards, 8 doz. buckram £52. John Myler: 1800 ells canvas £45. Richard Patrick: 40 grs woolcards, 30 grs combs, 1 cwt pack

thread, 6 grs inkhorns £43 16s 8d (24 Dec). Anthony Cage: 2000 ells canvas £50. William Handford: 10 doz. woolcards £5. John Harding: 900 ells canvas £22 10s. Richard Smyth: 110 reams paper, 18 grs playing cards £32 13s 4d. John Haull: 400 reams paper £53 6s 8d. [f. 65b] John Nicolson: 90 reams paper £12 (29 Dec).

1. Blank, but obviously canvas.

267. *James* of Flushing Cornilis Mychells
[f. 65] Humphrey Keil: 2 lasts barrelled fish £12 (24 Dec 1567).

268. *Saviour* of London (80) Dany Phillie; San Sebastián
[f. 65b] Richard Folkes: 10 tons Spanish iron £40 (29 Dec 1567). Thomas Robinson: 2 tons Spanish iron £8. Thomas Hewet: 10 tons Spanish iron £40. Francis Bowyer: 20 tons Spanish iron £80. William Richardson: 1 ton resin £5. Richard May: 5 tons Spanish iron £20. Robert Car: 40 cwt liquorice £20. Robert Dow: 10 tons Spanish iron £40. Richard Renolds: 12 hd Spanish wool £20. Edward Boyes: 5 tons Spanish iron £20 (30 Dec). [f. 66b] Nicholas Atkinson: 3 tons iron £12 (31 Dec).

269. *Bonadventure* of St. Omer (30) Lawrence Hawes; St. Omer
[f. 65b] Thomas Sound: 20 cwt madder £13 6s 8d (29 Dec 1567).

270. *Hopsak* of Amsterdam (200) Peter Peterson; Brouage
[f. 66] William Page: 60 weys great salt £60 (29 Dec 1567). [f. 79b] Peter Peterson: 2 tuns Rochelle wine *net* 1 tun 3s (20 Jan).

271. *Jonas* of Newcastle Walter Baylyf; Bordeaux
[f. 66] Richard Foster: 30 cwt prunes £15 (30 Dec 1567). William Silvester: 23 tuns Gascony wine *net* 19 tuns 57s. Thomas Cordall: 10 tuns Gascony wine *net* 9 tuns 27s. John Holand: 6 tuns Gascony wine *net* 4¾ tuns 13s 9d (3 Jan). [f. 66A] Robert Barker: 7 tuns Gascony wine *net* 7 tuns 21s.

272. *Bark Fox* of London (50) Thomas Pirrie
[f. 66b] Thomas Blanck: 20 pipes Seville oil *net* 18 pipes £72 (31 Dec 1567). John Hall: 10 butts sack *net* 9 butts 13s 6d (5 Jan). Thomas Walker: 5 butts sack *net* 5 butts 7s 6d, 12 cwt figs £8. Francis Banison: 20 pipes Seville oil *net* 18 pipes £72. John Thomas: 1 tun olives, 6 cwt figs £14 13s 4d. Reynold Barker: 10 butts sack *net* 9 butts 13s 6d, 7 cwt figs, 100 doz. squirts, 1 hhd olives, 30 lbs capers £17 6s 8d. Thomas Bainton: 14 hhds olives, 1 tun Seville oil £45 6s 8d (8 Jan). [f. 69b] Thomas Altham: 8 hhds train oil, 2 hhds olives £15 6s 8d (9 Jan).

273. *Lion* of Ipswich (80) William Searles; Spain
[f. 66b] George and John Barnes: 10 tuns sack *net* 9 tuns 27s, 2 hhds 6 brls olives £8 (2 Jan 1568). Henry Callis 'cum sociis': 14 butts sack *net* 13 butts 19s 6d. Lawrence Mello: 20 butts sack *net* 18 butts 27s (3 Jan). Edmund Hugan: 40 butts sack *net* 36 butts 54s. Edmund Flick: 10 butts sack *net* 9 butts 13s 6d (5 Jan). Robert Barker: 9½ tuns oil *net* 8½ tuns £68. Simon Broke: 200 ells Levant taffeta £16 13s 4d (7 Jan). Wolston Randall: 3 cwt

Algarve figs £2. Augustin Parker: 9 butts sack *net* 9 butts 13*s* 6*d* (8 Jan).
[f. 68*b*] Henry Richards: 6 butts sack *net* 5 butts 7*s* 6*d*.

274. *Trinetie* of Scarborough (45) John Skilton; Bordeaux
[f. 66*b*] Thomas Searle: 18 tuns Gascony wine *net* 16 tuns 48*s*, 2 tuns
vinegar £4 13*s* 4*d* (2 Jan 1568). George Lucas: 6 tuns Gascony wine *net*
4 tuns 12*s*, 1 tun vinegar £2 6*s* 8*d* (3 Jan). Margaret Chambrelain: 12 tuns
Gascony wine *net* 11 tuns 33*s* (5 Jan). [f. 70*b*] Robert Dalton: 36 cwt woad
£24 (12 Jan).

275. *Mary George* of Blakeney (80) Nicholas Wilkinson; Bordeaux
[f. 66A] John Mun: 120 cwt woad £80 (3 Jan 1568). William Crips: 35 cwt
prunes £17 10*s* (5 Jan). William Silvester: 105 cwt prunes, 1 hhd [ ],[1] 26
ballets woad £88 8*s* 4*d*. Thomas Searle: 22 tuns Gascony wine *net* 19 tuns
27*s*, 2 tuns vinegar £4 6*s* 8*d*. Francis Benison: 7 tuns Gascony wine *net*
6 tuns 18*s*. William Catcher: 4 tons resin, 4 tuns vinegar £27 (7 Jan).
Lawrence Mello: 8 tuns Gascony wine *net* 7 tuns 21*s*, 1 tun vinegar £2 6*s* 8*d*
(8 Jan). [f. 69*b*] Thomas Cordall: 3 tuns Gascony wine *net* 2¼ tuns 8*s* 3*d*
(9 Jan).

    1. Blank.

276. *Marygold* of Lynn (75) John Wylson; Bordeaux
[f. 66A] William Bond: 565 quintals prunes[1] £282 10*s* (3 Jan 1568).

    1. Or 153 pipes.

277. *Falcon* of Saltash (13) Bartholomew Pope; Galicia
[f. 66A*b*] John Hinchinson: 40 thou. oranges £13 6*s* 8*d* (5 Jan 1568).

278. *Marlin* of Newcastle (56) John Digton; Bordeaux
[f. 66A*b*] Henry Sakford: 7 tuns Gascony wine *net* 6 tuns 18*s* (5 Jan 1568).
Thomas Searle: 6 tuns Gascony wine *net* 4½ tuns 16*s* 6*d*, 1 tun vinegar
£2 6*s* 8*d* (7 Jan). Richard Culverwell: 10 tuns Gascony wine *net* 9 tuns 27*s*,
2 tons resin, 1 tun vinegar £12 6*s* 8*d* (8 Jan). Edward Hoy: 4 tuns Gascony
wine *net* 3 tuns 9*s*, 2 hhds vinegar £1 3*s* 4*d* (9 Jan). [f. 71] Thomas Robles:
14 pcs resin £6 13*s* 4*d* (12 Jan).

279. *Robert* of Aldeburgh (52) William Hugins; Bordeaux
[f. 66A*b*] Henry Sakford: 8 tons Gascony wine *net* 7 tuns 21*s* (5 Jan 1568).
Thomas Searle: 20 tuns Gascony wine *net* 18 tuns 54*s*, 2 tuns vinegar
£4 6*s* 8*d*. George Lucas: 6 tuns Gascony wine *net* 4 tuns 12*s*, 1 tun vinegar
£2 6*s* 8*d* (8 Jan). [f. 70*b*] Thomas Searle: 3 tuns Gascony wine *net* 3 tuns
9*s* (12 Jan).

280. *Grace of God* of Lee (70) Robert Smith; Bordeaux
[f. 67] George Bond: 24 tuns Gascony wine *net* 21½ tuns 64*s* 6*d*, 35 cwt
prunes £17 10*s* (5 Jan 1568). [f. 67] William Bond: 26 tuns Gascony wine
net 23½ tuns 70*s* 6*d*, 35 cwt prunes £17 10*s*.

281. *Nicolas* of Lee (50) Stephen Rede; Bordeaux
[f. 67*b*] Anthony Grigory and John Holansyd: 16 tuns Gascony wine *net* 14½ tuns 40*s* 6*d* (5 Jan 1568). Christopher Edwards: 10 tuns Gascony wine *net* 9 tuns 27*s*. Edward Batham: 10 tuns Gascony wine *net* 9 tuns 27*s*. [f. 69] John Langley: 3 tuns Gascony wine *net* 2 tuns 6*s* (8 Jan).

282. *Robert* of Ipswich (120) Richard Apleton; Malaga
[f. 67*b*] Richard Apleton 'cum sociis': 40 pcs raisins £10 (7 Jan 1568). Thomas Altham: 250 pcs Malaga raisins £62 10*s*. William Griffin: 200 pcs raisins £50. John Gyll: 4 doz. Spanish skins £12. William Allen: 650 ells Levant taffeta, 60 lbs sewing silk £114 3*s* 4*d*. Augustin Parker: 125 pcs raisins £31 5*s* (8 Jan). William Gryffen: 40 pcs raisins £10. Reynold Barker: 125 pcs raisins £31 5*s*. Robert Cutler: 2 tuns sack *net* 2 tuns 6*s*, 25 pcs raisins £6 5*s*. William Vaghan: 75 pcs raisins £18 15*s* (9 Jan). Alexander Scofilde: 15 butts sack *net* 14 butts 21*s* 6*d*. Gregory Yong: 4 cwt raisins of the sun £3 6*s* 8*d*. Thomas Boldnes: 10 cwt raisins of the sun £8 6*s* 8*d*. John Watson: 19 cwt raisins of the sun £15 6*s* 8*d*. Anthony Throgmorton: 80 pcs raisins £20 (10 Jan). Matthew Chambres: 100 pcs raisins £25. [f. 70*b*] John Gile: 30 lbs sewing silk, 12 pairs silk hose £46.

283. *William* of Burnham (10) Barnaby Nicolls; Flushing
[f. 67*b*] Barnaby Nicolls: 24 brls onions £1 13*s* 4*d* (7 Jan 1568).

284. *Burning Oven* of Danzig (80) Stephen Johnson; Bordeaux
[f. 68] Edward van Crog: 50 tuns Gascony wine *net* 45 tuns 135*s* (8 Jan 1568). [f. 73*b*] Stephen Johnson: 8 tuns Gascony wine *net* 6 tuns 18*s* (16 Jan).

285. *George* of Dordrecht (40) Cornilis Michell; Rouen
[f. 68*b*] John Marshall: 1500 ells canvas £37 10*s* (8 Jan 1568). Robert Sadler: 1000 ells canvas £25. Richard Morris: 1400 ells canvas £35. Richard Hills: 900 ells canvas £22 10*s*. John Millner: 1200 ells canvas £30. John Allot: 1400 ells canvas £35 (9 Jan). Henry Buckston: 50 ells canvas, 22 doz. napkins £5 13*s* 4*d*. John Marshall: 1600 ells canvas £40. William Bond: 1600 ells canvas £40. William Handford: 105 cwt prunes £52 10*s*. Richard Patrik: 20 grs woollen-lace for hats, 20 doz. woolcards, 12 grs playing cards, 10 grs combs £27 18*s* 4*d*. Thomas Starkey: 2000 ells canvas £50. John Olif: 700 ells canvas £17 10*s* (10 Jan). Anthony Gamage: 2400 ells canvas £60. William Dudsbury: 1000 ells canvas £25. [f. 70*b*] Hugh Offley: 30 cwt brazil £50.

286. *Anne Sackford* of London (55) John Renold of Ipswich; Spain
[f. 69] Henry Sackford: 150 pcs raisins £37 10*s* (8 Jan 1568). John Denavant: 500 pcs raisins £125. John Hawse: 350 pcs raisins, 11 doz. Spanish skins £114 5*s* (9 Jan). [f. 71] Godfrey Willson: 6 doz. Spanish skins £18 (12 Jan).

287. *Golden Lion* of Leith (50) John Colburne; Bordeaux
[f. 69] John Colburne: 48 tuns Gascony wine *net* 40 tuns 120*s* (8 Jan 1568).

288. *Bonadventure* of La Rochelle (80) Helin Chambrewse; Bordeaux
[f. 69] Count Arundel and Lord Lumley: 65 tuns Gascony wine *net* 38¾
tuns 114s 9d (8 Jan 1568).

289. *Mary Edward* of London (70) Edward Master; Andalusia
[f. 70] Richard Whitlok: 19 butts sack *net* 14 butts 21s (9 Jan 1568). John
Bird: 10 tuns sack *net* 8 tuns 24s. John Barnes: 10 tuns sack *net* 8 tuns 24s.
Thomas Blanck: 20 butts sack *net* 16 butts 24s. [f. 70b] William Shrew-
craste: 6 hhds olives £16 (10 Jan).

290. *Maudlen* of London (50) Andrew Markes; Rouen
[f. 70b] Hugh Offley: 25 doz. woolcards, 25 cwt prunes, 50 cwt brazil
£108 16s 8d (12 Jan 1568). Humphrey Broune: 24 doz. woolcards, 4 grs
inkhorns, 12 sum rose nails at 3s 4d the sum £16. Richard Morris: 2400 ells
canvas £60. John Raines: 1100 ells canvas £27 10s. William Chapman:
6 doz. horse combs, 6 doz. chafing dishes £2 18s 4d (13 Jan). William
Hanford: 240 reams paper £32. John Mylner: 900 ells canvas £22 10s.
Richard Patrick: 20 doz. woolcards, 10 doz. lbs thread, 6 grs inkhorns
£26 6s 8d. Robert Sadler: 1800 ells canvas, 100 reams paper £58 6s 8d. John
Olif: 2800 ells canvas £70. Reynold Barker: 800 ells canvas £20 (14 Jan).
Anthony Cage: 3000 ells canvas £75. Thomas Awder: 100 reams paper
£13 6s 8d (15 Jan). John Clint: 830 ells canvas £20 15s (16 Jan). [f. 74b]
Reynold Barker: 300 ells canvas[1] £8 15s (17 Jan).

    1. Noted as 'entered short'.

291. *Prymrose* of Harwich (100) Thomas Grey; Barbary
[f. 71] Edward Jackman: 186 quintals sugar and broken sugar, 1 qr 19 hhds
4 puncheons panele £669 10s (12 Jan 1568). Bernard Filde: 38 cwt sugar,
13 cwt almonds, 220 lbs succade, 50 lbs marmalade £163 10s. Gerard Gore:
103 quintals sugar, 12 lbs capers £355 6s 8d (13 Jan). William Wydnall:
60 cwt sugar £200. William Crompton: 4 cwt sugar £13 6s 8d. John Mun
and Thomas Cordell: 61 quintals sugar, 4 hhds panele £211 6s 8d. Sir
William Garret: 4 hhds 1 brl panele, 66 quintals sugar £240 16s 8d. Gerard
Gore: 21 hhds panele £42 (14 Jan). [f. 73] Thomas Grey: 2 tuns panele
£20 (15 Jan).

292. *Lion* of 'Gosborough'[1] (16) Henry Clerk; Biscay
[f. 71] William Hawkins: 6 tons resin £30 (12 Jan 1568).

    1. ? Gosport.

293. *Boptayle* of Wivenhoe (12) Edward Mark; Flushing
[f. 73] James Peye: 60 brls onions £4 (15 Jan 1568).

294. *Saker* of Lee (30) Richard Harrys; Antwerp
[f. 73] William Allen: 18 cwt estrige wool £15 (15 Jan 1568). James Harvie:
20 'funi plates', 6½ cwt black latten, 3 brass bottoms, 9 red copper bottoms
£12. John Pasfyld: 14 pair andirons with latten knops, 4 doz. pair iron
tongs and fireshovels, 24 pair iron creepers, 9 cwt iron wire, 4 pair latten

pipes for andirons £27. Roger Warfild: 12 cwt aniseed £20. George Colmer: 15 doz. lbs bottom pack thread £3. Francis Warren: 72 yds frizado £18. William Ludington: 1½ cwt candy sugar £5 (16 Jan). Robert Bladwell: 180 lbs ginger £13 10s. Richard Goderd and Robert Smith: 38 cwt madder £25 6s 8d (17 Jan). Thomas Starkey: 1200 ells 'clincent' canvas £16. Thomas Randall: 20 lbs satin silk £20 (19 Jan). Thomas Eaton: 18 pcs narrow worsted £9 (20 Jan). [f. 79b] Robert Broke: 30 cwt mull-madder £3 15s.

295. *Spledegle* of Amsterdam (30) Garet Jacobson; Amsterdam
[f. 73] Daniel van Eytson: 8 cwt estrige wool £6 13s 4d (15 Jan 1568).
[f. 78] Jerome Rice: 45 cwt estrige wool £37 (20 Jan).

296. *Primrose* of Lee (60) Robert Salmon; Antwerp
[f. 73b] Robert Broke: 64 cwt madder £42 13s 4d (16 Jan 1568). Edmund Burton: 13 cwt iron wire, 6 doz. hanging locks, 2 grs joiner's tools, 1 grs horse bells, 1¼ cwt iron wire, 1 half-brl head nails, 11 cwt frying pans £43. Richard Holiman: 11 cwt madder £7 6s 8d. John Lambert: 18 cwt battery £36. Nicholas Hewet: 12 pcs Holland cloth, 30 ells linsey-wolsey £15 1s 8d. Thomas Hale: 3½ cwt sugar candy, 140 lbs marmalade, 2 cwt white lead, drugs ad valorem 40s £21 6s 8d. Roger Warfilde: 6 cwt starch, 1 brl treacle, 2 brls litmus, 4 brls ochre, 2 hd lbs gum, 400 lbs matches £30 6s 8d. Thomas Heton: 120 yds velvet £90. Anthony Warfilde: 200 lbs nutmegs, 7 cwt saltpetre £45. William Coles: 12 cwt hops, 400 lbs cotton wool £19 6s 8d (17 Jan). Joan Bower: 35 doz. lbs bottom thread £7. Richard Goderd and Robert Smith: 36 cwt madder £24. Edward Bright: 32 cwt iron pans, 15 pair andirons, 15 pair tongs, 15 fireshovels, 30 pair coarse creepers, 12 pair tongs and shovels £30 13s 4d. Humphrey Fairfax: 24 cwt hops, 175 lbs cotton wool £17 16s 8d. Thomas Aldersay: 40 pcs grogram camlet, 26 yds velvet £72 3s 4d. Thomas Eaton: 1½ grs pinpillows, 2 doz. lbs wrought inkle, 8 doz. lbs Bruges thread, 2 thou. awl blades, 24 doz. lbs crewel, 16 doz. crewel pieces, 12 doz. lbs bottom thread, ½ cwt coarse pack thread £39 18s 4d. Robert Skarbrough: 6 close stools with pans, 6 close stools without pans, 5 doz. lbs bottom thread, 1 qr pack thread £3 13s 4d. John Colmer: 64 lbs nutmegs £10 13s 4d. Francis Warrin: 72 yds frizado £18 (19 Jan). Arthur Hall: 1 half-brl head nails £2. John Gardner: 49 cwt madder, 150 lbs ginger, 1 cwt onion seed, ½ cwt verdigris £46 15s. Thomas Gardner: 27 cwt madder £18. William Cokin: 24 cwt madder, 4 raw wolverine skins £18. Richard Hills: 14½ cwt onion seed £24 3s 4d. Gerson Hills: 12¼ cwt onion seed £20 8s 4d. Robert Exton: 30 Turnhout ticks, 30 lbs candy £11. William Towerson: 16 ells silk tapestry, 90 ells wool tapestry, 69 Turnhout ticks £30 3s 4d. Jacob Car: 10 cwt latten wire £20. James Canon: 9 doz. lbs thread, 1 grs Cologne thread, 2 thou. pack needles, 2 thou. balls, 1 grs small looking glasses £11. John Sutton: 60 Turnhout ticks £20. William Goodwin: 31 double pcs grogram camlet £82 13s 4d. Thomas Rose: 72 yds frizado £18. Ancelm Becket: 32 cwt soap, 11 cwt flax £35 10s. Henry Billingsley: 8 doz. lbs bottom thread, 1 hd lbs unwrought inkle £4 18s 4d. John Taylor: 120 doz. thou. pins £20. Thomas Starkey: 3000 ells 'clincent' canvas £45. Robert

Daunser: 5 cwt flax, 30 lbs 'poll' silk £35 (20 Jan). Robert Morris: 200 lbs pepper, 50 lbs nuts £25. John Eliots: 20 doz. thou. pins, 8 doz. lbs crewel, 16 doz. lbs wrought inkle, 3 grs small looking glasses £20 3s 4d. William Sherington: 60 half-pcs Genoa fustian £20. Julian Bemish: 620 lbs pepper £51 13s 4d. Thomas Gryme: 20 pcs Holland cloth, 150 grs Milan buttons £30 5s. Joan Bower: 40 pairs fireshovels and tongs £2 10s. Edmund Smith: 20 pcs narrow worsted, 20 pcs striped canvas £16 13s 4d. Robert Turvill: 20 lbs 'poll' silk £20. John Fitzwilliams: 30 cwt mull-madder £3 15s. Thomas Randall: 520 yds Levant taffeta £43 6s 8d. William Perry: drugs ad valorem £12 (21 Jan). [f. 80b] Thomas Walker: 700 lbs pepper £58 6s 8d.

297. *Egle*[1] of Antwerp (40) Anthony Cornilis; Antwerp
[f. 74] Anthony Warfilde: 4 cwt hops £2 (16 Jan 1568). Thomas Heton: 60 ells sarcenet, 60 yds damask £34. Richard Howle: 7 cwt argol £8 6s 8d (17 Jan). Robert Exton: 3 nests chests, 500 ells hair tapestry £18 13s 4d. John Car: 5 doz. piercers, 10 doz. locks, 8 doz. small gridirons and pottingers ad valorem 60s £3 13s 4d (19 Jan). Robert Taylor: 65 yds velvet £48 15s (20 Jan). Edward Hardingworth: 6 half-brls steel £36 (22 Jan). [f. 81b] Reynold Thirling: 24 cwt madder £16.

    1. Also the *Spledegle.*

298. *Ellen* of London (80) William Spender; Antwerp
[f. 74] Anthony Warfilde: 4 cwt hops £2 (16 Jan 1568). Thomas Bresie: 46 pcs mockado £30 13s 4d. Edmund Burton: 5 cwt frying pans, 27 doz. coarse sword blades £21 6s 8d (17 Jan). George Stockmed: 5 cwt flax £5. Thomas Aldersey: 420 ells sarcenet £70. Richard Holiman: 12 cwt estrige wool, 16 cwt madder £20 13s 4d. Thomas Heton: 80 yds velvet £60. John Pasfilde: 3 pair latten andirons, 1 cwt latten pipes £7 (19 Jan). William Coles: 30 lbs onion seed, 93 lbs nuts £65 10s. Thomas Gardner: 27 cwt madder, 3½ cwt saltpetre £22 16s 8d. Richard Bowdler: 6 cwt woad £4. William Towerson: 7 cwt feathers £10 10s. Henry Becher: 120 doz. thou. pins £20. James Canon: 6 doz. lbs bottom thread, 10 grs combs, 6 reams paper, 3 thou. balls, 12 doz. thou. pins, 2 cwt iron thread £12 16s 8d. Robert Tailor: 8 cwt hops £4. John Car: 20 cwt latten wire, 22 cwt iron wire £76 13s 4d. Thomas Davy: 11½ cwt iron wire £19 3s 4d. Robert Hungat: 10 lbs fringe £10. Henry Becher: 140 doz. thou. pins £23 6s 8d. William Luddington: 100 lbs cotton wool, 5 cwt white and red lead, 1½ cwt orpiment, 4 cwt red argol, 35 lbs sugar candy, drugs ad valorem 80s £17 15s. John Eliots: 14 doz. lbs crewel, 12 doz. lbs thread riband, 2 doz. crewel pieces, 6 doz. lbs Bruges thread, 4 doz. pcs Rennes boultel £33 18s 4d (20 Jan). Sir John York: 10,000 lbs pepper £83 6s 8d. William Sherington: 40 lbs ferret silk £16 13s 4d. Wolston Dixi: 1 double-roll Osnabrücks £33 6s 8d.[1] Christopher Jewkes: 24 cwt woad £16. Thomas Barker: 18 cwt battery £36. Thomas Longston: 6 cwt dates, 70 lbs cloves £29. George Breme: 9 cwt battery £18. John Lambert: 13 cwt iron pans £8 13s 4d. Roger Warfyld: 2 hhds olives, 100 lbs bay oil, 4 cwt saltpetre £12 13s 4d. John Alden: 589 lbs ginger, 400 lbs bay oil £49 10s. Thomas Eaton: 20 doz. crewel pieces, 2 doz. lbs wrought inkle, 5 doz. lbs Bruges thread, 10 doz. lbs bottom pack thread, 1 cwt coarse pack thread, 60 lbs

counters, 2 thou. thimbles £21 5s 8d. John Boorne: 2 half-pcs tripe de velours, 2 doz. lbs wrought inkle, 8 doz. lbs Bruges thread, 5 thou. thimbles, 1½ doz. lbs clavichord wire, 16 grs coarse morris bells, 5 thou. awl blades, 1½ doz. lbs crewel, 3 grs thread points, 16 doz. thou. pins, 6 doz. lbs pack thread, 18 grs coarse hat bands £32 18s. Richard Godderd and Robert Smith: 38 cwt madder £25 6s 8d (21 Jan). Richard Nott: drugs ad valorem £10. Robert Langham: 8 pcs Holland cloth, 14 pcs striped sackcloth £44 11s 8d. Richard Billam: 32 cwt madder £21 6s 8d. Nicholas Garnows: 48 cwt madder £32. John Langton: 15 pcs buckram £3 6s 8d. Julian Beymish: 40 cwt madder £26 13s 4d. Richard Cotton: 150 yds taffeta £50. Henry Billingsley: 200 butts Paris thread £20 (22 Jan). William Gifford: 32 pcs Milan fustian £32. [f. 81b] Anthony Scoloker: 5 grs wooden writing pens, 4½ doz. thou. needles, 2 grs lute strings £6.

> 1. The Book of Rates does not list double-rolls. From the valuation it does no seem that they were double the volume of a single-roll.

299. *Samson* of Bruges (60) Marten Frise; Bruges
[f. 74] Thomas Brasie: 168 pcs buckram £37 6s 8d (16 Jan 1568). Thomas Sound: 700 ells brown 50 ells white Hazebroucks, 13 pcs 'russels', 150 ells white Hazebroucks, 20 cwt madder £47 18s 4d (17 Jan). John Nicholson: 180 doz. hemp, 1150 clapholt £26 8s 4d (20 Jan). [f. 78b] Thomas House: 225 ells brown 175 ells white Hazebroucks, 10 pcs brown Holland cloth, 300 ells Hazebroucks £30.

300. *Unicorn* of St. Omer (23) Gilliam Mersye; St. Omer
[f. 74] John Atkinson: 2000 bunches onions, 120 bushels apples £10 6s 8d (16 Jan 1568).

301. *Grene Cloverblade* of Amsterdam (28) Garet Isbrant
[f. 75] Edward van Krog: 4 half-packs flax £16 (17 Jan 1568).

302. *Falcon* of Amsterdam (28) Allerd Allardson
[f. 75] Edward van Krog: 3 half-packs flax £12 (17 Jan 1568).

303. *Fortune* of Amsterdam (36) Cornilis Cornilison
[f. 75b] Edward van Krog: 3 half-packs flax £12 (17 Jan 1568).

304. *Asse* of Antwerp (40) John Joyce; Antwerp
[f. 75b] Garret Dews: 20 reams unbound books £2 (17 Jan 1568).

305. *Spledegle* of Antwerp (40) Barnard Peters; Antwerp
[f. 75b] Robert Broke: 32 cwt madder £21 (17 Jan 1568). Edward Harding-worth: 6 half-brls steel £36 (22 Jan). [f. 81] John Whit: 6 citherns, 6 gitterns, 4 small lutes, 6 lutes in cases £6.

306. *Mary* of Amsterdam (30) Nicholas Simonson; Amsterdam
[f. 76b] Hartik van Sprecleson: 660 ells soultwich £12 (19 Jan 1568).

307. *George* of Antwerp (70) Matthew Broune; Antwerp
[f. 77] Robert Exton: 8½ cwt unwrought flax £8 10s (19 Jan 1568).

308. *Fortune* Allbright [*sic*][1]
[f. 78] John Nicholson: 90 pcs buckram, 10 pcs Holland cloth £32 (20 Jan 1568). Francis Wight: 1000 ells Hazebroucks £25. [f. 80*b*] Thomas Planckney: 120 lbs silk cards £30 (21 Jan).

> 1. Perhaps Cornilis Albright's *Fortune* of Bruges, **303**.

309. *Sea Hors* of Amsterdam (30) Peter Post; Amsterdam
[f. 78*b*] Jerome Rice: 7 cwt estrige wool £5 16*s* 8*d* (20 Jan 1568).

310. *Falcon* of Bergen-op-Zoom Adrian Williamson; Bergen-op-Zoom
[f. 78*b*] Robert Skarborough: 7 cwt dressed flax £7 (20 Jan 1568). Ancelm Becket: 11½ cwt wrought flax £11 10*s*. Christopher Jewkes: 39 cwt hops, 15 cwt tow £23 5*s* (21 Jan). William Hewet: 13 brls rape oil £17 6*s* 8*d*. Christopher Jewkes: 10 cwt flax £10 (22 Jan). [f. 81*b*] Henry Bornes: 100 clapholt 5*s* (23 Jan).

311. *George* of Flushing Andrew Paules; Flushing
[f. 78*b*] Richard Nash: 45 cwt hops £22 10*s* (20 Jan 1568).

312. *George* of Antwerp (50) Jacob de Cooper; Antwerp
[f. 79] Thomas Barker: 9 cwt battery £18 (20 Jan 1568). Richard Billam: 250 doz. straw hats £8 6*s* 8*d* (21 Jan). [f. 81*b*] Reynold Thirling: 16 cwt madder £10 13*s* 4*d* (22 Jan).

313. *Swan* of Flushing (28) Peter Paull Slyne; Flushing
[f. 80] Michael Lion: 11 doz. lbs thread £7 6*s* 8*d* (21 Jan 1568). Martin Johnson: 3 pcs Holland cloth £3 11*s* 8*d*. Henry Alward: 40 pcs striped canvas with thread £13 6*s* 8*d*.

314. *Spledegle* of Antwerp (26) Giles Dornehoven; Antwerp
[f. 80] George Sowthac: 12 cwt figs £8 (21 Jan 1568).

315. *Sebastian* of Middleburg (12) Harman Milner; Middleburg
[f. 80] Thomas Kelley: 60 brls onions £4 (21 Jan 1568).

316. *Meareman* of Amsterdam (30) Peter Garetson; Amsterdam
[f. 80] Henry Bucston: 30 cwt undressed hemp £30 (21 Jan 1568).

317. *Crab* of Haarlem (30) Cornilis Adrianson; Amsterdam
[f. 80*b*] John Lence: 750 ells Osnabrücks £10 (21 Jan 1568).

318. *George* of Amsterdam (15) William Peterson; Amsterdam
[f. 80*b*] Richard Graunge: 500 small bundles white rods £8 6*s* 8*d* (21 Jan 1568).

319. *Owell* of Dordrecht (30) Jacob Florison; Dordrecht
[f. 80*b*] John Middleton: 150 bundles white rods £2 10*s* (21 Jan 1568).

320. *Sparrow Hawk* of Antwerp Matthew Brounge
[f. 80*b*] John Smyth: 4 chests Burgundy glass £8 (21 Jan 1568). Edmund
Brassy: 44 pcs narrow worsted £22. Thomas Davy: 6 cwt wrought flax £6
(22 Jan). [f. 81] Edward Hardingworth: 6 half-brls steel £36.

321. *Mary* of Amsterdam (28) Clais Simonson; Amsterdam
[f. 81] Thomas Sandford: 660 lings £24 (22 Jan 1568).

322. *Dolphin* of Dordrecht Sebrant Cornelis
[f. 81] Melchior van Aldenack: 6 awms Rhenish wine 6*s* (22 Jan 1568).
[f. 81*b*] Cornelis Nollet: 24 awms Rhenish wine 24*s*.

323. *Cloverblade* of Haarlem John Neveson
[f. 81*b*] Adam Cooper: 5 pcs Holland cloth £6 (23 Jan 1568).

324. *Angell* of Dordrecht (50) Tylman Cornilis; Dordrecht
[f. 81*b*] Reynold Thirling: 136 awms Rhenish wine 136*s*, 24 cwt hemp
£24 (30 Jan 1568). [f. 82] John Picknet: 12 cwt hops £6.

325. *Spledegle* of Dordrecht (50) Godfrey Dirickson; Dordrecht
[f. 82] Gawen van Alden: 138 awms Rhenish wine 138*s* (30 Jan 1568).

326. *William* of Maldon (40) John Gunby; Dordrecht
[f. 82] William Brouning: 10 awms Rhenish wine 10*s* (3 Feb 1568).

327. *Falcon* of Dordrecht (30) Adrian Francis; Dordrecht
[f. 82] Reynold Thirling: 120 awms Rhenish wine 120*s*, 24 cwt Cologne
hemp £24 (3 Feb 1568).

328. *Robert* of Saltash (24) John Brendjam; The Groyne
[f. 82] Randolph Joris: 24 thou. oranges £8 (3 Feb 1568).

329. *Mary Anne* of Brightlingsea (30) John Chandler; Bordeaux
[f. 82] Anthony Ratclif: 20 tuns Gascony wine *net* 18 tuns 54*s*, 3 tuns
vinegar £7 (3 Feb 1568).

330. *Mary Martin* of London John Ewstas; Barbary
[f. 82*b*] Gerard and Thomas Gore: '68 whole chests and half chests 15 tons
panele in 60 hhds all the sugar 105 quintals' £500 (4 Feb 1568). Anthony
Pillborrow: 5½ cwt sugar £18 6*s* 8*d*. Margaret Chambrelaine: 19 cwt
sugar £63 6*s* 8*d*. John Mun and Thomas Cordell: 35 cwt sugar, 12 hhds
2 butts 2 puncheons panele £163 6*s* 8*d*. Edward Jackman and Francis
Bowyer: 132½ cwt sugar, 42 hhds 5 puncheons panele £561 13*s* 4*d*. William
Widnall: 66 cwt sugar, 4 hhds panele £230. Henry Callys: 32 cwt sugar,
60 cwt panele £136 13*s* 4*d*. Sir William Gerrard: 65 cwt sugar, 1 tun
panele £216 13*s* 4*d* (5 Feb). John Watson: 9½ cwt sugar £31 13*s* 4*d*. Henry
Wallis: 2½ cwt sugar £8 6*s* 8*d*. Robert Fryer: 7½ cwt sugar £25. John
Eustas: 7 cwt sugar £23 6*s* 8*d*. John Freman: 3 cwt sugar £10. Thomas

Harvey: 5 cwt sugar £16 13s 4d. John Mun: 12 cwt sugar, 24 cwt panele £52. [f. 83b] Sir William Garrerd: 178 cwt panele £89 (6 Feb).

331. *Lyon* of London (80) Richard Bepell; La Rochelle
[f. 82b] John Broke 'cum sociis de Russia': 70 weys great salt £70 (4 Feb 1568).

332. *Thomas Allen* of London (140) Thomas Wade; La Rochelle
[f. 82b] Thomas Allen: 90 weys great salt £90 (4 Feb 1568). Richard Dane: 720 yds poldavis £24 (5 Feb). Robert Fryer: 11 tuns train oil £55. [f. 86] John Hill: 1½ tuns Rochelle wine [*sic*] (10 Feb).

333. *Bilkin* of Antwerp (6) Peter van Ward; Antwerp
[f. 83] Elizabeth Williams: 8 cwt hops £4 (4 Feb 1568).

334. *Spledegle* of Gouda (30) Lucas Williamson; Rouen
[f. 83b] Augustin Parker: 10 cwt prunes, 450 ells canvas £16 5s (9 Feb 1568). Robert Broke: 1300 ells canvas £32 10s. John Harding: 2000 ells canvas £50. Richard Morris: 1100 ells canvas £27 10s. Richard Hill: 900 ells canvas £22 10s. John Raines: 126 yds dornick, 60 doz. coarse earthenware bottles £14 11s 8d. Anthony Gamage: 2200 ells canvas £55. Humphrey Broune: 25 doz. woolcards, 1 grs crewel chain-lace, 1 grs inkhorns, 50 reams paper £20 6s 8d. Robert Sadler: 1200 ells canvas £16 (10 Feb). Richard Billam: 1300 ells canvas £32 10s. John Olif: 1800 ells canvas £45. William Handford: 18 grs playing cards, 100 lbs spun cotton, 20 lbs wrought crewel lace £24 6s 8d. John Marshall: 16 grs playing cards £16 (11 Feb). William Chapman: 25 sum small nails £4. Thomas Starkey: 1500 ells canvas, 8 hd 'lbs' canvas £57. Robert Barker: 32 cwt prunes, 900 ells canvas, 24 doz. woolcards £50 10s. Robert Barker: 4 doz. Rouen buckrams £6. John Broke 'cum sociis': 200 reams paper £26 13s 4d (12 Feb). Thomas Bolnuse: 1200 ells packing canvas £16. Wolston Dixi: 2000 ells packing canvas £26 13s 4d. [f. 91] Anthony Cage: 500 ells canvas £12 10s (13 Feb).

335. *Mary George* of London (50) Robert Osburn; Antwerp
[f. 83b] Christopher Jewkes: 6 cwt estrige wool £9 (9 Feb 1568). Robert Broke: 96 cwt madder £64. John Alden and Edmund Pigot: 16½ cwt onion seed £27 10s. Anthony Warfilde: 3 cwt candy, 75 lbs marmalade, 2 brls linseed oil £15 3s 4d. John Collmer: 19 cwt soap, 400 topnets figs, 100 pcs figs, 300 lbs crossbow thread £51 11s 8d. John Boorne: 6 doz. crewel pieces, 50 doz. lbs wrought inkle, 500 thimbles, 4 doz. thou. needles, ½ grs steel looking glasses, 20 doz. lbs bottom thread £16 3s 4d. William Coles: 12 cwt hops, 100 lbs cotton wool £9 6s 8d. Thomas Heton: 120 yds velvet £90. William Handford: 14 cwt hops, 1¼ cwt estrige wool £8. John Fitzwilliams: 22 cwt soap £16 10s. William Smith: 25 pcs watered camlet £25. Thomas Gardner: 2 lasts rape oil £32. Nicholas Spiring: 9¼ cwt sumach, 1 grs knives, 1 grs halfpennyware looking glasses £8 3s 4d (10 Feb). Henry Billingsley: 3 cwt iron thread £5. William Ludington: 10 cwt rice, 3½ cwt almonds, 160 lbs marmalade £20 13s 4d. Robert Hungat: 8 lbs silk fringe, 10 lbs Bruges silk £16 6s 8d. John Eliots: 16 doz.

lbs crewel, 12 doz. lbs wrought inkle, 1½ doz. lbs thread riband, 3 doz. lbs pack thread £22 8s 4d. Thomas Rose: 72 yds frizado £18. William Hewet: 6 cwt wrought flax £6. William Towerson: 250 ells wool tapestry, 245 ells hair tapestry, 8 doz. coarse cushion cloths, 1 doz. Ghentish carpets £31 15s (11 Feb). Richard Byllam: 20 cwt Castile soap £15. Thomas Barker: 12 cwt battery £24. Edmund Smith: 70 half-pcs Genoa fustian £23 6s 8d. John Lambert: 20 cwt iron pans £13 6s 8d (12 Feb). Thomas Brasie: 36 yds frizado, 55 yds dornick thread £19. William Gyfford: 40 cwt madder £26 13s 4d. [f. 90b] George Southack: 450 lbs pepper £37 10s.

336. *Jesus* of Newcastle (80) Robert Nessby; Bordeaux
[f. 83b] John White: 50 tuns Gascony wine *net* 44 tuns 132s (9 Feb 1568). [f. 95] Robert Nesby: 2 hhds wine 1s 6d (24 Feb).

337. *Bear* of Amsterdam (30) Adrian Francis; Rouen
[f. 84] Edmund Anselm: 8 cases Normandy glass £8 (9 Feb 1568). Robert Sadler: 140 reams paper, 60 reams loose cap-paper £26 13s 4d (10 Feb). [f. 85b] Thomas Walker: 50 cases Normandy glass £50.

338. *Crown of Thorn* of Antwerp (30) John Johnson; Antwerp
[f. 84] William Handford: 8 cwt hops, 1¾ cwt estrige wool £5 10s (9 Feb 1568).

339. *Jesus* of London (70) John Clerk; Antwerp
[f. 84b] John Alden and Edmund Pigot: 3 qrs treacle £1 10s (10 Feb 1568). William Ludington: 30 cwt madder £20. John Eliots: 36 doz. thou. pins, 3 doz. lbs thread riband, 4 grs morris bells £8 10s. John Jackman: 185 lbs nutmegs £30 16s 8d. William Coles: 182 lbs nutmegs £30 6s 8d. Wolston Dixi: 3000 ells minsters £33 6s 8d (11 Feb). Robert Bladwell: 6 cwt woad £4. Humphrey Fairfax: 400 lbs pepper £33 6s 8d. John Car: 1 half-brl small nails, 9 cwt latten wire £22. Thomas Hale: 400 lbs bay oil, 4 half-brls crossbow thread, 1 hd lbs treacle £13. Lawrence Wythers: 16 cwt madder £10 13s 4d. William Bower: 11½ hd rings £23. George Stockmed: 24 cwt madder £15 6s 8d. Francis Bowyer: 25 cwt Castile soap £18 15s. Roger Knott: 16 cwt battery £32. John Daniell: 1 last rape oil £17 6s 8d. William Hobs: 429 ells hair tapestry, 14 cradle rugs, 11 white rugs, 110 pcs lince, 2 lasts rape oil, 7 beds, 13 blankets, 11 cradle cloths £44 18s 4d. John Lambert: 8¾ cwt battery, 58½ cwt Castile soap £61 15s. William Hewet: 245 half-pcs Genoa fustian, 2 half-brls steel, 19 cwt estrige wool £109 16s 8d. Edmund Smith: 450 yds dornick thread £10 (12 Feb). Henry Billingsley: 50 doz. thou. pins, 20 grs harp strings, 10 doz. lbs bottom thread £11 13s 8d. Roger Warfilde: 200 lbs bay oil, 400 lbs pepper £36. Thomas Barker: 9 cwt battery £18. Robert Skarborow: 12 cwt madder £8. Robert Taylor: 32 cwt battery, 3½ cwt hops £23 1s 8d. Henry Beecher: 58 cwt madder £38 13s 4d. William Elkin: 84 yds frizado £21 (13 Feb). Thomas Langston: 300 lbs pepper £25. George Kightley: 10 pcs broad worsted, 4 pcs double mockado, 3 pcs watered camlet £15 13s 4d. Richard Pype: 117 pcs mockado £78. Thomas Gryme and

Robert Walkeden: 900 ells Normandy canvas, 13 pcs Holland cloth £29 1s 8d. Thomas Eaton: 6 grs coarse hat bands, 10 grs halfpennyware glasses, 6 grs horse bells, 24 doz. pincers, 120 lbs counters, 7 doz. lbs crewel, 10 doz. lbs bottom thread, 1 qr coarse pack thread, 9 cwt latten wire £38 8s 4d. John Isham: 30 pcs Naples fustian £45 (14 Feb). Henry Becher the younger: 3 cwt woad £2. Thomas Randall: 400 yds Levant taffeta £33 6s 8d. Anthony Scoloker: 48 grs minikins, boxes and pipes ad valorem 40s £26 (16 Feb). John Wanton: 195 lbs nutmegs, 65 lbs cinnamon £45 10s. John Pasfilde: 5 cwt iron thread, 6 cwt steel £12 6s 8d. Richard Godard and Robert Smith: 20 cwt madder £13 6s 8d. John Wells: 63 yds velvet, 60 yds satin £75 15s (17 Feb). Alexander Chisnall: 25 pcs broad worsted 'russels' £25 (20 Feb).[1] [f. 94b] Robert Hungat: 8 lbs silk fringe £8 (21 Feb).

1. Entered under *Mary Fortune*, master John Clerk [f. 94].

340. *Primrose* of Milton Henry Church; Antwerp

[f. 85] Ancelm Becket: 52 cwt madder £34 13s 4d (10 Feb 1568). William Ludington: 12 cwt aniseed, 225 lbs bay oil, 20 lbs green ginger, 18 lbs senna, 1½ cwt brimstone, 125 lbs cotton wool £25 6s 8d. John Eliots: 5 doz. lbs crewel, 10 doz. lbs thread riband, 16 doz. lbs Bruges thread, 8 grs morris bells, 3 grs small looking glasses £22 8s 4d. John Boorne: 2 doz. thou. needles, 20 grs coarse bells, 4 doz. lbs counters, 2 doz. lbs Bruges thread, 6 doz. lbs bottom thread, 3 grs glass buttons £11 16s 8d. William Coles: 7 cwt hops, 100 lbs cotton wool £6. Anthony Warfild: 11 cwt hops, 3½ cwt saltpetre, 200 lbs ginger £26 6s 8d. Wolston Dixi: 1600 ells Newcastle canvas £24 (11 Feb). Humphrey Fairefax: 225 lbs pepper, 100 lbs cinnamon, 4½ cwt hops, 1¼ cwt estrige wool £40. William Towerson: 630 ells hair tapestry, 2½ doz. Ghentish carpets £24 6s 8d. Nicholas Hewet: 2 tons iron, 2 half-brls head nails £14. John Spencer: 30 lbs mace, 6 cwt sugar, 75 lbs nutmegs £42 10s. Robert Taylor: 51 pcs watered camlet £51. John Car: 10 cwt latten wire £20. John Collmer: 5 cwt sugar, 64 lbs cloves, 64 lbs nutmegs, 20 lbs mace £50 5s. Edmund Burton: 2 cwt iron wire, 21 doz. chisels, 9 grs hanging locks, 5½ cwt loose black latten, 5 cwt dripping pans, 31 doz. sword blades £51 10s. Gerson Hills: 7 cwt hemp £7. Richard Byllam: 21 cwt madder £14. Thomas Starkey: 1500 ells minsters £16 13s 4d. Francis Bowyer: 25 cwt Castile soap £18 15s. Roger Knott: 16 cwt battery £32. Leonard Hollidaie: 10½ cwt Cologne hemp £10 10s. Edmund Smith: 16 pcs say, 2 bales Ulm fustian £46. Henry Becher: 26 doz. lbs piecing thread, 25½ doz. lbs Oudenaarde thread £51 13s 4d (12 Feb). Henry Smith: 200 doz. coarse hats, 30 doz. fine straw hats £7 18s 4d. William Hewet: 10 cwt unwrought flax, 2 half-brls head nails, 11 cwt madder £18. Roger Warfild: 400 lbs pepper £33 6s 8d. John White: 12 doz. lbs crewel, 72 yds frizado £28. John Sutton: 418 ells wool tapestry £20 18s 4d. Thomas Daunster: 20 doz. lbs thread, 4 doz. Beaupreau boultel, 10 doz. thou. pins £37 18s 4d. Abraham Smith: 117 yds taffeta £29. Thomas Barker: 18 cwt battery £36. Robert Scarborrow: 12 cwt madder £8. Robert Taylor: 48 cwt madder, 6 cwt hops £35. William Gifford: 72 yds frizado £18. Mark Gryme: 400 lbs silk nobs, 120 lbs short silk £43 6s 8d. William Elkin: 168 yds frizado £42 (13 Feb).

Thomas Eaton: 50 grs halfpennyware glasses, 40 doz. pcs say, 6 doz. lbs wrought inkle, 7 doz. thou. needles, 30 lbs clavichord wire, 2 doz. lbs purse wire, 2 grs wooden dials, 30 grs morris bells £51 6s 8d. John Isham: 40 cwt mull-madder, 60 yds velvet £50 (14 Feb). Thomas Randall: 160 lbs cochineal £26 13s 4d. Anthony Scoloker: boxes ad valorem £2 (16 Feb). William Pirry: 8 half-brls crossbow thread, 10 lbs senna, 2 half-brls treacle, drugs ad valorem 40s £11 8s 4d. Thomas Gardener: 3 cwt corn powder £5. John Colmer: 14 rolls coarse canvas £3 10s. William Gefford: 1 bale Milan fustian £16 (17 Feb). John Wells: 105 yds velvet £82 10s [f. 93b] Randal Collie: 2 cwt sugar £6 13s 4d (19 Feb).

341. *John Baptist* of London (70) William Hall; Antwerp
[f. 85] John Boorne: 30 doz. crewel pieces, 50 doz. thou. pins, 2 doz. lbs crewel, 10 doz. lbs bottom thread £27 (10 Feb 1568). John Alden and Edmund Pigot: 1625 lbs pepper £135 8s 4d. John Eliots: 10 doz. lbs crewel, 8 doz. lbs thread riband, 14 doz. crewel pieces £19 6s 8d. Thomas Chester: 1750 lbs pepper £144 6s 8d. Robert Stevens: 260 lbs pepper, 140 lbs ginger £32 16s 8d. James Harvie: 16 cwt battery £32. George Breme: 150 yds silk tapestry £25. Roger Warfild: 15 cwt aniseed, 200 bundles brown paper, 5 cwt hops, 100 lbs ginger £36 13s 4d (11 Feb). John Haidon: 50 pcs Genoa fustian £33 6s 8d. Wolston Dixi: 1200 ells Newcastle canvas, 1 double-roll Osnabrücks £51 6s 8d. Humphrey Fairefax: 3 cwt sugar candy £10. Nicholas Hewet: 1 half-brl great head nails, 12 cwt madder £20 13s 4d. Edward Bright: 3 half-brls small nails, 6 half-brl head nails, 8 cwt iron pans £29 6s 8d. John Colmer: 160 lbs ginger, 450 lbs pepper, 2 brls treacle £55 6s 8d. Robert Taylor: 72 yds frizado £18. William Bower: 5½ cwt flax £5 10s. Thomas Bower: 7 cwt iron pans, 8 cwt iron wire, 1 half-brl small nails £22. George Stockmed: 46 cwt madder £30 13s 4d. Edmund Smyth: 16 pcs say, 2 bales Ulm fustian £46. Henry Becher: 45 cwt woad £30 (12 Feb). Thomas Heton: 100 yds velvet £75. Henry Billingsley: 100 butts Paris thread £10. William Hewet: 15 cwt wrought flax £15. Sir John York: 5 cwt bay berries £3 6s 8d. John White: 72 yds frizado £18. William Coles: 30 cwt madder, 4 cwt liquorice £7 15s. John Lambert: 16 cwt iron pans £10 13s 4d. Henry Smith: 400 doz. coarse straw hats, 60 doz. fine straw hats £23 6s 8d. John Sutton: 400 ells wool tapestry, 280 ells hair tapestry £29 11s 8d. William Sherington: 45 lbs Bruges silk £45. Thomas Barker: 5 cwt battery £10. Robert Taylor: 32 cwt madder £21 6s 8d. Robert Hungat: 12 lbs silk fringe £12. Henry Beechar: 140 doz. thou. pins £23 6s 8d. Thomas Gardener: 2 lasts rape oil £32 (13 Feb). Richard Carill: 4 pcs Holland cloth £4 16s 8d. Thomas Longston: 5 cwt dates, 100 lbs cotton wool £13 6s 8d. Gerard Gore: 1 dyed cloth, 1 dyed 'kers'[1] £10. John Isham: 56 cwt mull-madder, 60 yds damask £31 (14 Feb). John Pasfilde: 8 cwt iron thread £13 6s 8d (16 Feb). William Pirry: 2½ cwt serpentine gunpowder, 250 lbs pepper, 2 cwt aniseed £26 10s. John Heydon: 142 yds velvet £106 10s. William Gefford: 60 lbs cochineal £10 (17 Feb). John Wells: 20 pcs narrow worsted, 70 pcs Genoa fustian £56 13s 4d. [f. 93b] Randal Collie: 4 cwt sugar, 10 lbs sugar candy £13 13s 5d (19 Feb).

1. ? kersey.

342. *Jonas* of Flushing Jacob Stephen
[f. 86] George Jenens: 4 lasts herring and fish, 3 brls salmon gills £28 10*s*
(10 Feb 1568).

343. *Fortune* of Flushing (22) Simon Johnson Yongenell; Flushing
[f. 87] Henry Violet: 2 lasts fish, 2½ lasts codsheads £17 (11 Feb 1568).
George Jenens: 4 lasts barrelled fish £24. [f. 92] Thomas Jenens: 1 last
fish £6 (14 Feb).

344. *Peter* of Flushing (15) Thomas Timeson; Flushing
[f. 87*b*] George Jenens: 2 lasts fish and herring £12 (11 Feb 1568). [f. 92]
Thomas Jenens: 6 brls herring £3 (14 Feb).

345. *Mychell* of Flushing (14) Peter Clayson; Flushing
[f. 88] Henry Violet: 480 lings, 2½ lasts codsheads, 10 brls fish £26 (11 Feb
1568).

346. *Spret* of Dieppe (10) John Plenes; Dieppe
[f. 88*b*] Richard Cokes: 100 doz. stone bottles £7 10*s* (11 Feb 1568).

347. *Jennet* of 'Purgant'¹ (46) Evan Carew; Nantes
[f. 89] William Bond: 46 tons prunes £230 (12 Feb 1568).
    1. Purquet near Quimper?

348. *Spledegle* of Antwerp (45) Joyes Daniell; Antwerp
[f. 89*b*] Nicholas Huet: 21 cwt woad £14 (12 Feb 1568). Thomas Barker:
9 cwt battery £18. Robert Skarbrough: 6 chamber stools with pans, 6
chamber stools without pans £2 15*s*. William Allen 'cum sociis': 16 cwt
estrige wool £13 6*s* 8*d* (13 Feb). Thomas Eaton: 120 doz. coarse 40 doz.
fine straw hats £10 13*s* 4*d*. Mary Peterson: 30 grs shirt strings £6. William
Hewet: 200 doz. coarse 10 doz. fine straw hats £8 6*s* 8*d*. [f. 92] Mark Gryme:
36 doz. 8 yds Cyprus cotton £6 2*s* 6*d* (14 Feb).

349. *Spledegle*¹ of Bruges (60) Francis Bowins; Bruges
[f. 90] Thomas Brasie: 153 pcs buckram £34 (12 Feb 1568). John Hall:
20 cwt madder £13 6*s* 8*d* (13 Feb). William Gelders: 150 doz. hemp
£18 15*s*. Thomas House: 24 pcs 'checker' bustian, 450 ells blue Hazebroucks £23 18*s* 4*d*. [f. 92] Matthew Colcloghe: 130 doz. hemp £16 5*s*
(14 Feb).
    1. Also the *Egle*.

350. *Falcon* of Flushing Peter Gaisire
[f. 90*b*] Henry Violet: 240 lings, 4 brls codsheads £8 13*s* 4*d* (12 Feb 1568).

351. *John* of Lee (14) Harry Freman; Flushing
[f. 92] James Pie: 40 brls onions, 20 brls walnuts £6 (14 Feb 1568).

352. *Mary Catherin*¹ (100) George Iyerland; Barbary
[f. 92*b*] Bernard Filde: 29 cwt sugar £96 13*s* 4*d* (16 Feb 1568). Sir William

Garret: 18 cwt sugar, 3½ tons panele £96 13s 4d. William Wydnall: 22 cwt sugar, 1 ton panele £83 6s 8d. Edward Jackman: 166 cwt sugar, 11 tons 1 hhd panele £665 16s 8d. Margaret Chambrelaine: 20 cwt sugar £66 13s 4d. Thomas Beynam: 40 cwt sugar £133 6s 8d (17 Feb). Gerard Gore: 105 cwt sugar, 30 hhds 50 cwt panele £450. Simon Laurance: 70 lbs sugar £2 6s 8d (19 Feb). George Iyerland: 5 cwt sugar £16 13s 4d. Henry Frost: 3 cwt sugar £10 (23 Feb). Robert Rout: 2 quintals sugar £6 13s 4d. Henry Walton: 90 lbs sugar £3 (26 Feb). [f. 95b] Henry Wallis and Thomas Turnebull: 1¼ cwt 10 lbs sugar £4 10s (27 Feb).

    1. No home port stated.

353. *Anne Gallant* of London (45) Arthur Pitts; Bordeaux
[f. 94] Thomas Searle: 27 tuns Gascony wine *net* 24 tuns,[1] 3 tuns vinegar £7 (20 Feb 1568). William Silvestre: 5 tuns Gascony wine *net* 4 tuns,[1] 1 tun vinegar, 30 cwt woad £22 6s 8d.

    1. No tonnage given.

354. *Peter* of Ipswich (80) John Backhouse; Barbary
[f. 94] Thomas Turnebull: 22 cwt sugar, 62 cwt panele £104 6s 8d (20 Feb 1568). Henry Callis 'cum sociis': 106 cwt sugar, 22 cwt panele £364 6s 8d (21 Feb). Edward Jackman: 66¼ cwt 1 brl panele £221 6s 8d. Bernard Filde: 17½ cwt sugar, 18 hhds 1 brl panele £104 11s 8d. Anthony Morris: 6½ cwt sugar £21 13s 4d. Reynold Holingeworth: 16 cwt sugar, 20 cwt panele £63 6s 8d. Matthew Filde and Richard Hills: 56½ cwt sugar, 30 cwt panele £203 6s 8d (23 Feb). Gerard Gore: 16 cwt sugar £53 6s 8d. John Watson: 23 cwt sugar £76 13s 4d. Richard Hopkins: 26 cwt sugar, 18 cwt scomes, 12 hhds panele £125 13s 4d. Robert How: 41 cwt sugar, 63 cwt panele £168 3s 4d. [f. 95] John Kell: 10 cwt sugar £33 6s 8d (24 Feb).

355. *Holigost* of St. Malo (16) Gilliam Clement; St. Malo
[f. 94b] Charles Vanart: 9 tuns Spanish sack 27s (23 Feb 1568).

356. *George* of London (60) William Thomson; Spain
[f. 95] George Saunders: 43 pipes oil *net* 38 pipes £95 (26 Feb 1568). Simon Brooke: 18 pipes Seville oil *net* 16 pipes £64. [f. 95b] John Spencer: 21½ tuns train oil *net* 16 tuns £80 (27 Feb).

357. *Rosse* of Plymouth John Dowk; Bay of Cadiz
[f. 95] Richard Hyll: 175 lbs cinnamon £35 (27 Feb 1568). George Saunders: 8 hhds olives £21 6s 8d. John Hawse: 22 doz. Seville skins £66 (28 Feb). Henry Becher: 150 pcs raisins £37 10s. Robert Dow: 8 butts sack *net* 7 butts 10s 6d. Richard Busby: 85 lbs mace £27 6s 8d. Godfrey Willson: 17 butts sack *net* 15 butts 22s 6d. John Watson: 10 butts sack *net* 9 butts 13s 6d, 1 hhd olives, 2½ cwt figs £5 (1 Mar). Cuthbert Brand: 1 tun sack 3s. Lawrence Mello: 10 butts sack *net* 9 butts 13s 6d. Richard Renolds: 13½ tuns sack *net* 12 tuns 36s, 2 hhds olives, 1 hhd cuit, 150 lbs grain berries £30 6s 8d. John Barker: 8 cwt figs £5 6s 8d. William Sharcrost: 165 doz. hand baskets, 100 doz. cork £33 14s (4 Mar). [f. 103] Richard Stapers: 80 lbs satin silk, 80 yds Spanish taffeta £96 (9 Mar).

358. *James* of Newcastle Nicholas Madeson; Seville
[f. 95] Richard May and Humphrey Fayrefax: 10 tuns Seville oil *net* 9 tuns £72 (27 Feb 1568). John Broke 'et sociis de Russia': 100 butts sack *net* 90 butts 270*s*. Simon Brooke: 20 butts sack *net* 18 butts 27*s* (28 Feb). Thomas Walker and Richard Saltinstall: 10 butts sack *net* 9 butts 13*s* 6*d*. [f. 96*b*] Nicholas Madison: 2 tuns sack *net* 2 tuns 6*s* (1 Mar).

359. *Star* of Antwerp (50) Peter Williamson; Antwerp
[f. 95*b*] Thomas Barker: 9 cwt battery £18 (28 Feb 1568). John Jackman: 300 bundles brown paper £10. Thomas Eaton: 300 doz. straw hats £10 (1 Mar). Humphrey Toy: 5 reams unbound books 10*s* (4 Mar). Jerome Rice: 16 cwt battery £32 (6 Mar). [f. 103] Edward Hardannaght: 6 half-brls steel £36 (9 Mar).

360. *Christopher* of London William Langley; Rouen
[f. 96] John Harding: 1600 ells canvas £40 (1 Mar 1568). Richard Morris: 1800 ells canvas £45. Anthony Gamage: 2700 ells Normandy canvas £65. Thomas Cambell: 1150 ells canvas £28 15*s*. Edward Bowes: 10 grs crewel chain-lace, 3 grs inkhorns, 2 grs playing cards, 16 grs combs £20 10*s*. Humphrey Broune: 20 doz. woolcards, 4 grs crewel-lace, 40 reams loose paper £31 6*s* 8*d*. William Handford: 50 grs pennyware combs, 20 lbs cotton-lace £26. Richard Renolds: 300 butts thread £30. Robert Broke: 130 quintals prunes, 60 cwt brazil £165. Robert Sadler: 2500 ells canvas £62 10*s* (3 Mar). John Milner: 2000 ells canvas £50. Wolston Dixi: 1200 ells canvas £30. Richard Hill: 140 reams paper £18 13*s* 4*d*. Anthony Cage: 2400 ells canvas £60. Robert Broke: 1800 lbs grains £60. Hugh Offley: 300 reams paper £40. Thomas Fido: 3 cwt prunes £1 10*s*. William Bond: 800 ells canvas £20 (4 Mar). Thomas Starkey: packing canvas,[1] 60 reams paper £32 (5 Mar). Matthew Colcloghe: 1800 ells coarse packing canvas, 10 thou. teazles £27 6*s* 8*d*. Richard Patrick: 60 reams paper, 12 cwt prunes £14. Richard Billam: 1500 ells packing canvas, 120 reams paper £36. [f. 113*b*] Thomas Walker: 500 lbs grains, 30 cwt prunes £31 13*s* 4*d* (20 Mar).

    1. Quantity not stated.

361. *Yong Egle* of Antwerp Anthony Cornilis the younger
[f. 96] Garret Dews: 20 reams unbound books £2 (1 Mar 1568). Francis Tooke: 5 cwt hops, 50 lbs cotton wool, 200 bundles brown paper £10 16*s* 8*d*. William Megs: 2 pipes rape oil £8 (3 Mar). [f. 97*b*] Thomas Hale: 6 cwt hops £3.

362. *Black Drake* of Amsterdam (36) Lucas Garretson
[f. 96*b*] Edward van Krog: 7 half-packs bundle-flax £28 (1 Mar 1568).

363. *Falcon* of Antwerp (40) Christian Johnson; Antwerp
[f. 96*b*] William Handford: 8 cwt hops, 50 lbs cotton wool £5 13*s* 4*d* (1 Mar 1568).

364. *Christofer* of Flushing (5) Garret Cornilison; Flushing
[f. 97] George Jenens: 2 lasts fish £12 (3 Mar 1568).

365. *Lyon* of Lee (60) John Boner; Antwerp
[f. 97*b*] John Car: 18 cwt latten wire, 2 cwt varnish £37 6*s* 8*d* (3 Mar 1568). Roger Knot: 17 cwt battery £34. Roger Warfilde: 3 cwt gunpowder, 3 cwt barley, 100 lbs turnsole £11 6*s* 8*d*. Thomas and Edmund Brasie: 20 pcs mockado £13 6*s* 8*d*. John Lambert: 1200 ells Vitré canvas £20. William Handford: 12 cwt hops £6. George Stockmed: 2 lasts rape oil £32. William Salkins: 12 cwt Cologne hemp £12. Edmund Smith: 20 pcs mockado, 28 half-pcs Genoa fustian £22 13*s* 4*d* (4 Mar). Anthony Warfilde: 3 cwt hops, 600 lbs bay oil, 40 lbs argentum vivum £12 3*s* 4*d*. John Spencer and Thomas Page: 214 lbs pepper, ½ cwt turmeric £19 10*s*. Gerard and Thomas Gore: 4 half-brls orchil £4. Thomas Cranfilde: 60 half-pcs Genoa fustian £20. James Harvie: 4 doz. whip-saws £6. Gerson and Barnabas Hills: 8 cwt Cologne hemp £8. Thomas Barker: 9 cwt battery £18. Richard Billam: 3 cwt hops £1 10*s*. William Bower: 1 bale fustian, 8 cwt madder £20 6*s* 8*d*. William Luddington: 6 cwt soap, 1 last rape oil £20 10*s*. Edward Jackman: 24 brls rape oil £32. John Eliots: 48 doz. thou. pins, 12 grs coarse bells, 4 doz. thou. needles, 8 doz. lbs piecing thread, 2 doz. lbs crewel, ½ cwt pack thread, 6 doz. lbs Bruges thread £25 6*s* 8*d*. John Borne: 50 doz. thou. pins, 6 doz. lbs Bruges thread, 4 thou. awl blades, 3 doz. lbs wrought inkle, 3 doz. lbs coarse crewel, 5 doz. crewel pieces, 5 doz. lbs bottom thread £21 13*s* 4*d*. Nicholas Spering: 5½ grs coarse knives, 2 doz. coarse gold weights £8 15*s*. John Pasfilde: 5 cwt iron creepers, 3 cwt iron wire £8 6*s* 8*d*. William Croft: 7 cwt madder £4 13*s* 4*d*. Nicholas Hewet: 35 cwt madder, 200 doz. coarse 10 doz. fine straw hats, 7 cwt dripping pans £36 6*s* 8*d*. Henry Beecher: 144 yds frizado £36 (5 Mar). Henry Byllingsley: 65 doz. thou. pins, 6 doz. lbs bottom thread £12. Thomas Longston: 200 lbs pepper, 16 cwt madder £27 6*s* 8*d*. John Taylor: 120 doz. thou. pins £20. William Gyfford: 72 yds frizado £18. William Towerson: 20 reams unbound books, 20 ticks £8 13*s* 4*d*. John Fitzwilliams: 35 cwt madder £23 6*s* 8*d*. William Hobs: 27 small white rugs, 11 doz. sealed carpets, 10 doz. lince £38 6*s* 8*d*. Robert Skarborow: 12 close stools without pans £1 10*s*. Robert Bladwell: 300 lbs pepper £25. John White: 24 cwt madder, 12 doz. lbs crewel £26 (6 Mar). Randal Manning: 30 pcs Holland cloth, 210 yds green dornick £40 13*s* 4*d*. George and John Barnes: 27 cwt sugar £90. William Pirri: 4 doz. lince, 200 ells hair tapestry, 16 ticks, 10 cwt soap £19 3*s* 4*d*. Thomas Rose: 74 pcs mockado £49 6*s* 8*d*. Thomas Parker: 16 pcs Milan fustian £16. Thomas Gryme and Robert Walkeden: 33 pcs Holland cloth £39 11*s* 8*d*. Thomas Eaton: 100 pcs mockado £66 13*s* 4*d*. William Brounesmyth: 30 paving tiles, 100 ells Hazebroucks, 3 doz. painted boxes, 1 doz. white boxes, 20 great 20 small chimney backs, 100 bundles brown paper, 100 doz. galley pots £11 13*s* 4*d*. Robert Scarboro: 50 pcs mockado £33 6*s* 8*d*. Nicholas Luddington: 24 cwt madder £16 (8 Mar). [f. 102*b*] William Sherington: 20 lbs Bruges silk £20.

366. *Angell* of Flushing (7) Cornilis Bastianson; Flushing
[f. 97*b*] George Jenens: 5 lasts 4 brls fish and herrings £32 (3 Mar 1568).

366a. *Angell* of Hamburg (60) Henricks Alverman; Hamburg.[1]

1. One entry, in the name of Daniel van Eitson, and marked 'vacat quia exivit' [f. 97*b*].

367. *Mary Thomas* of Lee (70) John Coke; Antwerp

[f. 97*b*] Roger Warfilde: 40 cwt soap, 200 lbs crossbow thread, 1 hd lbs cyperus £34 3*s* 4*d* (3 Mar 1568). John Alden and Edmund Pigot: 350 lbs bay oil, 4½ cwt almonds, 44 lbs argentum vivum, 2 half-brls treacle, 7½ cwt onion seed, 40 lbs white hellebore, 24 lbs wormseed £33 10*s*. John Daniell: 13 brls rape oil £17 6*s* 8*d*. Roger Knot: 16 cwt battery £32. William Handford: 16 cwt hops £8. William Salkins: 12 cwt Cologne hemp £12. William Coles: 6 cwt hops £3 (4 Mar). John Passfilde: 2 half-brls head nails, 19 chimney backs £7 1*s* 8*d*. Thomas Cranefild: 60 half-pcs Genoa fustian £20. William Hewet: 1½ tons iron, 2 bales fustian, 13 cwt estrige wool, 200 doz. coarse 10 doz. fine straw hats £58 6*s* 8*d*. Thomas Barker: 9 cwt battery £18. Richard Billam: 3 cwt hops £1 10*s*. Richard Hills: 12 cwt Cologne hemp £12. William Luddington: 6 cwt soap, 2 lasts rape oil, 5 cwt aniseed £43 13*s* 4*d*. Henry Hungat: 30 pcs mockado £20. George and John Barnes: 27 cwt sugar £90. John Borne: 2 grs thread points, 4 grs coarse bells, 2½ thou. awl blades, 2 thou. needles, 6 doz. lbs bottom thread £5 5*s*. William Thowerson: 370 ells wool tapestry, 550 ells hair tapestry, 3 doz. Ghentish carpets, 8½ doz. coarse cushion cloths £51 10*s*. George Stockmed: 12 cwt madder £8. Arthur Haull: 6 cwt white plates, 1 ton 'ames' iron, 20 cwt frying pans, 100 doubles, 5 cwt fireshovel plates £29. Thomas Hale: 24 cwt madder, 12 cwt sumach, 6 cwt hops, 4 cwt dates, 4 firkins Flemish treacle, 1 cwt 20 lbs candy £37. Nicholas Hewett: 18 doz. drinking glasses 13*s* 4*d*. Thomas Eaton: 30 doz. lbs wrought inkle, 2 thou. thimbles, 15 doz. thou. pins, 25 doz. pcs say, 3 doz. lbs bottom thread, ½ cwt pack thread, 2 doz. lbs crewel £39 5*s*. Henry Beecher: 7 grs check points, 16 doz. worsted checks, 10 doz. lbs bottom thread, 6 doz. lbs piecing thread, 25 doz. thou. needles, 170 doz. thou. pins £74 16*s* 8*d* (5 Mar). Thomas Heaton: 30 pcs mockado £20. Henry Byllingsley: 60 doz. thou. pins, 10 doz. lbs bottom thread £12. Thomas Longston: 200 lbs pepper £16 13*s* 4*d*. Francis Warren: 144 yds frizado £36. Anthony Brinckle: 29 pcs Milan fustian £29. John Colmer: 1 last rape oil £16. John Sutton: 100 Turnhout ticks £33 6*s* 8*d*. Humphrey Whitlok: 100 Turnhout ticks £33 6*s* 8*d*. William Bower: 40 cwt madder £26 13*s* 4*d*. John Fitzwilliams: 42 cwt madder £28. Thomas Starkey: 1500 ells minsters, 600 ells Troys canvas, 20 pcs Olonne cloth £39. Robert Bladwell: 3 cwt sugar, 50 lbs sugar candy £11 13*s* 4*d*. Randal Manning: 4 hd Castile canvas,[1] 18 pcs Holland cloth, 90 yds green dornick £29 11*s* 8*d* (6 Mar). William Pirri: 250 ells hair tapestry, 3 doz. lince £7 5*s*. Thomas Parker: 6 Venice carpets, 6 pcs dornick with thread, 30 pcs single mockado, 13 pcs caddis dornick £13 10*s*. Thomas Gryme: 20 pcs Holland cloth £24. William Brounesmyth: 1000 paving stones, 25 reams paper, 1 grs rubbing brushes, 30 lbs pepper, 20 lbs nutmegs £10 6*s* 8*d*. Thomas Parker: 16 pcs Milan fustian £16 (8 Mar). Nicholas Luddington: 30 cwt madder £20. Thomas Randall: 200 ells Levant taffeta £16 13*s* 4*d*. Christopher Jewkes: 40 half-pcs striped canvas £10. [f. 109*b*] John Isham: 30 cwt madder, 40 pcs narrow worsted £23 15*s* (17 Mar).

---

1. Soap was first written in, then corrected to canvas. No such canvas appears in the Book of Rates, but see a further consignment for Manning in **576**.

368. *George* of Antwerp (45) Matis Goras; Antwerp
[f. 97*b*] John Thomas: 22 thou. teazles £7 6*s* 8*d* (3 Mar 1568). George Stockmed: 2 pipes oil £8. John Jackman: 200 bundles brown paper £6 13*s* 4*d*. Reynold Thirling: 32 cwt madder £21 6*s* 8*d* (4 Mar). Hartik van Sprecleson: 2 packs flax £16. William Coles: 182 lbs ginger £13 13*s* 4*d*. [f. 100] John Smyth: 2 chests Burgundy glass £4.

369. *Claverblade* of Amsterdam (36) John Garretson; Amsterdam
[f. 99] Edward van Crog: 4 half-packs flax £16 (4 Mar 1568).

370. *Angell* of Dordrecht (30) Nicholas Gilbert; Dordrecht
[f. 99*b*] Walter Lyn: 16 awms Rhenish wine 16*s* (4 Mar 1568).

371. *Hog* of Dordrecht (40) Thomas Lawrence; Dordrecht
[f. 100] Thomas Clark: 6 awms Rhenish wine 6*s* (4 Mar 1568). [f. 104*b*] Thomas Lawrence: 8 awms Rhenish wine 8*s* (11 Mar).

372. *Mary Flower* of Lee (70) Robert Pope; La Rochelle.
[f. 101] Robert Pope: 35 weys great salt £35 (5 Mar 1568).

373. *Broom* of Amsterdam (30) Jacob Bothe
[f. 101*b*] Edward van Crog: 5 half-packs flax £20 (6 Mar 1568). Court Ellers: 1500 ells Osnabrücks £40.

374. *Swan* of Flushing Peter Pale
[f. 102] George Jenens: 16 brls fish £8 (6 Mar 1568).

375. *Golden World* of Amsterdam[1] (30) John Gawson; Amsterdam
[f. 102*b*] William Cocks: 22 cwt hops £11 10*s* (9 Mar 1568).

    1. But see **195, 505**.

376. *Buck* of Amsterdam (16) Cornilis Henrickson; Amsterdam
[f. 103] Hartik van Sprecleson: 600 ells soultwich £10 (9 Mar 1568).

377. *Swan* of Antwerp (30) Adrian Zegarson; Antwerp
[f. 103] Hartik van Sprecleson: 2 packs flax £16 (9 Mar 1568). John Smith: 2 cases Burgundy glass £4. Henry Billingsley: 200 doz. straw hats £6 13*s* 4*d*.

378. *Egle* of Bergen-op-Zoom (40) Thomas Johnson; Bergen-op-Zoom
[f. 103] John Collmer: 1 last rape oil £16 (9 Mar 1568). George Stockmed: wrought flax[1] £11. William Hobs: 4 lasts rape oil £64. Ancelm Becket: 23¼ cwt flax £23 5*s* (10 Mar). Christopher Jewkes: 15 cwt hops, 10 cwt tow £10 16*s* 8*d*. Thomas Eaton: 7 cwt wrought flax £7. [f. 104] William Hewet: 39 brls rape oil *net* 36 brls £48 (11 Mar).

    1. No quantity stated; the valuation indicates 11 cwt.

379. *Seadog* of Amsterdam (30) Cornilis Claison; Amsterdam
[f. 103] Edward van Crog: 6 half-packs bundle-flax £24 (9 Mar 1568).

Court Ellers: 3000 ells Osnabrücks £40 (10 Mar). William Page: 1½ lasts soap £12. [f. 105] Jacob Dews: 5 cwt flax £3 6s 8d (12 Mar).

380. *Grace of God* of London (45) Richard Tye; Rouen
[f. 103b] William Bond: 800 ells canvas £20 (10 Mar 1568). Robert Sadler: 2000 ells canvas £50. Wolston Dixi: 1500 ells canvas £37 10s. John Allot: 1400 ells canvas £35. Richard Billam: 1600 ells canvas £40. Humphrey Broune: 50 reams paper, 1 cwt pack thread, 2 grs wicker rattles £9. John Raynes: 60 doz. earthenware bottles £4 10s. Thomas Cambell: 2100 ells canvas £52 10s. James Morley: 2800 ells canvas £70. John Harding: 2250 ells canvas £56 5s (11 Mar). Hugh Offley: 1300 ells canvas, 20 cwt brazil £65 16s 8d. George Beche: 200 ells canvas £5. John Marshall: 800 ells canvas £20. John Wanton: 49 doz. woolcards £24 10s. Thomas Starkey: 2000 ells canvas £50 (12 Mar). [f. 109] Anthony Cage: 1600 ells canvas £40 (17 Mar).

381. *Angell* of Hamburg (50) Harman Bondman; Hamburg
[f. 104] John Myller: 3960 ells middlegood, 50 doz. tankards £46 (11 Mar 1568). Hartik van Sprecleson: 1620 ells soultwich £27. William Sherington: 2280 ells hedlack, 15 cwt copperas £26 10s. Daniel van Eytson: 4 hd Hamburg cloth, 840 ells soultwich, 3000 ells Osnabrücks, 33 cwt estrige wool, 960 ells middlegood £100 3s 4d. John Rainkin: 2160 ells soultwich, 1680 ells hinderlands £57. Daniel van Crog: 3 packs flax, 720 ells soultwich £36 (12 Mar). Edward van Crog: 3 half-packs flax, 16 cwt cordage, 540 ells middlegood, 6 cwt estrige wool £33 13s 4d. Yogham Kelinghusson: 90 lbs copperas, 20 cwt estrige wool £61 13s 4d. [f. 105b] Michel Rozenbargh: 32 cwt estrige wool £26 13s 4d (13 Mar).

382. *Whit Falcon* of Hamburg (50) Harman Crutman; Hamburg
[f. 104] John Myler: 2640 ells middlegood £29 6s 8d (11 Mar 1568). William Sherington: 2160 ells hedlack, 15 cwt copperas £25 10s. Otte Frolik: 3360 ells middlegood, 960 ells soultwich £53 6s 8d. John Reinkin: 1340 ells soultwich, 1680 ells hinderlands £45. Daniel van Crog: 3 packs flax, 720 ells soultwich, 20 cwt cables £49 6s 8d (12 Mar). Matthew Hope: 1 last croplings £6 13s 4d. Edward van Crog: 1680 ells middlegood, 2 half-packs flax, 6 cwt estrige wool, 35 cwt cordage £55. Court Ellers: 1680 ells middlegood £18 13s 4d. Michael Rozenbargh: 32 cwt estrige wool £26 13s 4d (13 Mar). [f. 106b] Jerome Ryse: 1680 ells middlegood, 1560 ells soultwich, 6 lasts stockfish £58 (15 Mar).

383. *George* of Purmerend (4) Sebrant Cornilis; Rouen
[f. 105b] Robert Harison: 2 grs woollen edging for hats, 12 doz. brushes £3 18s 4d (13 Mar 1568). Richard Patrik: 30 doz. woolcards, 6 grs inkhorns, 30 grs woollen edging at 3s the gross, 100 single grs coarse points, 1½ cwt pack thread, 12 leather standishes, 4 doz. brushes, 20 grs combs £36 6s 8d. Richard Renolds: 12 cwt almonds £24. Thomas Bolnust: 1100 ells canvas £27 10s. Humphrey Broune: 3 cwt pack thread, 12 sum rose nails £7. John Allot: 2200 ells canvas £55. Thomas Carter: 250 ells Normandy canvas £6 5s. John Harding: 1200 ells canvas £30 (15 Mar). Thomas

Awder: 900 ells canvas £22 10s. John Ranes: 20 doz. coarse earthenware bottles, 5 cases coarse Normandy glass, 18 coarse quilts £13 11s 8d. Edmund Ansell: 1500 ells canvas £37 10s. Edward Osborne: 1400 ells canvas £35. Richard Hyll: 1000 ells canvas £25. Anthony Gamage: 800 ells Normandy canvas £20. John Bodleigh: 2500 ells canvas £62 10s. Thomas Starke: 1300 ells canvas £32 10s (16 Mar). Anthony Cage: 2000 ells packing canvas £26 13s 4d (17 Mar). [f. 109b] Richard Smith: 1300 ells packing canvas, 12 thou. teazles £21 6s 8d.

384. *Bell* of Flushing (40) Leonard Bame; Rouen
[f. 105b] Robert Harison: 110 reams paper £14 13s 4d (13 Mar 1568). Richard Patrik: 300 reams paper, 30 doz. woolcards, 2 grs ounce balances, 20 grs combs, 8 grs inkhorns, 12 grs tin pinpillows at 3s the gross, 15 grs playing cards, 12 doz. brushes £72 3s 4d. Hugh Offley: 2000 ells canvas £50. Humphrey Broune: 25 grs combs, 1 cwt pack thread, 4 grs inkhorns, 5 grs crewel chain-lace £17. James Morley: 600 ells canvas, 12 grs crewel lace £17 (15 Mar). John Harding: 1200 ells canvas £30. Richard Morrys: 1400 ells canvas £35. John Watson: 1400 ells canvas £35. John Ranes: 8 doz. coarse quilts, 112 yds coarse dornick £13 3s 4d. Edmund Ansell: 600 ells canvas, 100 yds dornick £20. John Mylner: 900 ells canvas £22 10s. Anthony Cage: 1800 ells canvas £45 (16 Mar). [f. 111b] John Wanton: 1300 lbs grains £43 6s 8d (18 Mar).

385. *John* of Flushing (50) John White; Rouen
[f. 105b] Hugh Offley: 2200 ells canvas £55 (13 Mar 1568). Richard Patrick: 100 reams paper, 50 doz. woolcards, 10 grs inkhorns £43 6s 8d. James Morley: 1600 ells canvas £40 (15 Mar). Robert Broke: 3250 lbs grains £108 6s 8d. Richard Morrys: 1300 ells canvas £32 10s. Thomas Fydo: 500 lbs grains £16 13s 4d. Robert Sadler: 1900 ells canvas, 120 reams paper £63 10s. Richard Smyth: 28 doz. woolcards £14. John Bodleigh: 2200 ells canvas £55. William Bond: 700 ells canvas £17 10s (16 Mar). Thomas Starkey: 1400 ells canvas £35. William Didsbury: 1100 ells canvas £27 10s (17 Mar). Thomas Cambell: 2400 ells packing canvas £32. John Allot: 2200 ells canvas £29 6s 8d. [f. 109b] Anthony Cage: 2100 ells packing canvas £28.

386. *Egle*[1] of Flushing (50) Lion Lamson;[2] Rouen
[f. 106] Matthew Colcloghe: 2000 ells canvas £50 (13 Mar 1568). Hugh Offley: 1305 ells canvas £32 10s (15 Mar). Richard Smyth: 2800 ells canvas £70. John Mylner: 1000 ells canvas £25. Thomas Starke: 2400 ells canvas £60 (16 Mar). Anthony Cage: 1300 ells canvas £32 10s. Richard Morris: 2100 ells packing canvas £28 (17 Mar). John Harding: 1600 ells packing canvas £21 6s 8d. Thomas Cambell: 1400 ells packing canvas £18 13s 4d. [f. 126b] Richard Morrys: 15 cwt brazil £25 (8 Apr).

    1. Also called the *Falcon*.
    2. Also Lionson.

387. *Swan* of Ostend (30) Jedion Gilson; Ostend
[f. 106] Thomas Kelley: 85 cwt hops £42 10s (15 Mar 1568).

388. *Falcon* of Lee (55) John Boner the younger; Antwerp
[f. 107*b*] George Collimer: 120 doz. thou. pins, 6 doz. lbs bottom thread
£21 5*s* (16 Mar 1568). George Stockmed: 2 pipes Seville oil £8. Nicholas
Hewet: 17 cwt frying pans £11 6*s* 8*d*. William Hewet: 16 cwt estrige wool,
7½ cwt latten wire £28 6*s* 8*d*. Anthony Warfild: 4 cwt hops, 3 brls linseed
oil £6. Thomas Brazie: 30 pcs broad worsted £30. Richard Bowdler:
54½ cwt woad £35. William Handford: 14 cwt hops £7. Roger Warfilde:
6 hd lbs treacle £12. John Lambert: 1800 ells Vitré canvas £30. John
Fitzwilliams: 40 cwt madder £26 13*s* 4*d*. Thomas Brasie: 14 pcs narrow
worsted £22. John Isham: 40 cwt mull-madder, 72 yds frizado £23 (17
Mar). John Boorne: 40 doz. thou. pins, 10 thou. awl blades, 5 doz. crewel
pieces, 1 doz. lbs clavichord wire, 2 grs thread points, 2 doz. lbs wrought
inkle, 3 doz. lbs counters £16 18*s* 8*d*. Ancelm Becket: 16 cwt madder
£10 13*s* 4*d*. John Eliots: 6 doz. lbs crewel, 14 doz. lbs thread riband, 1 cwt
coarse pack thread £15 13*s* 4*d*. Francis Benison: 4500 ells Vitré canvas £75.
George and John Barnes: 15 cwt sugar £50. Thomas Gardiner: 400 lbs
pepper, 1½ cwt rice £34 15*s*. John Colmer: 90 lbs mace £30. Henry Byllingsley: 30 doz. lbs Bruges thread, 3 doz. pcs boultel £27 5*s*. Anthony
Brincklow: 36½ cwt Flemish madder £24 6*s* 8*d*. Thomas Davy: 10 cwt
frying pans £6 13*s* 4*d*. Thomas Laurence: 50 doz. thou. pins, 10 doz.
lbs bottom thread £10 6*s* 8*d*. Thomas Starkey: 1500 ells Osnabrücks £20.
William Luddington: 150 lbs pepper, 50 lbs cinnamon, 30 cwt madder
£42 10*s* (18 Mar). Baldwin Durham: 3 bales Ulm fustian £45. John
Woodward: 120 yds Levant taffeta, 80 yds satin £46. Thomas Longston:
12 cwt madder, 10 cwt soap, 200 lbs cotton wool, 60 lbs cloves £37 3*s* 4*d*.
Thomas Hale: 7 cwt aniseed, 2 cwt bay berries £13. Richard Billam:
9 cwt hops £4 10*s*. George Keightley: 24 cwt madder £16. Thomas Eaton:
18 cwt madder £12. Francis Tooke: 150 lbs pepper, 1 cwt aniseed £13 16*s* 8*d*.
Thomas Rose: 55 doz. lbs bottom thread £11 (19 Mar). Roger Knot:
21 cwt frying pans £14. Randal Manyng: 1 cwt aniseed £1 13*s* 4*d*. William
Towerson: 300 doz. straw hats £10. John Sutton: 300 ells hair tapestry,
5 doz. lince, 110 doz. coarse straw hats £17 8*s*. Robert Scarboro: 50 pcs
mockado £33 6*s* 8*d*. John Alden: 15 cwt soap, 4 cwt hemp £15 5*s*. [f. 114]
Gervais Simons: 4 pair 'vents' martens' tails £1 10*s* (20 Mar).

389. *Edward* of Milton (70) William Harris; Antwerp
[f. 107*b*] George Stockmed: 1 pipe 1 caroteel Seville oil £6 (16 Mar 1568).
Nicholas Hewet: 17 cwt frying pans, 200 doz. coarse 10 doz. fine straw
hats £19 13*s* 4*d*. Roger Warfilde: 1 cwt candy, 15 cwt sumach £13 6*s* 8*d*.
Henry Becher: 122 doz. thou. pins £20 6*s* 8*d*. William Hewet: 17 cwt
estrige wool, 250 lbs pepper £35. Edmund Smith: 40 pcs mockado
£26 13*s* 4*d*. Nicholas Spering: 3 doz. coarse standishes, 8 doz. coarse gold
weights, 20 grs copper bands, 3 grs coarse single knives, ½ grs crewel
girdles £9 11*s* 8*d*. Randolph Vezie: 7½ cwt hops £3 15*s*. Robert Stephanes:
175 lbs ginger £13 3*s* 4*d*. William Handfford: 20 cwt hops £10. Jacob
Lambert: 18 cwt battery £36. Thomas Brasy: 73 pcs Genoa fustian
£48 13*s* 4*d*. Godfrey Walkeden: 24 pcs Holland cloth £28 16*s*. William
Colles: 32 cwt madder, 525 lbs cotton wool, 175 lbs ginger, 10½ cwt Castile
soap £59 15*s*. William Hobbs: 134 Turnhout ticks, 32 sealed carpets

£48 8s. John Fitzwilliams: 60 cwt madder £40. John Car: 24 pair andirons with tongs and fireshovels £9 6s 8d (17 Mar). William Elkin: 24 pcs Holland cloth, 13 half-pcs canvas striped with silk £32 1s 8d. Ancelm Becket: 22 cwt madder £14 13s 4d. Thomas Davy: 45 pcs mockado £30. John Alden and Edmund Pigot: 3 cwt red lead, 4¾ cwt almonds, 3 brls painter's oil, 4 hd lbs treacle, 4 half-brls crossbow thread £27 1s 8d. John Eliots: 10 doz. crewel pieces, 8 doz. lbs crewel, 4 grs thread points, 10 thou. awl blades, 50 lbs counters, 1 thou. thimbles, 12 lbs bristles, 4 doz. lbs Bruges thread, 30 doz. thou. pins £28. Francis Benison: 4200 ells Vitré canvas £70. George and John Barnes: 17½ cwt sugar £58 6s 8d. Thomas Gardiner: 4 cwt aniseed, 200 lbs pepper £23 6s 8d. Francis Warren: 36 cwt madder £24. William Marten: 20 pcs single mockado, 17 pcs double mockado £24 13s 4d. Robert Scarboro: 13 cwt madder £8 13s 4d. Henry Byllyngsley: 100 doz. thou. pins £16 13s 4d. Anthony Brincklow: 36½ cwt Flemish madder £24 6s 8d. Thomas Randall: 15 cwt madder, 50 ells sarcenet, 8 doz. yds Cyprus cotton £19 18s 4d. Bartholomew Dod: 80 cwt madder £53 6s 8d. Randal Maning: 23 pcs Holland cloth £27 13s 4d. Thomas Laurence: 10 pcs Holland cloth £12. Thomas Starkey: 1500 ells minsters £16 13s 4d. William Luddington: 150 lbs pepper, 6½ cwt aniseed, 1¼ cwt red lead, 1¾ cwt brimstone, 3 qrs serpentine gunpowder, 18 cwt madder £37 8s (18 Mar). John Pasfilde: a great branch with 24 candlesticks at £3, 1 doz. candlesticks, 2 latten chafing dishes, 1 fireshovel and tongs of latten, 1 grs small balances, 52 lbs pile weights £5 11s 8d. Baldwin Durham: 3 bales Ulm fustian £45. Stephen Slany: 48 pcs Holland cloth £57 11s 8d. John Spencer: 150 lbs nutmegs, 150 lbs ginger, 60 lbs mace, 125 lbs cyperus, 1 cwt turmeric £61 13s 4d. John Woodward: 100 yds sarcenet, 75 yds damask £46 13s 4d. John Wanton: 58 cwt madder £38 13s 4d. Thomas Longston: 12 cwt madder, 10 cwt soap, 200 lbs cotton wool £20 10s. Thomas Hale: 30 lbs mace, drugs ad valorem £8, 50 lbs cyperus, 125 lbs verdigris, 2 brls treacle, 4 cwt hops £29 8s 4d. Richard Billam: 4 cwt hops £2. William Sherington: 30 lbs raw dyed silk £10. George Keightley: 24 cwt madder £16. Thomas Eaton: 18 cwt madder, 12 grs thread points, 3 doz. crewel pieces, 7 doz. lbs Bruges thread £24 3s 4d. Edmund Burton: 3 half-brls head nails, ½ ton iron, 150 doz. straw hats £13 10s (19 Mar). Wolston Dixi: 360 yds green dornick, 5 pcs Holland cloth £14. [f. 113] William Towerson: 10 doz. blue lince, 4 doz. Ghentish carpets, 300 ells hair tapestry £23 10s.

390. *Spledegle* of Dordrecht (40) Adrian Henricks; Dordrecht
[f. 107b] Adrian Henricks: 300 bundles green rods small band £1 13s 4d (16 Mar 1568).

391. *Red Lion* of Amsterdam (15) Simon Allerson; Amsterdam
[f. 108] Edward van Crog: 5 half-packs flax £20 (16 Mar 1568). [f. 112b] James Dews: 15 cwt hops, 100 wainscots, 100 spars £12 10s (18 Mar).

392. *Pellican* of Middleburg (20) Harman Johnson; Rouen
[f. 108] Thomas Walker: 10 cases glass £10 (16 Mar 1568). [f. 109] John Raines: 13 cases glass £13 (17 Mar).

393. *Fortune* of Bruges (50) Cornilis Albright; Bruges
[f. 108] Thomas Brasye: 165 pcs buckram £36 13*s* 4*d* (16 Mar 1568).
Richard Renolds: 800 ells brown canvas, 400 ells white Hazebroucks £30.
[f. 111*b*] Thomas House:¹ 2½ hd blue linen thread £6 5*s* (18 Mar).

> 1. Entered under the *Michell*, Cornilis Albright. Linen thread at this valuation
> does not appear in the Book of Rates.

394. *Michell* of Flushing (14) Peter Cleisson; Flushing
[f. 108*b*] John Violet: 960 lings £32 (16 Mar 1568). Thomas Sandford:
6 brls codsheads, 240 coal-fish £3. [f. 124*b*] Richard Mouse: 840 lings, 3
lasts barrelled fish £46 (3 Apr).

395. *Pellican* of Flushing John Cornilis; Flushing¹
[f. 109] Anthony Cage: 1200 ells canvas £30 (16 Mar 1568). John Raynes:
10 cases Normandy glass £10 (19 Mar). Humphrey Broune: 120 reams
paper £16 (20 Mar). John Allot: 1400 ells canvas £35. John Harding: 500
ells canvas £12 10*s*. Richard Pattrick: 60 grs combs, 3 grs narrow lace for
hats at 3*s* the gross, 50 single grs points £37 10*s*. John Bodleigh: 800 ells
brown canvas, 1300 ells packing canvas £37 6*s* 8*d*. Matthew Colcloghe:
1150 ells canvas £28 15*s* (22 Mar). William Handford: 12 grs pennyware
combs, 50 lbs cotton-lace, 40 lbs crewel-lace cost 3*s* 4*d* the lb, 12 lbs
wrought inkle, 6 grs thread-lace cost 1*s* 8*d* the gross £22 16*s* 8*d*. William
Hobson: 160 reams small paper, ½ cwt pack thread, 25 grs 'box combs',
12 grs paper combs, 2 grs ounce balances, 3 grs inkhorns, 2 grs spectacles,
2 doz. lbs piecing thread, 3 doz. wicker bottles, 3 doz. pipes, 1 doz. coarse
brushes, 10 grs playing cards £58 6*s* 8*d* (23 Mar). Thomas Starkey: 2800
ells canvas £70. [f. 126*b*] Richard Morrys: 20 cwt brazil £33 6*s* 8*d* (8 Apr).

> 1. But the cargo suggests Rouen: see above, p. xix.

396. *Margaret* of Amsterdam (40) Raire Cornilis; Amsterdam
[f. 110*b*] Court Ellers: 3000 ells Osnabrücks £40 (17 Mar 1568).

397. *Jonas* of Flushing (24) Jacob Stophles; Flushing
[f. 112] John Violet: 1200 lings £40 (18 Mar 1568). [f. 113] Thomas Sandford: 8 brls herrings £4 (19 Mar).

398. *Pellican* of Middelburg (30) Palls Lambert; Rouen
[f. 112] Peter van der Wall: 28 tuns French wine *net* 24 tuns 72*s* (18 Mar
1568).

399. *John* of Emden (20) Claise Peterson; Emden
[f. 113] James Heth: 51 cwt hops £15 10*s* (19 Mar 1568).

400. *Morryan* of Flushing Joyse Garretson
[f. 113] Thomas Sandford: 6 brls codsheads £1 (19 Mar 1568).

401. *John* of Lee (18) John Raphe; Flushing
[f. 113*b*] James Pye: 11 cwt hops £5 10*s* (20 Mar 1568).

402. *Falcon* of Antwerp (30) Vincent Johnson; Antwerp
[f. 113*b*] Hartik van Sprecleson: 3 packs 1 half-pack flax £28 (20 Mar 1568). Anthony Warfild: 3 cwt hops £1 10*s*. George Stockmed: 150 bundles brown paper £5. [f. 115*b*] John White: 6 Venice lutes with cases £6 (26 Mar).

403. *Pellican* of Antwerp Brumball Jacobson
[f. 114] William Wood: 6 cwt estrige wool £5 (20 Mar 1568).

404. *Romayne* of Antwerp[1] (40) Paul Limport; Antwerp
[f. 114] Hartik van Sprecleson: 1 pack flax £8 (22 Mar 1568). [f. 115] John Pycknett: 12 cwt hops £6 (23 Mar).

    1. Antwerp is a correction for Hamburg.

405. *Samson* of Bruges (45) Marten Fryse; Bruges
[f. 114] Richard Renolds: 500 ells canvas £12 10*s* (22 Mar 1568). Thomas House: 2500 ells brown Hazebroucks, 23 pcs 3 half-pcs canvas striped with crewel, 50 lbs garden seed ad valorem 40*s* £72 13*s* 4*d*. Richard Harris: 80 brls apples £4 (23 Mar). Thomas Cleve: 156 pcs buckram £34 13*s* 4*d*. Thomas Brasie: 150 pcs buckram £33 6*s* 8*d*. [f. 115] Thomas Sound: 6 cwt madder, 300 ells brown Hazebroucks £10.

406. *Peter* of Flushing (15) Anthony Antonison; Flushing
[f. 114] Richard Mouse: 6 brls Scotch salmon, 6 brls 'sea gills' £13 10*s* (22 Mar 1568).

407. *Rose Campe* of Heusden (40) Cornilis Garetson; Heusden
[f. 114*b*] Richard Nash: 24 cwt hops £12 (23 Mar 1568).

408. *Peter* of Lee (47) John Tyllar; Bordeaux
[f. 114*b*] Thomas Pen: 40 tuns Gascony wine *net* 30¾ tuns 92*s* 3*d*, 5 tuns vinegar £11 13*s* 4*d* (23 Mar 1568).

409. *Christofer* of Antwerp (50) Christian Cornilis; Antwerp
[f. 115] Hartik van Sprecleson: 1 pack flax £8 (24 Mar 1568). John White: 25 doz. basil skins £10 (26 Mar). [f. 116] John Brooke: 6 Venice lutes £6.

410. *Spredegle* of Dordrecht (40) Godfrey Dirickson; Dordrecht
[f. 115] John Olyf: 100 bundles white rods small band, 20 doz. small wicker baskets ad valorem 13*s* 4*d* £2 6*s* 8*d* (24 Mar 1568).

411. *Crab* of Haarlem John Evartson
[f. 115] Mary Peterson: 13 pcs Holland cloth £15 12*s* (24 Mar 1568).

412. *Mary Flower* of Brightlingsea (58) Francis Harvie; Bordeaux
[f. 115] Steven Skidmore 'et sociis': 13 tuns Gascony wine *net* 11 tuns 33*s*, 1 tun vinegar £2 6*s* 8*d* (24 Mar 1568). Edmund Burd: 34½ tuns Gascony wine *net* 28 tuns 84*s*, 3 tuns vinegar £7, 7 tuns corrupt wine £22 10*s*.

413. *Barbary* of Brightlingsea (40) John Smaly; Bordeaux
[f. 115*b*] Steven Skidmore 'et sociis': 31 tuns Gascony wine *net* 26 tuns
78*s*, 3 tuns vinegar £7 (26 Mar 1568).

414. *Grace of God* of Lee (50) John Stevens; Rouen
[f. 115*b*] John Harding: 1200 ells canvas £30 (26 Mar 1568). Thomas
Starkey: 700 ells canvas £17 10*s*. Humphrey Broune: 30 doz. woolcards,
1 grs inkhorns, 1 grs crewel lace, 60 reams cap-paper £24 3*s* 4*d*. Hugh
Offley: 90 reams paper, 1000 ells canvas £37. Anthony Cage: 2000 ells
canvas £50. Thomas Bolnust: 1100 ells canvas £27 10*s*. John Bodleigh:
3400 ells canvas £85 (27 Mar). Henry Buxston: 950 ells canvas £23 15*s*.
Anthony Gamage: 100 reams paper £13 6*s* 8*d*. John Allot: 1000 ells
canvas £25. Richard Morys: 2300 ells packing canvas £30 13*s* 4*d* (29 Mar).
William Hobbs: 760 reams paper, 1 cwt pack thread £22 13*s* 4*d*. John
Wanton: 48 doz. woolcards £24. William Plaisden: 1200 ells canvas £30.
Robert Sadler: 1600 ells canvas, 60 reams loose paper £48. [f. 118*b*]
Christopher Pears: 800 ells canvas £20.

415. *Bark Allen* of London (80) John Pearson of Harwich; Spain
[f. 115*b*] William Allen: 28 tuns train oil *net* 24 tuns, 70 doz. hand baskets
£132 (26 Mar 1568). John Spencer: 20 pipes oil *net* 16 pipes £64. Edward
Jackman: 20 pipes Seville oil *net* 18 pipes £72. George and John Barne:
10 tuns oil *net* 9 tuns £72 (27 Mar). Thomas Blank: 10 tuns oil *net* 8 tuns
£64. [f. 126*b*] Thomas Banester: 30 doz. felt hats £20 (8 Apr).

416. *Marygold* of London (45) Thomas Andros; Rouen
[f. 115*b*] John Milner: 1300 ells canvas £32 10*s* (26 Mar 1568). Hugh
Offley: 800 ells canvas, 80 reams paper, 48 doz. woolcards £54 13*s* 4*d*.
Richard Lee: 900 ells canvas £22 10*s*. Anthony Cage: 2000 ells canvas £50.
John Bodleigh: 3200 ells brown canvas £80 (27 Mar). Richard Morris:
2300 ells packing canvas £30 13*s* 4*d* (29 Mar). Thomas Bolnest: 2100 ells
packing canvas £28. John Allot: 2300 ells packing canvas £30 13*s* 4*d*.
William Hobs: 130 reams paper, 22 cwt prunes, 6 grs inkhorns, 1 doz.
flaskets covered with leather £31 10*s*. William Handford: 120 reams paper
£16. [f. 118*b*] Christopher Pears: 1200 ells canvas £30.

417. *Grace* of Rye (23) William Harman; Vigo
[f. 116] George Barnes: 7 thou. oranges £2 6*s* 8*d* (26 Mar 1568).

418. *Mary and John* of London (50) John Dyet; Bordeaux
[f. 116] Harry Wayte: 28 tuns Gascony wine *net* 24 tuns 72*s*, 4 tuns vinegar
£9 6*s* 8*d*, 4 tuns 3 hhds corrupt wine £14 5*s* (26 Mar 1568). [f. 199] John
Lendall: 3 tuns Gascony wine *net* 2 tuns 6*s* (30 Mar).

419. *Mary Jarmane* of Lynn (57) William Crag; Bordeaux
[f. 116*b*] Thomas Robley: 4 tuns Gascony wine *net* 3 tuns 9*s* (27 Mar
1568). John Lendall: 22 tuns Gascony wine *net* 17¾ tuns 53*s* 3*d*, 1 tun
1 hhd corrupt wine £3 15*s*, 1 tun vinegar £3 10*s*. Richard Whitelock: 4 tuns
Gascony wine *net* 3 tuns 9*s*, 4 tuns corrupt wine £12, 1½ tuns vinegar £3 10*s*.

420. *Jesus* of Dartmouth (56) Thomas Tucker; Bordeaux
[f. 116*b*] Thomas Searle: 42 tuns Gascony wine *net* 37¼ tuns 111*s* 9*d*, 6 tuns corrupt wine £19 10*s*, 3 tuns vinegar £7 (27 Mar 1568).

421. *Mary Flower* of Lee (55) John North; Bordeaux
[f. 116*b*] Thomas Searle: 44 tuns 2 hhds Gascony wine *net* 38 tuns 114*s*, 10 tuns corrupt wine £30, 2 tuns vinegar £4 13*s* 4*d* (27 Mar 1568).

422. *Peter* of Lee (60) Robert Cockerell; Bordeaux
[f. 116*b*] Anthony Ratclif: 3 tuns 3 hhds Gascony wine *net* 2¼ tuns 3*s* 9*d*, 1 tun 3 hhds corrupt wine £5 5*s* (27 Mar 1568). Thomas Searle: 250 pcs resin and pitch £41 13*s* 4*d* (29 Mar). Henry Waight: 2 tuns wine *net* 1 tun 3*s*, 1 tun corrupt wine £3 (30 Mar). [f. 125] Thomas Maynard: 3 tuns French wine *net* 2 tuns 6*s* (3 Apr).

423. *Greyhound* of Lee (80) William Mott; Bordeaux
[f. 117] Edward Osborne: 15 tuns Gascony wine *net* 13 tuns 39*s*, 11 tuns 3 hhds corrupt wine £35 5*s*, 5 tuns vinegar £11 13*s* 4*d* (27 Mar 1568). Thomas Pen: 12 tuns Gascony wine *net* 10 tuns 30*s*, 3 tuns corrupt wine £9, 6 hhds vinegar £3 10*s*. William Mot: 12 cakes resin £2 (5 Apr). [f. 125*b*] Lawrence Mello and Edward Osburne: 5 tuns Gascony wine *net* 4 tuns 12*s*.

424. *Margaret* of Lee (50) Thomas Barret; Bordeaux
[f. 117] William Bond: 155 quintals prunes £77 10*s* (27 Mar 1568). William Bond: 1 tun Gascony wine 3*s*, 5 tuns 3 hhds corrupt wine £17 5*s*. George Bond: 2½ tuns Gascony wine *net* 1 tun,[1] 5 tuns 3 hhds corrupt wine £17 5*s*. Edward Osburne: 3 hhds vinegar, 15 cakes resin £4 5*s*, 4 tuns Gascony wine *net* 3 tuns 9*s* (29 Mar). [f. 118*b*] Thomas Searle: 7½ tuns corrupt wine £22 10*s*, 2 tuns 3 hhds Gascony wine 8*s* 3*d*, 3 tuns vinegar, 7½ cwt feathers £18 5*s*.

    1. No subsidy given.

425. *Mary Anne* of London (60) Thomas Dale; Bordeaux
[f. 117*b*] Christopher Edwards: 35 tuns Gascony wine *net* 30 tuns 90*s*, 2 tuns vinegar, 1 ton resin £9 13*s* 4*d* (27 Mar 1568). [f. 119] Edward Sheffilde: 6½ tuns Gascony wine *net* 3 tuns 9*s*, 2½ tuns corrupt wine £7 10*s*, 1 tun vinegar £2 6*s* 8*d* (31 Mar).

426. *Primrose* of Newcastle (90) Thomas Gray; Bordeaux
[f. 117*b*] Nicholas Culverwell: 34 tuns Gascony wine *net* 30 tuns 90*s*, 4 tuns corrupt wine £12, 1 tun vinegar, 5 cwt resin £3 11*s* 8*d* (27 Mar 1568). [f. 124] Thomas Gray: 4 tuns Gascony wine *net* 2¾ tuns 8*s* 3*d* (2 Apr).

427. *Francis* of Fécamp (45) John Mansier; La Rochelle
[f. 117*b*] William Catcher: 32 weys great salt £32 (29 Mar 1568).

428. *John Baptist* of London (45) Robert Temple; Bordeaux
[f. 117*b*] Anthony Ratclif: 6 tuns Gascony wine *net* 5¼ tuns 15*s* 9*d*, 3 tuns 3 hhds corrupt wine £11 5*s*, 1½ tuns vinegar £3 10*s* (29 Mar 1568). Robert Temple: 12 tuns corrupt wine *net* 10½ tuns £31 10*s*, 2 tuns wine.[1] [f. 118*b*] William Bond: 9½ tuns corrupt wine £28 10*s*, 2 tuns Gascony wine 6*s*.

    1. No subsidy given.

429. *William* of Gorkum (30) Jacob Jacobson; Gorkum
[f. 118] Jacob Cornilis: 44 awms Rhenish wine 44*s* (29 Mar 1568). [f. 123*b*] Melchior van Aldenek: 12 awms Rhenish wine 12*s* (2 Apr).

430. *Cressaunt* of Fécamp John Mansire[1]
[f. 118*b*] William Crother: 32 weys bay salt £32 (29 Mar 1568).

    1. Despite the similarity of the masters' names, the size of their cargoes suggests that the *Francis* (**427**) and the *Cressaunt* are different ships.

431. *Egle* of Dordrecht Morgan Dirickson
[f. 119] John Freman: 300 stone pots £1 10*s* (30 Mar 1568).

432. *Marten* of Newcastle (50) John Ray; Bordeaux
[f. 119] Henry Sackford: 5 tuns Gascony wine *net* 4 tuns 12*s* (30 Mar 1568). Robert Barker: 9 tuns Gascony wine *net* 8 tuns 24*s* (1 Apr). John Skrivener: 18 tuns Gascony wine *net* 16 tuns 48*s*, 7 tuns corrupt wine £21. John Skrivener: 18 cwt woad, 56 cakes resin £21 6*s* 8*d* (5 Apr). [f. 127*b*] Richard Rotherforth 'et sociis': 2 tuns Gascony wine *net* 1½ tuns 4*s* 6*d* (13/14 Apr [*sic*]).

433. *Mary fortune* of Lee (70) John Morce; Antwerp
[f. 119] Wolston Dixi: 600 ells Bar canvas, 24 pcs Holland cloth £40 16*s* 8*d* (31 Mar 1568). Edward Bright: 6 half-brls head nails, 2 half-brls small nails £20. Edward Doughty: 19¼ cwt soap £14 8*s* 4*d*. George Stockmed: 5 cwt wrought flax £5. Nicholas Hewet: 6½ cwt oakum £1 11*s* 6*d*. William Towerson: 20 cwt feathers £30. Richard Billam: 28 cwt madder £18 13*s* 4*d* (1 Apr). Baldwin Durham: 120 half-pcs Genoa fustian, 60 lbs ferret silk £64. Thomas Gardener: 400 lbs matches £3 6*s* 8*d*. Alexander Sherington: 90 yds taffeta £30. John Alden and Edmund Pigot: 3 qrs 8 lbs mace, 175 lbs ginger, 45 lbs wormseed, 14 cwt aniseed, 9½ cwt bay berries £75. Roland Earlington: 100 lbs crossbow thread £1 13*s* 4*d*. Philip Watkins: 48 lbs ferret silk £19 3*s* 4*d*. Thomas Castelyn: 36 cwt madder £24. William Colls and John Newman: 6 tons 'ames' iron £30. John Lambert: 3000 ells minsters, 16 cwt battery, 3¼ cwt broad latten plates £72 6*s* 8*d*. Henry Smyth: 160 doz. coarse 30 doz. fine straw hats £10 6*s* 8*d* (2 Apr). John Pasfield: 1 half-brl small nails, 1 doz. fireshovels and iron tongs £4 13*s* 4*d*. Thomas Hale: 50 lbs cinnamon, drugs ad valorem 20*s*, 1 cwt ireos, 1½ cwt barley, 8 cwt brazil, 20 doz. empty barrels £20 16*s* 8*d*. Thomas Bowyer: 3 half-brls head nails £6. Henry Byllingsley: 20 lbs Spanish silk £24. Thomas Lawrence: 80 doz. thou. pins £13 6*s* 8*d*. George Breme: 28 cwt frying pans £18 13*s* 4*d*. Roger Warffild: 3 cwt caraway seed, 1 cwt copperas £2 13*s* 4*d*.

Robert Brook: 48 cwt madder £32. William Sherington: 30 doz. yds Cyprus cotton £6. Robert King: 3 half-packs flax £12. George Collymore: 12 pcs caddis dornick, 20 doz. checks, 2 doz. pcs caddis riband, 16 great grs thread points, 4 doz. lbs bottom pack thread £25 16*s*. Arthur Hale: 2 half-brls head nails, 80 doubles, 5 cwt fireshovel plates £9. Godfrey Walkeden: 19 pcs Holland cloth £22 16*s*. William Smyth: 50 doz. lbs inkle £33 6*s* 8*d*. Robert Stephens: 228 lbs pepper, 256 lbs ginger £38 3s 4*d*. William Hobbs: 436 ells hair tapestry, 11 doz. 8 lince, 3 doz. coarse carpets £34 12*s*. Thomas Cranfild: 60 half-pcs Genoa fustian £20. John Eliotts: 20 doz. thou. pins, 6 doz. lbs crewel, 1 cwt coarse pack thread, 4 grs half-pennyware glasses, 36 yds frizado £19 10*s*. Thomas Randal: 6 doz. packing sheets, 100 yds sackcloth £12 6*s* 8*d*. Humphrey Fayrefax: 3 brls Flemish treacle £6. William Luddington: 225 lbs cotton wool £7 10*s*. Bartholomew Dod: 30 pcs narrow worsted £15. John Fytzwilliams: 20 cwt soap £15. Thomas Aldersey: 65 pcs Genoa fustian, 70 ells sarcenet, 40 ells taffeta sarcenet £61 13*s* 4*d*. Thomas Eaton: 16 doz. lbs Bruges thread, 15 doz. thou. needles, 6 grs minikins, 4 grs hat bands, 2 thou. thimbles, 10 doz. pcs say £35 13*s* 4*d*. John Woodward: 70 yds velvet, 25 yds black satin £63 15*s*. John Isham: 72 yds frizado £18. Thomas Longston: 300 lbs pepper, 350 lbs cotton wool £36 13*s* 4*d*. Robert Scarboro: 12 cwt madder £8. Thomas Parker: 15 pcs wool dornick, 6 lbs sister's thread, 6 doz. coarse cauls £9 8*s* 4*d*. Anthony Fytton: 56 cwt madder £37 6*s* 8*d* (3 Apr). Francis Benizon: 87½ cwt Toulouse woad £58 6*s* 8*d*. Thomas Rise: 2 bales Ulm fustian £30. Nicholas Luddington: 21 cwt madder £14. Thomas Parker: 14 pcs woollen dornick £7. Anthony Fytton: 200 lbs pepper, 300 lbs ginger, 45 lbs mace £54 3*s* 4*d* (5 Apr). Henry Becher the younger: 40 cwt mull-madder, 32 half-pcs striped canvas, 5 grs points £12 16*s* 8*d* (10 Apr). Sir John York: 7 cwt bay berries £5 6*s* 8*d*. [f. 127*b*] John Sutton: 10 doz. lince, 200 ells hair tapestry £14 3*s* 4*d*.

434. *Sea Horse* of Amsterdam[1] (36) Henry Crite; Hamburg
[f. 119*b*] Hartik van Sprecleson: 960 ells soultwich, 50 cwt tarred rope, 2 packs flax, 1 brl potash £67 16*s* 8*d* (31 Mar 1568). Daniel van Crow: 2 packs flax, 720 ells soultwich, 28 cwt flax, 13 cwt cables, 12 cwt hawsers £64 (1 Apr). Dirick van Holt: 2640 ells middlegood, 1440 ells soultwich £53 6*s* 8*d*. Matthew Hope: 1320 ells middlegood £14 13*s* 4*d*. Court Ellers: 1320 ells middlegood £14 13*s* 4*d*. Alard Bartrinck: 6 cwt hops, 4 cwt flax £5 13*s* 4*d*. Otte Frolyk: 3840 ells middlegood, 3000 ells Osnabrücks £82 13*s* 4*d*. John Rainkin: 3840 ells soultwich, 1440 ells middlegood, 2 hd ells white Hamburg cloth £85. William Sherington: 68 cwt copperas £34 (2 Apr). Jerome Ryce: 3160 ells soultwich £36. William Luddington: 13 cwt estrige wool £10 16*s* 8*d*. [f. 125*b*] Edward van Crog: 48 cwt cables and hawsers £32 (3 Apr).

    1. Or of Hamburg.

435. *Swallow* of London Giles Gray
[f. 119*b*] Francis Bowyer: 26 cwt Castile soap £19 10*s* (31 Mar 1568). Nicholas Hewet: 6½ cwt oakum £1 11*s* 6*d*. Edmund Burton: 158 Turnhout

ticks £52 13s 4d. William Towerson: 320 ells hair tapestry, 450 ells wool tapestry, 2 doz. Ghentish carpets, 1 doz. Brussels ticks £36 10s. William Elkin: 72 yds frizado £18 (1 Apr). Henry Hungat: 70 pcs striped canvas £35. Richard Billam: 40 cwt madder £26 13s 4d. Alexander Sherington: 80 yds taffeta £26 13s 4d. James Harvie: 17 cwt battery £34. Roland Earlington: 100 doz. thou. pins £16 13s 4d. Thomas Gardner: 300 lbs ginger £22 10s. John Sutton: 20 doz. lince, 24 Brussels ticks, 1 Turnhout tick £31 6s 8d. William Coles and John Newman: 6 tons 'ames' iron £30. Baldwin Derham: 120 half-pcs Genoa fustian, 60 lbs ferret silk £64. Lucas Lane: 260 lbs ginger, 86 lbs cloves £40. Thomas Castelyn: 22 cwt madder £15. Sir John York: 600 lbs pepper, 30 lbs mace £60. John Car: ironware ad valorem £20, 1 grs small gridirons, 1 grs hammers, 1 grs 'slight' locks £24 (2 Apr). William Hobbs: 4½ doz. coarse carpets, 3 doz. 7 pcs lince £9 3s 4d. Thomas Laurence: 50 doz. thou. pins £8 6s 8d. George Breme: 30 cwt frying pans £20. Nicholas Spering: 10 doz. basil skins, 1 grs coarse knives, 10 doz. brazen gold weights, 3 grs coarse 'catlins', 10 doz. small writing tables, 6 grs steel buttons, 1 doz. counters, 2 grs coarse razors, 6 doz. lbs bottom pack thread, 8 comb cases, 2 grs leather points, 48 doz. thou. pins, 24 coarse lutes with cases £29. Thomas Daunster: 144 yds frizado £36. Robert Brook: 48 cwt madder £32. William Sherington: 100 ells sarcenet £16 13s 4d. Robert King: 4 half-packs flax, 5 cwt rope-yarn £19 6s 8d. Richard Billingsley: 22 doz. lbs bottom pack thread, 40 doz. thou. coarse pins, 30 grs harp strings £13 1s 4d. John Fitzwilliams: 36 cwt madder £24. Thomas Davies: 16 cwt madder £10 13s 4d. Roger Warfild: 3 brls treacle, 300 lbs cotton wool, 2 hd lbs marking stones £22 13s 4d. John Spencer: 164 lbs ginger, 25 lbs wormseed, 50 lbs senna £17 6s 8d. Thomas Randal: 12½ cwt madder, 100 yds taffeta £42 6s 8d. Humphrey Fayrefax: 250 lbs Genoa treacle, 3 brls Flemish treacle £14 6s 8d. Nicholas Warner: 68 doz. basil leather £27 12s. Thomas Aldersey: 60 pcs Genoa fustian £40. Thomas Eaton: 3 doz. lbs Bruges thread, 5 doz. lbs wrought inkle, 3 doz. crewel pieces, 10 grs morris bells, 5 doz. thou. needles, 25 doz. thou. pins, 3 thou. awl blades £18 13s 4d. John Woodward: 66 yds velvet £49 10s. John Isham: 30 pcs broad worsted, 150 yds velvet £142 10s. Bartholomew Dod: 41 yds velvet, 160 ells sarcenet £57 8s 4d. Thomas Longston: 350 lbs cotton wool, 150 lbs ginger £22 18s. Anthony Fytton: 35 cwt madder, 100 lbs cotton wool, 70 lbs candy £29 (3 Apr). Francis Benizen: 87½ cwt Toulouse woad £58 6s 8d. John Borne: 4 grs thread points, 2 doz. crewel pieces, 10 doz. thou. pins, 4 doz. lbs crewel, 24 pcs Rennes boultel, 2 thou. thimbles, 3 doz. lbs counters, 2 grs coarse bells, 4 doz. lbs Bruges thread, 10 doz. lbs bottom pack thread £20 16s. John Grene: 24 cwt madder, 27 pcs Holland cloth £48 8s. Nicholas Luddington: 24 cwt madder £16. Thomas Starkey: 1500 ells Osnabrücks £20. Richard Hyll: 6 cwt woad £4 (5 Apr). Henry Becher the younger: 30 cwt mull-madder, 70 pcs striped canvas with thread £27 1s 8d (10 Apr). [f. 127] William Smith: 22 pcs narrow worsted £11.

436. *Miryman* of Amsterdam (30) Peter Garetson; Amsterdam [f. 120] Thomas Sanford: 48 cwt hops £24 (1 Apr 1568).

437. *Pelican* of Hamburg (36) Adrian Cornilison; Hamburg
[f. 120] Daniel Brandes: 3000 ells Osnabrücks £40 (1 Apr 1568). William Meggs: 10 lasts soap ashes £30 (2 Apr). [f. 125] Edward van Crog: 3000 ells Osnabrücks £40 (3 Apr).

438. *Mereman* of Amsterdam (25) Sybart Jacobson; Amsterdam
[f. 123*b*] Randal Starkey: 8 cwt hops £4 (2 Apr 1568).

439. *Claverblad* of Amsterdam (36) Garet Isbrand; Amsterdam
[f. 123*b*] John Rainkin: 3000 ells Osnabrücks £40 (2 Apr 1568).

440. *Jesus* of Milton (12) Edmund Laurence
[f. 125] John Hall: 120 doz. hemp £15 (3 Apr 1568).

441. *Mary* of St. Valéry-en-Caux (40) John Vasslet; Bordeaux
[f. 125] George Claperton: 29 tuns Gascony wine *net* 26 tuns 78*s*, 3 tuns corrupt wine £9 (3 Apr 1568).

442. *Angell* of Dordrecht (40) Corst Eyngell; Dordrecht
[f. 125*b*] Nicholas Rodrigo: 15 awms Rhenish wine 15*s* (5 Apr 1568).

443. *Elizabeth* of London (60) Robert Burrell; Spain
[f. 126] Robert How: 15 butts sack *net* 14 butts 21*s* (6 Apr 1568). Henry Callys 'et sociis': 32 butts sack *net* 29 butts 87*s*. Thomas Turnebull: 4 butts sack *net* 4 butts 6*s*. Thomas Blanck: 5 tuns Seville oil *net* 4½ tuns £36. Henry Richards: 3 butts sack *net* 3 butts 4*s* 6*d*. [f. 126*b*] John Bird: 200 pcs raisins £50 (7 Apr).

444. *Egle* of Bruges (60) Francis Bowens; Bruges
[f. 126] Thomas Howse: 1750 ells brown 350 ells white Hazebroucks, 32 pcs white bustian, 3 pcs Ulm fustian, 2 pcs Genoa fustian, 10 pcs mockado £74 6*s* 8*d* (6 Apr 1568). William Gelders: 140 doz. hemp £17 10*s* (7 Apr). [f. 126*b*] William Harrys: 26 brls walnuts £4 6*s* 8*d* (8 Apr).

445. *Angell* of Bergen-op-Zoom (30) Cornilis Adrianson; Bergen-op-Zoom
[f. 126] Robert Wilkinson: 10 weys bay salt £10 (6 Apr 1568). [f. 126*b*] Robert Exton: 4½ cwt flax £4 10*s* (8 Apr).

446. *Swallow* of St. Malo (10) John Bassyn; St. Malo
[f. 126*b*] William Collin: 10 tuns sack *net* 9 tuns 27*s* (9 Apr 1568).

447. *Francis* of St. Malo (18) Edmund Obie; St. Malo
[f. 126*b*] Peter Sersett: 30 butts sack *net* 27 butts 40*s* 6*d* (9 Apr 1568).

448. *Paskall* of Plymouth (30) Thomas Pears; Spain
[f. 127] Gregory Cox: 58 butts sack *net* 52 butts 78*s* (9 Apr 1568).

449. *Peter* of London (55) Ralph Goodwyn; Bordeaux
[f. 127] Robert Fryer: 50 cwt prunes £25 (9 Apr 1568). [f. 127*b*] William Page: 25 pcs resin £4 3*s* 4*d* (13/14 Apr).

450. *Confidence* of London (48) Erasmus Kidball
[f. 127] William Bulley: 32 weys great salt £32 (9 Apr 1568).

451. *Luce* of 'Ello'¹ (50) John Goodwell; La Rochelle
[f. 127] Robert Fryer: 36 weys great salt £36 (9 Apr 1568).

    1. ? Ellough, Suffolk.

452. *Mary* of Brightlingsea Thomas Page; Bourgneuf
[f. 127] John Broke 'cum sociis Russia': 30 weys great salt £30 (9 Apr 1568).

453. *Trinity Richard* of London (58) Richard Clerk; Bordeaux
[f. 127] Edward Sheffilde: 3 tons resin £15 (10 Apr 1568). Henry Sackford: 11 tuns Gascony wine *net* 9½ tuns 28s 6d, 2 tuns vinegar £4 13s 4d. [f. 127b] John Elmes: 6 tuns Gascony wine *net* 5 tuns 15s, 1 tun vinegar £2 6s 8d (13/14 Apr).

454. *John Evangelist* of Newcastle (80) Mark Barber; The Bay
[f. 127b] Edward Barteram and Laurence Rigsby: 50 weys great salt £50 (12 Apr 1568).

455. *Sprite* of St. Malo (16) Giles Clement; St. Malo
[f. 127b] Charles van Hart: 7 tuns sack 21s (13/14 Apr 1568).

456. *John* of London (40) Thomas Turner; Rouen¹
[f. 128] John Harding: 1200 ells canvas £30 (22 Apr 1568). Thomas Cambell: 1000 ells canvas, 4½ doz. chafing dishes £26 10s. John Milner: 1300 ells canvas £32 10s. John Marshall: 2000 ells canvas £50. Miles Gray: 900 ells canvas £22 10s. Henry Buckston: 900 ells canvas £22 10s. Thomas Bolnust: 900 ells canvas £22 10s. Edward Jackman and Francis Bowyer: 400 ells canvas £10. Anthony Cage: 1200 ells canvas £30. Thomas Starkey: 1700 ells canvas £42 10s. Richard Morris: 2000 ells canvas £50. Matthew Colcloghe: 11 puncheons French wine *net* 8 puncheons 8s. Anthony Gamage: 1000 ells canvas £25. John Bodleigh: 350 ells canvas £8 15s. Matthew Colcloghe: 2300 ells canvas £57 10s. Richard Smith: 1800 ells canvas £45. William Hobson: 172 reams paper £22 18s 4d. Humphrey Broune: 20 sum rose nails £4. Oliver Fysher: 1800 ells canvas £45 (23 Apr). Richard Patrick: 10 thou. teazles £3 6s 8d (24 Apr). Richard Renold: 2400 ells packing canvas £32. Richard Morrys: 2000 ells canvas £50. [f. 137] John Clint: 300 ells canvas £7 10s (27 Apr).

    1. The first entry after Easter.

457. *Hearon* of Lee (40) John Davis; Rouen
[f. 128] Richard Smith: 1800 ells canvas £45 (22 Apr 1568). Anthony Gamage: 2400 ells canvas £60. John Marshall: 600 ells canvas £15. William Hobson: 6½ cwt shaven latten £13. Henry Buxton: 950 ells canvas £23 15s. Robert Sadler: 1400 ells canvas £35 (23 Apr). Oliver Fysher: 600 ells canvas £15. John Allot: 1100 ells canvas £27 10s. Edward Jackman:

300 ells canvas £7 10s. Hugh Offley: 1600 ells canvas £40. Richard Patrick: 10 doz. woolcards, 20 grs narrow woollen lace for hats, 20 grs lead tablets, 5 grs spectacles, 3 grs needle cases, 3 doz. sleeves of thread, 30 doz. lbs thread, 3 grs inkhorns £36 16s 8d. Thomas Bolnust: 1600 ells packing canvas £21 6s 8d (24 Apr). John Mylner: 1300 ells canvas £32 10s. George Beche: 1 hd 2 qrs [*sic*] coarse canvas £3 15s. Robert Sandler: 600 ells Normandy canvas £15. Anthony Cage: 2400 ells canvas £60 (26 Apr). [f. 135] Robert Harreson: 10 grs wooden combs, I grs ounce balances, 10 sum nails £8 10s.

458. *Thomas* of Sandwich John Daunger
[f. 128b] John Marshall: 1600 ells canvas £40 (22 Apr 1568). Richard Patrik: 12 grs lead brooches at 3s the gross, 2 grs spectacle cases, 2 grs ounce balances, 12 grs combs, 3 grs needle cases, 2 grs inkhorns, 25 grs lead tablets at 2s 6d, 40 reams paper £18 (23 Apr). Robert Sadler: 800 ells packing canvas, 110 reams paper £34 13s 4d. Humphrey Broune: 3 grs inkhorns, 5 grs crewel chain-lace £4 16s 8d. Oliver Fysher: 800 ells canvas, 300 ells narrow working canvas £27 10s. Edward Jackman: 500 ells canvas £12 10s. Hugh Offley: 1600 ells canvas £40. Matthew Colclough: 1900 ells packing canvas, 5 thou. teazles £27 (24 Apr). John Myller: 1100 ells canvas, 20 reams paper £27 10s. John Challimer: 14 grs playing cards £14 (27 Apr). [f. 141b] Hugh Offley: 150 reams cap-paper £20 (28 Apr).

459. *Verge* of Venice Nicholas Stephano
[f. 129] Anthony Donato: 24 butts muscatel *net* 22 butts 33s (22 Apr 1568). Placito Ragozin: 11 butts muscatel *net* 10 butts 15s (23 Apr). [f. 133b] Bastian Rizo: 12 butts muscatel *net* 12 butts 18s (24 Apr).[1]

1. The wines were entered on Benedict Spinola's licence: see above **53** n. 3.

460. *Falcon* of Flushing (20) Peter Gaisier; Flushing
[f. 129] Richard Mouse: 3 lasts fish, 300 lings £28 (23 Apr 1568).

461. *Sea Rider* of Antwerp (40) Jacob Lawrance; Antwerp
[f. 129] Bartholomew Dod: 8 cwt hops £4 (23 Apr 1568). Robert Broke: 36 cwt hops £18. John Jackman: 36 cwt hops £18. William Coles: 16 cwt hops £8. Michael Lyon: 100 pcs canvas striped with crewel £33 6s 8d (24 Apr). John Colimer: 10 cwt hops £5. Thomas Gardner: 16 cwt hops £8. Robert Stephens: 6 cwt hops £3. Humphrey Fayrefax: 42 cwt hops £21. John Spencer: 10 cwt hops £5. [f. 134] John White: 6 slight citherns, 8 gitterns, 2 small lutes £5 3s 4d (26 Apr).

462. *Mary Grace* of Lee (50) John Pett; Antwerp
[f. 129] Henry Becher the younger: 120 doz. thou. pins, 20 doz. worsted checks £30 (23 Apr 1568). John Lambert: 17 cwt battery £34. Edward Jackman: 18 cwt Castile soap, 24 cwt hops £25 10s. William Hobbs: 735 ells hair tapestry, 7 pcs and 3 doz. Ghentish carpets, 5½ doz. lince £34. Nicholas Hewet: 1 half-brl great nails, 1 half-brl small nails £6 (24 Apr). Roger Warfyld: 20 cwt sumach, 4 cwt hops £15 6s 8d. William Salkins:

16 cwt hemp £16. John Fitzwilliams: 50 cwt mull-madder £6 5s (26 Apr). Francis Keightly: 90 yds Florence taffeta, 50 ells Florence sarcenet, 11 yds Lucca velvet £46 11s 8d. William Towerson: 4 cwt hops £2. Thomas Hale: 600 lbs cotton wool £20. Edmund Doughty: 39 cwt Castile soap £29 5s. John Elyetts: 10 doz. pcs thread riband, 2 thou. thimbles, 3 doz. lbs Bruges thread, 270 lbs shaven latten, 5 doz. crewel pieces, 1 doz. lbs bristles, 2 doz. lbs wrought inkle, 5 grs coarse copper hat bands £15 16s 8d. John Pasfyld: 7 cwt iron creepers, 1 hd lbs crossbow laths, 3 doz. halbert heads £10. Roland Erlington: 20 pcs mockado, 50 doz. thou. pins, 11 doz. lbs piecing thread, 6 doz. lbs bottom pack thread £37 10s. Richard Hill: 15 cwt Cologne hemp £15. James Harvie: 40 cwt madder £5. Thomas Aldersey: 40 pcs single grogram £53 6s 8d (27 Apr). John Borne: 8 doz. lbs Bruges thread, 2 grs thread points, 6 doz. lbs crewel, 3 doz. lbs counters, 3 grs coarse bells, 16 grs coarse copper hat bands, 2 thou. thimbles, 3 grs halfpennyware looking glasses, 20 doz. thou. pins, 4 thou. awl blades, 3 doz. thou. needles, 20 doz. yds Cyprus cotton £28 3s 4d. Robert Taylor: 3 cwt hops £1 10s. William Sherington: 600 ells sarcenet £10. Thomas Thorp: 6 cwt hops £3. Robert Hungat: 200 ells wool and hair tapestry £10. John Mun: 30 doz. lbs white thread, 60 doz. thou. pins, ½ grs pin pillows, 3 doz. lbs wrought inkle, 6 grs inkle points, 1 doz. lbs coarse inkle, 2 brls crossbow thread, 2 grs knives £41 3s 4d. John Keightly: 50 pcs Genoa fustian £33 6s 8d. Robert Taylor: 2 cwt hops, 20 pcs boultel £5. Robert Bye: 75 cwt woad £50 (28 Apr). Thomas Eaton: 15 doz. lbs wrought inkle, 1 hd lbs unwrought inkle, 20 doz. yds Cyprus cotton, 6 grs halfpennyware glasses, ½ doz. lbs crewel £18 15s. Thomas Parker: 35 pcs dornick with wool £17 10s. Stephen Woodrof: 48 cwt mull-madder £6. William Barret: 15 cwt madder £10. Anthony Warfild: 3 cwt hops £1 10s (29 Apr). John Wodard: 80 pcs boultel £16 (30 Apr). [f. 144b] John Isham: 1 dyed cloth, 40 pcs mockado, 675 yds Ulm fustian £57 13s 4d.

463. *Beniamin* of Lee (80) John Dryver; Antwerp
[f. 129] Henry Becher the younger: 120 doz. thou. pins, 10 doz. worsted checks, 5 great grs points, 2 pcs coarse striped sackcloth £32 10s (23 Apr 1568). Edmund Burton: 11½ cwt white plates, 2½ cwt shaven latten, 6 doz. files cost 5s, 60 lbs counters, 60 lbs curtain rings £17 8s 4d. William Coles: 38 cwt hops £19. George Breme: 30 cwt kettle bands £20. Robert Broke: 48 cwt hops £24. Thomas Randall: 136 doz. yds Cyprus cotton £27 5s. James Harvie: 17 cwt battery, 4 doz. whip-saws £40 (24 Apr). John Collimer: 2 chests candy, 4 cwt aniseed £12. Alexander Sherington: 200 yds taffeta £66 13s 4d. William Luddington: 6½ cwt aniseed, 12 cwt madder £16 13s 4d. William Cocks: 20 cwt woad £13 6s 8d. George Collimer: 110 doz. thou. pins, 10 pcs dornick, 50 doz. lute strings, 8 doz. lbs bottom pack thread £26 8s. Richard Pipe: 2 doz. large crystal looking glasses, 6 chamber stools without pans £4 15s. Arthur Hall: 3 half-brls head nails, 2 cwt shaven latten, 1 grs small files, 1 grs small hanging locks, 48 yds frizado, apothecary drugs ad valorem £3, 6 Brussels ticks £30 10s. George Keightly: 16 cwt madder £10 13s 4d (26 Apr). William Towerson: 6 cwt feathers £9. Thomas Hale: 6½ cwt aniseed, 13 cwt sumach £17 6s 8d. John Elyetts: 10 doz. lbs thread pieces, 4 doz. thou. pins, 3 doz. lbs

Bruges thread, 1 doz. lbs inkle, 3 doz. lbs coarse crewel, 2 cwt coarse pack thread £18 3s 4d. George Stockmed: 120 doz. hemp, 400 lbs pepper £48 1s 8d. John Car: 24 cwt iron pans, 60 iron doubles, 80 iron plates for fireshovels[1] £20 6s 8d. William Cockin: 38 cwt madder £4 15s. John York: 600 lbs pepper, 150 lbs ginger £61 15s. Thomas Longston: 16 cwt soap, 12 cwt estrige wool £22. Robert Exton: 400 ells canvas £10 (27 Apr). Richard Billam: 4 cwt hops £2. Thomas Castlin: 25½ cwt coarse madder £17. Thomas Aldersey: 40 single pcs mockado, 30 yds satin, 25 yds damask, 210 ells sarcenet £85 3s 4d. John Borne: 10 doz. lbs wrought inkle, 80 doz. thou. pins, 4 doz. lbs crewel, 1 doz. crewel pieces £23 16s 8d. Robert Taylor: 24 cwt madder £16. William Sherington: 150 ells sarcenet £25. Thomas Laurence: 8 doz. checks, 10 doz. lbs bottom pack thread, 30 lbs silk nobs £7. Henry Smyth: 37½ doz. lbs narrow inkle, 36 lbs Spanish silk, 5 doz. lbs bottom pack thread £62. Mark Gryme: 100 ells Levant taffeta £8 6s 8d. Thomas Barker: 8½ cwt battery £17. John Sutton: 250 doz. coarse straw hats £8 6s 8d. Phillip Watkins: 32 cwt madder, 72 lbs ferret silk £47 3s 4d. Phillip Jones: 2 cwt garbled dates, 2½ hd Flemish treacle £6 (28 Apr). Steven White: 28 cwt woad £18 13s 4d. Thomas Cranfild: 27 cwt mull-madder £3 6s 8d. Edmund Smyth: 8 cwt mull-madder £1. Thomas Eaton: 50 doz. thou. pins, 3 thou. thimbles, 100 lbs counters, 10 doz. lbs crewel £22 16s 8d. William Hewet: 24 cwt mull-madder, 200 doz. straw hats £9 13s 4d. Edmund Roberts: 30 cwt woad £20. Robert Bladwell: 200 lbs pepper, 2 cwt aniseed £19 6s 8d. John Coniers: 108 half-pcs Genoa fustian £36 6s 8d. Robert Bye: 3 bales fustian £45. Anthony Skolokor: ear picks, washing balls and boxes ad valorem £5. Anthony Warfyld: 2 cwt red lead £1 10s. Robert Bye: 50 pcs mockado £33 6s 8d (29 Apr). Anthony Fytton: 140 lbs nutmegs, drugs ad valorem 80s £27 6s 8d (30 Apr). John Isham: 1 dyed cloth, 24 yds frizado £14. [f. 148] Richard Hills: 13 cwt flax £13 (6 May).

1. Weighing 3½ cwt.

464. *George* of Antwerp John de Bare;[1] Antwerp
[f. 129] Bartholomew Dod: 12 cwt hops £6 (23 Apr 1568). Thomas Thorp: 1 cwt corn powder £1 13s 4d (27 Apr). William Wood: 6 doz. counterfeit Spanish skins £18 (29 Apr). [f. 144] Anthony Warfild: 300 bundles paper £10.

1. Or Bardmaker.

465. *Primrose* of Lee (70) Henry Church; Antwerp
[f. 129] Edmund Burton: 5 grs hanging locks, 27 doz. joiner's tools, 4½ cwt shaven latten, 2 pair latten andirons £22 13s 4d (23 Apr 1568). John Lambert: 1400 ells Trois tapestry canvas £23 6s 8d. Edward Bright: 2 half-brls small nails, 24 pair small iron creepers,[1] 3 cwt varnish £11. Edward Jackman: 20 cwt Castile soap £15. Nicholas Hewet: 10½ cwt frying pans £7 (24 Apr). James Harvie: 48 cwt madder £32. Roger Warfyld: 9 cwt candy, 8 cwt hops £34. William Salkins: 16 cwt hemp £16. Robert Scarboro: 27 doz. yds Cyprus cotton, 12 cwt madder £13 8s. Richard Cotton: 45 doz. yds Cyprus cotton £9. William Luddington: 80 lbs candy, 2½ cwt green

copperas, 20 lbs serpentine gunpowder £4 3s 4d. John Fitzwilliams: 50 cwt mull-madder £6 5s (26 Apr). John Jackman: 24 cwt hops £12. Robert Brook: 12 cwt hops £6. Thomas Hale: 3 brls litmus, 6½ cwt saltpetre, 80 lbs candy, 70 lbs cyperus, 1 firkin painter's oil £17. Robert Taylor: 102 yds velvet £76 10s. Edmund Doughty: 33 cwt Castile soap £24 15s. William Hewet: 18 cwt madder £12. John Gresham: 140 yds Lucca taffeta £46 13s 4d. Richard Hill: 18 cwt Cologne hemp £18. Roger Knot: 8½ cwt battery, 1½ cwt black latten £19 5s. Arthur Hall: 4½ cwt white latten £6 15s (27 Apr). Robert Exton: 300 doz. straw hats £10. Richard Billam: 4 cwt hops, 5 cwt madder £5 6s 8d. Thomas Aldersey: 55 yds Lucca velvet £41 5s. Thomas Brasie: 101 pcs Genoa fustian £67 6s 8d. Anthony Warfild: 6 cwt hops £3. Nicholas Garnows: 45 pcs mockado £30. Robert Taylor: 12½ cwt hops £6 5s. John Wanton: 57 cwt madder £37 6s 8d. William Sherington: 60 ells sarcenet £10. Richard Billingsley: 20 doz. thou. pins, 30 grs harp strings, 3 grs minikins, 12 doz. lbs bottom pack thread, 3 cwt white latten £13 13s 4d. Henry Smyth: 4 doz. lbs broad inkle, 24 lbs Paris silk £8 13s 4d. Thomas Parker: 9 pcs dornick with wool, 1 bale fustian £20 10s. John Sutton: 2 packs flax £16. John Hutton: 190 doz. thou. pins, 6 doz. cap bands £39 13s 4d. John Spencer: 150 lbs white copperas £2 10s (28 Apr). William Towerson: 7 cwt hops, 3 cwt feathers £8. Hugh Bradborne: 20 cwt brazil £33 6s 8d. John Travers: 50 pcs say £50. Robert By: 60 cwt woad, 2 bales fustian £70. John Woodward: 80 yds velvet, 20 yds damask £68. Alexander Chisnall: 28 pcs broad worsted, 3 bales Ulm fustian £73. Thomas Eaton: 8 doz. lbs Bruges thread, 6 doz. lbs crewel, 3 thou. tacks, 40 lbs counters, 3 doz. thou. needles, 2 cwt shaven latten, 24 doz. crewel pieces, 10 doz. thou. pins, 2 grs half-pennyware glasses, 10 doz. yds Cyprus cotton, 20 lbs clavichord wire, 3 grs minikins £37 13s 4d. Geoffrey Goffe: 100 ells flax and hair, 2 doz. lince £4 16s 8d. Robert Bladwell: 3 cwt sugar, 20 lbs nutmegs £13 6s 8d. Francis Warrin: 75 cwt woad £50. Gerard Gore: 4 dyed cloths £32. Stephen Woodrof: 64 cwt mull-madder £8. William Barret: 16 cwt madder £10 13s 4d. Martin Wood: 4 cwt orchil £4 (29 Apr). Richard Pipe: 50 pcs mockado £33 6s 8d. John Isham: 120 pcs boultel £24 (30 Apr). [f. 147] George Keightley: 50 yds satin, 160 yds 'caffaes' taffeta £75 16s 8d (5 May).

1. Weighing 1½ cwt.

466. *Hound* of Lee (50) John Salmon; Antwerp
[f. 129b] William Coles: 30 cwt hops £15 (23 Apr 1568). John Lambert: 3000 ells minsters £33 6s 8d. Thomas Randall: 160 yds Levant taffeta £13 6s 8d. Nicholas Hewet: 21 cwt frying pans £14 (24 Apr). Roger War-fyld: 10 cwt sumach £6 13s 4d. Alexander Sherington: 200 yds taffeta £66 13s 4d. William Luddington: 6½ cwt aniseed, 75 lbs ginger, 1 cwt red lead, 1 brl ochre, 12 cwt madder £24. George Collimer: 90 doz. thou. pins £15. Edmund Smyth: 2 bales Ulm fustian £30. Thomas Bowyer: 8 cwt iron pans, 1 half-brl small nails, 3 hd iron plates, 10 pair iron andirons, 20 pair creepers, 6 doz. candlesticks, 1 grs slight iron ladles, 12 lbs crossbow thread, 3 doz. trunks, 1 brl varnish, 1 doz. chimney rakes,[1]

1 doz. gridirons £23 1*s* 8*d*. Nicholas Spering: 8 doz. lbs pack thread, 8 grs coarse knives, 10 doz. small gold weights, 6 lbs wire, 8 Cologne lutes, 3 grs harp strings £15 11*s* 8*d*. George Keightly: 19½ cwt madder £13 (26 Apr). William Towerson: 260 ells hair tapestry, 380 ells wool tapestry, 2½ doz. Ghentish carpets £31 8*s* 4*d*. Thomas Hale: 6½ cwt aniseed, 4 half-brls crossbow thread, 8 lbs coloquintida £12 8*s*. Robert Taylor: 2 pcs stammel £20. John Sutton: 30 Turnhout ticks, 86 counterfeit Turnhout ticks, 7 doz. cushions, 160 ells silk tapestry £85 16*s* 8*d*. John Car: 8 cwt iron pans, 7 hd plates, 25 cwt 'Lukes' iron £16 5*s*. William Cockin: 26 cwt mull-madder £4 5*s*. Thomas Longston: 12 cwt soap, 12 cwt estrige wool £19. Mark Grime: 300 stone pots, 25 doz. chamois £11 10*s* (27 Apr). Thomas Castlin: 16 cwt coarse madder £10 13*s* 4*d*. Thomas and Edmund Brasye: 1 bale Ulm fustian, 44 pcs narrow worsted £37. Robert Taylor: 5½ cwt hops £2 15*s*. Francis Benison: 167½ cwt woad £112. William Sherington: 120 ells sarcenet £20. Thomas Daunster: 30 doz. lbs narrow inkle, 10 doz. lbs Bruges thread, 4 doz. lbs bottom pack thread, 7 pcs Holland cloth £35 18*s*. John Keightly: 50 pcs fustian £33 6*s* 8*d*. Thomas Barker: 9 cwt battery, 1½ cwt black latten £19. Phillip Watkins: 32 cwt madder £21 6*s* 8*d*. Henry Beecher: 70 doz. thou. pins £11 13*s* 4*d* (28 Apr). William Hewet: 8 cwt hops, 22 cwt mull-madder £6 13*s* 8*d*. Thomas Cranefild: 20 cwt mull-madder, 3¼ cwt hemp £6. Robert Bye: 68 pcs mockado £45 6*s* 8*d*. John Woodward: 18 half-pcs canvas striped with silk £4 10*s*. Robert Bladwell: 250 lbs pepper £20 16*s* 8*d*. John Coniers: 96 half-pcs Genoa fustian £32. Henry Smyth: 23 doz. lbs narrow inkle, 5 doz. lbs bottom pack thread, 15 lbs raw undyed silk £21 6*s* 8*d*. Henry Billingsley: 40 doz. thou. pins, 10 doz. lbs bottom thread £8 13*s* 4*d*. Robert Bye: 48 pcs watered camlet, 7 pcs mockado £52 13*s* 4*d* (29 Apr). Anthony Warfild: drugs ad valorem £4. John Isham: 36 pcs narrow worsted, 5 cwt dressed flax £23 (30 Apr). [f. 148] Richard Hills: 40 half-pcs Genoa fustian, 100 ells Levant taffeta £21 13*s* 4*d* (6 May).

1. Or 'racks'.

467. *Spredegle* of Antwerp (40) Peter Johnson; Antwerp
[f. 129*b*] Hartik van Sprecleson: 2 packs flax £16 (23 Apr 1568). John Jackman: 36 cwt hops £18. Nicholas Hewet: 28 cwt hops £14 (24 Apr). [f. 146*b*] Edward Hardinworth: 8 half-brls steel £48 (4 May).

468. *Black Egle* of Amsterdam (30) Cornilis Frederickson; Amsterdam
[f. 129*b*] John Edmunds: 30 brls fish £15 (23 Apr 1568). John Rainckin: 420 ells padduck, 720 ells middlegood, 3000 ells Osnabrücks £52 5*s*. Daniel van Eyston: 960 ells middlegood £10 13*s* 4*d* (26 Apr). [f. 136*b*] Otte Frolick: 3000 ells Osnabrücks £40.

469. *Christopher* of Antwerp Garet Rose
[f. 130] John Jackman: 44 cwt hops £22 (23 Apr 1568). William Coles: 52 cwt hops £26. John Collimer: 28 cwt hops £14 (24 Apr). Anthony Warfild: 3 cwt hops £1 10*s* (27 Apr). [f. 139] Lucas Lane: 10 cwt hops £5.

470. *Andris* of Antwerp (40) Jacob Cornilis; Antwerp
[f. 130] John Jackman: 36 cwt hops £18 (23 Apr 1568). John Colimer:

46 cwt hops £23 (24 Apr). John Spencer: 16 cwt hops £8. Thomas Hale: 20 cwt hops £10 (26 Apr). [f. 138] Anthony Warfild: 12 cwt hops £6 (27 Apr).

471. *Fortune* of Antwerp (40) John Dorne; Antwerp
[f. 130] John Jackman: 34 cwt hops £17 (23 Apr 1568). Robert Broke: 36 cwt hops £18. John Colimer: 16 cwt hops £8 (24 Apr). John Spencer: 12 cwt hops £6. Richard Billam: 12 cwt hops £6 (27 Apr). [f. 146b] Edward Hardingworth: 4 half-brls steel £24 (4 May).

472. *Charitie* of London (100) John Webb; Alicante
[f. 131] Lawrence Mello: 12 butts Alicante wine *net* 11 butts 16s 6d (23 Apr 1568). Richard Staper: 21 cwt rice, 9 cwt almonds £35 10s (28 Apr). [f. 141b] Richard Staper: 150 pcs raisins, 20 cwt raisins of the sun, 5 tons beryllia ad valorem £6 13s 4d, 25 cwt liquorice £73 6s 8d.

473. *Spredegle* of Antwerp (40) Daniel Peters; Antwerp
[f. 132] John Collimer: 22 cwt hops £11 (24 Apr 1568). Thomas Hale: 10 cwt hops £5 (26 Apr). John Jackman: 20 cwt hops £10 (28 Apr). [f. 142b] Hartik van Sprecleson: 2 packs flax £16.

474. *Saker* of Lee (28) John Harrys
[f. 132] Thomas Sound: 400 ells brown 100 ells blue Hazebroucks, 9 pcs brown 'russels' £21 6s 8d (24 Apr 1568). [f. 136b] Thomas House: 400 ells Vitré canvas, 6 cases glasses £12 13s 4d (26 Apr).

475. *Mary* of Antwerp (50) John Rick; Antwerp
[f. 133] John Spencer: 6 cwt hops £3 (24 Apr 1568). Thomas Thorp: 8 cwt hops £4 (28 Apr). Robert Stephens: 6 cwt hops £3. Lucas Lane: 6 cwt hops £3. Humphrey Fayrefax: 48 cwt hops £24. William Coles: 26 cwt hops £13. [f. 144b] Edward Jackman: 48 cwt hops £24 (30 Apr).

476. *Asse* of Antwerp (40) Francis Peters; Antwerp
[f. 133] John Spencer: 22 cwt hops £11 (24 Apr 1568). John Jackman: 22 cwt hops £11 (28 Apr). Robert Stephens: 6 cwt hops £3. [f. 143b] Arnold Lobley: 36 cwt hops £18 (29 Apr).

477. *Black Dragon*[1] of Amsterdam (30) Lucas Garretson
[f. 133] Thomas Sandford: 1200 lings £40 (24 Apr 1568). Edward van Crog: 6 half-packs bundle-flax, 1220 ells middlegood £38 13s 4d (26 Apr). Hartik van Sprecleson: 1 pack flax £8. [f. 137b] Francis Arbeto: 3400 bundles ton-flax £2 (27 Apr).

1. Or *Drake*.

478. *Bear* of Amsterdam (30) Adrian Francis
[f. 133b] William Megs: 3 brls potash, 100 wainscots £11 10s (24 Apr 1568). Edward van Crog: 4 half-packs bundle-flax, 1400 ells middlegood £32 (26 Apr). Hartik van Sprecleson: 1500 ells Osnabrücks £20. Otte Frolick:

1440 ells middlegood £16. [f. 138*b*] John Edmunds: 300 staplefish, 240 lings, 30 brls fish £27 10*s* (27 Apr).

479. *Pellican* of Amsterdam (30) Naning Thomas
[f. 133*b*] William Meggs: 6 lasts soap ashes, 100 wainscots £22 (24 Apr 1568). John Smyth: 4 weys Rhenish glass £10 (26 Apr). [f. 144*b*] Court Ellers: 1500 yds Osnabrücks £20 (30 Apr).

480. *Pellican* of Amsterdam (30) Tyman Cornilis; Amsterdam
[f. 133*b*] William Meggs: 4 lasts ashes £12 (24 Apr 1568). Edward van Crog: 2 half-packs bundle-flax, 1440 ells middlegood £24 (26 Apr). Hartik van Sprecleson: 780 ells soultwich, 3000 ells Osnabrücks £53. Otte Frolick: 720 ells soultwich £12. Daniel van Eitzen: 1680 ells soultwich £28 (27 Apr). Harry Boore: 4 weys Rhenish glass £10. [f. 142*b*] John Myller: 840 ells middlegood £9 6*s* 8*d* (28 Apr).

481. *Lefe Grase* of Amsterdam (30) Jacob Jacobson; Amsterdam
[f. 135*b*] Edward van Crog: 700 wainscots £18 (26 Apr 1568).

482. *Claverblad* of Amsterdam (40) Garret Johnson; Amsterdam
[f. 135*b*] Edward van Crog: 6 half-packs bundle-flax, 1440 ells middlegood £40 (26 Apr 1568). Hartik van Sprecleson: 1500 ells Osnabrücks £20. Daniel van Eytson: 960 ells middlegood £10 13*s* 4*d*. Otte Frolick: 720 ells middlegood, 1500 ells Osnabrücks £28. [f. 138*b*] John Edmunds: 1200 staplefish, 960 lings £50 (27 Apr).

483. *Falcon* of Amsterdam (24) Alard Allardson; Amsterdam
[f. 136] Edward van Crog: 2400 clapholt £6 (26 Apr 1568).

484. *Unicorn* of Amsterdam (36) Peter Peterson; Amsterdam
[f. 136] Daniel van Eytson: 1920 ells middlegood £21 6*s* 8*d* (26 Apr 1568). [f. 141*b*] Edward van Crog: 1200 ells middlegood £13 6*s* 8*d* (28 Apr).

485. *World* of Amsterdam (36) Peter English; Amsterdam
[f. 136] Daniel van Eytson: 1440 ells soultwich £28 (26 Apr 1568). Otte Frolick: 1560 ells middlegood £17 6*s* 8*d*. Mary Peterson: 13 pcs Holland cloth £15 13*s* 4*d* (28 Apr). [f. 141*b*] Edward van Crog: 1200 ells middlegood £13 6*s* 8*d*.

486. *Fortune* of Flushing (35) Simon Cornilis; Flushing
[f. 137] Simon Cornilis: 22 butts sack *net* 20 butts 30*s* (26 Apr 1568). James Heath: 27 cwt hops £13 10*s*.

487. *James* of Antwerp Simon Joyce
[f. 137] John Smyth: 2 chests Burgundy glass £4 (27 Apr 1568). Humphrey Lawton: 5 cwt estrige wool, 4 doz. Flanders skins, 24 reams writing paper, 400 paste boards, 6 doz. calf-forrel £21 10*s*. Robert Fermer: 72 lbs ferret silk £30 (3 May). [f. 145] Benedict Spinola:[1] 7 butts sweet wine *net* 6 butts 9*s*.

1. Entered under the *Ass.* master Simon Joyse.

488. *Angel*[1] of Bergen-op-Zoom (40) Andrew Williamson; Bergen-op-Zoom
[f. 141] Robert Exton: 9 cwt flax £9 (28 Apr 1568). Ancelm Becket: 12 cwt flax £12. William Hewet: 6½ cwt quartern-flax £6 10s (29 Apr). Thomas Davy: 4½ cwt unwrought flax £4 10s. Christopher Jewkes: 10 cwt tow, 15 cwt hops, 10 cwt flax £20 16s 8d. Nicholas Hewet: 6 cwt oakum, 6 cwt wrought flax £7 10s (30 Apr). [f. 145] John Boylson: 9½ cwt flax £9 10s.

    1. Also the *Falcon*.

489. *Catt* of Amsterdam (35) Eggle Cornilison; Amsterdam
[f. 141] Hartik van Sprecleson: 1920 ells soultwich £32 (28 Apr 1568). Edward van Crog: 600 wainscots, 600 ells middlegood £30 13s 4d. Henry Weyghtman: 2 lasts 360 croplings £15 6s 8d. [f. 143] John Kellinghouson: 2 lasts 240 croplings £14 13s 4d (29 Apr).

490. *An* of Antwerp (45) Barthel Paules; Antwerp
[f. 142] Humphrey Fayrefax: 6 cwt tow £2 (28 Apr 1568). Nicholas Hewet: 27 cwt hops £13 10s. Garret Dewes: 20 reams unbound books £2 (29 Apr). William Hammond: 50 doz. straw hats £1 13s 4d. Thomas Eaton: 8 doz. lbs crewel, 4 doz. curtain rings, 4 grs Jews' trumps £10 13s 4d (30 Apr). [f. 146b] Edward Hardingworth: 6 half-brls steel £36 (4 May).

491. *Cock* of Bruges (60) Jacob Albright; Bruges
[f. 143] Nicholas Burden: 60 brls apples, 1 brl 'all manner of seeds' at 33s £4 13s 4d (29 Apr 1568). John Mun: 16 doz. lbs Bruges thread, 1 doz. lbs inkle, 1 grs dolls £11 10s. Thomas Howse: 1050 ells brown 300 ells blue Hazebroucks, 4 doz. lbs brown thread, 1 pc. blue say, 2 pcs Ulm fustian, 18 cwt hops £48 8s. [f. 143b] William Gelders: 20 pcs mockado, 10 pcs bustian £20.

492. *George* of Antwerp Jacob de Cooper
[f. 143b] John Jackman: 26 cwt hops, 100 bundles brown paper £16 6s 8d (29 Apr 1568). Alard Bartrinck: 5 cwt hops £2 10s (4 May). [f. 148] Edward Hardannoght: 6 half-brls steel £36 (6 May).

493. *Jenet* of Saltash (16) John Williamson of Millbrook; San Sebastián
[f. 144] Stephen Hekins: 16 tons resin £80 (30 Apr 1568).

494. *Jonas* of Flushing (24) Jacob Stoffles; Flushing
[f. 144b] John Edmunds: 480 lings, 20 brls fish £26 (30 Apr 1568).

495. *Falcon* of Flushing Peter Peterson
[f. 144b] John Edmunds: 480 lings £16 (30 Apr 1568).

496. *Morian* of Flushing (18) Joise Garetson; Flushing
[f. 145] John Edmunds: 2 lasts fish, 120 lings £16 (3 May 1568).

497. *Spredegle* of Antwerp Giles Dorne; Antwerp
[f. 145] Henry Billingsley: 150 butts Paris thread £15 (3 May 1568).
George Bisshop: 40 reams unbound books, 2 rolls maps ad valorem
40s £6 (4 May). Lucas Harison: 40 reams unbound books, 54 reams paper,
12 doz. parchment skins £15 2s 6d. John Spencer: 28 cwt hops £14.
[f. 147] John Colmer: 20 cwt hops £10.

498. *Pellican* of Flushing (20) John Cornilis
[f. 145] Thomas Kelley: 14 weys white salt £18 13s 4d (3 May 1568).

499. *Spledegle* of Amsterdam (30) Cornilis Peterson
[f. 145] Edward van Crog: 650 wainscots, 1200 clapholt £29 (3 May 1568).

500. *Grey falcon* of Hamburg (70) Peter Alverman
[f. 145] Hartik van Sprecleson: 1080 ells middlegood, 900 ells soultwich
£27 (4 May 1568). Luder van Dorne: 1 pack flax £8. John Myller: 1200 ells
padduck, 840 ells middlegood, 720 ells soultwich £33 6s 8d. Otte Frolik:
1440 ells soultwich, 7680 ells middlegood £109 6s 8d. Matthew Hope:
24 cwt estrige wool £20. Court Ellers: 1500 ells Osnabrücks, 720 ells
middlegood, 9 hd Hamburg brown cloth £52 10s. Daniel van Crog: 720
ells middlegood £8. John Killinghowse: 13 cwt estrige wool £10 16s 8d.
Daniel Brandes: 840 ells middlegood £9 6s 8d. Alard Bartrinck: 2520 ells
middlegood £28. Jerome Risse: 1800 ells middlegood, 1440 ells soultwich,
240 ells padduck £46 8s. [f. 147b] Edward van Crog: 45 cwt cordage, 1
half-pack flax, 3720 ells middlegood, 6 cwt estrige wool £80 6s 8d (5 May).

501. *Angell* of Hamburg (80) Henrik Alverman; Hamburg
[f. 145b] Hartik van Sprecleson: 1200 ells middlegood, 900 ells soultwich,
360 ells padduck £31 18s 8d (4 May 1568). Daniel van Eitson: 1920 ells
middlegood, 480 ells padduck, 3000 ells Osnabrücks, 2 hd brown Hamburg
cloth, 16 cwt hops £78 2s 6d. Luder van Dorne: 2 packs flax £16. John
Myller: 720 ells soultwich, 600 ells padduck £18. Matthew Hope: 12 cwt
estrige wool, 600 ells soultwich £20. Daniel van Crog: 720 ells middlegood,
1 half-pack flax, 4 cwt estrige flocks[1] £15 6s 8d. John Killinghowse: 13 cwt
estrige wool, 1 last 1080 croplings £23 10s. John Rainkin: 1 double-roll
Osnabrücks, 1560 ells soultwich, 9 hd Hamburg cloth, 900 ells middlegood
£94. Daniel Brandes: 1680 ells middlegood £18 13s 4d. Alard Bartrinck:
1920 ells middlegood, 6 cwt estrige wool £26 6s 8d. Edward van Crog:
1800 ells middlegood, 8 cwt estrige wool, 35 cwt cordage £50 (5 May).
[f. 147] John Rainkin: 1680 ells middlegood £18 13s 4d.

1. See **520** n.

502. *Sparrow Hauk* of Antwerp Mattis Brounge[1]
[f. 146] Thomas Parker: 35 pcs double carrels £17 10s (4 May 1568).
Hartik van Sprecleson: 2 packs flax £16. [f. 148] Edward Hardannoght:
6 half-brls steel £36 (6 May).

1. Also Brouning.

503. *John* of Antwerp (10) Jacob Joryson; Antwerp
[f. 146*b*] Hartik van Sprecleson: 1 pack flax £8 (4 May 1568). Richard Cotton: 80 yds taffeta £26 13*s* 4*d* (5 May). Lancelot Yong: 3 chests Burgundy glass £6. Edward Hardannoght: 6 half-brls steel £36 (6 May). [f. 148*b*] Mary Peterson: 9 pcs cambric £18.

504. *Sampson* of Bruges (40) Marten Fryse; Bruges
[f. 146*b*] Matthew Colcloth: 30 cwt hops, 12 doz. hemp £16 10*s* (4 May 1568). Thomas Howse: 50 pcs bustian, 5 doz. Flanders skins, 10 pcs brown Holland cloth, 50 ells Hazebroucks, 5 cwt hops £64 1*s* 8*d* (5 May). [f. 147*b*] William Gelders: 40 pcs white bustian £16 13*s* 4*d*.

505. *Golden World* of Emden (30) John Gosson
[f. 147] Michael Lyon: 40 doz. lbs thread £2 3*s* 4*d* (4 May 1568).

506. *John* of Lee (18) John Raffe; Sluis
[f. 147] James Pye: 30 brls loose apples £1 10*s* (5 May 1568).

507. *Cockelain* of Dunkirk (6) Serle Clincker; Dunkirk
[f. 147*b*] James Ward: 27 cwt hops £13 10*s* (5 May 1568).

508. *Nightingale* of Amsterdam (25) Claise Simonsson; Amsterdam
[f. 147*b*] William Allen: 9000 ells Osnabrücks £120 (5 May 1568). John Rainkin: 6000 ells Osnabrücks £60 (6 May). [f. 148*b*] John Rainkin: 360 ells padduck, 1680 ells middlegood £22 5*s* (7 May).

509. *Peter* of Flushing (15) Anthony Antonison; Flushing
[f. 148] James Heath: 15 cwt hops £7 10*s* (6 May 1568).

510. *Falcon* of London (4) [*sic*] Dignatus Garlof; Danzig
[f. 148] Alard Bartinck: 63 cwt copperas £31 10*s* (6 May 1568). Court Ellers: 14 firkins sturgeon £9 6*s* 8*d*. George Mylner: 10 half-packs 1 pack flax, 110 cwt,[1] 2 cwt cordage, 10 cwt onion seed £147 6*s* 8*d*. Dunstan Walton: 23 cwt cordage £15 6*s* 8*d* (7 May). Robert Collet: 4 packs flax, 2 lasts 5 brls pitch £36 16*s*. Edmund Boldero: 2 packs flax £16. Thomas Russell: 8½ lasts pitch £17. William Cockin: 5 lasts pitch £10. Richard Garney: 13¾ packs flax £110. Robert Hilson: 10 packs flax, 7 lasts pitch, 1200 clapholt £98. [f. 149] William Francland: 4 packs bale-flax £32.

    1. Commodity not stated.

511. *An Gallant* of Milton (40) William Morkock; Hamburg
[f. 148*b*] William Luddington: 32 cwt estrige wool £26 13*s* 4*d* (7 May 1568). William Allen: 33 cwt madder, 27 cwt copperas, 2000 clapholt £40 10*s*. Hartik van Sprecleson: 420 ells soultwich £7 (10 May). [f. 149] Jerome Rice: 1800 ells soultwich £30.

512. *Cleverblade* of Amsterdam (40) William Thomas; Amsterdam
[f. 149] William Megs: 24 cwt hops £12 (10 May 1568). John Myller:

3000 ells Osnabrücks £40 (11 May). Court Ellers: 20 firkins sturgeon £13 6s 8d. [f. 150] Thomas Ivie: 12 cwt hops £6 (12 May).

513. *Red Lyon* of Amsterdam (30) Simon Allardson; Amsterdam
[f. 149] William Page: 1½ lasts Flemish soap £12 (10 May 1568). [f. 149b] James Dewes: 30 cwt hops £15 (11 May).

514. *Christopher* of London Thomas Wilson; Rouen
[f. 149] Anthony Gamage: 1400 ells canvas £35 (11 May 1568). Humphrey Broune: 3 grs crewel chain-lace, 1 grs ounce balances £3. Oliver Fysher: 1400 ells canvas, 1½ cwt pack thread, ½ cwt feathers £38 5s. Richard Renolds: 16 doz. buckrams £24 (12 May). Robert Sadler: 1400 ells canvas, 140 reams paper £53 13s 4d. John Harding: 1800 ells canvas £45. Anthony Cage: 1200 ells canvas £30. John Boodleigh: 2200 ells canvas £55. Wolston Dixi: 2200 ells Normandy canvas £55. John Mylner: 900 ells canvas £22 10s. John Marshall: 600 ells canvas £15. John Wanton: 47 doz. wool-cards £23 10s (13 May). William Hobson: 120 reams paper, 40 doz. wool-cards, 6 hhds vinegar, 1 cwt pack thread £41 3s 4d. Henry Cletherow: 60 reams cap-paper £8. Richard Billam: 1 tun French wine *net* ½ tun 1s 6d (15 May). [f. 152] John Broke 'pro socio Russia': 860 reams paper £114 13s 4d (17 May).

515. *William* of London (60) Thomas Foster
[f. 149] Richard May: 8 tons Spanish iron £32 (11 May 1568). Edward Boyes: 5 tons Spanish iron £20 (12 May). Thomas Turnebull: 5 tons Spanish iron £20. Thomas Hewet: 5 tons Spanish iron £20. Richard Folkes: 5 tons Spanish iron £20. Roger Winston: 5 tons Spanish iron £20. Roger Winston: 9 sacks liquorice £4. Roger Winston: 3½ tuns train oil £17 10s. Francis Bowyer: 20 tons Spanish iron £80. [f. 151] Nicholas Alkins: 3½ tons Spanish iron, 30 hd yellow resin, 6 ballets woad £29 10s.

516. *Jesus* of Dover John Howe; Rouen
[f. 149b] Humphrey Broune: 30 doz. woolcards, 1 grs inkhorns, 80 reams paper £26 3s 4d (11 May 1568). Oliver Fysher: 1400 ells canvas £35. Anthony Gamage: 1400 ells canvas, 16 doz. woolcards, 6 coarse quilts £44 3s 4d. Richard Renolds: 16 doz. buckrams £24 (12 May). John Allot: 1400 ells canvas £35. Matthew Colclothe: 1200 ells canvas, 26 doz. wool-cards £43. Henry Wayte: 120 reams paper, 16 doz. woolcards £24. Richard Patrick: 40 reams paper, 10 grs inkhorns, 10 grs lead tablets, 35 grs woollen edging, 16 grs playing cards, 1 hd lbs round cord, 80 grs points at 8d the gross £48 16s 8d. John Harding: 600 ells canvas £15. Thomas Campbell: 1500 ells brown canvas, 50 doz. wicker bottles £39 15s. Anthony Cage: 1800 ells canvas £45. John Boodleigh: 2400 ells canvas £60. Wolston Dixi: 1200 ells brown canvas £30. John Mylner: 900 ells canvas £22 10s. John Marshall: 800 ells canvas £20. John Olyff: 800 ells canvas £20. Hugh Offley: 2000 ells canvas £50. Edward Best: 650 ells canvas £16 5s (13 May). William Hobson: 8 grs combs, 8 doz. rackets, 2 grs penners and horns, 2 grs ungilt spectacle cases, 3 doz. heath brushes, 6 doz. wooden pipes £7 13s 4d. William Didsbury: 1600 ells canvas £40 (14 May). [f. 152] Robert Cage: 1800 ells canvas £45.

517. *Kylleard* of Dieppe Martin Duhard
[f. 151*b*] Thomas Byckner: 2 tuns French wine *net* 1 tun 3*s* (13 May 1568).

518. *Ark* of Amsterdam (50) Cornilis Laurence; Amsterdam
[f. 151*b*] Robert Taylor: 40 cwt hops £20 (13 May 1568).

519. *World* of Amsterdam Albert Garretson
[f. 152] William Long: 12 cwt hops 6*s* [*sic*][1] (14 May 1568).

> 1. The valuation should be £6.

520. *Grehound* of Antwerp (30) Edward Paules; Antwerp
[f. 152] John Spencer: 6 cwt hops £3 (15 May 1568). John Boorne: 20 doz. thou. pins, 2 grs knives, 4 doz. crewel pieces, 6 doz. thou. needles, 8 grs minikins, 40 grs coarse bells, 30 doz. lbs bottom thread, 6 grs halfpenny-ware glasses, 4 grs pennyware glasses, 2 thou. thimbles £38 10*s* (17 May). John Colmer: 6 cwt hops £3. Thomas Welffcrast: 1 cwt flocks[1] 13*s* 4*d* (19 May). Frank Adams: 6 cwt hops, 2 cwt flocks £4 6*s* 8*d*. [f. 157*b*] Edward Hardingworth: 6 half-brls steel £36 (20 May).

> 1. The Book of Rates lists flocks for the subsidy outwards only; the charge was the same as here.

521. *Michell* of Flushing (14) P. Peterson
[f. 152] John Edmunds: 240 lings, 480 coal-fish £12 (15 May 1568).

522. *John Bonadventure* of London (60) Richard Say; Antwerp
[f. 152*b*] Thomas Bressie: 84 pcs Genoa fustian £56 (17 May 1568). William Salkins: 16 cwt Cologne hemp £16. John Elietts: 6 doz. lbs crewel, 50 lbs unwrought inkle, 10 grs morris and horse bells, 1 doz. crewel pieces, 12½ pcs coarse short carpets, 1 cwt coarse pack thread £13 10*s*. John Borne: 5 cwt hemp £5. George Breme: 12 cwt frying pans, 3 cwt kettle bands £10. William Elkin: 15 pcs Holland cloth £18. Richard Hills: 20 cwt Cologne hemp £20. Edward Bright: 18 cwt iron pans, 100 iron doubles, 2 cwt iron plates, 32 chimney backs £24 6*s* 8*d*. John Spencer: 3 qrs cloves, 8 cwt bay berries, 150 bundles brown paper £29 1*s* 8*d*. John Mun: 6 cwt flax, 3½ cwt pack thread, 10 doz. lbs bottom thread £11 13*s* 4*d*. Thomas Randall: 90 lbs cochineal £15. Robert Exton: 15 cwt madder £10. John Pasfyld: 7 cwt iron pans, 80 iron doubles £7 6*s* 8*d*. Francis Waight: 66 pcs Genoa fustian £44. Edmund Burton: 7 grs small files, 1 doz. chisels, 2 grs carving tools, 60 lbs curtain rings, 4 thou. awl blades, 8 doz. whip-saws, 6 doz. two-hand-saws, 2 pair latten andirons £25 5*s*. William Towerson: 550 ells hair tapestry, 2 cwt hops £28 10*s*. Roland Erlington: 25 doz. lbs Oudenaarde thread, 10 doz. lbs bottom thread, 24 grs harp strings £20 13*s* 4*d* (18 May). John Car: iron-works ad valorem £20. Alexander Sherington: 260 yds taffeta £86 13*s* 4*d*. Thomas Eaton: 3 doz. thou. needles, 6 thou. pack needles, 3 doz. lbs wrought inkle, 20 grs morris bells, 4 doz. crewel pieces, 10 doz. lbs bottom thread, ½ cwt pack thread £16 13*s* 4*d*. Edward Ocleshaw: 48 lbs silk £48. Lawrence Withers: 24 cwt madder £16. Thomas

Davie: 1 half-brl head nails, 1 hhd small nails £10. Thomas Manship: 28 cwt hops £14. John Barker: 70 pcs fustian, 30 pcs narrow worsted £61 13s 4d. William Luddington: 12 cwt madder, 7 cwt bay berries, 15 cwt argol, 5 cwt aniseed £38 10s. William Sherington: 2 bales fustian, 80 yds taffeta, 20 lbs silk £76 13s 4d. George Stockmed: 5 cwt flax, 100 bundles brown paper £8 6s 8d. Thomas Daunster: 40 pcs Holland cloth £48. Edmund Smith: 2 bales Ulm fustian, 45 pcs watered camlet, 30 pcs mockado £95 (19 May). Thomas Cranfild: 56 half-pcs Genoa fustian £18 13s 4d. John Lambert: 24 cwt iron pans £16. Henry Becher: 109 doz. thou. paper pins £18 3s 4d. William Barret: 1 half-brl head nails, 1 half-brl small nails, 100 iron doubles £9 6s 8d. Roger Warfild: 400 lbs pepper, 2 brls litmus, 8 cwt aniseed, 4 cwt hops £50 13s 4d. Roger Knott: 21 cwt dripping pans £14. Thomas Castlin: 7½ cwt sugar £25. Hugh Bradborne: 60 cwt madder, 5 cwt brazil £15 16s 8d. Thomas Gryme: 50 pcs Holland cloth £60. Francis Warrin: 40 cwt madder £26 13s 4d. William Hewet: 178 half-pcs Genoa fustian, 6 cwt single white plates £64 6s 8d. William Hobbs: 7 doz. Ghentish carpets, 226 ells coarse hair tapestry, 11 doz. lince, 200 Turnhout ticks, 3½ doz. Ghentish beds, 17 lince £99 2s 6d. Thomas Blanck: 80 pcs Genoa fustian £53 6s 8d. Thomas Hale: 2½ cwt gum arabic, pumice-stone ad valorem 6s 8d, 1 lb green ginger, 4 lbs epithyme, 4 lbs cucumber seed £4 2s 8d. Richard Pipe: 50 pcs mockado £33 6s 8d. Edmund Hugen: 70 pcs fustian £46 13s 4d. John Gresham: 85 yds velvet, 27 yds taffeta £72 15s. John Gresham: 85 yds velvet, 27 yds taffeta, 25 doz. yds Cyprus cotton £77 15s. Anthony Brinckle: 300 yds Bruges satin £30 (20 May). Robert Bey: 3 bales fustian, 56 lbs ferret silk £64 3s 4d. Vincent Randall: 42 pcs narrow worsted £21. Thomas Parker: 1 bale Ulm fustian £15. Nicholas Hewet: 2 cwt single plates, 8 half-pcs Genoa fustian, 10 cwt wrought flax £15 6s 8d. Francis Keightly: 30 yds velvet, 120 yds Levant taffeta £30 10s. John Isham: 30 pcs broad worsted, 60 pcs mockado, 80 yds damask, 70 pcs Genoa fustian £148 13s 4d. Henry Smyth: 14 doz. lbs inkle, 10 lbs Bruges silk, 20 doz. yds Cyprus cotton, 10 lbs raw silk £26 13s 4d. William Perry: 300 lbs pepper, 40 lbs wormseed, 20 lbs senna £30 10s. Robert Luce: 60 pcs mockado £40 (21 May). [f. 158b] William Smith: 16 pcs Milan fustian, 60 pcs boultel £28 (22 May).

523. *Trinity* of Erith (50) William Ferris; Antwerp
[f. 152b] Thomas Bressie: 30 pcs broad worsted £30 (17 May 1568). Thomas Collimer: 30 doz. thou. pins, 10 doz. lbs bottom thread, 5 doz. lbs checks, 8 pcs dornick £14 16s 8d. Ancelm Becket: 3½ cwt hops £7 15s. George Breme: 14 cwt frying pans £9 6s 8d. Edward Bright: 18 cwt iron pans, 100 iron doubles, 1 ton 13 cwt iron £23 5s. William Salkins: 12 cwt Cologne hemp £12. John Pasfyld: 10 cwt battery, 20 iron chimney backs £21 13s 4d. Richard Billingsley: 6 doz. lbs thread, 12 doz. lbs bottom thread, 50 doz. thou. pins, 40 grs harp strings £18 (18 May). John Car: 3 cwt varnish, 8 cwt iron plates £10 6s 8d. Alexander Sherington: 220 yds taffeta £73 6s 8d. Thomas Eaton: 3 doz. lbs crewel, 6 doz. crewel pieces, 2 doz. lbs wrought inkle, 15 doz. thou. needles, 2 grs coarse hat bands, 6 lbs clavichord wire, 2 thou. thimbles, 2 pcs dornick £25 1s 8d. Thomas Davie: 18 cwt madder £12. Lawrence Withers: 16 cwt madder £10 13s 4d.

Thomas Manship: 24 cwt hops £12. William Sherington: 2 bales Ulm fustian, 200 yds taffeta £96 13s 4d. Hugh Bradborne: 64 cwt madder £42 13s 4d. Edward Ockleshaw: 40 lbs silk £40. William Luddington: 33 cwt madder, 225 lbs bay oil £25. Thomas Daunster: 20 pcs Holland cloth, 12 grs knives £40. George Stockmed: 200 bundles brown paper £6 13s 4d. John Barker: 70 pcs Genoa fustian £46 13s 4d. Henry Becher: 69 doz. thou. paper-pins, 15 doz. lbs bottom thread, 10 doz. worsted checks, 16 pcs canvas striped with crewel £25. William Goodwyn: 150 yds satin, 30 yds damask £67 10s (19 May). William Tench: 1 half-brl head nails, 1 half-brl small nails £6. Roger Knott: 30 cwt iron pans £20. Roger Warfild: 20 cwt bay berries, 4 cwt ireos, 7 cwt hops £20 16s 8d. John Whit: 14 doz. lbs worsted yarn £11 13s 4d. Nicholas Hewet: 15 cwt madder, 10 cwt frying pans, 2 cwt single white plates £14. Thomas Thorp: 12 cwt hops, 400 lbs crossbow thread £14 13s 4d. Richard Billam: 56 cwt madder £27 6s 8d. John Lambert: 18 cwt iron pans £12. Francis Warren: 60 cwt woad £40. William Hobbs: 9 cwt wrought flax £9 5s. Thomas Blanck: 80 pcs Genoa fustian £53 6s 8d. Thomas Hale: 650 lbs pepper, 160 lbs ginger £66 3s 4d. Edmund Hugen: 70 pcs fustian £46 13s 4d. George Bence: 8 cwt battery £16. William Hewet: 5 cwt white plates, 5 cwt wrought flax £8 6s 8d (20 May). Anthony Fytton: 2½ cwt aniseed, drugs ad valorem 32s £5 16s 8d. Martin Wood: 20 lbs thrown silk, 24 lbs Spanish silk, 2 lbs chain-lace £40. John Isham: 80 pcs Genoa fustian, 120 ells sarcenet, 30 pcs narrow worsted £88 6s 8d. Vincent Randall: 30 pcs narrow worsted, 6 pcs camlet, 6 pcs mockado £25. Edmund Hill: 50 lbs cinnamon, 16 lbs mace, 10 lbs wormseed £16 6s 8d. William Perry: 4 cwt aniseed, 150 lbs pepper, 30 lbs senna £21 8s 4d. Robert Bye: 5 cwt wrought flax, 30 pcs canvas with thread, 20 pcs thread dornick, 30 half-pcs Genoa fustian £31 13s 4d (22 May). Thomas Parker: 60 pcs canvas striped with thread, 12 pcs thread dornick £24. [f. 159] William Smyth: 150 butts thread, 40 pcs boultel £23.

524. *Falcon* of Dordrecht (30) Adrian Dottell; Dordrecht
[f. 152b] John Borne: 22 cwt white plates, 16 cwt latten plates £37 6s 8d (17 May 1568). [f. 154] Cornelis Nollet: 24 awms Rhenish wine 24s (18 May).

525. *William Bonadventure* of London (80) Thomas Lawson; Bordeaux
[f. 153] Thomas Pen: 25½ cwt woad £17 (17 May 1568).

526. *Jesus* of London (80) John Clerk; Bourgneuf
[f. 153] Thomas Robley: 60 weys great salt £60 (17 May 1568).

527. *Mary Edward* of London (60) Edward Maister; St. Martin
[f. 153b] Robert Fryer: 37 weys bay salt £37 (17 May 1568). [f. 157] Richard Pipe: 3 weys bay salt £3 (19 May).

528. *Pellican* of Antwerp William Adrianson
[f. 155] Humphrey Toy: 10 reams unbound books £1 (18 May 1568).
[f. 158b] Edward Hardannaght: 6 half-brls steel £36 (21 May).

529. *Egle* of Antwerp A. Cornilis
[f. 156*b*] Thomas Hale: 100 bundles brown paper £3 3*s* 4*d* (19 May 1568).
[f. 159] Henry Smyth: 20 lbs Bruges silk, 12 pcs Rennes boultel, 12 doz. lbs
thread £18 5*s*. (22 May).

530. *Spledegle* of Antwerp (22) Barnard Peters; Antwerp
[f. 157] Richard Hill: 23¾ cwt Cologne hemp £23 15*s* (19 May 1568).
Edward Hardingworth: 6 half-brls steel £36 (20 May). Edward Hardingworth: 6 half-brls steel £36. [f. 158] John Jackman: 200 bundles brown
paper £6 13*s* 4*d*.

531. *Spledegle* of Dordrecht (50) Godfrey Derickson; Dordrecht
[f. 158*b*] Reynold Thirling: 134 cwt hemp £134 (22 May 1568). Richard
Hills: 38½ cwt hemp £38 10*s* (24 May). Reynold Thirling: 85 awms
Rhenish wine 85*s* (25 May). [f. 159] Bartholomew Broune: 29 awms
Rhenish wine 29*s*.

532. *Little Bark* of Danzig Hans Lang; Danzig
[f. 159*b*] William Conrad: 6 cwt estrige wool £5 (26 May 1568).

533. *Lawrance* of Plymouth (30) John Haies; Biscay
[f. 159*b*] William Hawkes: 40 thou. oranges and lemons £13 6*s* 8*d* (26 May
1568).

534. *Saviour* of Aldeburgh (50) Thomas Beversham; Port St. Mary
[f. 159*b*] Thomas Walker: 80 butts sack *net* 72 butts 108*s* (26 May 1568).
Nicholas Wydnall: 3 butts sack 4*s* 6*d* (31 May). [f. 162] William Bond:
16 cwt aniseed £26 13*s* 4*d*.

535. *Grace of God* of Lee (30) John Stevens; Rouen
[f. 159*b*] Robert Fryer: 4 tuns Gascony wine *net* 3½ tuns 10*s* 6*d* (26 May
1568). Henry Waite: 3 tuns Gascony wine *net* 2½ tuns 7*s* 6*d* (27 May).
William Hobson: 6 grs crewel lace, 4 sum saddler's nails £4 15*s* 8*d*. Richard
Billam: 6 doz. small iron pots £1 10*s*. John de Soles: 4 tuns French wine
net 3 tuns 9*s*, 1 tun corrupt wine £3. Oliver Fisher: 300 ells packing canvas,
1 puncheon vinegar, 200 ells broad cushion canvas, 160 butts Lyons thread
£25 15*s*. [f. 160] Anthony Gamage: 1 tun vinegar £2 6*s* 8*d* (29 May).

536. *Margaret* of Amsterdam (30) Roger Cornilis; Amsterdam
[f. 159*b*] Alard Bartinck: 40 firkins sturgeon £26 13*s* 4*d* (27 May 1568).

537. *James* of Aldeburgh (36) Robert Beversham; Brouage
[f. 159*b*] Robert Beversham: 20 weys great salt £20 (27 May 1568).

538. *Mary fortune* of London (28) Richard Mills; Brouage
[f. 159*b*] Richard Mills: 20 weys great salt £20 (27 May 1568).

539. *Grace of God* of Lee (60) Thomas Boyse; Antwerp
[f. 160] George Breame: 8 cwt frying pans £5 6*s* 8*d* (29 May 1568). William

Salkins: 42¼ cwt hemp, 925 ells packing canvas £54 11s 8d. Richard Hills: 30 cwt hemp £30. Richard Billam: 12 cwt hops £6 (31 May). John Pasfild: 1 half-brl small nails, 1 quarter-brl head nails, 7 cwt frying pans, 6 doz. white halbert heads at 10s the dozen, 4 doz. wooden beams £14 13s 4d. Robert Broke: 24 cwt hops £12. Thomas Davy: 5½ cwt flax £5 10s. Thomas Daunster: 15 cwt estrige wool £12 10s. John Eliets: 5 doz. weaver's shuttles, 6 doz. lbs bottom thread, 8 doz. thou. pins, 10 thou. awl blades, 3 doz. lbs crewel, 4 doz. lbs Bruges thread, 5 doz. thread pieces, 3 doz. crewel pieces, 10 grs horse bells, 30 lbs unwrought inkle £18 18s 4d. George Stockmed: 100 doz. hemp £12 10s. John Carr: 32 cwt iron pans, 25 cwt 'ames' iron £27 11s. John Borne: 1 thou. trenchers, 4 grs halfpennyware comb brushes, 4 grs pennyware comb brushes, 2 grs hair brushes £6 13s 4d. William Towerson: 260 ells wool tapestry, 1½ doz. Ghentish carpets £15 5s. John Jackman: 425 lbs ginger £31 18s. Edmund Smyth: 12 cwt woad, 2 bales Ulm fustian £38. John Coniers: 3 bales Ulm fustian £45. Nicholas Hewet: 370 hand-doubles £12 6s 8d. Ancelm Becket: 6 cwt flax £6. Thomas Brasie: 97 pcs Genoa fustian, 98 yds velvet £138 3s 4d (1 June). Thomas Gardyner: 2½ cwt aniseed, 50 lbs quicksilver, 200 lbs pepper £25 1s 8d. Randal Manning: 16 pcs Holland cloth £19 3s 4d. Thomas Aldersey: 60 pcs mockado, 145 yds velvet £148. William Luddington: 19 cwt estrige wool, 7 cwt aniseed, 36 lbs cloves, 3 cwt brimstone £35 3s 4d. William Elkin: 144 yds frizado £36. John Colymer: 60 lbs mace, 450 lbs ginger, 450 lbs pepper £91 5s. Richard Hill: 50 single pcs Genoa fustian £33 6s 8d. Edward Jackman: 550 lbs pepper, 4 cwt aniseed, 6 cwt bay berries, 36 cwt mull-madder £59 13s 4d. Thomas Parker: 27 pcs wool dornick, 1 bale Ulm fustian £28 10s. Thomas Longston: 200 lbs pepper, 28 cwt hops £30 13s 4d. Henry Becher: 50 doz. thou. pins, 20 doz. lbs bottom pack thread, 20 pcs canvas striped with thread, 14 doz. worsted checks £26. Thomas Starkey: 600 ells canvas £12. Roger Ramsey: 16 cwt madder £10 13s 4d. John Sutton: 98 Turnhout ticks, 7 doz. lince, 330 ells hair tapestry, 3 counterfeit Turnhout ticks £49 18s. Thomas Rose: 4 bales fustian £60 (2 June). Thomas Randall: 60 lbs ferret silk, 10 doz. yds Cyprus cotton £20 16s 8d. John Spencer: 2 cwt aniseed, 200 lbs pepper, 150 lbs ginger, 40 lbs wormseed, 106 doz. hemp £48 6s 8d. William Gifford: 2½ pcs stammel £25. William Smyth: 30 pcs broad worsted £30. Thomas Hale: 6 cwt hops, 2 cwt red lead, 2 lbs manna, 30 lbs nigella, 40 lbs cloves £18 10s. Roger Warfild: 4 cwt hops, 8 cwt sumach, 4 hd paper £40 13s 4d (3 June). Henry Becher: 11 cwt wrought flax £11. Anthony Fytton: 7 cwt liquorice, 200 lbs cotton wool £10 3s 4d. Edmund Hill: 11 cwt sugar £5 10s. John Isham: 20 pcs mockado, 20 pcs narrow worsted, 30 pcs canvas striped with thread, 42 half-pcs Genoa fustian, 48 yds frizado £59 6s 8d. Edmund Smyth: 6 pcs grogram camlet £8. Sir William Chester: 35 cwt panele and molasses £17 10s. Stephen Slany: 9 pcs 'greens and blues'[1] £6 (4 June). [f. 168] Nicholas Luddington: 17½ cwt madder £11 6s 8d (5 June).

---

1. Probably dornick cloth. Green dornick is listed but not blue in the Book of Rates.

540. *Marygold* of Lee (70) John Wilson; Antwerp
[f. 160] Edmund Burton: 9 cwt iron thread, 8 grs small files at 10*s*, 6 doz. dog chains, 60 lbs counters, 16 cwt frying pans, 48 doz. coarse sword blades £63 3*s* 4*d* (29 May 1568). Henry Becher: 109 doz. thou. pins, 203 yds taffeta, 200 half-pcs Genoa fustian £152 10*s*. John Lambert: 13 cwt battery £26. Gerson Hills: 38 cwt hemp £38. Richard Hills: 41 cwt hemp £41. John Pasfilde: 1 half-brl small nails, 1 quarter-brl head nails, 100 iron doubles £8 6*s* 8*d* (31 May). Roger Knott: 7 cwt battery £14. Thomas Daunster: 220 doz. thou. pins £36 13*s* 4*d*. John Kelk: 48 doz. thou. pins, 8 doz. thou. needles £16. John Car: 32 cwt iron pans, 110 iron doubles, 5 cwt fireshovel plates £28 6*s* 8*d*. Richard Billingsley: 20 lbs silk nobs, [   ][1] harp strings, 5 doz. lbs Bruges thread, 20 doz. thou. pins, 20 doz. lbs bottom pack thread £14 13*s* 4*d*. John Jackman: 525 lbs ginger £39 6*s* 8*d*. Nicholas Hewet: 15 pair andirons, 2½ doz. fireshovels and tongs £6. Randal Manning: 1½ cwt aniseed £2 (1 June). Thomas Aldersey: 65 pcs grogram camlet, 57 yds grogram silk £105 13*s* 4*d*. William Sherington: 56 yds taffeta £18 13*s* 4*d*. Anthony Warfild: 400 lbs pepper £33 6*s* 8*d*. William Luddington: 20 cwt estrige wool, 16 lbs mace, 5 cwt aniseed £30 6*s* 8*d*. Edward Jackman: 300 lbs pepper, 4 cwt bay berries, 2 cwt aniseed, 36 cwt mull-madder £34 16*s* 8*d*. William Elkin: 144 yds frizado £36. John Hutton: 39 doz. thou. pins, 10 lbs ferret silk, 8 lbs Bruges silk £13 10*s*. Thomas Parker: 2 bales Ulm fustian £30. Thomas Longston: 200 lbs pepper, 26 cwt hops £29 13*s* 4*d*. Francis Keighly: 46 pcs Ghentish cloth £55 3*s* 4*d*. John Sutton: 54 Turnhout ticks, 80 counterfeit Turnhout ticks £44 13*s* 4*d*. Thomas Randall: 125 yds velvet £113 15*s*. Edward Bright: 2 half-brls small nails, 3 doz. whip-saws, 5 doz. two-hand-saws, 10 doz. hand-saws £15 16*s* 8*d*. Thomas Eaton: 3 doz. lbs inkle, 1 grs thread lace, 2 doz. crewel pieces, 3 doz. lbs crewel, 4 grs horse bells, 8 grs minikins, 2 doz. lbs bottom pack thread, 15 grs halfpennyware glasses, 1 doz. thou. needles, 1 thou. thimbles, 40 pcs mockado £42 18*s* 4*d*. John Mun: 250 ells [*sic*] pack thread £3 6*s* 8*d* (2 June). Alexander Sherington: 160 yds taffeta, 30 lbs Genoa silk £83 6*s* 8*d*. John Spencer: 35 lbs mace, 1½ cwt turmeric, 46 lbs nutmegs £24 6*s* 8*d*. William Smyth: 46 pcs narrow worsted £46. Thomas Hale: 420 lbs pepper £35. John Woodward: 140 yds velvet, 14 pcs sackcloth, 19 half-pcs[2] striped canvas £143 3*s* 4*d*. Christopher Jewkes: 8 pcs Holland cloth £9 8*s* 4*d*. Roger Warfild: 4 cwt hops, 400 lbs matches, 3 cwt caraway seed £8 6*s* 8*d* (3 June). Anthony Fytton: 7 cwt liquorice, 200 lbs cotton wool £10 3*s* 4*d*. John Collymer: 8 cwt sumach, 5 cwt flax £10 6*s* 8*d*. Edmund Smyth: 40 yds Genoa satin £18. John Isham: 72 yds frizado, 40 pcs narrow worsted, 20 pcs mockado, 34 half-pcs Genoa fustian £62 13*s* 4*d*. Thomas Brasy: 36 yds frizado, 30 pcs thread dornick, 10 pcs narrow worsted £24. Thomas Rose: 5 cwt wrought flax, 30 half-pcs Genoa fustian £15. Sir William Chester: 35 cwt panele molasses £17 10*s*. Richard Hills: 36 pcs canvas striped with thread, 60 half-pcs Genoa fustian £32 [f. 167] Robert Turvill: 60 yds satin £27.

    1. Blank.   2. Or 19½ pcs.

541. *Crown Dorne* of Antwerp John Johnson; Antwerp
[f. 160] John Spencer: 28 cwt hops £14 (29 May 1568). Humphrey Toy:

20 reams unbound books £2 (31 May). John Colmer: 28 cwt hops £14. Alard Bartrinck: 36 cwt hops £18. George Lubkin: 1500 ells Osnabrücks £20. Richard May: 120 yds Spanish taffeta £24 (1 June). [f. 167] Peter Bowlan: 2½ grs German knives, 3 grs coarse wrought knives without hafts £8 5s (3 June).

542. *Jonas* of Flushing (24) Jacob Stoffles; Flushing
[f. 160] Richard Storey: 720 lings, 10 brls fish £29 (29 May 1568).

543. *Lion* of Amsterdam (30) Raire Cornilis; Amsterdam
[f. 160b] John Smith: 4 weys Rhenish glass £10 (29 May 1568).

544. *Swan* of Rotterdam (25) Henrick Johnson; Rotterdam
[f. 160b] John Benet: 39 cwt hops £19 10s (29 May 1568).

545. *Michell* of Flushing (14) Peter Claison; Flushing
[f. 160b] Humphrey Keel: 5 lasts fish, 120 lings £34 (29 May 1568).

546. *Ass* of Antwerp (40) John Jasper; Antwerp
[f. 161] Alard Bartrinck: 36 cwt hops £18 (31 May 1568). John Car: 56 iron chimney backs £9 6s 8d. John Jackman: 100 bundles brown paper £3 6s 8d. George Lubkin: 1500 ells Osnabrücks £20. Henry Alward: 24 doz. lbs Oudenaarde thread £16 (1 June). Edward Hardingworth: 6 half-brls steel £36. Hartik van Sprecleson: 16 cwt estrige wool £13 6s 8d. [f. 167] Peter Rowland: 4 doz. sword blades £2 13s 4d (3 June).

547. *Croune* of Bergen-op-Zoom (30) Govert Albright; Bergen-op-Zoom
[f. 161b] George Stockmed: 5 cwt wrought flax £5 (31 May 1568). Nicholas Hewet: 6½ cwt flax £6 10s. Ancelm Becket: 19½ cwt flax £19 10s. Robert Luce: 7 cwt wrought flax £7 (1 June). William Hobs: 1½ lasts rape oil, 5 cwt flax £29. Henry Duce: 6 cwt flax £6. Randal Starkey: 6½ cwt tow £2 3s 4d (2 June). [f. 167] Phillip Harper: 13 weys white salt, 3 weys bay salt £20 6s 8d (3 June).

548. *Angell* of Bruges (60) Lucas Albright; Bruges
[f. 162b] Thomas Brasie: 162 pcs buckram £36 (1 June 1568). Thomas Howse: 45 pcs bustian £30. Owen Rydley: 200 lbs silk nobs £6 13s 4d (2 June). [f. 166] William Barnard: 60 cwt madder £40 (3 June).

549. *Falcon* of Amsterdam (28) Alard Allardson
[f. 164b] John Edmunds: 18 brls fish £9 (1 June 1568). John Violet: 1200 lings, 12 brls fish £46. Thomas Sandford: 600 lings £20. [f. 166b] Alard Bartrinck: 1500 ells Osnabrücks £20 (3 June).

550. *Fortune* of Aldeburgh (60) Thomas Johnson; La Rochelle
[f. 165] Thomas Johnson: 43 weys great salt £43 (2 June 1568).

551. *Bark Bond* of London (70) John Benet; Cadiz
[f. 165] William Bond: 115 butts sack *net* 103 butts 310s (2 June 1568).

552. *Pellican* of Königsberg (100) Albert Rode; Königsberg
[f. 166] Luder van Dorne: 54 lasts pitch, 14½ lasts tar, 9 lasts soap ashes, 12 half-packs flax, 1 quintal wax £215 (3 June 1568). [f. 166*b*] William Vaughan 'et sociis': 12 lasts pitch, 1 last tar, 1 pack 1 half-pack flax, 83 cwt cordage £97 6*s* 8*d*.

553. *Pellican* of London (40) Henry Wright; Cadiz
[f. 167*b*] Anthony Pilboro: 15 butts sack *net* 13 butts 19*s* 3*d* (4 June 1568). John Bird: 6 butts sack *net* 6 butts 9*s*. John Chaplin: 9 butts sack *net* 8 butts 12*s*. Hector Nonns: 19 butts sack *net* 17 butts 25*s* 6*d*. [f. 168] Thomas Garret: 8 butts sack *net* 8 butts 12*s* (5 June).

554. *Mereman* of Amsterdam (34) Dirick Simonson; Haarlem
[f. 167*b*] Richard Mouse: 6 lasts barrelled fish, 120 lings £40 (5 June 1568). Thomas Sanford: 960 staplefish, 1 last barrelled fish £18. [f. 168*b*] Court Ellers: 7 half-packs flax £28 (10 June).

555. *Mary george* of London Robert Osburn; Rouen
[f. 168] Richard Morris: 1400 ells canvas, 1 tun vinegar £37 6*s* 8*d* (10 June 1568). Anthony Gamage: 2600 ells canvas £65. John Allot: 2800 ells canvas £70. Matthew Colclogh: 1250 ells canvas £31 5*s*. Francis Benizen: 3500 ells canvas £86 5*s*. John Bodleigh: 1900 ells canvas £31 3*s* 4*d*. Henry Wayt: 5 doz. iron pots £1 5*s*. Robert Sadler: 1600 ells canvas £40. Richard Patrick: 120 reams paper, 35 doz. woolcards £33 10*s*. John Harding: 4 tuns French wine *net* 3 tuns 9*s*. Henry Buxton: 1850 ells canvas £46 5*s* (11 June). Humphrey Broune: 11 grs crewel chain-lace, 2 thou. pack needles, 4 grs inkhorns, 3 qrs pack thread £11. Hugh Offley: 500 ells canvas £12 10*s*. Anthony Cage: 1600 ells canvas £40. John Harding: 500 ells canvas £12 10*s*. Robert Broke: 2700 ells coarse canvas £36. John Myller: 300 ells canvas £7 10*s*. Thomas Starkey: 900 ells canvas £22 10*s*. [f. 171] John Baptist: 2 tuns French wine 6*s* (12 June).

556. *Marygold* of London Thomas Andros; Rouen
[f. 168] Richard Morris: 800 ells canvas £20 (10 June 1568). Oliver Fisher: 700 ells canvas £17 10*s*. Robert Broke: 1800 ells canvas £45. Matthew Colcloghe: 1250 ells canvas £31 5*s*. Francis Benizen: 850 ells canvas £21 5*s*. John Bodleigh: 1400 ells brown canvas £35. Henry Wayt: 24 doz. woolcards, 5 doz. iron pots £13 5*s*. John Raynes: 750 ells canvas £18 15*s*. William Handford: 120 reams paper £16. Edmund Ansell: 280 yds French dornick, 5 doz. buckrams £21. Robert Sadler: 220 ells canvas £55. Richard Patrick: 120 reams paper, 35 doz. woolcards, 12 grs combs, 6 grs ink-horns £39 10*s*. Wolston Dixi: 1700 ells Normandy canvas £42 10*s* (11 June). Robert Cage: 600 ells canvas £15. William Hobson: 8 doz. French buck-rams, 2 cwt French pack thread £15 6*s* 8*d*. Thomas Cordell: 13 doz. buckrams £19 10*s*. Humphrey Broune: 30 reams paper £4. Hugh Offley: 500 ells canvas £12 10*s*. Anthony Cage: 2500 ells canvas £62 10*s*. John Harding: 2200 ells canvas £55. John Allot: 3200 ells packing canvas £42 13*s* 4*d*. John Myller: 1500 ells canvas £37 10*s*. Anthony Gamage: 3100 ells packing canvas £41 6*s* 8*d*. Arthur Hannson: 2200 ells canvas £55 (12 June). [f. 171] John Ollyff: 3200 ells canvas £80.

557. *Jonas* of Newcastle (70) Walter Bayly; Danzig
[f. 168*b*] William Cockin: 3 packs bale-flax £24 (10 June 1568). Robert
Bayly: 1 pack flax, 5 tons faggot iron £33. Robert Hilson: 36 cwt cordage
£24. Ezekiel Best: 2 packs flax £16. George Milner: 1½ packs and 2 cwt
flax, 40 cwt cordage £40. Richard Gurney: 5 tons Spanish iron, 10 quarter-
packs flax £40 (11 June). Thomas Allen: 3 packs flax £24. Edmund
Boldero: 120 bales flax £7 (12 June). [f. 173*b*] Thomas Randall:[1] 2125
wainscots, 4800 clapholt, 3½ lasts tar, 1 last pitch £106 (17 June).

> 1. Entered under the *Jonas*, master [John] Read (see **560**). The cargo is obviously
> more appropriate here.

558. *Hart* of London (110) Thomas King; Spain
[f. 169] Thomas Altham: 16 pipes oil *net* 15 pipes £37 10*s* (10 June 1568).
John Spencer: 20 pipes Seville oil *net* 17 pipes £68. John Spark: 10 doz.
Spanish skins £30 (11 June). William Crompton: 5 tuns Seville oil *net*
4½ tuns £36. Thomas Cordell: 6 tuns Seville oil *net* 5½ tuns £44. Edward
Jackman: 20 pipes Seville oil *net* 18 pipes £72. Christopher Hodson:
50 tuns oil *net* 45 tuns £225. John Cooper: 1 tun Seville oil £8 (14 June).
[f. 171*b*] John Gill: 29 doz. felt hats £19 6*s* 8*d* (15 June).

559. *Fortune* of Königsberg (120) Joachim Bred; Königsberg
[f. 171] Joachim Bred: 1000 wainscots, 2400 clapholt, 2 lasts tar, 2 lasts
pitch, 1 quarter-pack flax, 30 bundles bast-ropes, 1 shock bast-ropes £64
(12 June 1568). Luder van Dorne: 6 lasts soap ashes, 5 lasts tar, 2 half-
packs flax, 12 lasts 10 brls pitch £61 13*s* 4*d*.

560. *Spredegle* of Amsterdam (40) John Read; Amsterdam
[f. 171] John Vyolet: 5 lasts barrelled fish, 120 lings £34 (12 June 1568).
Thomas Sandford: 3 lasts barrelled fish £18. [f. 171*b*] John Smith: 6 weys
Rhenish glass £15 (14 June).

561. *Black egle* of Amsterdam (30) Cornilis Fredrickson; Amsterdam
[f. 171*b*] Richard Mouse: 8 lasts fish, 200 staplefish £51 (14 June 1568).

562. *Michell* of Flushing (14) Peter Peterson
[f. 171*b*] Humphrey Keile: 360 lings £14 (14 June 1568).

563. *Daniell* of Danzig (200) Hans Grote; Danzig
[f. 171*b*] Alard Bartrinck: 13 firkins sturgeon £8 13*s* 4*d* (15 June 1568).
Edmund Boldero: 3 packs flax £24 (16 June). Robert Hilson: 1 pack flax,
2400 clapholt, 1 shock deals, 8 bundles chests[1] £24 10*s*. William Jamys:
5 packs flax £40. William Cockin: 5 packs flax, 18 cwt feathers, 10 lasts
tar £87. Thomas Allyn: 10 lasts tar, 240 oars, 6 packs flax £76. Gervais
Simons: 30 lasts pitch £60. George Mylner: 3 packs flax, 7 lasts tar, 30
chests, 60 basts £45 3*s* 4*d*. Richard Gurney: 2 packs flax £16. Dunstan
Walton: 23 lasts pitch £46 (17 June). Robert Barker: 2 packs flax £16.
Robert Collet: 3 packs flax, 1 half-shock deals, 200 wainscots £35 15*s*
(18 June). Thomas Russell: 2 packs hemp,[2] 4 lasts 4 brls pitch, 93 Danzig
chests £69 6*s* 8*d*. Michael Rozenberch: 15 lasts pitch £30 (23 June).

[f. 177*b*] Jerome Rise: 2 half-packs 1 quarter-pack flax, 2400 clapholt, 60 spruce deals £23 10*s*.

    1. Or 4½ nests.
    2. By the sack of 3 cwt in the Book of Rates.

564. *Rose* of Danzig (200) Hans White; Danzig
[f. 171*b*] Alard Bartrinck: 16 firkins sturgeon £10 13*s* 4*d* (15 June 1568). Edmund Boldero: 1 pack flax £8 (16 June). William Cockin: 102 cwt cordage, 3 packs flax, 15 lasts pitch, 10 lasts tar £142. Richard Lewys: 2 packs flax £16. John More: 10 lasts pitch, 9 lasts tar £38. Thomas Allyn: 20 lasts pitch, 10 lasts tar, 5 packs flax, 100 wainscots £104. Gervais Simons: 2 packs flax £16. George Mylner: 7 packs flax, 5 lasts pitch £66. William Franckland: 3 packs flax £24. Richard Gurney: 6 packs flax, 6 vats eels £60. Robert Collet: 5 packs flax, 3 lasts horn-tips, 360 soap boxes £49 10*s* (18 June). [f. 174] Thomas Russell: 17 lasts 2 brls pitch £34 6*s* 8*d*.

565. *Spledegle* of Antwerp (40) Joyes Daniell; Antwerp
[f. 171*b*] Thomas Brasie: 2 bales Ulm fustian £30 (15 June 1568). Thomas Parker: 22 pcs dornick wool £11 (16 June). Thomas Aldersey: 115 yds satin, 27 yds damask £96 1*s* 8*d*. Thomas Randall: 310 yds Levant taffeta £25 16*s* 8*d* (17 June). Thomas Eaton: 5 doz. Spanish skins, 4 doz. of thread [*sic*] £17 13*s* 4*d*. [f. 174*b*] Peter Roland: 9 doz. sword blades £6 (21 June).

566. *Fortune* of Flushing (22) Simon Yongenell
[f. 171*b*] Humphrey Keile: 360 lings £12 (15 June 1568).

567. *St. George* of Danzig (200) Jacob Wyldcat; Danzig
[f. 172] Edmund Boldero: 3 packs flax, 5 lasts pitch £34 (16 June 1568). William Jamys: 7 packs flax £56. Robert Hilson: 4 packs flax, 10 lasts pitch, 1 shock deals, 1200 clapholt, 480 soap boxes £67 16*s*. John More: 10 lasts pitch, 9 lasts tar £38. Richard Lewys: 2 packs flax £16. Gervais Simons: 4 packs flax £32. George Mylner: 3 packs flax, 7 lasts tar, 10 nests chests, 60 basts £45 3*s* 4*d*. Ezekiel Best: 3 packs flax £24 (17 June). Dunstan Walton: 60 cwt cordage £40. Robert Barker: 26 cwt cordage £17 6*s* 8*d*. Thomas Russell: 16½ lasts tar £33 (18 June). Matthew Hope: 3 vats eels £6 (19 June). [f. 190*b*] Alard Bartrinck: 13 lasts tar, 4 tons iron £46 (5 July).

568. *Angell* of Bergen-op-Zoom (30) Cornilis Adrianson
[f. 173*b*] Henry Bornes: 16 cwt oakum £4 (18 June 1568). Ancelm Becket: 12 cwt flax £12. William Bower: 6 cwt flax £6 (19 June). William Hewet: 6 cwt flax, 12 brls rape oil, 9 cwt oakum £24 5*s*. [f. 174] William Hobbs: 4¾ cwt flax £4 15*s*.

569. *John Evangelist* of Rochester (40) John Mardall; 'out of the *John Thomas* that came from Emden'.
[f. 173*b*] Francis Tooke: 104 cwt hops £52 (18 June 1568).

570. *Unicorn* of Nieuwpoort (24) Giles Lukes; Nieuwpoort
[f. 174] Thomas Kelley: 81 cwt hops £40 10*s* (18 June 1568).

571. *Unicorn* of Amsterdam (20) John Peterson; Arnemuiden
[f. 174*b*] Phillip Harper: 8 weys bay salt £8 (21 June 1568).

572. *Swan* of Antwerp (28) Adrian Zegarson; Antwerp
[f. 174*b*] Robert Broke: 58 cwt hops £29 (21 June 1568). Matthew Colcloghe: 9 lasts pitch £18 (22 June). William Cooper: 10 doz. coarse gloves, 50 yds 'garding' velvet, 1 grs hooks, 6 pcs tinsel, 6 citherns, 18 halbert heads, 1 bugle cost £2, 16 lbs white thread £55 16*s* 8*d* (25 June).
[f. 186] John Whit: 6 Cologne lutes £1 10*s* (1 July).

573. *Yongegle* of Antwerp Anthony Cornilis
[f. 174*b*] Robert Broke: 40 cwt hops £20 (21 June 1568).

574. *Prymrose* of Lee (60) John Clerk
[f. 174*b*] Robert Broke: 32 cwt hops £16 (22 June 1568). Richard Hills: 15 cwt hemp £15. John Lambert: 27 cwt battery £54. William Coles and John Newman: 20 cwt aniseed £33 6*s* 8*d*. George Breme: 10 cwt battery £20. John Car: ironmongers' ware ad valorem £20. Ancelm Becket: 16 cwt madder, 6 cwt flax £16 13*s* 4*d*. Edward Jackman: 1 last rape oil £16. Roger Warfyld: 4 brls ochre, 1500 lbs crossbow thread, 12 cwt alum, 10 cwt liquorice, 2 hd treacle £34 10*s*. Thomas Brasie: 1 bale Ulm fustian, 74 pcs mockado £64 6*s* 8*d* (23 June). William Hobbs: 753 ells hair tapestry, 8 doz. Ghentish beds, 9 doz. lince, 75 Turnhout ticks £66 3*s* 4*d*. Thomas Daunster: 100 doz. thou. pins, 15 doz. lbs Bruges thread, 3 doz. Beaupreau boultel, 5 doz. lbs bottom pack thread £34 18*s* 4*d*. John Alden: drugs ad valorem £5 6*s* 8*d*. Sir John York: 600 lbs pepper £50. John Isham: 80 Genoa fustian [*sic*], 100 pcs Genoa fustian, 60 pcs mockado £140. Thomas Gardener: 400 lbs pepper, 1½ cwt coriander seed, 200 lbs stavesacre £37 13*s* 4*d*. Humphrey Whitelock: 6½ doz. Turnhout ticks, 4 doz. and 1 counterfeit Turnhout ticks £42. Nicholas Hewet: 1 half-brl great head nails £2. Robert Exton: 4 hd 22 lbs copper wire, 15 ticks £13 5*s*. Alexander Sherington: 36 lbs silk, 80 yds sarcenet, 4 yds taffeta £76. George Colymer: 210 butts Paris thread, 24 pcs Beaupreau boultel, 12 doz. lbs bottom thread £28 3*s* 4*d*. Thomas Eaton: 10 doz. thou. pins, 1 grs pincers, 75 lbs counters, 6 doz. small hammers, 6 doz. lbs crewel, 4 doz. crewel pieces, 6 thou. awl blades, 4 doz. thou. needles £20. Richard Billingsley: 100 butts black thread, 10 doz. lbs bottom thread, 40 grs harp strings £14 13*s* 4*d*. Thomas Rose: 40 pcs mockado £26 13*s* 4*d*. Thomas Davie: 2½ tons iron, 10 cwt frying pans, 5 pair iron andirons, 5 cwt flax £25 16*s* 8*d*. Robert Luce: 7 cwt wrought flax £7. Lawrence Wether: 4½ tons 'ames' iron £22 10*s*. William Salkins: 24 cwt Cologne hemp £24. Henry Becher: 85 pcs Genoa fustian, 65 cwt woad £100. Thomas Aldersey: 437 ells sarcenet £72 16*s* 8*d*. Thomas Blanck: 20 pcs say £20. William Towerson: 12 cwt feathers £18 (25 June). John Borne: 6 doz. lbs coarse crewel, 4 grs coarse knives, 10 doz. thou. pins, 5 doz. Rennes boultel, 8 doz. crewel pieces £28 13*s* 4*d*. Richard Pope: 60 pcs mockado £40. Francis Bowyer: 204 yds black velvet, 60 yds

black satin £180. Nicholas Ludington: 460 lbs pepper £38 6s 8d. Richard Byllam: 140 Turnhout ticks £46 13s 4d. John Woodward: 2 bales Ulm fustian £30. George Stockmed: 5 cwt flax £5. William Goodwyn: 310 yds Levant taffeta £25 16s 8d. Francis Keightley: 45 yds velvet, 32 yds satin, 20 yds damask £55 13s 4d. William Smyth: 60 pcs Genoa fustian, 50 doz. lbs inkle £73 6s 8d. Matthew Fyld: 22 pcs narrow worsted £11. Thomas Thorp: 430 lbs pepper, 10 cwt aniseed, 30 lbs nigella, 'L' lbs 'sine alexandrie' £55 3s 4d. Thomas Barker: 9 cwt battery, 30 cwt plates £24. Anthony Brinckelo: 900 ells harnesdale cloth, 6 cwt woad £40. Thomas Hale: 25 lbs mace, 40s in drugs, 60 lbs turnsole, 1 cwt barley, 3 cwt alum, 3 brls painters' oil, 410 lbs pepper, 40 lbs senna, 40 lbs cinnamon, 24 lbs ginger, 30 lbs wormseed, 6 cwt hops £78 10s. William Sherington: 2 bales Ulm fustian, 150 ells sarcenet £55 (26 June). Robert Taylor: 16 cwt madder £10 13s 4d. Richard Goddard: 26 cwt madder £17 6s 8d. William Hewet: 7 cwt dressed flax £7. Edmund Smyth: 24 cwt woad, 5 cwt wrought flax, 45 pcs narrow worsted £43 10s. Thomas Parker: 83 pcs dornick with wool, 21 pcs bustian, 7 lbs sister's thread £56 3s 4d. John Boylson: 70 pcs Genoa fustian, 5 cwt flax, 3 cwt estrige wool £54 3s 4d. Anthony Fytton: 14 cwt sumach, 1 hd 20 lbs treacle, 2 cwt gum arabic, 180 lbs pepper, 120 lbs ginger £42. Thomas Longston: 30 lbs cloves £7 10s. George Sotherton: 12 cwt Cologne hemp £12 (30 June). Martin Wood: 45 lbs ferret silk, 22 lbs Bruges silk, 6 lbs fringe silk, 1½ lbs Venice gold £50 16s 8d. [f. 185] Thomas Starkey: 3000 ells minsters £33 6s 8d.

575. *Swallo* of Alkmaar (12) Frederick Rairson; Amsterdam
[f. 174b] Thomas Sanford: 600 lings, 1½ lasts fish £29 (22 June 1568).
[f. 175] John Violet: 2½ lasts fish £15.

576. *Ellen* of London (60) William Spender; Antwerp
[f. 175] William Coles: 125 lbs pepper, 90 lbs nutmegs £100 8s 4d. (22 June 1568). Gerson Hills: 27½ cwt Cologne hemp £27 10s. Richard Hills: 14 cwt hemp £14. Thomas Aldersey: 65 yds satin, 57 yds damask, 50 pcs grogram camlet £110 15s. Thomas Brasie: 30 pcs broad worsted, 48 pcs narrow worsted £54 (23 June). William Cockin: 2150 raw rumney budge £53 15s. Robert Exton: 34 Turnhout ticks £11 6s 8d. William Hobbs: 653 ells hair tapestry, 6½ doz. lince, 2 doz. Ghentish beds £29 10s. Thomas Daunster: 120 pcs boultel £24. John Alden: 100 doz. empty barrels £10. Edward Bright: 1 half-brl small nails, 1 half-brl head nails £6. William Luddington: 6 cwt aniseed £10. Randal Manning: 480 ells harnesdale cloth, 15 pcs 'blues',¹ 300 ells Castile canvas £33 15s. Nicholas Hewet: 20 cwt frying pans £13 6s 8d. John Fitzwilliams: 30 cwt madder £20. Thomas Eaton: 10 doz. lbs Bruges thread, 4 doz. lbs inkle, 1 grs thread lace, 1 grs wooden dials, 3 thou. thimbles, 6 doz. crewel pieces, 1 doz. lbs bottom pack thread £12 16s 8d. Thomas Rose: 40 pcs mockado £26 13s 4d. George Collymer: 12 doz. worsted girdlings, 10 pcs single dornick, 20 doz. lbs bottom thread, 5 doz. lbs narrow inkle £18 6s 8d. Robert Luce: 6 cwt wrought flax £6. William Bond: 8 pcs sackcloth £20. Bartholomew Dod: 125 yds velvet £93 15s (25 June). Edmund Smyth: 36 cwt woad, 170 half-pcs Genoa fustian, 2 bales Ulm fustian, 40 pcs single mockado

£137 6s 8d. William Towerson: 70 ells wool tapestry, 600 ells hair tapestry £23 10s. Wolston Dixi: 1200 ells harnesdale cloth £48. John Borne: 60 doz. thou. pins, 3 grs checkered points of thread, 2 thou. thimbles, 4 doz. thou. needles, 4 doz. coarse crewel pieces, 5 doz. lbs Bruges thread, 5 doz. lbs crewel £24 6s 8d. John Eliets: 70 doz. thou. pins, 2 thou. thimbles, 4 doz. thou. needles, 4 doz. lbs wrought inkle, 2 doz. lbs crewel, 10 doz. crewel pieces, 6 doz. lbs Bruges thread, 3 doz. lbs pack thread, 4 doz. minikins, 3 thou. awl blades £33 8s. John Woodward: 2 bales Ulm fustian £30. Geoffrey Walkeden: 16 Turnhout ticks, 3 pcs diaper for table cloths, 9 pcs diaper for napkins, 1 pc damask for napkins and towelling £32 3s 4d. Francis Vazey: 184 yds frizado £54. Henry Becher: 20 reams paper, 50 doz. thou. pins, 1 hd lbs inkle, 18 cwt woad £26 6s 8d. Alexander Sherington: 200 yds Levant taffeta £16 13s 4d. Thomas Thorp: 2 cwt corn powder, 9 cwt hops £7 16s 8d. William Hewet: 4 cwt mull-madder £1 15s. William Smyth: 80 pcs Genoa fustian £53 6s 8d. John Lambert: 21 cwt iron pans £14. William Sherington: 2 bales Ulm fustian, 80 yds taffeta £56 13s 4d (26 June). Thomas Hale: 9 cwt liquorice £4 10s. Thomas Randall: 80 yds taffeta £26 13s 4d. Robert Taylor: 16 cwt madder £10 13s 4d. John Pasfyld: 1½ cwt ireos, 3 qrs cyperus, 4 doz. wooden beams, 6 pair small andirons £4 13s 4d. John Boylson: 100 yds black velvet £75. Edward Doughty: 220 ells caddis tapestry £22. James Canon: 20 lbs coarse copper gold thread, 29 doz. quilted nightcaps £6. Robert Bladwell: 150 lbs pepper, 1 cwt aniseed, 20 lbs nutmegs £17 3s 4d. Richard Goddard: 26 cwt madder £17 6s 8d. John Flower: 300 lbs pepper £25. Robert Scarboro: 60 pcs mockado £40. William Allyn: 2 dressed and dyed cloths £16. Nicholas Spering: 2 grs knives £3 (28 June). [f. 185] Martin Wood: 60 lbs ferret silk, 18 lbs Bruges silk, 4 lbs fringe silk, 50 lbs nobs £48 13s 4d (30 June).

    1. See **539** n.

577. *Grace of God* of Lee (60) Robert Samon; Antwerp
[f. 175] Gerson Hills: 20 cwt Cologne hemp £20 (22 June 1568).

578. *William* of Dover (20) Robert Edge; Calais
[f. 175b] Bonchan Taddey: 4 tuns French wine *net* 4 tuns 12s (22 June 1568). [f. 197] Acerbo Velutella: 9½ tuns French wine *net* 8 tuns 24s (12 July).

579. *Jonas* of Flushing Jacob Stoffles
[f. 176] William Bond: 19 tuns Coniac wine *net* 14¾ tuns 44s 3d (23 June 1568).

580. *Falcon* of Antwerp (30) Christian Johnson; Antwerp
[f. 176] Thomas Gardener: 14 cwt hops £7 (23 June 1568). Nicholas Hewet: 1380 ells harnesdale cloth £55 5s. [f. 178] William Cooper: 5 boxes glass bugles ad valorem £3, 5 doz. hour glasses £8 (25 June).

581. *Killiard* of Dieppe (25) Martin Duylliard; Dieppe
[f. 176b] Lewis Tyrill: 5 hhds French wine *net* 4 hhds 3s (23 June 1568). [f. 177b] Hugh Offley: 30 cwt brazil £50.

582. *Bear* of Amsterdam (30) Adrian Francis; Amsterdam
[f. 178] Thomas Jenens: 5 lasts barrelled fish, 600 staplefish £39 (25 June 1568). Richard Mouse: 200 staplefish, 2 lasts barrelled fish £15. John Edmunds: 30 brls fish, 200 staplefish £18. Edward van Crog: 2 packs bundle-flax £16. Alard Bartrinck: 13 pcs Gelders cloth £15 13s 4d. [f. 181b] Garbrom Bower: 27 pcs Gelders cloth £32 8s 4d (26 June).

583. *Elizabeth* of Newcastle Nicholas Peters; Danzig
[f. 179] Edmund Boldero: 5 packs flax £40 (25 June 1568). George Mylner: 2 packs flax £16. Dunstan Walton: 13 cwt wax £39. William Cockin: 2 packs bale-flax¹ £14. Ezekiel Best: 3 packs flax £24 (26 June). Richard Gurney: 1 pack flax £8. Thomas Allyn: 9 half-packs flax, 630 yds poldavis, 5 tons iron, 200 clapholt £82 10s. William James: 4 packs flax £32. William Cockin: 5 half-packs 3 quarter-packs flax, 29 cwt cables £45 6s 8d. Robert Barker: 1 pack 1 half-pack flax £12. Robert Collet: 3 packs flax £24 (28 June). [f. 185] Gervais Simons: 2 packs 1 quarter-pack flax £18 (30 June).

    1. Containing 240 bales.

584. *Mary Fortune* of London (70) John Morcok; Sanlucar
[f. 179] George Sowthack: 20 tuns sack *net* 17 tuns 51s, 15 tuns Seville oil *net* 13 tuns £104 (23 June 1568). Robert Bladwell: 10 tuns oil *net* 8 tuns £64 (26 June). John Thomas: 5 tuns Seville oil *net* 4½ tuns £36. [f. 182] William Allen: 10 pipes Seville oil *net* 9 pipes £36.

585. *Grace* of Rye (30) William Harman; Vigo
[f. 179b] Thomas Draper: 40 thou. oranges and lemons £13 6s 8d (25 June 1568).

586. *Nightingale* of Newcastle John Mychelson; Danzig
[f. 180] Thomas Allen: 3 packs bale-flax £24 (25 June 1568). Dunstan Walton: 3 packs 1 half-pack flax, 45 cwt cordage £58. William Cockin: 2 packs¹ bale-flax £14. Thomas Russell: 6 half-packs 5 quarter-packs flax £34 (26 June). Robert Hilson: 6 packs flax £48 (28 June). Robert Lambert: 1 pack flax £8. [f. 184b] William James: 9 lasts pitch, 10 quarter-packs flax, 6 tons iron, 200 clapholt, 43 quintals cordage £88 (30 June).

    1. Containing 240 bales.

587. *Mary Fortune* of Newcastle Edward Johnson; Danzig
[f. 180] William Cockin: 2 packs bale-flax¹ £14 (25 June 1568). Robert Hilson: 8 packs flax £64 (28 June). Robert Lambert: 3 packs flax £24. William James: 200 clapholt, 52 quintals cordage, 4 half-packs flax £42 (30 June). [f. 188] Thomas Russell: 8 lasts pitch, 7 tons faggot iron, 3 packs flax, 8 firkins sturgeon, 3 packs hemp £140 6s 8d (2 July).

    1. Containing 240 bales.

588. *Salamon* of Lee (30) Thomas Wilkins; Oléron
[f. 180] Thomas Wilkins: 22 weys bay salt £22 (25 June 1568).

589. *Peter* of Dunkirk (40) Peter Lewkin; Dunkirk
[f. 180*b*] John Hall: 150 doz. hemp £18 15*s* (26 June 1568). [f. 183] Thomas Sound: 500 ells white Hazebroucks £12 10*s* (28 June).

590. *Primrose* of Harwich (120) Thomas Gray; Narva
[f. 181] William Wynter: 20 packs flax,[1] 160 cwt tallow, 22 cwt wax, 700 raw hides £346 6*s* 8*d* (26 June 1568).

    1. Containing 1028 bundles.

591. *Mary Gold* of Harwich (80) Lawrence Hayward; Barbary
[f. 181*b*] Anthony Pylboro: 7 cwt sugar £23 6*s* 8*d* (26 June 1568). John Digby: 10½ cwt sugar £35. Robert Barker: 79 cwt sugar £264 6*s* 8*d*. John Kell: 12 cwt sugar £40 (28 June). John Mun: 17 cwt sugar £56 13*s* 4*d*. Richard Hopkins: 22 cwt sugar £73 6*s* 8*d*. Henry Callys: 10½ cwt sugar £35. William Crompton: 41 cwt sugar £136 13*s* 4*d*. Edward Jackman: 62 cwt sugar and sugar powder, 125 lbs ostrich feathers £237 18*s* 11*d*. Barnard Fyld: 85 quintals sugar £283 6*s* 8*d*. Robert How: 74 cwt sugar £246 13*s* 4*d*. Gerard Gore: 10 hhds panele £25 (30 June). [f. 185*b*] Leonard Holingworth: 62 cwt sugar £206 13*s* 4*d*.

592. *Bark Aldersey* of London (70) Thomas Rickman; Cadiz
[f. 182*b*] Edmund Hugan: 20 butts sack *net* 17 butts £25 10*s* (28 June 1568). William Shacrost: 13 tuns 3 brls sack *net* 12 tuns 35*s*, 6 cwt brimstone £2. Robert How: 7 butts sack *net* 7 butts 10*s* 6*d*. Henry Callys: 10 butts sack *net* 9 butts 13*s* 6*d*. John Bird: 60 lbs grain berries £10 (2 July). [f. 188] James Gryffyth: 2 tuns sack 6*s*.

593. *Bark Gray* of London Robert Gray; Danzig
[f. 182*b*] George Mylner: 2 packs flax £16 (28 June 1568). William Cockin: 4 packs flax £32. Robert Collet: 4 packs flax, 1½ shock 17 pair tables, 5 grs tablemen £34 13*s* 4*d*. Edmund Boldero: 420 bales flax, 180 bales loose-flax £30 6*s* 8*d*. Thomas Allyn: 6 half-packs flax, 2730 yds poldavis £143 (30 June). Richard Gurney: 2 packs flax £16. Gervais Simons: 2 packs flax £16. Alard Bartrinck: 22½ firkins sturgeon £15 (1 July). William Coper: 2 half-packs flax £8. [f. 188] Thomas Russell: 1 half-pack hemp[1] £10 (2 July).

    1. An alternative reading could be 1½ packs.

594. *George* of Antwerp (50) Matis Goras; Antwerp
[f. 182*b*] Robert Brooke: 52 cwt hops £26 (28 June 1568). Edward Jackman: 32 cwt hops £16. Edmund Burton: 19 cwt iron wire, 12 grs horse bells, 2 grs hanging locks, 24 doz. snuffers, 6 grs 'chaps', 10 cwt single white plates £47 10*s* (30 June). [f. 186*b*] Ancelm Becket: 8 cwt madder £5 6*s* 8*d* (1 July).

595. *Lamb* of Hamburg (40) Hans van Lubbeck; Hamburg
[f. 182*b*] Hartik van Sprecleson: 20 cwt tarred ropes, 8 cwt copperas £17 6*s* 8*d* (28 June 1568). Daniel van Eitson: 1200 ells padduck, 2160 ells

hinderlands, 960 ells middlegood £49 13s 4d. Daniel van Crog: 25 cwt cables, 12 hd 'trosies', 1320 ells soultwich £46 13s 4d. William Luddington: 30 cwt copperas £15 (30 June). George Lubkin: 8 lasts pitch, 1320 ells soultwich £38. William Allyn: 53 cwt copperas £26 10s. John Rainkin: 780 ells soultwich £13 (1 July). Daniel Brandes: 3480 ells middlegood £52. Alard Bartrinck: 3 packs flax, 2 chests glass £28. Jerome Ryce: 600 ells middlegood £6 13s 4d. John Myller: 720 ells middlegood, 720 ells soultwich £20. Yogham Killinghewson: 16 cwt estrige wool, 24 cwt hops £25 6s 8d. Jerome Rice: 4½ hd Hamburg cloth £9 (2 July). [f. 191] Matthew Hope: 1200 ells middlegood, 1 half-pack flax £17 6s 8d (5 July).

596. *World* of Haarlem (36) Peter English; Haarlem
[f. 182b] Alard Bartrinck: 12 pcs Gelders cloth £14 6s 8d (28 June 1568).
[f. 183] Edward van Crog: 6 half-packs flax, 99 pcs buckram £46 (2 July).

597. *Mychell* of Amsterdam (35) Laurence Lobranson; Amsterdam
[f. 183] Richard Mouse: 5½ lasts barrelled fish, 500 staplefish £40 10s (28 June 1568). John Edmunds: 4 lasts green fish, 200 staplefish £27.
[f. 184b] Thomas Jenens: 6 lasts barrelled fish, 500 staplefish £43 10s (30 June).

598. *Mary* of Hamburg (50) Harder Grob; Hamburg
[f. 183] Daniel van Eytson: 2160 ells hinderlands, 1920 ells middlegood, 480 ells padduck £53 1s 8d (28 June 1568). Daniel van Crog: 20 cwt cables, 24 hd 'trosies', 480 ells middlegood, 720 ells soultwich, 3 packs flax £71 6s 8d. Henry Dale: 80 lbs latten plates, 80 lbs narrow latten plates, 80 lbs copper wire, 90 lbs broad iron plates £5 8s 4d (30 June). William Luddington: 12 cwt estrige wool £10. George Lubkin: 1320 ells soultwich £22. William Allyn: 52 cwt copperas £26. John Rainkin: 1680 ells middlegood £18 13s 4d (1 July). Daniel Brandes: 3120 ells middlegood £34 13s 4d. Otte Frolick: 2400 ells soultwich, 4800 ells middlegood £93 6s 8d. Alard Bartrinck: 1 pack flax, 720 ells middlegood, 60 doz. small trenchers £16 10s. Jerome Ryce: 720 ells middlegood, 600 ells soultwich £18. Court Ellers: 1 pack flax £8. John Myller: 720 ells middlegood £8. Christopher Hargrave: 1 qr cloves £6 5s. Yogham Killinghowson: 16 cwt estrige wool, 24 hd wool, 25 cwt hops £45 16s 8d. James Holmes: 24 cwt madder £16. Daniel van Krog: 600 ells soultwich £10 (2 July). [f. 189] Edward van Crog: 16 cwt madder £10 13s 4d.

599. *Black Dragon* of Hamburg[1] (36) Luce Garretson; Hamburg
[f. 183] Alard Bartrinck: 13 pcs Gelders cloth £15 13s 4d (28 June 1568). William Page: 9 lasts ashes, 200 Marienburg deals, 3½ lasts soap, 5 lasts pitch £81 13s 4d (30 June). Thomas Sandford: 480 lings, 200 staplefish £19. George Lubkin: 4500 ells Osnabrücks £60. [f. 189] Edward van Crog: 4 half-packs flax £16 (2 July).

1. Perhaps in error for Amsterdam: see **150, 362, 477, 824**. If so, the port of departure should read Amsterdam.

600. *Black Hulk* of Stavoren (160) Alker Wybrands; Danzig
[f. 183*b*] Robert Hilson: 8½ lasts pitch £17 (28 June 1568). [f. 185*b*] William Jenens: 1800 wainscots, 17 lasts pitch, 2400 clapholt £112 (30 June).

601. *Jerusalem* of Amsterdam (40) Jacob Garretson
[f. 184] Thomas Sandford: 1 last barrelled fish £6 (30 June 1568). [f. 184*b*] William Page: 2 lasts Flemish soap £16.

602. *Pellican* of Amsterdam (30) Tyman Cornilis; Amsterdam
[f. 184*b*] William Page: ½ hd barlings, 100 spruce deals, 80 oars, 100 wainscots £20 13*s* 4*d* (30 June 1568). Thomas Jenens: 3 lasts barrelled fish £18. Thomas Sandford: 1½ lasts barrelled fish £9. [f. 188] Nicholas Spencer: 8 half-pcs Holland cloth £4 16*s* 8*d* (2 July).

603. *Pellican* of Antwerp (30) Brumball Jacobson; Antwerp
[f. 184*b*] Robert Brok: 62 cwt hops, 24 cwt madder £47 (30 June 1568). William Luddington: 20 cwt argol £20. William Cockin: 1720 rumney budge skins £43 10*s* (1 July). John Ramsey: 17½ cwt battery £35. John Car: 7½ hd iron plates £5. Henry Billingsley: 150 butts Paris thread, 20 doz. lbs bottom thread, 10 pcs thread dornick £22 6*s* 8*d*. Edward Bright: 32 cwt madder £21 6*s* 8*d* (2 July). George Lubkin: 1500 ells Osnabrücks, 6 cwt estrige wool £25. [f. 189*b*] William Cowper: 2 doz. halbert heads £2 (3 July).

604. *Unicorn* of Amsterdam Peter Claison
[f. 185*b*] Robert Cox: 15 weys bay salt £15 (30 June 1568).

605. *Martha* of York John Beam; Antwerp
[f. 186] George Breme: 8 cwt battery £16 (1 July 1568). Thomas Gardiner: 100 lbs quicksilver, 50 lbs mace £23 6*s* 8*d*. John Ramsey: 28 cwt battery £56. John Car: 36 pair andirons with creepers, tongs and fireshovels £14. Thomas Castlin: 16 pcs Ghentish cloth £19 3*s* 4*d* (2 July). Thomas Aldersey: 80 pcs mockado £53 6*s* 8*d*. Thomas Longston: 4 cwt aniseed, 400 lbs pepper £40. William Allyn: 219 cwt prunes £109 10*s*. Thomas Starky: 30 pcs Olonne cloth £20. William Hewet: 18 cwt madder £12. Robert Bladwell: 300 lbs pepper £25. William Sherington: 110 yds taffeta £36 13*s* 4*d* (3 July). Martin Wood: 40 lbs Spanish and satin silk £40. [f. 190] Thomas Blanck: 20 pcs say £20.

606. *Cock* of Bruges (60) Jacob Albright; Bruges
[f. 186] Matthew Colclough: 5½ lasts pitch £11 (1 July 1568). Francis Wyght: 81 half-pcs 3 pcs bustian, 100 ells white Hazebroucks, 6½ doz. lbs thread £35 16*s* 8*d* (2 July). [f. 190] Adrian Adrianson: 100 great bundles white rods £3 6*s* 8*d* (3 July).

607. *Mychell* of Antwerp (50) William Peters; Antwerp
[f. 186*b*] Robert Broke: 50 cwt hops £25 (1 July 1568). Thomas Howse: 69 half-pcs 5 pcs bustian, 100 ells Hazebroucks, 6 doz. lbs brown thread, 8 pcs Genoa fustian, 2 pcs grogram, 2 pcs say £42 16*s* 8*d*. Roger Warfyld:

400 lbs pepper, 2 brls litmus, 4 cwt coriander seed £40 13s 4d (2 July). John Jackman: 200 bundles brown paper £6 13s 4d. William Cockin: 1720 rumney budge skins £43. Thomas Aldersey: 210 yds sarcenet £35. Wolston Dixi: 45 pcs Ghentish and Bar canvas £54. Robert Bladwell: 400 lbs pepper £33 6s 8d. William Cowper: 3 doz. halbert heads £3 (3 July). Henry Byllingsley: 40 doz. thou. pins, 5 doz. lbs Bruges thread, 6 doz. lbs bottom pack thread £11 3s 4d. [f. 191] William Long: 20 cwt hops £10 (5 July).

608. *Sea Rider* of Flushing (25) Gomer Antewurs; Flushing
[f. 187] Peter van Clewall: 17 tuns French wine *net* 15 tuns 45s (1 July 1568).

609. *Thompson* of Southwold (40) Thomas Wright; Bourgneuf
[f. 187b] Robert Broke: 28 weys bay salt £28 (1 July 1568).

610. *Lyon* of Roscoff (80) Evan Jacob; Sanlucar
[f. 187b] Evan Jacques: 48 butts sack *net* 43 butts 64s 6d (2 July 1568). Robert Bladwell: 34 pipes oil £120, 2 butts sack 3s. [f. 189b] Gilbert Cotton: 14 butts sack *net* 13 butts 19s 2d, 30 pipes oil *net* 26 pipes £104 (3 July).

611. *Spledegle* of Flushing Vincent Simondson
[f. 188] Mary Peters: 250 ells coarse 'housewaies' thread £6 6s (2 July 1568).
[f. 206] Phillip Halfpenny: 13 tuns corrupt wine *net* 9 tuns £27 (16 July).

612. *Sea Dog* of Amsterdam (30) Cornilis Claison; Amsterdam
[f. 189] Thomas Jenens: 600 lings, 800 staplefish £32 (3 July 1568). John Violet: 600 lings, 900 staplefish £33 10s. [f. 189b] Richard Mowse: 600 lings, 800 staplefish £32.

613. *Falkon* of London Thomas Grene; Rouen
[f. 189] John Bodleygh: 1100 ells canvas £27 10s (3 July 1568). Humphrey Brown: 160 reams paper and loose paper, 800 paste boards £24. Richard Folsam: 1200 ells canvas £30. Robert Sadler: 1300 ells canvas, 160 reams paper, 20 reams loose paper £56 11s. Thomas Campbell: 1500 ells brown canvas £37 10s. Hugh Offley: 1500 ells canvas £37 10s. Richard Smyth: 2400 ells canvas £60. Francis Benizen: 2600 ells canvas £66 5s. Oliver Fysher: 1600 ells canvas £40. John Olyf: 3400 ells coarse canvas £45 6s 8d (5 July). Anthony Gamage: 2200 ells canvas £29 6s 8d. Wolston Dixi: 2400 ells coarse canvas £32. Richard Morrys: 2000 ells canvas £26 13s 4d. Arthur Handson: 12 thou. teazles, 20 reams paper £6 13s 1d. [f. 191b] Thomas Starkey: 3500 ells canvas £87 10s.

614. *Margaret* of Dover Stephen Anderson; Rouen
[f. 190] John Bodleigh: 2000 ells canvas £50 (5 July 1568). John Harding: 1100 ells canvas £27 10s. Thomas Campbell: 1000 ells brown canvas £25. Matthew Colclough: 10 puncheons French wine *net* $2\frac{2}{3}$ tuns 8s. Henry Wayt: 3 tuns French wine *net* $2\frac{1}{2}$ tuns 7s 6d, 5 doz. buckrams £7 10s.

Arthur Hanson: 6 doz. buckrams £9. Anthony Gamage: 1300 ells canvas, 8 doz. old buckrams £44 10s. Hugh Offley: 1000 ells canvas £25. Thomas Davie: 1000 ells canvas £25 (6 July). Robert Sadler: 1000 ells canvas £25. John Olyf: 2000 ells canvas £50. Humphrey Broune: 100 reams paper, 60 reams loose paper £21 6s 8d. [f. 200b] Richard Smyth: 1400 ells packing canvas, 80 yds Tours taffeta £32 (14 July).

615. *Angell* of Hamburg (50) Henrik Alverman; Hamburg
[f. 190] Hartik van Sprecleson: 1200 ells soultwich £20 (5 July 1568). Daniel van Eytzen: 3 packs ton-flax £24. Alard Bartrinck: 1 pack flax £8. Otte Frolick: 1440 ells soultwich £24. Daniel van Crog: 600 ells soultwich £10 (6 July). Edward van Crog: 4320 ells middlegood £48 (7 July). [f. 194b] Daniel Brandes: 3120 ells middlegood £34 13s 4d (8 July).

616. *Hopsack* of Amsterdam (30) Peter Peterson; Amsterdam
[f. 190b] Gervais Simonds: 6 cwt feathers £9 (5 July 1568). Robert Hilson: 8½ lasts pitch, 6½ lasts tar £81 (7 July). William James: 17 lasts pitch, 1 nest chests, 2000 clapholt £39 13s 4d. Dunstan Walton: 23 lasts pitch, 6 lasts tar, 1200 clapholt £61 (8 July). [f. 194b] Thomas Russell: 25 lasts 10 brls pitch, 7 lasts 10 brls tar, 550 oars £89 6s 8d.

617. *Sampson* of Hamburg Hening Crow
[f. 190b] Gervais Simonds: 120 bales flax £7 (5 July 1568). William Cokin: 3 packs flax, 35 cwt cordage, 17 cwt feathers £72 16s 8d. George Millner: 2 packs flax £16 (6 July). Thomas Allyn: 10 lasts pitch, 5 packs flax £60. William Franckland: 3 packs bale-flax £24. Robert Hylson: 4 packs flax £32 (7 July). Robert Barker: 3½ packs flax £28. Clement Draper: 20 lasts tar, 2 packs flax, 360 bales hemp £77. William Jenens: 4 packs flax £32. Richard Gurney: 7 packs flax £54 [*sic*]. Robert Collet: 15 lasts pitch, 5 lasts tar, 1800 clapholt, 5 shocks boxes, 1 pc. mazer wood £46 (8 July). John Ranckin: 4 packs flax £32. Thomas Russell: 2½ packs hemp £50. [f. 198] Luder van Dorne: 9½ lasts tar £19 (13 July).

618. *Black Falcon* of Veere John Martyn; Rouen
[f. 190b] Jacques Fyshet 'et sociis': 26 tuns French wine *net* 20 tuns 60s, 2 tuns corrupt wine £6 (5 July 1568).

619. *Swallo* of Dieppe (20) Nicholas Tribart; Dieppe
[f. 190b] Henry Waite: 2 tuns Rochelle wine *net* 1 tun 3s, 8 tuns corrupt wine £24 (5 July 1568). [f. 192] Christopher Pereson: 10 cases glass £10 (6 July).

620. *Barbary* of Harwich (12) John Gray; Rouen
[f. 191b] Henry Waite: 8 tuns French wine *net* 7 tuns 21s (5 July 1568).

621. *Ellen* of Scarborough Richard Thorp; Nantes
[f. 191b] John Crosswet: 4 tuns Nantes wine *net* 2 tuns 6s, 12 tuns corrupt wine £36 (5 July 1568).

622. *Alberyes* of Dieppe (10) John Machen; Dieppe
[f. 191*b*] Hugh Offley: 50 cwt brazil £83 6*s* 8*d* (5 July 1568).

623. *Ballet* of Dieppe (18) Richard Browmantyne; Dieppe
[f. 191*b*] John Varry: 1 tun Rochelle wine, 3½ tuns Burgundy wine *net* 4 tuns 12*s* (5 July 1568).

624. *Greyhound* of Lee (26) Henry Rawlins; Antwerp
[f. 192] Thomas Aldersay: 64 yds velvet £48 (6 July 1568). William Luddington: 800 lbs pepper £66 13*s* 4*d*. William Colles: 10 cwt alum £16 13*s* 4*d*. Edward Bright: 6 hd iron plates, 1½ cwt creepers £5. Thomas Brasie: 2 bales Ulm fustian £30 (7 July). Wolston Dixi: 50 pcs Ghentish [*sic*] £60. Gervais Simons: 1150 raw budge skins, 120 raw fox skins £32 15*s*. William Gifford: 60 yds velvet £45. William Sherington: 15 doz. yds Cyprus cotton £3. George Bond: 70 cwt prunes £35. William Hobbs: 164 Turnhout ticks, 3½ doz. sealed beds £59 18*s* 4*d*. John Spencer: 3 cwt hops £1 15*s*. Edmund Smyth: 1 bale Ulm fustian £15. Thomas Parker: 24 pcs dornick with wool £12. John Sutton: 80 Turnhout ticks £26 13*s* 4*d* (8 July). Thomas Rose: 2 bales Ulm fustian £30. Thomas Eaton: 36 doz. yds Cyprus cotton, 5 doz. thou. needles, 3 grs minikins, 7 grs halfpenny-ware glasses, 40 lbs counters £17 5*s*. Edmund Roberts: 200 reams paper £26 13*s* 4*d*. John Borne: 15 yds Cyprus cotton, 1 grs coarse hour glasses, 10 doz. lbs bottom pack thread, 1 doz. lbs crewel £6 3*s* 4*d*. John Alsopp: 80 cwt woad £53 6*s* 8*d* (9 July). Sir William Chester: 4 cwt panele molasses £2. John Eliets: 17 doz. thou. pins, 2 doz. lbs crewel, 5 doz. lbs thread, 6 doz. lbs bottom pack thread, 2 doz. thou. needles, 4 thou. awl blades £12 8*s* 4*d*. [f. 196*b*] Thomas Longston: 400 lbs pepper, 10 cwt prunes £38 6*s* 8*d* (10 July).

625. *Sampson* of Antwerp Adrian Williamson
[f. 192] John Jackman: 100 bundles brown paper £3 6*s* 8*d* (6 July 1568).

626. *Fortune* of Bruges (50) Cornilis Albright; Bruges
[f. 192*b*] Thomas Brasie: 162 pcs buckram £36 (7 July 1568).

627. *Barthelemew* of London (60) Richard Cokes; Antwerp
[f. 193] Gervais Simons: 1080 raw budge skins £27 (7 July 1568). William Ramsey 'per' John Lambert: 24½ cwt battery £49 (8 July). Thomas Daunster: 65 doz. yds Cyprus cotton, 2 doz. pcs Beaupreau boultel £17 16*s* 8*d* (8 July). Thomas Rose: 2 bales Ulm fustian £30. William Smyth: 40 pcs camlet £40. George Stockmed: 5 cwt wrought flax £5. Sir John York: 600 lbs pepper £50. William Hewet: 5½ cwt wrought flax £5 10*s*. Henry Becher: 88 pcs Genoa fustian, 100 cwt woad £125. George Cullymer: 20 doz. lbs Oudenaarde thread, 12 doz. lbs bottom pack thread £15 1*s* 8*d*. Thomas Aldersey: 45 pcs single grogram camlet £60. George Bond: 50 cwt prunes £25. John Boorne: 2 thou. thimbles, 2 doz. lbs crewel, 4 doz. lbs inkle, 8 thou. awl blades, 40 doz. thou. pins, 5 grs thread points, 2 doz. crewel pieces, 16 doz. lbs pack thread £21 15*s*. William Sherington: 100 ells sarcenet, 40 lbs ferret silk £33 6*s* 8*d*. Richard

Billingsley: 60 doz. thou. pins, 10 doz. lbs bottom thread, 50 butts black thread, 5 doz. lbs Bruges thread £20 6s 8d (9 July). Charles Morgain: 225 lbs pepper, 71 lbs cloves £36 10s. Edmund Smyth: 2 bales Ulm fustian £30. Thomas Gardner: 100 lbs isinglass, 1¼ cwt starch, 75 lbs cloves £20 8s 4d. Thomas Eaton: 10 doz. lbs crewel, 1 grs wooden dials, 18 thou. awl blades, 6 grs minikins, 12 lbs clavichord wire, 4 doz. thou. needles, 15 doz. lbs narrow inkle, 1 grs thread-lace, 4 doz. crewel pieces £34 16s 8d. John Sutton: 45 Turnhout ticks, 25 counterfeit Turnhout ticks £23 6s 8d. Alexander Sherington: 200 ells sarcenet £33 6s 8d. George Breme: 7 cwt battery £14. Robert Taylor: 4 cwt hops £2. Robert Morris: 2 brls litmus, 150 bundles brown paper, 4 cwt hops £9. John Eliets: 10 doz. thou. pins, 4 doz. lbs crewel, 1 thou. thimbles, 4 doz. lbs counters, 6 grs copper hat bands, 10 thou. awl blades, 8 doz. lbs Bruges thread, 4 doz. lbs bottom pack thread, 3 doz. thread pieces £23 1s 8d. James Sturtivant: 3 packs flax £24. [f. 196b] Thomas Longston: 400 lbs pepper, 15 cwt prunes £40 16s 8d (10 July).

628. *Mychell* of Bruges (50) Cornilis Alben; Bruges
[f. 193] Thomas Howse: 30 half-pcs bustian, 1 pc. fustian, 10 pcs brown Holland cloth £23 (7 July 1568). Thomas Sound: 16 cwt madder, 7 pcs coarse cloth £19 1s 8d. William Gelders: 20 pcs bustian £13 6s 8d (8 July). [f. 195] Adam Coper: 12 half-pcs bustian £8 6s 8d (9 July).

629. *Anne* of 'Barlam' (10) John Cook; Dunkirk
[f. 193b] William Page: 6 cwt hops £3 (7 July 1568).

630. *Sampson* of Bruges (60) Marten Fryze; Bruges
[f. 193b] William Gelders: 30 pcs bustian £20 (8 July 1568).

631. *Grace of God* of London (50) Thomas Wilson; St. Martin
[f. 195] Richard May: 26 weys bay salt £26 (8 July 1568). [f. 214b] John Fuller: 14 weys bay salt £14 (29 July).

632. *George* of Newcastle John Tymoth; Danzig
[f. 195b] William Cokin: 16 cwt feathers £24 (9 July 1568). Thomas Allen: 3 packs flax £24 (10 July). Robert Best: 4 packs 1 half-pack flax £36. Edmund Ardimer: 12 Danzig chests £2 13s 4d (13 July). Robert Colet: 21 cwt cordage, 3 brls potash £21 10s. Thomas Russell: 4 packs hemp, 4 packs flax, 8 lasts 8 brls ashes, 20 firkins sturgeon, 4 tons spruce iron, 15 cwt tarred ropes, 140 cwt cordage £274. Robert Hylson: 3 packs flax £24 (14 July). William James: 36 cwt copper, 3 packs flax, ½ ton iron, 26 cwt cordage £115 16s 8d. [f. 206] Alard Bartrinck: 10 firkins sturgeon £6 13s 4d (16 July).

633. *Egle* of Arnemuiden (15) Hubright Jacobson; Arnemuiden
[f. 196] William Yonger: 4 weys white salt, 7 weys bay salt £12 6s 8d (9 July 1568).

634. *George* of Antwerp (40) Barthell Mychelson; Antwerp
[f. 196b] Thomas Thorp: 16 cwt hops £8 (10 July 1568). Thomas Hacker:

26 cwt hops £13. [f. 197] Garret Dowse: 20 reams unbound books £2 (12 July).

635. *Grace of God* of London Richard Tye; Rouen
[f. 196b] Francis Beneson: 1550 ells canvas £38 15s (12 July 1568). Humphrey Brown: 180 reams paper, 12 reams loose paper £25 13s 4d. William Plaisden: 1000 ells canvas £25 (13 July). William Disby: 1300 ells canvas £32 10s. Richard Smyth: 1700 ells canvas £42 10s. Robert Cage: 1700 ells canvas £42 10s. Henry Wayt: 100 reams paper, 5 doz. iron pots £15. John Allot: 1400 ells canvas £35. Edmund Ansell: 10 doz. buckrams, 100 yds dornick £20. Richard Morris: 1400 ells canvas £35. John Harding: 2000 ells canvas £50. Robert Sadler: 600 ells canvas, 100 reams paper £28 6s 8d. Thomas Starkey: 800 ells canvas £20 (14 July). William Handford: 30 lbs pack thread, 16 grs penny combs, 5 grs inkhorns, 10 grs crewel lace £16 11s 8d. George Beche: 500 ells canvas £12 10s. [f. 201] John Olyf: 1600 ells canvas £40.

636. *Hearn* of London (40) John Davis; Rouen
[f. 196b] Arthur Hanson: 150 reams paper £20 (12 July 1568). Richard Renold: 20 doz. pcs French buckram £30 (13 July). Richard Smyth: 210 yds Tours taffeta £35. John Bodleigh: 1000 ells canvas £25. Thomas Campbell: 1800 ells canvas £45. John Allot: 1600 ells canvas £40. John Harding: 1100 ells canvas £27 10s. Anthony Gamage: 1800 ells canvas £45. Hugh Offley: 1400 ells canvas £35. William Handford: 40 doz. woolcards £20 (14 July). Humphrey Broune: 60 reams paper, 50 reams loose paper, 1 thou. loose trenchers, 600 ells canvas £29 18s 4d. Anthony Cage: 800 ells canvas £20 (16 July). John Olyff: 2100 ells canvas £28. [f. 205b] John Harding: 45 yds silk grogram, 50 yds Tours taffeta £23 6s 8d.

637. *Pellican* of Amsterdam (30) Nanyng Thomas; Amsterdam
[f. 196b] Mary Peterson: 12 pcs Holland cloth £14 8s 4d (12 July 1568). [f. 200] John Coppin: 1 last barrelled fish £6 (14 July).

638. *Nightingale* of Amsterdam (30) Cleise Simonson; Amsterdam
[f. 197] Mary Peterson: 19 pcs Holland cloth £22 16s 8d. John Lense: 40 pcs Holland cloth £48 (13 July). [f. 202] Edward van Krog: 650 wainscots £26 (15 July).

639. *Elizabeth* of Maidstone Richard Startup; Rouen
[f. 197] Humphrey Browne: 240 reams paper £32 (12 July 1568). Richard Patrik: 8 doz. quilts, 120 reams paper, 30 grs combs, 20 grs woollen edging at 3s the gross, 9 great grs points at 8d the gross, 6 grs inkhorns £51 6s 8d. Thomas Cambell: 800 ells brown canvas, 10 sum rose nails £22 10s (13 July). John Bodleigh: 500 ells canvas £12 10s. Luder van Dorne: 5 puncheons French wine *net* 1¾ tuns 4s. John Gardner: 7 tuns French wine *net* 6 tuns 18s. John Harding: 1500 ells canvas £37 10s. Robert Sadler: 800 ells canvas, 20 reams loose paper £22 13s 4d. Anthony Gamage: 1800 ells canvas £45. Hugh Offley: 100 reams paper, 10 grs playing cards £23 6s 8d. Richard Hyll: 2000 ells canvas £50 (14 July). John Olyf: 1600 ells canvas £40. [f. 205b] Anthony Cage: 1000 ells canvas £25 (16 July).

640. *Michell* of Flushing (14) [*sic*]
[f. 197] Thomas Sanford: 720 lings £24 (12 July 1568).

641. *Confidence* of London (45) Erasmus Kidball
[f. 197] William Bulley: 32 weys great salt £32 (12 July 1568).

642. *John* of Saucats (40) John Auger; Rouen
[f. 197*b*] Richard Renold: 3 tuns vinegar £7 (13 July 1568). Richard Smyth: 1200 ells canvas £30. John Bodleigh: 800 ells canvas £20. Richard Morris: 1400 ells canvas £35. Robert Sadler: 1300 ells canvas, 80 reams paper £43 3*s* 4*d*. Thomas Starkey: 700 ells canvas £17 10*s* (14 July). Richard Patrick: 110 reams paper, 4 grs quarter combs, 6 grs inkhorns, 25 grs tin tablets, 15 grs woollen edging £32 8*s*. John Allot: 1400 ells canvas £18 13*s* 4*d*. Hugh Offley: 600 ells canvas, 10 cwt prunes £14 6*s* 8*d*.
[f. 201] Humphrey Broune: 20 grs playing cards £20.

643. *Harry*[1] of Lee (25) William Drifyld; Antwerp
[f. 197*b*] George Stockmed: 12 cwt wrought flax £12 (13 July 1568). Thomas Randall: 60 yds taffeta £20 (14 July). Richard Byllam: 20 cwt madder £13 6*s* 8*d*. William Bowyer: 7 cwt hops £3 10*s*. William Cockin: 1620 raw rumney budge skins £42. William Cooles: 500 lbs pepper, 170 lbs nutmegs £70. Francis Wotton: 45 doz. yds Cyprus cotton £9. John Eliets: 40 doz. thou. pins, 20 doz. lbs inkle, 3 doz. lbs crewel, 2 doz. lbs Bruges thread, 3 doz. thread pieces, 2 grs looking glasses £26 12*s*. Thomas Gardner: 2 cwt gunpowder, 3 qrs turnsole £5 3*s* 4*d* (15 July). William Hobbs: 58 Turnhout ticks, 13 Ghentish carpets £20 19*s*. Thomas Cranfyld: 80 yds Spanish taffeta £16. Sir John York: 400 lbs pepper £33 6*s* 8*d*. William Atkins: 1 bale fustian £15. Thomas Bowyer: 3 hd iron plates, 14 doz. small candlesticks, 12 lbs pack thread, 2 cwt varnish, 2 bundles steel, 12 doz. bodkins, 6 doz. pincers cost 6*s* 8*d*, 6 cwt iron wire, 30 wisps coarse steel, 2 cwt iron wire, 7 hd nails, 4 sum small nails, 2 grs Jews' trumps, 2 grs small locks, 9 grs files, 50 lbs curtain rings, 3 grs pincers, 1 grs dog chains, 6 doz. snuffers, 12 lbs pile weights, 20 lbs 'iruns', 5 grs joiners' tools, 1 grs iron horns, 1 grs hammers, 5 grs horse bells, 1 grs 'sirrills' cost 10*s*, 10 thou. tacks, 3 mark shears, 1 thou. roses for head pieces, 2 grs 'tressel garnet', 6 doz. compasses, 2 doz. hatchets, 500 awl blades, 6 doz. wooden gimlets £51 18*s*. Nicholas Hewet: 1 half-brl small nails £4. Randal Maning:[2] harnesdale cloth £32. John Car: 1 half-brl small nails, 8 hd plates, 10 cwt iron wire £26. Edmund Burton: 1 half-brl head nails, 12 bundles steel £10. Henry Billingsley: 33 doz. lbs thread, 36 doz. thou. pins, 15 doz. lbs pack thread £31. Roger Warfild: 4 cwt almonds, 1 cwt candy, 2 cwt copperas, 6 brls yellow ochre £16 6*s* 8*d* (16 July). Robert Broke: 850 lbs pepper £70 16*s* 8*d*. Anthony Fytton: 6 half-brls crossbow thread, drugs ad valorem 200*s* £15. John Wanton: 1050 lbs pepper, 80 lbs mace £114 3*s* 4*d*. Edmund Smyth: 1 bale fustian £15. John Sutton: 11 doz. lince £8 5*s*. John Isham: 100 pcs mockado, 50 pcs narrow worsted £91 13*s* 4*d*. Wolston Dixi: 48 pcs Holland cloth £57 13*s* 4*d*. Edward Bright: 9 cwt iron pans, 1 cwt double plates, 15 cwt square iron, 1 ton iron £15 5*s*. Thomas Eaton: 10 doz. crewel pieces, 3 doz. lbs wrought inkle,

2 doz. lbs crewel, 4 doz. lbs bottom pack thread £9 10s. Thomas Parker: 78 pcs dornick with wool £26. Thomas Brasye: 4 bales Ulm fustian £60. Matthew Fyld: 22 pcs grogram camlet, 66 half-pcs Genoa fustian £52 6s 8d. John Passfyld: 7 cwt iron wire, 7 cwt iron creepers, 7 doz. coarse sword blades, 1½ cwt black latten £23 5s. John Alden: 5 cwt liquorice, 14 cwt argol, 975 lbs pepper, 18¼ hd 'sanderstock' £130 15s (17 July). Anthony Fytton: 3 half-brls crossbow thread £2 10s. [f. 208b] Stephen Slany: 52 pcs Holland cloth £62 6s 8d (20 July).

1. Or *Hare.*
2. Quantity illegible.

644. *Mary George* of London (70) Jacob Fryer; La Rochelle
[f. 198] Thomas Sotcham: 40 weys bay salt £40 (13 July 1568).

645. *Christofer* of Harwich (30) John Alden; Spain
[f. 198] Robert Barker: 6 pipes Seville oil £24 (13 July 1568).

646. *Wildman* of Harlingen (80) Vibram Charson; Danzig
[f. 199] Jerome Beale: 20 lasts pitch, 48 cwt copperas, 5 lasts ashes, 2 lasts 6 brls ashes, 1200 clapholt, 12 chests, 16 lasts tar £124 3s 4d (13 July 1568). Dunstan Walton: 3½ lasts ashes £10 (14 July). [f. 199b] Thomas Allyn: 10 lasts pitch £20.

647. *Mary Katherine* of Lee (50) Robert Parnell; Antwerp
[f. 199b] John Lambert: 12 cwt unwrought flax £8 (14 July 1568). George Stockmed: 13½ cwt wrought flax, 24 cwt flax £29. William Sherington: 1440 ells 'spruce' canvas £16. William Bowyer: 9 cwt hops £4 10s. Francis Wotton: 45 doz. yds Cyprus cotton £9. Thomas Gardener: 2 cwt corn-powder, 400 lbs pepper, 3 cwt aniseed £40 (15 July). William Towerson: 18 ells wool tapestry, 12 doz. Ghentish carpets £18 18s 4d. John Borne: 30 doz. thou. pins, 1 doz. lbs crewel, 4 doz. lbs counters, 6 thou. awl blades, ½ thou. thimbles, 10 grs coarse copper bands, 2 doz. lbs inkle, 2 doz. crewel pieces, 2 grs thread points £15 3s 4d. William Hobbs: 104 Turnhout ticks, 19 lince £48 18s. Richard Billingsley: 20 doz. lbs narrow inkle, 16 doz. lbs inkle, 12 thou. balls £36. Henry Beecher: 10 doz. lbs Bruges thread, 14 doz. lbs inkle, 8 doz. thou. needles, 10 doz. lbs piecing thread £37 6s 8d. William Atkins: 1 bale fustian £15. John Alsopp: 80 cwt woad £53 6s 8d. Thomas Bowyer: 16 cwt iron pans, 3 brls small nails, 2½ cwt fireshovels and tongs ad valorem 36s £24 10s. Nicholas Hewet: 3 cwt iron bands, 1 half-brl head nails £4. William Gifford: 50 yds satin £22 10s. John Car: 1 half-brl small nails, 11 cwt iron wire, 4 bundles coarse steel £12 6s 8d. Edmund Burton: 76½ cwt 'ames' iron, 120 doubles, 2¾ cwt fireshovel plates, 3 half-brls head nails £30 6s 8d. Thomas Longston: 10 cwt estrige wool, 60 lbs cloves £23 6s 8d (16 July). William Sherington: 3 bales Ulm fustian, 120 ells sarcenet £65. Edmund Smyth: 2 bales Ulm fustian £30. William Hewet: 11 cwt wrought flax £11. Anthony Fytton: 100 lbs nigella, 90 lbs quicksilver, 3 cwt corn powder £14 6s 8d. Robert Broke: 40 cwt mull-madder, 700 lbs pepper £63 6s 8d. Thomas Aldersey: 40 pcs grogram camlet £53 6s 8d. Sir John York: 5 cwt aniseed, 38 lbs

mace, 20 lbs nutmegs £35 3*s* 4*d*. William Colles: 6 cwt aniseed, 200 lbs pepper, 70 lbs nutmegs £36 6*s* 8*d*. John Isham: 120 pcs mockado £80. Edward Bright: 17 cwt iron pans £11 6*s* 8*d*. Thomas Eaton: 6 doz. crewel pieces, 10 doz. thou. pins, 4 doz. lbs bottom pack thread £5 10*s*. Alexander Sherington: 300 ells sarcenet £50. Richard Byllam: 48 cwt madder £32. Matthew Fyld: 160 ells Bologna sarcenet, 110 half-pcs Genoa fustian £63 6*s* 8*d*. John Pasfyld: 16 cwt iron wire £26 13*s* 4*d*. Edmund Hugan: 40 pcs Genoa fustian £26 13*s* 4*d* (17 July). John Spencer: 30 lbs senna, 30 lbs copperas £2 15*s*. Stephen Woodrof: 1200 yds poldavis £40. John Wanton: 6 cwt aniseed, 400 lbs pepper £41 6*s* 8*d* (19 July). John Sutton: 320 ells hair tapestry, 6 doz. lince £15 3*s* 4*d*. John Alden: 20 cwt liquorice, 8 cwt glue £14. [f. 208*b*] Thomas Castlyn: 3 small packs flax £24 (20 July).

648. *Blockhouse* of Stavoren (200) Martin Johnson; Danzig
[f. 199*b*] Robert Hylson: 17 lasts 2 brls pitch, 15 brls soap ashes £38 1*s* 8*d* (14 July 1568). [f. 204*b*] William James: 1100 wainscots, 3600 clapholt £53 (16 July).

649. *Falcon* of Dordrecht (30) Adrian Duttel; Dordrecht
[f. 200] Reynold Thirling: 36 cwt hemp, 10 cwt shaven latten £56 (14 July 1568). Melchior van Aldenik: 21 awms Rhenish wine 21*s* (16 July). [f. 207*b*] Edward Hardinaght: 16 half-brls steel £96 (17 July).

650. *Andris* of Antwerp Jacob Cornilis
[f. 200] William Hobson: 2½ doz. troy weights, 56 lbs counters, 2 thou. thimbles, 5 grs wooden dials, 8 thou. pack needles, 1 grs spectacles, 20 grs morris bells, 4 doz. balances, 3 doz. standishes 'cum aliis' £46 13*s* 4*d* (14 July 1568).

651. *Egle* of Middelburg (30) Cornilis Chewt; Middelburg
[f. 200*b*] John Valyam: 18 tuns French wine *net* 15½ tuns 50*s* (14 July 1568).

652. *Red Lyon* of Amsterdam (30) Simon Allardson; Amsterdam
[f. 200*b*] John Lense: 300 ells Osnabrücks £4 (14 July 1568). Matthew Colclough: 10 lasts pitch £20 (15 July). [f. 202] Edward van Krog: 5 packs bundle-flax £40.

653. *Andrew* of Antwerp (40) Cornilis Johnson Sprite; Antwerp
[f. 201*b*] Thomas Gardener: 3 cwt aniseed, 150 lbs ginger, 200 lbs pepper £31 18*s* 4*d* (15 July 1568). William Megs: 24 brls soap £16. Daniel van Krow: 1 pack flax £8. John Alden: 50 lbs senna, 3 qrs 7 lbs wormseed, 312 lbs ginger, 44 lbs quicksilver £38 5*s* (16 July). William Allyn: 16 pcs Holland cloth, 5 pcs canvas striped with silk £21 13*s* 4*d* (17 July). William Cowper: 5 doz. knitted petticoats, 3 doz. thread petticoats, 6 doz. stammel hose, 12 doz. coarse gloves, 1 bed of silk with furniture ad valorem 200*s* £38 16*s* 8*d*. William Hobson: 200 lbs crossbow thread, 10 grs coarse dolls, 4 grs horse bells, 4 doz. lbs pack thread, 100 bundles paper £7. John Whit: 5 pcs Holland cloth, 13 ells cambric £8. [f. 208] William Elkin: 18 pcs linen cloth £21 13*s* 4*d* (19 July).

654. *Grene Claverblade* of Amsterdam (30) Garet Isbram; Amsterdam
[f. 201*b*] Richard Mouse: 2 lasts barrelled fish £12 (15 July 1568). Thomas Jenens: 2 lasts barrelled fish £12. [f. 202] John Edmunds: 20 brls fish £10.

655. *Owl* of Amsterdam (36) Jacob Peterson
[f. 202] Thomas Jenens: 3 lasts 4 brls fish, 360 lings, 400 staplefish £38 (15 July 1568). John Violet: 3 lasts 4 brls fish, 400 staplefish, 360 lings £37. [f. 203] Richard Mouse: 3 lasts 4 brls fish, 400 staplefish, 240 lings £34.

656. *George* of Purmerend Sibram Cornilis
[f. 202] John Violet: 5 lasts 4 brls fish, 240 lings, 200 staplefish £43 (15 July 1568).

657. *Peter* of Lee (40) John Tyler; Rouen
[f. 203*b*] John Harding: 1250 ells canvas £31 5*s* (16 July 1568). Hugh Offley: 2400 ells canvas, 12 grs playing cards, 5 reams cap-paper £78 13*s* 4*d*. Thomas Campbell: 1000 ells canvas £25. Oliver Fysher: 1300 ells canvas £32 10*s*. Humphrey Broune: 100 reams paper £13 6*s* 8*d*, 10 tuns French wine *net* 6 tuns 18*s*, 1½ tuns corrupt wine £4 10*s*. Robert Sadler: 2200 ells canvas £55 (17 July). John Olyf: 1000 ells canvas £25. Anthony Gamage: 2200 ells canvas £55. Richard Patrick: 230 reams paper, 1 doz. quilts, 40 grs combs, 15 grs cards, 20 grs woollen-lace, 100 grs points £61 8*s*. John Allot: 1400 ells canvas £35. [f. 208] John Myller: 1000 ells canvas £25 (19 July).

658. *Swan* of Flushing (38) John van Lorson; Amsterdam
[f. 204] Thomas Sandford: 600 lings, 960 coal-fish £28 (16 July 1568). [f. 207] Humphrey Kele: 2 tuns Coniac wine *net* 2 tuns 6*s* (17 July).

659. *Audry James* of London John Burrell of Ratcliff; Spain
[f. 204*b*] William Wydnell: 5 tuns oil *net* 4½ tuns £36 (16 July 1568). James Hawes: 18 tuns Seville oil *net* 16 tuns £128. Anthony Pylborogh: 5 tuns Seville oil *net* 4½ tuns £36. Edward Jackman: 20 pipes Seville oil *net* 17 pipes £68. Simon Brook: 5 tuns Seville oil *net* 4½ tuns £36. Edward Osborne: 5 tuns Seville oil *net* 4½ tuns £36. George Barnes: 20 butts sack *net* 18 butts 27*s* (17 July). Thomas Altham: 10 pipes Seville oil *net* 9 pipes £36. Reynold Barker: 5 tuns Seville oil *net* 4½ tuns £36 13*s* 4*d*. [f. 209] Robert Cogan: 10 doz. Spanish skins £30 (20 July).

660. *Black Egle* of Amsterdam (30) Cornilis Frederickson; Amsterdam
[f. 205*b*] Mary Peterson: 4 pcs Holland cloth £4 16*s* 8*d* (16 July 1568). [f. 206*b*] William Page: 12 lasts 'rouse' ashes £36 (17 July).

661. *Pellican* of Middelburg (36) Harman Johnson; Middelburg
[f. 206] Richard Eswick: 22 tuns 3 hhds Gascony wine *net* 18 tuns 54*s*, 5 tuns 3 hhds corrupt wine £17 5*s* (17 July).

662. *Fortune* of Middelburg (18) John Kettle; Middelburg
[f. 207] Simon de Starkey: 14 tuns Coniac wine *net* 10 tuns 30*s* (17 July 1568).

663. *Spredegle* of Dordrecht (50) Godfrey Dirickson; Dordrecht
[f. 207] Adrian Adrianson: 200 bundles white rods £3 6*s* 8*d* (17 July 1568).

664. *Owl* of Dordrecht (40) Jacob Floryson; Dordrecht
[f. 207] Adrian Adrianson: 300 bundles white rods £5 (17 July 1568).
[f. 207*b*] John Irelond: 300 cast stone pots £1 10*s* (19 July).

665. *Fortune* of Flushing (25) Simon Johnson; Flushing
[f. 207] Thomas Sandford: 480 lings, 600 coal-fish £22 (17 July 1568).
[f. 207*b*] Richard Knight: 4 tuns French wine *net* 3 tuns 9*s* (19 July).

666. *Falcon* of Haarlem S. Dirickson
[f. 208] John Violet: 3 lasts fish, 400 staplefish £24 (19 July 1568). Richard Mouse: 3 lasts barrelled fish, 200 staplefish, 120 lings £25. [f. 208] Thomas Jenens: 40 brls fish, 400 staplefish £26 (20 July).

667. *Swan* of Dordrecht (40) Dirick Jeniface; Dordrecht
[f. 208] John Johnson: 350 small bundles white rods £5 16*s* 8*d* (19 July 1568).

668. *Grene Falcon* of Dordrecht (40) John Tyson
[f. 208] John Johnson: 300 small bundles white rods £5 (19 July 1568).
[f. 208*b*] Melchior van Aldeneck: 40 awms Rhenish wine 40*s* (20 July).

669. *Christopher* of Antwerp (50) Christian Cornilis; Antwerp
[f. 208*b*] Matthew Colclough: 10 lasts pitch £20 (20 July 1568). Robert Brook: 60 cwt brazil £100. Roger Warffild: 6 cwt aniseed, 4 cwt argol, 100 bundles brown paper £15 6*s* 8*d*. Peter Vegelman: 4 tuns Gascony wine *net* 3 tuns 9*s*. Stephen Slany: 5 pcs fine Holland cloth £6 (22 July). Nicholas Luddington: 24 cwt madder £16. [f. 211*b*] Fernando Pointz: 400 yds Levant taffeta £33 6*s* 8*d* (29 July).

670. *Spredegle* of Amsterdam (40) John Read; Amsterdam
[f. 208*b*] Thomas Sandford: 800 staplefish, 3 lasts barrelled fish £30 (20 July 1568). Humphrey Keel: 2 lasts 2 brls fish, 600 lings £35. [f. 209] Thomas Hecker: 8 lasts ashes, 480 lings, 16 small cutting boards £40 16*s* 8*d*.

671. *Mereman* of Haarlem (40) Walter Simonson; Haarlem
[f. 208*b*] William Page: 8 lasts soap ashes £24 (20 July 1568). [f. 209] Mary Peterson: 5 pcs 1 half-pc. Holland cloth £6 13*s* 4*d*.

672. *Mychell* of Amsterdam (29) Henrick Johnson; Amsterdam
[f. 208*b*] William Page: 25 lasts soap ashes £75 (20 July 1568).

673. *Nightingale* D. Allardson [*sic*]
[f. 209] Edward van Krog: 2200 clapholt £4 10*s* (22 July 1568).

674. *Red Swan* of Bruges (60) Adrian Matyson; Bruges
[f. 209] William Gelders: 66 pcs buckram £14 13*s* 4*d* (22 July 1568).

Thomas Brazie: 162 pcs buckram £36. Lewis Sohire: 20 tuns corrupt French wine *net* 18 tuns £54. Owen Ridley: 57 doz. hemp £8. [f. 210] Thomas House: 75 pcs bustian, 12 pcs fustian £33 (23 July).

675. *Angell* of Dordrecht (40) Christian Angle; Dordrecht
[f. 209*b*] Walter Lyn: 80 awms Rhenish wine 80*s* (22 July 1568).

676. *Esperance* of Dieppe (15) Towsen Nicolas; Dieppe
[f. 209*b*] Hugh Offley: 30 cwt brazil £50 (22 July 1568). John Varry: 4 tuns Rochelle wine *net* 2½ tuns 6*s* 6*d*, 1½ tuns corrupt wine £4 10*s*.

677. *Christopher* of London (60) William Langley; Rouen
[f. 210] Matthew Colclogh: 5 tuns French wine *net* 3⅔ tuns 11*s*, 4 tuns corrupt wine £12, 3 tuns vinegar £7 (26 July 1568). John Bodleigh: 1200 ells canvas £16. Harry Buxton: 1200 ells canvas £30. Arthur Hansson: 2000 ells canvas £50. Robert Sadler: 1200 ells canvas £30. Richard Patrick: 100 reams paper, 1 doz. quilts, 25 grs combs, 6 doz. ounce balances, 20 small grs points, 6 doz. heath brushes, 18 grs playing cards £41 12*s*. Richard Renolds: 150 reams printing paper £20 (27 July). John Harding: 4 tuns vinegar £9 6*s* 8*d*. Richard Billam: 3 doz. small iron pots 15*s*. Richard Hyll: 3000 ells canvas £75 (28 July). Robert Cage: 2000 ells canvas £50. Walter Coppinger: 100 lbs rhubarb £66 13*s* 4*d*. Humphrey Broune: 80 reams paper, 12 grs playing cards £22 13*s* 4*d*. [f. 216*b*] John Hopworth: 30 doz. stone bottles £2 5*s* (31 July).

678. *Phenex* of Hull (50) Walter Hall; Rouen
[f. 210] Oliver Fissher: 600 ells canvas £15 (26 July 1568). Thomas Cambell: 1800 ells canvas £45. Richard Morris: 1400 ells canvas £35. Richard Renolds: 5 tuns French wine *net* 4 tuns 12*s*, 2 tuns corrupt wine £6, 4 tuns vinegar £10 13*s* 4*d*. Robert Sadler: 1400 ells canvas, 160 reams paper £56 6*s* 8*d*. John Milner: 1600 ells canvas £40. Harry Wayte: 27 grs playing cards, 12 doz. woolcards, 5 doz. iron pots £34 5*s*. William Handford: 30 doz. woolcards, 25 grs crewel lace £31 13*s* 4*d*. John Marshall: 2200 ells canvas £29 6*s* 8*d* (27 July). William Hobson: 22 grs combs in boxes, 12 grs crewel lace, 6 grs penners and horns, 2 doz. coarse gun flasks, 4 doz. wooden pipes, 11 grs playing cards £30 1*s* 8*d*. John Olyf: 800 ells canvas £20. Robert Fryer: 6 tuns French wine *net* 5 tuns 15*s*. Anthony Gamage: 1200 ells canvas £30 (28 July). Humphrey Broune: 100 reams paper, 12 grs playing cards £25 6*s* 8*d*. William Dale: 12 doz. woolcards, 30 reams paper, 20 reams loose cap-paper, 50 grs loose penny trenchers £21 (29 July). [f. 215*b*] Anthony Cage: 500 ells canvas £12 10*s* (30 July).

679. *Bark Collet* of London (120) Jacob Riddam; Spain
[f. 210] Thomas Turnebull: 10 pipes oil *net* 9 pipes £36 (26 July 1568). John Mun: 10 pipes oil *net* 9 pipes £36 (27 July). John Barne: 40 tuns train oil *net* 36 tuns £180. Robert How: 12 butts sack *net* 11 butts 16*s* 6*d* (28 July). Thomas Collet: 10 tuns sack *net* 9 tuns 27*s*, 5 tuns oil *net* 4½ tuns £36. Edward Osborne: 10 pipes Seville oil *net* 9 pipes £36. John Watson: 10 pipes Seville oil *net* 9 pipes £36. Robert Chambrelaine: 10 pipes oil

net 9 pipes £36. Cuthbert Brand: 8 butts sack 12*s*. John Spencer: 10 pipes Seville oil *net* 9 pipes £36. James Hawes: 6 butts sack 9*s*. Reynold Hollingworth: 9 pipes oil £36. Reynold Barker: 5 tuns Seville oil *net* 4½ tuns £36 (29 July). [f. 215*b*] William Thomas: 4½ cwt alum £7 10*s* (30 July).

680. *Elizabeth* of London (50) Thomas Harrison; Spain
[f. 210*b*] Francis Bowyer: 10 tons Spanish iron £40 (26 July 1568). Richard Folks: 5 tons Spanish iron £20. Edward Boies: 5 tons Spanish iron £20. Richard May: 5 tons Spanish iron £20. [f. 211*b*] William Silvester: 10 tuns Spanish iron £40.

681. *Pellican* of London (50) Richard Gyddy; Andalusia
[f. 210*b*] Thomas Turnebull: 20 butts sherry sack *net* 18 butts 27*s*, 20 pipes oil *net* 18 pipes £72 (26 July 1568). Robert Soll: 8 tuns sack *net* 16 butts 24*s*. Reynold Holinworth: 10 pipes oil *net* 9 pipes £36. Robert Fryer: 10 pipes oil *net* 9 pipes £36 (27 July). Richard Grange: 2 butts sack 3*s* (28 July). [f. 214*b*] Edmund Flyck: 10 pipes Seville oil *net* 9 pipes £36 (29 July).

682. *Christopher* of London (40) Thomas Wilson; Rouen
[f. 211] Robert Sadler: 80 reams paper £10 13*s* 4*d* (26 July 1568). Hugh Offley: 600 ells canvas, 20 grs playing cards £35. Lawrence Mello: 10 tuns corrupt wine £30, 5 tuns vinegar £11 13*s* 4*d*. Thomas Starky: 900 ells canvas £22 10*s* (28 July). Anthony Gamage: 1100 ells canvas £27 10*s*. [f. 213*b*] Humphrey Broune: 600 ells canvas, 110 reams paper £29 13*s* 4*d*.

683. *Lyon* of Ipswich (80) William Searles; Spain
[f. 211] Richard Staper: 10 pipes Seville oil *net* 9 pipes £36 (26 July 1568). Thomas Altham: 20 pipes oil *net* 18 pipes £72. John Mun: 10 butts sack *net* 9 butts 13*s* 10*d* (27 July). Lawrence Mello: 20 butts sack *net* 18 butts 27*s*. William Vagham: 4 tuns oil £32. Robert Barker: 6 tuns oil *net* 5½ tuns £44. Robert Cutter: 5 tuns oil *net* 4½ tuns £36. Robert Fryer: 20 butts sack *net* 18 butts 27*s*. James Hawes: 13 doz. Spanish skins £39. Emanuel Wolley: 4 pipes Seville oil £16. Emanuel Wolley: 1 tun sack 3*s*, 140 doz. cork £4. Edmund Flick: 5 tuns sack *net* 4½ tuns 13*s* 6*d* (28 July). Ralph More: 5 tuns Seville oil *net* 4½ tuns £36. William Cutter: 5 tuns Seville oil *net* 4½ tuns £36. [f. 215*b*] William Thomas: 4½ cwt alum £7 10*s* (30 July).

684. *Christ* of London (90) Bartholomew Storm; Andalusia
[f. 212] Edward Jackman: 10 pipes Seville oil *net* 9 pipes £36 (27 July 1568). Richard Venables: 10 pipes Seville oil *net* 9 pipes £36. Robert Fryer: 20 butts sack *net* 18 butts 27*s*. George Barne: 10 tuns Seville oil *net* 9 tuns £72 (28 July). William Shacrost: 6 tuns oil *net* 5½ tuns, 100 doz. hand baskets, 10 hd lbs cork, 60 yds Spanish taffeta £72 3*s* 4*d*, 1 tun sack *net* 2 butts 3*s*. John Watson: 10 pipes oil *net* 9 pipes £36. Cuthbert Brand: 10 pipes oil *net* 9 pipes £36. Margaret Chambarlaine: 6 pipes oil £24. Edmund Hugan: 10 butts sack *net* 9 butts 13*s* 6*d*. John Spencer: 18 pipes oil *net* 16 pipes £64. [f. 214*b*] Henry Becher: 10 pipes Seville oil *net* 9 pipes £36 (29 July).

685. *Katharine* of London (80) Thomas Pollard; Sanlucar
[f. 212*b*] Henry Hungat: 12 weys white salt, 14 cwt bast-cables £21 13*s* 4*d* (28 July 1568). Edmund Hugan: 5 pipes oil £20. [f. 215*b*] Robert Barker: 1 tun oil £8 (30 July).

686. *Star* of London John Podge; Rouen
[f. 213*b*] Richard Morris: 1400 ells canvas £35 (28 July 1568). Oliver Fysher: 2100 ells canvas £52 10*s*. Thomas Longston: 40 cwt dates, 60 cwt prunes £110 (29 July). Robert Sadler: 600 ells canvas, 80 reams paper, 40 reams loose paper £31. William Hobson: 12 doz. lbs piecing thread, 4 grs spectacles, 80 butts Lyons thread, 10 pcs boultel £28. Anthony Cage: 400 ells canvas £10 (30 July). [f. 215*b*] Thomas Starky: 400 ells canvas £10.

687. *Little Lyon* of Dieppe (19) Gillam Angle; Dieppe
[f. 213*b*] Jacques Fyshet: 2 tuns French wine *net* 1½ tuns 4*s* 6*d*, 2 tuns corrupt wine £6 (28 July 1568). [f. 214*b*] Humphrey Broune: 2 tuns French wine *net* 1½ tuns 4*s* 6*d*, 200 ells canvas, 1 tun corrupt wine £8.

688. *Bonadventure* of Dieppe (20) John Malbraunch; Dieppe
[f. 213*b*] Jacques Fyshet: 6 hhds Gascony wine *net* 4 hhds 3*s* (28 July 1568).

689. *Richard Arundell* of London (90) Richard Twid; Barbary
[f. 214*b*] Gerard Gore: 141 cwt sugar, 35 cwt dates £545 (28 July 1568). Reynold Hollinworth: 18 cwt sugar £60 (29 July). Edward Jackman: 14 cwt sugar, 126 cwt dates, 9 hhds panele £323 3*s* 4*d*. William Wydnall: 75 cwt sugar, 20 cwt panele £260. Sir William Garrard: 9 cwt sugar, 2 hhds panele, 62 cwt dates £159. John Mun: 36 cwt sugar £120. John Whit: 1 hhd panele £2 10*s* (30 July). [f. 215*b*] Anthony Moslye: 64 cwt sugar £213 6*s* 8*d*.

690. *Egle* of Middelburg Laurence Senson
[f. 214*b*] Andrew de Loe: 5 tuns French wine *net* 4 tuns 12*s* (28 July 1568).

691. *Jesus* of Aldeburgh (60) John Smyth
[f. 215*b*] Thomas Altham: 10 pipes oil *net* 9 pipes £36 (30 July 1568). John Raven: 10 pipes oil *net* 9 pipes £36. John Baker: 5 tuns Seville oil *net* 4½ tuns £36. George Saunders: 30 pipes train oil *net* 24 pipes £60. John Hall: 10 pipes oil *net* 9 pipes £36. Thomas Blanck: 5 tuns Seville oil *net* 4½ tuns £36 (31 July). Edward Osburne: 10 pipes Seville oil *net* 9 pipes £36. [f. 217] Thomas Mawe: 40 doz. cork, 40 doz. hand baskets £12 (3 Aug).

692. *Barbera* of Venice (400) Nicholas de Cortsolo; Venice
[f. 216] Mark Anthony Balinsa: 647 butts 49 caroteels malmsey and muscatel *net* 482 butts 723*s* (31 July 1568). [f. 217] Jacob Bisken: 53 butts 33 caroteels sweet wine *net* 35 butts 52*s* 6*d* (7 Aug).[1]

1. Wines by licence of Benedict Spinola: see **53** n. 3.

693. *Peter* of 'Barling' (10) William Odyam; Faversham [*sic*]
[f. 216] Thomas Sound: 200 ells white 200 ells brown Hazebroucks £9
(31 July 1568).

694. *John* of Poole (26) Leonard Nicoll; Spain
[f. 216*b*] Thomas Bainton: 24 tuns sack *net* 21 tuns 63*s* (31 July 1568).
Godfrey Wilson: 80 yds single Spanish taffeta £16 (3 Aug). [f. 217] Thomas
Bampton: 14 doz. Spanish skins £42.

695. *Mary Fortune* of Aldeburgh (50) Thomas Johnson; The Bay
[f. 216*b*] Thomas Johnson: 36 weys bay salt £36 (31 July 1568).

696. *John* of Flushing Jacob Hubright
[f. 216*b*] Peter van der Wall: 18 tuns corrupt Gascony wine £54 (31 July
1568).

697. *Blew Falcon* of Amsterdam N. Johnson
[f. 216*b*] Humphrey Broune: 2 millstones £4 (3 Aug 1568).

698. *Unicorn* of St. Omer Jacob Stephen
[f. 216*b*] Owen Rydley: 6 cwt hops £3 (3 Aug 1568).

699. *Flying Gost* of Zaandam (130) Cornilis Johnson; Danzig
[f. 216*b*] William James: 17 lasts pitch, 2 shocks deal, 1350 wainscots,
2400 clapholt, 100 oars £113 (3 Aug 1568).

700. *Lumbarda* of Candy (200) Matheo de Candy; Candy
[f. 217] Theodoro Lumbardo: 240 butts 40 caroteels sweet wine *net* 178
butts 267*s* (6 Aug 1568). [f. 236] Theodoro Lumbardo: 30 caroteels sweet
wine *net* 6 butts 9*s* (20 Aug).
    1. Wines by Spinola's licence: see **53** n. 3.

701. *Cock* of Dordrecht (50) Govert Francis; Dordrecht
[f. 217] Andrew Banbery: 200 bundles white rods £3 6*s* 8*d* (6 Aug 1568).
[f. 217*b*] Cornelis Nollet: 56 awms Rhenish wine 56*s* (7 Aug).

702. *Sacre* of Lee (28) John Harris; Antwerp
[f. 217] Thomas Randall: 42 yds velvet, 100 ells sarcenet £48 3*s* 4*d* (7 Aug
1568). William Colles: 75 lbs quicksilver, 33 lbs mace £16. George
Stockmed: 700 lbs pepper £58 6*s* 8*d*. John Car: 2 half-brls small nails,
244 iron plates £14. John Jackman: 350 lbs ginger £26 5*s*. Roger Morry:
6 cwt madder £14 13*s* 4*d* (9 Aug). Peter Honnyngborne: 11 cwt kettles
£23. William Cockin: 13020 raw rumney budge skins £33. William
Luddington: 150 lbs pepper, 50 lbs cloves, 36 lbs turmeric, 1¼ cwt bay
berries, 1½ cwt white lead, 50 lbs marking stones £29. Alexander Sherington: 120 yds taffeta £40. Roger Knot: 7½ cwt battery £15. John Spencer:
200 lbs pepper, 3½ cwt bay berries £19. Sir John York: 125 lbs cinnamon,
75 lbs cloves £43 15*s*. Thomas Gawdbie: 18 pcs Holland cloth, 13 pcs
cambric £47 13*s* 4*d*. Thomas Gardiner: 400 lbs pepper, 3½ cwt saltpetre,

75 lbs quicksilver, 4½ cwt aniseed, 1 cwt coriander seed £48 16s 8d. John Eliets: 10 doz. lbs crewel, 8 doz. crewel pieces, 3 grs halfpennyware glasses, 4 doz. thou. needles, 2 thou. thimbles, 4 thou. tacks, 1 thou. bodkins, 50 lbs counters, 6 doz. weaver's shuttles, 1 cwt pack thread £24 5s. Thomas Aldersey: 80 pcs mockado £53 6s 8d. George Stockmed: 600 lbs pepper £50. Richard Billingsley: 10 doz. lbs bottom thread, 30 grs harp strings, 7 doz. lbs Bruges thread £8 13s 4d (10 Aug). John Wanton: 450 lbs pepper £37 10s. Francis Tuck: 400 lbs pepper £33 6s 8d. Henry Becher: 88 pcs Genoa fustian £58 13s 4d. Edward Best: 540 ells harnesdale cloth £21 12s. Edward Bright: 5 lasts soap ashes, 38 cwt madder, 1 half-brl small nails, 1 half-brl head nails £44 6s 8d. Nicholas Spering: 12 grs copper bands, 4 doz. coarse comb brushes, 4 doz. coarse gold weights, 9 doz. looking glasses £14. Nicholas Luddington: 40 cwt madder £26 13s 4d. William Hobbs: 12 brls grey soap £8. James Cannon: 26 lbs coarse copper gold upon thread, 6 doz. coarse quilted night caps of linen at 5s the dozen £4 (11 Aug). Randal Manning: 12 pcs Holland cloth £14 8s 4d. Matthew Fyld: 20 pcs mockado £13 6s 8d. Richard Pipe: 50 pcs mockado £33 6s 8d. [f. 224] Sir Christopher Draper: 20 pcs poldavis £20 (13 Aug).

703. *Mary George* of London (100) Peter Richardson; Antwerp
[f. 217] Thomas Randall: 64 doz. washing balls £5 5s (7 Aug 1568). William Hewet: 21½ cwt estrige wool £17 18s 4d. Thomas Bowyer: 2 hd iron plates, 4 doz. wooden beams at 40s, 30 pair andirons with fireshovels and tongs, 46 pair creepers £16. John Car: 13 pair latten andirons, 2 doz. small bed pans, 18 doz. latten candle plates, 18 trunks, 10 thou. balls £41 11s 8d. John Lambert: 114 cwt unwrought flax £76. John Jackman: 260 lbs pepper, 2 cwt liquorice, 12 lbs vermilion, 18 lbs quicksilver, 40 lbs long pepper, 2 cwt bay berries, 150 lbs quicksilver £45 15s. Thomas Cambell: 10 lasts soap ashes £30. Robert Trapham: 14 cwt iron pans £9 6s 8d (9 Aug). John Alden: 72 cwt liquorice, 4¼ cwt saltpetre, 8½ cwt alum, 12 Antwerp lutes £60 10s. Nicholas Garnous: 40 pcs double mockado £26 13s 4d. Thomas Longston: 11 cwt estrige wool £9 3s 4d. William Luddington: 150 lbs pepper, 7½ cwt liquorice £16. William Towerson: 140 ells wool tapestry £7. Roger Knot: 20 cwt battery £40. Matthew Cradrok: 8 pcs Holland cloth £9 16s 8d. James Harvie: 4 doz. whip-saws, 1 doz. tenon-saws £6 6s 8d. John Spencer: 214 lbs pepper, 75 lbs nutmegs, 25 lbs mace, 20 lbs vermilion, 4 cwt aniseed £45. Thomas Gawdbie: 28 pcs Holland cloth £33 13s 4d. Thomas Parker: 13 pcs dornick with wool, 6 pcs bustian £10 10s. Thomas Gardner: 3½ cwt saltpetre £4 15s. Roger Warfyld: 2 cwt candy, 2 cwt varnish, 15 cwt orpiment, 300 lbs crossbow thread, 2 brls orchil £21 10s. Richard Billingsley: 10 doz. lbs narrow inkle, 40 doz. thou. pins, 12 pcs Beaupreau boultel, 5 doz. lbs bottom thread £16 15s (10 Aug). John Borne: 16 grs coarse copper bands, 10 grs thread points, 50 doz. thou. pins, 1 thou. thimbles, 4 doz. lbs bottom thread £17 8s 4d. Francis Tuck: 100 lbs cloves £25. Richard Billam: 48 cwt madder £32. Henry Becher: 25 doz. lbs inkle, 10 doz. lbs Bruges thread, 7 doz. thou. needles, 10 doz. check pieces £35 6s 8d. Edward Bright: 40 cwt madder £26 13s 4d. William Hobbs: 4½ doz. sealed carpets, 23 blankets, 3 doz. lince, 53 ells hair tapestry, 31 pcs linen cloth, 1 last rape

oil £75 8s 4d. Robert Taylor: 60 cwt mull-madder £7 10s. Thomas Castlin: 60 cwt madder £40. Thomas Hecker: 300 bundles brown paper, 8 bundles small basts £12. Thomas Eaton: 20 doz. lbs Bruges thread, 4 doz. lbs inkle, 150 lbs counters, 9 doz. thou. needles, 1 grs horse bells, 2 doz. lbs bottom pack thread, 5 doz. crewel pieces, 1 thou. awl blades, 6 grs thread points, 24 grs halfpennyware glasses £40 8s 4d. Randal Manning: 13 pcs Holland cloth £15 13s 4d (11 Aug). Stephen Slany: 40 pcs Holland cloth £48. Thomas Thorp: 1½ cwt corn powder £2 10s. John Boylson: 60 pcs mockado £40. William Sherington: 2 half-packs flax, 60 pcs boultel £20 (12 Aug). John Wanton: 15 cwt prunes, 7 cwt bay berries, 63 cwt mull-madder £20. William Colles: 6 cwt dates, 20 cwt prunes £22. Francis Benizen: 3½ hd lbs inkle £11 13s 4d. Robert Walkeden: 600 ells 'clincent' canvas £9. Edmund Burton: 14 cwt iron pans, 22 doz. lince £25 10s. George Stockmed: 2 half-packs unwrought flax, 5 cwt wrought flax £13. Matthew Fyld: 30 pcs camlet and grogram, 30 pcs narrow worsted £55. [f. 223b] Sir William Chester: 190 half-pcs Genoa fustian £63 6s 8d.

704. *Sea Rider* of Antwerp (40) Jacob Laurence; Antwerp
[f. 217b] Hartik van Sprecleson: 3 packs flax £24 (7 Aug 1568). John Jackman: 100 bundles brown paper £3 6s 8d. Thomas Barker: 27 cwt battery £54 (9 Aug). Peter Honnyngborne: 5½ cwt kettles £11. John Smyth: 2 chests Burgundy glass £4. Robert Broke: 24 cwt hops, 42 cwt madder £40. George Byshop: 1 roll with maps ad valorem £2. Thomas Thorp: 100 pcs raisins £25 (10 Aug). [f. 222] Randal Manning: 175 lbs pepper £14 11s 8d (11 Aug).

705. *Swan* of Antwerp Adrian Johnson; Antwerp
[f. 218] William Hewet: 6 cwt wrought flax £6 (7 Aug 1568).

706. *Mychell* of Flushing Peter Claison
[f. 219] Thomas Sandford: 720 lings £24 (9 Aug 1568). [f. 219b] Michael Lyon: 10 pcs sackcloth striped with thread, 4 pcs coarse linen cloth, 12 doz. lbs Bruges thread £37 16s 8d.

707. *Swan* of Amsterdam (30) Jacob Tyson; Amsterdam
[f. 219] Edward van Crog: 600 wainscots, 1600 clapholt £28 (9 Aug 1568).

708. *Fortune* of Amsterdam (30) Eyffe Cornilis; Amsterdam
[f. 219b] William Megs: 23 lasts soap ashes, 1 last black soap £77 (9 Aug 1568). John Violet: 400 staplefish, 360 lings, 2 lasts barrelled fish £30 (10 Aug). Richard Mouse: 720 lings, 18 brls fish, 800 staplefish £45. John Edmunds: 12 brls fish, 480 lings, 600 staplefish £31. [f. 222b] Thomas Beam: 3 pcs Holland cloth £3 13s 4d (11 Aug).

709. *Margaret* of Amsterdam (30) Raire Cornilis; Amsterdam
[f. 219b] William Megs: 1 last black soap £8 (9 Aug 1568). Adam Cooper: 11 pcs linen cloth £13 3s 4d. William Page: 1 last soap £8 (10 Aug). John Lence: 31 pcs Holland cloth £37 3s 4d. [f. 222b] Humphrey Kele: 240 lings £8 (12 Aug).

710. *John* of London (40) Stephen Read; Antwerp

[f. 220] George Stockmed: 600 lbs pepper, 80 lbs ginger £56 (9 Aug 1568). Edmund Burton: 18¾ cwt battery, 14½ cwt iron wire, 10 doz. whip-saws, 8 doz. two-hand-saws, 21 doz. snuffers, 18 doz. pincers, 6 grs carving tools, 12 thou. awl blades, 4 doz. planing irons, 3 grs goldsmith's files, 30 grs horse bells, 60 lbs counters, 1½ grs small hanging locks, 60 lbs curtain rings, 44 sum card nails £107 (12 Aug). Roger Knot: 23 cwt battery £46 (14 Aug). Sir John York: 600 lbs pepper, 350 lbs ginger £76 5s (16 Aug). John Jackman: 340 lbs ginger £25 10s. Robert Scarboro: 7 cwt madder £4 13s 4d. Stephen Slany: 40 pcs Holland cloth £48. John Spencer: 214 lbs pepper, 1½ cwt cumin, 1¼ cwt turmeric, 25 lbs mace, 30 lbs quicksilver, 6 cwt bay berries £38 6s 8d. John Car: 10 cwt iron wire £16 13s 4d. Thomas Eaton: 6 doz. lbs crewel, 4 doz. crewel pieces, 1 thou. awl blades, 2 thou. thimbles, 7 grs halfpennyware glasses £25 1s 8d. John Eliets: 70 doz. thou. pins, 8 doz. lbs crewel, 5 doz. thou. needles, 8 grs horse bells, 4 doz. crewel pieces, 4 doz. thread pieces, 3 doz. lbs inkle, 4 doz. lbs Bruges thread £34. Geoffrey Walkeden: 20 pcs Holland cloth, 400 ells Castile canvas £30. Edward Bright: 5 lasts soap ashes, 3 half-brls head nails, 1½ grs small locks, 4 doz. horse locks, 1½ grs gate locks, 2 grs joiner's tools, 7 grs horse bells, 9 cwt battery £44 8s 4d. John Alden: 4 cwt saltpetre, 7 cwt red lead, 12½ cwt aniseed, 6 cwt arsenic and rosalger, 1¾ cwt marking stones, 43 lbs garbled mace, 35 lbs vermilion £53 16s 8d. Roger Warfild: 4 hd lbs gum, 4 cwt caraway seed, 7 cwt argol, 2 half-brls treacle, 2 cwt white lead, 1½ cwt candy £24 16s. John Mun: 40 doz. lbs Oudenaarde thread, 1 doz. lbs crewel yarn, 15 doz. pcs caddis riband, 4 great grs thread points, 6 doz. cloth pinpillows, 1 doz. comb cases garnished with wooden combs, 4 doz. leather bags, 4 doz. large looking glasses, 36 doz. thread cards, 3 doz. lbs piecing thread, 2 grs single knives £50 10s (17 Aug). William Hobbs: 316 ells hair tapestry, 5 doz. 8 sealed carpets, 1 last grey soap £27 8s. Nicholas Hewet: 20 pair iron andirons, 20 tongs, 20 fireshovels £8 13s 4d. Thomas Starkey: 48 pcs Olonne cloth £32. John Borne: 14 doz. lbs bottom pack thread, 6 grs thread points, 3 doz. crewel pieces, 30 doz. thou. pins, 2 doz. lbs coarse crewel £14. Nicholas Luddington: 40 cwt madder £26 13s 4d. Thomas Rose: 15 pcs Genoa fustian, 15 pcs mockado £20. William Towerson: 130 ells wool tapestry, 5½ doz. Ghentish carpets £14 15s. Sir Christopher Draper: 20 pcs poldavis £20. Thomas Thorp: 400 lbs pepper £33 6s 8d. Francis Tooke: 3 cwt aniseed, 20 lbs senna £6 10s. Henry Becher: 52 doz. lbs Oudenaarde thread, 9 pcs Genoa fustian £40 13s 4d (18 Aug). John Sutton: 28 doz. lince £21. Robert Scarboro: 6 cwt madder £4. Randal Manyng: 18 pcs Ghentish cloth £21 13s 4d. Thomas Gaudby: 20 pcs Holland cloth £24. Thomas Gardner: 5 cwt aniseed, 3 cwt starch, 300 lbs matches £11 3s 4d. [f. 233b] Robert Taylor: 250 yds Levant taffeta, 30 yds Lucca taffeta £30 16s 8d.

711. *Mychell* of Amsterdam (35) Laurence Lobranson; Amsterdam

[f. 220] Thomas Jenens: 4 lasts barrelled fish, 200 staplefish £27 (10 Aug 1568). John Violet: 4 lasts barrelled fish £24. Richard Mouse: 4 lasts barrelled fish, 200 staplefish £27. John Edmunds: 30 brls fish, 100 staplefish £16 10s. [f. 222b] Alard Bartrinck: 25 pcs Gelders cloth £31 8s 4d (12 Aug).

712. *Grene Dragon* of Haarlem (35) Arnold Christ; Haarlem
[f. 220b] Thomas Jenens: 4 lasts barrelled fish, 120 lings, 200 staplefish £31 (10 Aug 1568). John Violet: 200 staplefish, 120 lings, 3 lasts barrelled fish £25. Richard Mouse: 3 lasts barrelled fish, 100 staplefish £19 10s. John Edmunds: 30 brls fish, 120 lings, 100 staplefish £20 10s. [f. 222] Thomas Sandford: 2 lasts barrelled fish £12 (11 Aug).

713. *Jerusalem* of Amsterdam (40) Jacob Garretson; Amsterdam
[f. 220b] Thomas Jenens: 500 staplefish, 360 lings £19 (10 Aug 1568). John Violet: 4½ lasts fish £27. Luder van Dorne: 10 half-packs bale-flax £40 (12 Aug).[1] [f. 228b] Edward van Krog: 150 wainscots, 1200 clapholt £9 (17 Aug).

> 1. An entry was made under the *Jerusalem* on 13 August in the name of Jasper van de Lam. This has been erased and transferred to the aliens' book [f. 223b].

714. *Mary George* of London (80) John Fryer; The Bay
[f. 220b] Thomas Shotsam: 14 weys bay salt £14 (10 Aug 1568).

715. *Lyon* of London (75) John Dunstan; Russia
[f. 220b] John Brook 'et sociis': 74 tuns train oil *net* 66 tuns £330 (10 Aug 1568).

716. *Mary Fortune* of Newcastle (50) Lionel Reveley; Danzig
[f. 221b] Thomas Allyn: 20 cwt rough hemp £20 (10 Aug 1568). William Cockin: 7 lasts ashes, 36 cwt cordage, 4 cwt feathers £51 (12 Aug). Thomas Russell: 40 cwt cables £26 13s 4d. Robert Collet: 30 cwt cordage, 24 cwt madder £36. [f. 234b] Dunstan Walton: 21 cwt wax £63 (19 Aug).

717. *Cock* of Bruges (60) Jacob Albright; Bruges
[f. 222] John Olyff: 200 bundles white rods, 5 doz. baskets £17 3s 4d (11 Aug 1568). Thomas Brasie: 156 pcs buckram £34 13s 4d.

718. *Pellican* of Haarlem (30) Garret Dirickson; Amsterdam
[f. 222b] Adam Cooper: 3 pcs Holland cloth £3 13s 4d (12 Aug 1568). [f. 226] Alard Bartrinck: 30 pcs Gelders cloth £36 (16 Aug).

719. *Whit Falcon* of Amsterdam Cornilis Johnson; Amsterdam
[f. 223] William Cockin: 2 lasts ashes £6 (12 Aug 1568). Thomas Allyn: 10 lasts pitch, 2400 clapholt, 150 wainscots, 200 spruce deals, 1100 rasters £101 (13 Aug). [f. 224] Edmund Boldero: 10 lasts pitch £20 (14 Aug).

720. *Thre Kings* of Flushing (14) Marten Mychelson; Flushing
[f. 223b] Humphrey Kele: 360 lings £12 (13 Aug 1568).

721. *Black Egle* of Middelburg Cornilis Jobson; Middelburg
[f. 224] John Clayson: 18 tuns Gascony wine *net* 12 tuns 36s, 3 tuns corrupt wine £10 10s (13 Aug 1568).

722. *Romaine* of Antwerp (40) Paul Lumpet; Antwerp
[f. 224] Roger Warfild: 28 cwt hops £14 (13 Aug 1568). Thomas Barker: 18 cwt battery £36 (16 Aug). Court Ellers: 16 cwt estrige wool £13 6s 8d (18 Aug). [f. 235b] Robert Hungat: 30 lbs Bruges silk £22 10s (20 Aug).

723. *Sea Dog* of Amsterdam (30) Cornilis Claison; Amsterdam
[f. 224] John Edmund: 120 lings, 400 staplefish, 18 brls fish £19 (14 Aug 1568). [f. 225b] Thomas Jenens: 360 lings, 500 staplefish, 30 brls fish £34 10s (16 Aug).

724. *Owl* of Amsterdam (35) Jacob Peterson; Amsterdam
[f. 224] John Edmund: 240 lings, 800 staplefish £20 (14 Aug 1568). John Violet: 1200 staplefish, 960 lings £50 (16 Aug). [f. 226] Richard Mouse: 600 lings, 1000 staplefish £35.

725. *Bucket* of Flushing (20) John Snow; Flushing
[f. 224] Humphrey Kele: 6 tuns corrupt French wine £18, 600 lings, 7 cwt hops £23 10s (14 Aug 1568).

726. *Falcon* of Flushing Peter Gaisire
[f. 224b] Martin Prety: 6 half-pcs bustian £2 (14 Aug 1568).

727. *Hart* of Bergen-op-Zoom (25) Thomas Johnson; Bergen-op-Zoom
[f. 224b] George Stockmed: 10 cwt wrought flax £10 (14 Aug 1568). Thomas Eaton: 7 cwt wrought flax £7. Arthur Hale: 12½ cwt flax £12 10s (16 Aug). Ancelm Becket: 20¾ cwt flax £20 15s. Nicholas Hewet: 36 cwt oakum, 6 cwt wrought flax £15 (17 Aug). John Boylson: 16 cwt unwrought flax £10 13s 4d. Robert Luce: 12 cwt wrought flax £12. Robert Scarboro: 10 cwt wrought flax £10. John Mun: 3 doz. playing tables £2 5s (18 Aug). [f. 231] Roger Morrey: 4 cwt flax £4.

728. *Pellican* of London (150) Stephen Johnson; Danzig
[f. 224b] Richard Gurney: 3 packs flax £24 (14 Aug 1568). Alard Bartrinck: 2 half-packs flax, 1800 clapholt, 19 firkins sturgeon £25 10s (16 Aug). William Cockin: 5 lasts soap ashes £15. Gervais Simons: 4 lasts soap ashes £12 (17 Aug). Robert Hilson: 2 packs hemp, 4½ lasts pitch £49. George Mylner: 6 lasts soap ashes, 1 pack 2 half-packs flax £34. Richard Gurney: 1 pack 1 half-pack flax, 12 cwt hemp, 12 kegs eels £26. Edmund Boldero: 6 lasts ashes £18. William James: 9 packs 1 half-pack flax, 20 lasts ashes £136. Dunstan Walton: 30 lasts ashes £90 (19 Aug). [f. 236] John Watson: 15 chests £3 6s 8d (20 Aug).

729. *Swepstake*[1] of Lee (60) John Morse; Antwerp
[f. 224b] William Colles: 170 lbs ginger £12 15s (14 Aug 1568). Robert Trapham: 14 cwt frying pans £9 6s 8d (16 Aug). Nicholas Warner: 900 ells canvas £12. Roger Knot: 16 cwt battery £32. Anthony Warfyld: 400 lbs pepper £33 6s 8d. Robert Brook: 900 lbs pepper £75. William Sherington: 40 lbs ferret silk, 120 yds taffeta £56 13s 4d. Thomas Eaton: 10 doz. lbs crewel, 4 doz. thou. needles, 4 doz. crewel pieces, 20 lbs clavi-

chord wire, 3 grs thread points, 1 grs thread-lace, 3 doz. lbs wrought inkle, 4 pcs dornick with wool, 5 grs halfpennyware glasses £21 18s.[2] George Stockmed: 275 lbs ginger £20 12s. Lawrence Wethers: 1 last Flemish soap £8. Thomas Longston: 22 cwt coarse madder, 450 lbs pepper, 30 lbs cloves £47 15s (17 Aug). William Gyfford: 50 pcs grogram camlet £66 13s 4d. Wolston Dixi: 52 pcs Holland cloth £62 8s 4d. Thomas Randall: 400 yds Levant taffeta, 50 yds satin £55 16s 8d. Henry Bradborne: 48 cwt madder, 30 cwt brazil £82. Thomas Aldersey: 320 ells sarcenet £53 6s 8d. Robert Exton: 5¼ cwt feathers £7 16s 8d. John Alden: 50 doz. empty barrels £5. William Hobbs: 436 ells hair tapestry, 2 doz. 9 sealed carpets, 38 Turnhout ticks £31 6s 8d. Richard Billingsley: 50 doz. thou. pins, 10 doz. lbs bottom thread, 20 grs harp strings £10 6s 8d. John Car: 3 half-brls steel, 30 cwt iron pans, 150 iron doubles, 18 pair andirons with the furniture, 6 doz. iron gridirons, 8 doz. hammers £52 18s. John Borne: 20 doz. lbs bottom pack thread, 10 doz. lbs Bruges thread, 8 doz. lbs inkle, 1½ thou. thimbles, 4 doz. crewel pieces, 6 lbs coarse crewel £18 13s 4d. Peter Honyngborne: 7½ cwt kettles, 7 cwt dripping pans £19 13s 4d. John Spencer: 125 lbs ginger, 3 qrs coriander seed, 1¼ cwt copperas £10 18s. Nicholas Spering: 6 doz. lbs bottom pack thread, 3 grs knives, 27 doz. looking glasses, 6 doz. writing tables, 2 doz. standishes, 4 doz. gilt snuffers, 13 doz. coarse gold weights, 6 doz. petticoats, 120 razors, 1 grs coarse dolls £26 8s. William Towerson: 840 ells wool tapestry, 550 ells hair tapestry, 5 doz. coarse cushion cloths £66 6s 8d. John Eliets: 8 doz. thread pieces, 12 doz. crewel pieces, 4 grs thread points, 80 doz. thou. pins, 4 doz. lbs crewel, 2 thou. thimbles, 4 doz. lbs Bruges thread, 2 great grs dog bells £32 13s 4d. Thomas Thorp: 2 cwt corn powder £3 6s 8d. John Woodward: 2 bales Ulm fustian £30. Thomas Grymes: 30 pcs Holland cloth £36 (18 Aug). John Mun: 11 pcs Holland cloth £13 5s. John Lambert: 31 cwt iron pans £20 13s 4d. Nicholas Ludington: 9 cwt tow, 450 lbs pepper, 3½ cwt aniseed £45 3s 4d. Thomas Parker: 12 doz. quilted caps, 31 lbs sister's thread, 30 pcs bustian, 8 pcs dornick with wool £28 8s. Anthony Fytton: 4 cwt aniseed, 6 firkins litmus £11 6s 8d. Richard Billam: 40 cwt madder £26 13s 4d. George Colimer: 12 thou. tennis balls £12. William Elkin: 144 yds frizado £36. Edmund Burton: 42 cwt madder, 8 cwt black plates, 1 half-brl head nails, 4 cwt iron pans £15 5s. Thomas Gardiner: 1¼ cwt gunpowder, 2 half-brls litmus £4 1s 8d. Thomas Gaudbie: 630 ells harnesdale cloth £25 3s 4d. William Bower: 1 last soap, 10 hd plates £14 13s 4d. William Hewet: 2 half-brls steel, 12 cwt flax £24. John Collymer: 2 brls Flemish treacle £4. Robert Scarboro: 12 chamber stools without pans £1 10s. Stephen Slany: 50 pcs Holland cloth £60. Nicholas Spering: 5 grs coarse knives, 1 grs halfpennyware glasses, 6 wooden standishes, 40 lbs counters £9 10s. William Bond: 32 cwt rope-yarn £21 6s 8d (19 Aug). [f. 235] Francis Tooke: 300 lbs pepper, 20 lbs senna, 20 lbs cinnamon £30 10s.

1. Or *Mary Fortune*.
2. This and subsequent entries are made under the *Mary Fortune*.

730. *Prime Rose* of Milton (60) Henry Church; Antwerp
[f. 224b] William Colles: 175 lbs nutmegs, 26 lbs mace £37 16s 8d. (14 Aug

1568). Thomas Barker: 6 cwt battery £12 (16 Aug). William Bower: 1 last grey soap, 10 cwt double plates, 6 cwt single plates, 20 cwt iron wire £52. John Jackman: 450 lbs pepper £37 10s. William Sherington: 100 ells sarcenet £6 13s 4d. John Lambert: 32 cwt battery £65. Thomas Eaton: 4 pcs dornick with wool, 6 doz. lbs crewel, 8 doz. lbs thread points, 10 doz. crewel pieces, 3 doz. lbs wrought inkle, 3 grs halfpennyware glasses £17 16s 8d. George Stockmed: 5 cwt wrought flax £5. Richard Pipe: 60 pcs mockado £40. Ancelm Becket: 6 cwt flax £6. Thomas Longston: 22 cwt mull-madder, 450 lbs pepper £40 5s (17 Aug). Thomas Randall: 140 yds Levant taffeta £11 13s 4d. Henry Bradborne: 48 cwt madder, 20 cwt brazil £65 6s 8d. Thomas Aldersey: 90 pcs mockado £60. Robert Exton: 1 pack flax, 7 cwt feathers £18 10s. John Alden: 7 cwt dates, 46 lbs cinnamon, 114 lbs ginger £33 15s. William Hobbs: 1 last grey soap £8. Richard Billingsley: 10 doz. lbs bottom pack thread, 5 doz. lbs Bruges thread, 15 doz. thou. pins, 12 pcs Beaupreau boultel £10 3s 4d. John Car: 30 cwt 'ames' iron, 27 cwt iron pans, 4 hd iron plates, 3½ cwt varnish, ironmongery ad valorem £25 £55 10s. John Borne: 80 doz. thou. pins, 6 grs pennyware glasses, 8 doz. lbs coarse crewel £22 8s. Thomas Castlin: 5 cwt sugar £16. Roland Erlington: 26 doz. lbs Bruges thread, 4 doz. lbs bottom pack thread £18 1s 8d. Sir William Chester: 30 pcs Holland cloth £36. Peter Honyngborne: 7½ cwt kettles, 2 lbs iron wire, 4 cwt furnace plates £22 6s 8d. William Towerson: 340 ells wool tapestry, 160 ells hair tapestry, 14 doz. coarse cushion cloths, 8 counterfeit Turnhout ticks, 11 cwt feathers £58 6s 8d. John Isham: 90 pcs Genoa fustian £60. Roger Warfyld: 2 brls treacle, 3 cwt white lead, 6 cwt red lead, 20 cwt sumach, 24 cwt hops, 150 lbs gum, 20 cwt liquorice £53. John Woodward: 1 bale Ulm fustian £15. Edward Bright: 17 cwt iron pans, 6 cwt iron double plates,[1] 6 pair latten andirons, 1 half-brl head nails, 1 half-brl small nails, 15 pair iron andirons, 15 fireshovels, 15 pair tongs, 20 pair small creepers £34 16s 8d. John Sutton: 100 Turnhout ticks £33 6s 8d (18 Aug). John Mun: 10 thou. balls, 42 half-pcs Genoa fustian, 12 doz. lbs bottom thread, 50 lbs crossbow thread £27 18s. Robert Brook: 46 cwt mull-madder, 15 cwt hops, 7½ cwt aniseed £23 5s. Roger Warfild: 21 cwt prunes, 3 brls litmus, 75 lbs turmeric, 3 cwt fenugreek, 1½ cwt candy £23. Anthony Fytton: 2 cwt aniseed, drugs ad valorem 80s £6 13s 4d. William Hewet: 3 half-brls head nails, 12 cwt flax £18. Alexander Skovild: 10 cwt wrought flax £10. Thomas Gardiner: 1¼ cwt gunpowder, 50 lbs pepper, 100 bundles brown paper £9 11s 8d. John Sturtyvant: 18 pcs Holland cloth, 1 half-pc Holland cloth £22 3s 4d. Edmund Brasey: 103 pcs Genoa fustian £68 13s 4d. Nicholas Luddington: 9 cwt coarse tow, 2 cwt rice, 63 lbs mace, 28 cwt madder £41 13s 4d. Robert Walkeden: 40 pcs Holland cloth £48. Sir John York: 16 cwt liquorice, 600 lbs pepper £58. Thomas Gaudby: 20 pcs Holland cloth, 600 ells harnesdale cloth £48. Robert Brook: 8 cwt madder £5 6s 8d. [f. 235] Robert Taylor: 4 cwt hops £2 (19 Aug).

1. Containing 121 plates.

731. *Angell* of Bergen-op-Zoom (30) Cornilis Adrianson; Bergen-op-Zoom [f. 225] Phillip Harper: 14 weys white salt, 100 earthenware pots and pans £19 (16 Aug 1568). [f. 235] Henry Barnes: 33 cwt oakum £8 5s (19 Aug).

732. *Mychell* of Amsterdam Henrick Johnson
[f. 225*b*] Thomas Jenens: 1200 lings, 2000 staplefish £70 (16 Aug 1568).

733. *Spledegle* of Dordrecht Godfrey or Garret Dirickson
[f. 226*b*] Reynold Thirling: 3000 bowstaves £50 (16 Aug 1568). John Fitzwilliams: 24 awms Rhenish wine 24*s*, 8 tons 'ames' iron £40 (17 Aug).
[f. 233*b*] Barthelmew Browers: 21 awms Rhenish wine 21*s* (18 Aug).

734. *Angell* of Hamburg (80) Harman Bondman; Hamburg
[f. 226*b*] Matthew Hope: 3360 ells middlegood, 720 ells soultwich, 360 ells padduck £42 13*s* 4*d* (16 Aug 1568). Otte Frolick: 1440 ells soultwich, 600 ells middlegood £30 13*s* 4*d*. Edward van Krog: 1 pack flax, 40 cwt cordage £34 13*s* 4*d* (17 Aug). Daniel van Crow: 40 cwt cordage, 1200 ells soultwich, 5 hd ells brown Hamburg cloth £56 13*s* 4*d*. Luder van Dorne: 2 packs flax £16 (18 Aug). Otte Frolik: 4½ hd ells Hamburg cloth £9. John Rainckin: 300 ells Hazebroucks, 6 hd ells Hamburg cloth £21.
[f. 233*b*] Court Ellers: 8 hd ells Hamburg cloth £16.

735. *Myryman* of Amsterdam (34) Dirick Simons; Amsterdam
[f. 226*b*] Humphrey Kele: 30 brls fish, 240 lings £23 (16 Aug 1568).

736. *George* of Purmerend (40) Sebrant Cornilis; Purmerend
[f. 226*b*] Humphrey Kele: 18 brls fish, 840 lings £37 (16 Aug 1568). Thomas Hecker: 840 lings, 20 brls fish £38 (17 Aug). John Owldam: 3 half-packs flax £12 (18 Aug). John Haynes: 18 brls fish £9. [f. 234] John Edmunds: 18 brls fish £9 (19 Aug).

737. *Egle* of Middelburg Mychell Jacobson
[f. 227] Andrew de Loe: 5 tuns French wine *net* 4 tuns 12*s*, 10 tuns corrupt wine £30 (16 Aug 1568).

738. *Tomeling* of Bergen-op-Zoom (50) John Tomeling; Bergen-op-Zoom
[f. 227*b*] William Gyfford: 21 cwt flax £21 (17 Aug 1568). William Hobbs: 22 cwt wrought flax, 1 last rape oil £38. [f. 228] Thomas Starkey: 8 cwt flax £8.

739. *Spredegle* of Antwerp (40) Peter Johnson; Antwerp
[f. 230] John Jackman: 100 bundles brown paper £3 6*s* 8*d* (17 Aug 1568). Thomas Longston: 20 cwt hops £10. Hartik van Sprecleson: 1 pack flax £8 (18 Aug). Adam Cooper: 458 ells canvas £11 5*s*. [f. 233] Robert Brook: 50 cwt 'certain' brazil £66 13*s* 4*d*.

740. *White Falcon* of Amsterdam Claise Cornilis; Amsterdam
[f. 230] Edmund Ardymar: 8 shocks drinking cans, 30 white boards, 4 shocks boxes £4 6*s* 8*d* (17 Aug 1568). [f. 231] William Harrys: 12 Danzig chests £2 13*s* 4*d* (18 Aug).

741. *Peter* of London (60) Richard Clark; Danzig
[f. 230*b*] Richard Gurney: 2 packs flax £16 (17 Aug 1568). William James:

6 packs flax £48 (19 Aug). Richard Clark: 3 lasts ashes £9. [f. 235*b*] Thomas Russell: 4 half-packs flax, 25 cwt wax, 20 cwt cordage £124 6*s* 8*d* (20 Aug).

742. *Falcon* of St. Omer (30) Symon de Harder; St. Omer
[f. 230*b*] John Atkinson: 3500 bunches onions £14 11*s* 8*d* (17 Aug 1568).

743. *Red Fox* of Antwerp (150) Matis Sanders; Danzig
[f. 231] Thomas Russell: 8 lasts 4 brls pitch, 8 lasts 4 brls soap ashes, 2400 clapholt, 2 lasts tar £51 13*s* 4*d* (18 Aug 1568). Gervais Simons: 1 nest chests, 6 pair playing tables, 5 shocks thick trenchers £4. Dunstan Walton: 10 lasts ashes, 10 lasts pitch £50 (19 Aug). [f. 235] John Watson: 30 chests £6 13*s* 4*d*.

744. *Samson* of Bruges (50) Marten Frize; Bruges
[f. 231*b*] Matthew Colclogh: 14 packs flax £112 (18 Aug 1568).

745. *Ann Galland* of Milton (40) William Morecock; Hamburg
[f. 231*b*] William Sherington: 83 cwt copperas £41 10*s* (18 Aug 1568).

746. *Helmet* of Dordrecht Garret Bowenson
[f. 232] John Olyff: 350 white rods small band £5 16*s* 8*d* (18 Aug 1568).

747. *Anne* of Colchester (30) Matthew Pykas; Danzig
[f. 232] Robert Lambert: 8½ tons iron, 4 cables, 22 cwt small warps, 5 cwt wax, 2 half-packs flax £80 3*s* 4*d* (18 Aug 1568).

748. *Mary Thomas* of Lee (60) John Cock; Antwerp
[f. 233] William Hewet: 20 cwt green copperas £10 (18 Aug 1568).

749. *Diamond* of Lee (60) Richard Haddock; Antwerp
[f. 233] William Hewet: 33 cwt green copperas £16 10*s* (18 Aug 1568).

750. *Cock* Adrianson [*sic*]
[f. 233*b*] Court Ellers: 16 cwt estrige wool £13 6*s* 8*d* (18 Aug 1568). William Hobson: 2 grs 'chaps', 3 doz. lbs curtain rings, 3 grs looking glasses, 4 doz. lbs thread, 40 butts Lyons thread, 2 grs knives, 20 grs harp strings, 2 doz. lbs wrought inkle, 3 doz. yds narrow Cyprus cotton, 10 doz. lbs flax, 4 grs rubbing brushes, 100 lbs matches £29 11*s* 8*d* (19 Aug). John Jenyngs: 5 cwt gum arabic £5. Denis Bald: haberdashery ad valorem £20. Thomas Barker: 18 cwt battery £36 (20 Aug). [f. 237] Thomas Hecker: 8 bundles basts £2 (21 Aug).

751. *Mary Thomas* of London (25) William Dixson; The Bay
[f. 233*b*] William Dixson: 26 weys bay salt £26 (18 Aug 1568).

752. *An Galland* of Brightlingsea (40) Stephen Upchurch; Oléron
[f. 234] Stephen Upchurch: 25 weys bay salt £25 (18 Aug 1568).

753. *Remeyre* of 'Marlin' (28) Jacques Daniell; Nantes
[f. 234] Mark Hamelyn: 8 tuns French wine *net* 6 tuns 18*s*, 10 tuns corrupt wine £30 (19 Aug 1568).

754. *John Baptist* of London (65) Thomas Perry; Danzig
[f. 234] John Foxsall: 8 packs flax, 10 lasts soap ashes, 6 tons 'spruce' iron £124 (19 Aug 1568). Dunstan Walton: 13½ cwt wax £40 10*s*. William James: 4 packs 4 half-packs flax £48. Richard Gurney: 2 packs flax £16. [f. 235] Thomas Russell: 6 packs flax £48.

755. *Edward* of London (50) Christopher Hubbord; The Bay
[f. 234*b*] Christopher Hubbord: 35 weys bay salt £35 (19 Aug 1568).

756. *Grace of God* of Lee (40) John Stephens; Rouen
[f. 234*b*] William Handford: 100 butts Paris thread, 10 grs pennyware combs, 4 pcs working canvas, 10 grs crewel lace £26 13*s* 4*d* (19 Aug 1568). Humphrey Broune: 10 sum rose nails, 10 grs latten buckles, 2 grs coarse bells, 2½ grs crewel chain-lace, 1 thou. needles, 9 doz. inkhorns £8 13*s* 4*d*. Robert Sadler: 1200 ells canvas £30. John Bodleigh: 2200 ells brown canvas £55 (20 Aug). John Newton: 20 grs playing cards £20. Henry Waight: 10 grs playing cards, 10 cwt prunes, 2 brls yellow ochre £16 10*s*. Richard Morris: 1400 ells canvas £35. John Olyf: 1000 ells canvas £25. Richard Smyth: 100 reams paper £13 6*s* 8*d*. Oliver Fyssher: 1400 ells canvas £18 13*s* 4*d*. Anthony Gamage: 1000 ells canvas £25. John Harding: 500 ells canvas £12 10*s*. Robert Bennet: 200 ells canvas, 50 reams paper £11 13*s* 4*d*. Thomas Awder: 700 ells canvas £17 10*s* (21 Aug). Thomas Awder: 20 grs combs, 20 doz. woolcards, 4 grs inkhorns, 2 grs ounce balances, 100 ells brown cushion canvas £26 10*s*. Sir John York: 60 yds grogram £20. Robert Cage: 700 ells canvas £17 10*s*. [f. 238] Anthony Cage: 1000 ells canvas £25 (23 Aug).

757. *Ronaldo* of Venice (500) George Solvano; Venice
[f. 234*b*] Anthony Donato: 380 butts malmseys and muscatels *net* 165 butts 247*s* 6*d* (19 Aug 1568). Innocento Lacatelli: 160 butts 61 caroteels sweet wine *net* 106 butts 159*s* (26 Aug). Jacob Spinola: 100 butts 8 caroteels sweet wine and malmseys *net* 85 butts 127*s* 6*d*. Michel Gibley: 50 butts sweet wine *net* 50 butts 75*s*. Baptist de John: 120 butts, 12½ butts and caroteels sweet wine *net* 79½ butts 119*s* 3*d* (27 Aug). George Barbarigo: 50 butts sweet wine *net* 32 butts 48*s*. Mark Dingley: 40 cwt currants £60 (30 Aug). [f. 241*b*] William Coper: 28 cwt currants £42 (31 Aug).[1]

    1. Wine imports on Spinola's licence: see **53**.

758. *James* of Flushing (24) Cornilis Mychelson; Flushing
[f. 235] Henrick Bovinge: 31 awms Rhenish wine 31*s* (19 Aug 1568).

759. *John* of London (40) Thomas Turner; Rouen
[f. 235*b*] Henry Buxton: 900 ells canvas £22 10*s* (20 Aug 1568). John Bodleigh: 1100 ells canvas £14 13*s* 4*d*. Thomas Starkey: 1000 ells canvas

£25. Wolston Dixi: 2150 ells canvas £53 15s. Oliver Fysher: 1400 ells canvas £35. Hugh Offley: 800 ells canvas £20. Robert Sadler: 60 reams paper, 1000 ells canvas £33. Richard Patrick: 20 doz. lbs thread, 12 doz. ounce balances, 40 grs dolls, 25 grs narrow edging for hats, 12 grs combs £36 10s. Humphrey Broune: 12 grs crewel chain-lace, 2 thou. needles, 8 grs halfpennyware glasses, 10 grs halfpenny combs, 4 grs inkhorns £13 10s. William Hobson: 18 grs playing cards, 6 grs hawk bells, 18 butts Lyons thread, 50 reams paper £35 8s 4d (21 Aug). Richard Folsam: 500 ells canvas £12 10s. Robert Cage: 1600 ells canvas £40. Edmund Ansell: 11 cases Normandy glass £11 (23 Aug). John Allot: 1800 ells canvas, 7 thou. teazles £26 6s 8d. Edward Osborne: 2400 ells coarse canvas £32. Sir John York: 16 cwt dates, 24 cwt prunes £44. [f. 238] Anthony Cage: 1000 ells canvas, 1 bale black thread £35.

760. *Elizabeth* of London (40) William Tyllor; Rouen
[f. 235b] Richard Morris: 800 ells canvas £20 (20 Aug 1568). Oliver Fisher: 1300 ells canvas £32 10s. John Harding: 1000 ells canvas, 8 grs playing cards £33. Hugh Offley: 32 cwt prunes, 140 reams paper £33 13s 4d. John Newton: 60 reams paper, 13 grs playing cards £21. Robert Sadler: 800 ells canvas £20. Thomas Awder: 70 reams paper £9 6s 8d (21 Aug). Thomas Howse: 192 reams paper £26 (23 Aug). John Olyf: 800 ells canvas £20 (24 Aug). [f. 238b] John Allot: 800 ells canvas £20.

761. *Pellican* of London (30) James Steward; Narva
[f. 236] John Brook 'et sociis': 128 cwt cables, 260 cwt untarred ropes, 7 hd 'rogesens' down, 240 hides £268 13s 4d (20 Aug 1568).

762. *Falcon* of Antwerp (25) Daniel Peters; Antwerp
[f. 237] Thomas Thorp: 12 cwt hops £6 (21 Aug 1568).

763. *Mychell* of Bruges (60) Cornilis Albright; Bruges
[f. 237] Richard Renolds: 18 cwt Bruges madder £12 (21 Aug 1568). Thomas Sownd: 24 cwt madder £16. [f. 237b] Thomas Howse: 41 half-pcs bustian, 5 pcs Genoa fustian, 6 half-pcs sackcloth, 2 pcs say, 1 half-pc. canvas striped with silk £26 15s (23 Aug).

764. *Swallow* of Dieppe (18) Nicholas Tribart; Dieppe
[f. 237b] Henry Wayght: 30 cwt brazil £50 (23 Aug 1568). Jacques Fyshet 'et sociis': 12 tuns Gascony wine *net* 11 tuns 33s. [f. 238] John Varrey: 2 tuns Gascony wine *net* 2 tuns 6s.

765. *Jesus* of Flushing Peter Williamson
[f. 237b] Barthel Cornilis: 5 tuns French wine *net* 4 tuns 12s (23 Aug 1568).

766. *Swan* of Flushing Adrian Cornilis; Flushing
[f. 237b] Barthel Cornilis: 5 tuns French wine *net* 4 tuns 12s, 3 tuns corrupt wine £9 (23 Aug 1568).

123

767. *Mary George* of London (45) Robert Osburn; Rouen
[f. 238] John Bingley: 12 brls yellow ochre £8 (24 Aug 1568). Oliver Fysher: 2200 ells canvas £55. Henry Waight: 120 cwt prunes, 20 doz. woolcards £16. Hugh Offley: 500 ells canvas, 60 reams paper £20 10s. William Handford: 17 grs playing cards £17 (26 Aug). Anthony Gamage: 1200 ells canvas £30. Edmund Ansell: 18 grs playing cards £18. John Bodleigh: 600 ells canvas £15. William Silvester: 10 cwt prunes £5. John Newton: 12 grs playing cards, 60 reams paper £20. William Plaisden: 1200 ells canvas £30. Thomas Howse: 192 reams printing paper £25 13s 4d. William Hobson: 32 doz. woolcards, 8 grs crewel lace £21 6s 8d. John Raines: 1100 ells coarse canvas, 15 doz. woolcards £35. John Allot: 2600 ells coarse canvas £34 6s 8d (27 Aug). John Olyff: 2400 ells canvas £32. Richard Morrys: 1800 ells canvas £24. Robert Sadler: 1400 ells canvas, 80 reams paper, 10 cwt prunes £50 13s 4d. John Marshall: 15 cwt prunes £7 10s. Thomas Awder: 700 ells canvas £17 10s (30 Aug). [f. 241] Robert Cross: 700 ells canvas £17 10s.

768. *Pellican* of St. Omer (20) Cornilis de Keyser; St. Omer
[f. 238] John Atkinson: 3500 bunches onions £14 11s (24 Aug 1568).

769. *Mary and John* of London (50) John Diet; Bilbao
[f. 238] Francis Bowyer: 20 tons Spanish iron £80 (24 Aug 1568). Anthony Pilboro: 3 tons Spanish iron £12. Edward Boyes: 5 tons iron £20 (26 Aug). Richard May: 8 tons Spanish iron £32. Richard Foulkes: 20 tons Spanish iron £80. Roger Wilson: 5 tons Spanish iron £20. [f. 240] Robert Jaques: 2 tons Spanish iron £8 (27 Aug).

770. *Pellican* of Amsterdam (35) Adrian Cornilis; Amsterdam
[f. 238b] John Violet: 1500 staplefish, 1200 lings, 35 brls fish £80 (24 Aug 1568).

771. *John* of Faversham Alexander Dawson; Rouen
[f. 239b] John Bodleigh: 700 ells canvas £17 10s (26 Aug 1568). Thomas Starkey: 1200 ells canvas £30 (27 Aug). John Mylner: 1400 ells canvas £35. William Handford: 20 grs combs, 3 doz. woolcards, 200 lbs unspun cotton, 1 cwt pack thread, 2 grs inkhorns £20 16s 8d. Humphrey Broune: 25 doz. woolcards, 3 grs crewel chain-lace, 600 ells coarse canvas, 20 reams loose paper £32 3s 4d. Henry Wayt: 5 doz. iron pots £1 5s. John Marshall: 15 cwt prunes £7 10s. Richard Patrick: 150 grs points, 20 grs tin tablets for children, 6 grs spectacles, 10 grs combs, 1 grs ounce balances, 15 grs tooth picks, 6 doz. taffeta caps, 10 doz. steel glasses, 2 doz. children's girdles of velvet, 3 doz. barber's cases £20 13s 4d. Walter Gillingdon: 500 ells canvas £12 10s. John Allot: 400 ells canvas £10 (28 Aug). William Thwates: 100 ells canvas, 2 doz. napkins £2 18s 4d. John Olyf: 800 ells canvas £20 (30 Aug). Robert Sadler: 60 reams paper, 120 reams loose paper £24. Anthony Cage: 1000 ells canvas £25 (31 Aug). [f. 242] John Myller: 100 ells canvas £2 10s.

772. *Hart* of Amsterdam (44) Claise Dirickson; Danzig
[f. 239*b*] Robert Hilson: 30 lasts rye £75 (27 Aug 1568). [f. 241] William James: 13 lasts pitch £26 (30 Aug).

773. *Sampson* of Veere (120) Berent Rotkerson; Danzig
[f. 240] Thomas Russell: 2400 clapholt, 600 wainscots, 8 lasts 4 brls pitch, 4 lasts 2 brls tar, 9 lasts soap ashes, 9 chests £84 (27 Aug 1568). [f. 241] Edmund Ardymer: 24 Danzig chests £5 6*s* 8*d* (30 Aug).

774. *Jesus* of Ipswich (40) Thomas Lucas; Danzig
[f. 240] Thomas Russell: 6 packs flax £48 (27 Aug 1568). William Cardinall: 13 lasts soap ashes, 2 packs 1 half-pack flax, 200 clapholt, 12 cwt hemp £83 (28 Aug). [f. 241] William James: 8 half-packs flax £32 (30 Aug).

775. *Fortune* of Flushing Simon Johnson
[f. 240] Richard Knight: 5 tuns French wine *net* 4 tuns 12*s* (27 Aug 1568).

776. *Hound* of Lee (50) John Salmon; Sluis
[f. 240*b*] Matthew Colcloth: 27 cwt unwrought flax £18 (28 Aug 1568).

777. *Halk* of Spaarndam (35) Hubright Johnson
[f. 241] Richard Mouse: 960 lings, 1600 staplefish, 3 lasts barrelled fish £74 (30 Aug 1568).

778. *Mychell* of Flushing (14) Peter Peterson; Flushing
[f. 241] Thomas Sandford: 480 lings, 400 staplefish £22 (30 Aug 1568).

779. *Wolf* of Amsterdam (30) Garret Johnson; Amsterdam
[f. 241] Edward van Krog: 1 pack ton-flax £8 (30 Aug 1568). Luder van Dorne: 3 packs ton-flax £24 (31 Aug). [f. 241*b*] William Meggs: 2 lasts soap £16.

780. *Spredegle* of Amsterdam (30) Cornilis Frederickson; Amsterdam
[f. 241*b*] Luder van Dorne: 2 packs ton-flax £16 (31 Aug 1568).

781. *Edward* of Milton (60) William Harison; Antwerp
[f. 241*b*] John Jackman: 24 cwt Castile soap, 150 lbs ginger £29 5*s* (31 Aug 1568). William Cockin: 600 foin tails, 20 mantles foin potes, 33 pair 'vents' £28 10*s* (1 Sept). James Harvie: 3½ doz. whip-saws, 1 doz. tenon-saws £5 11*s* 8*d*. William Hobbs: 974 ells hair tapestry, 16 pcs white blanket, 3½ doz. sealed carpets, 2 doz. blue lince, 1 last rape oil £63 5*s*. John Spencer: 100 bundles brown paper £3 6*s* 8*d*. William Gifford: 6 cwt unwrought flax £3 6*s* 8*d*. John Flower: 16 cwt estrige wool £13 16*s* 8*d*. Edward Bright: 8 doz. carpenter's saws, 8½ cwt iron pans £8. Thomas Gardiner: 1 cwt gunpowder, 50 bundles brown paper, 4 cwt aniseed, 200 lbs pepper £25 6*s* 8*d*. William Towerson: 750 ells wool tapestry, 16 doz. Ghentish carpets, 1 doz. cushion cloths, 6 cwt feathers £72. Roger Warfild: 2 brls argol, 1 cwt candy, 400 lbs matches, 18 cwt soap, 6 cwt almonds, 100 bundles brown paper, 6 cwt starch £43 10*s*. Alexander Sherington: 3 bales

Ulm fustian £45. Thomas Brasie: 106 pcs unwatered camlet, 2 bales Ulm fustian £151. William Colles: 48 cwt madder, 8 cwt hops £36. Edmund Smyth: 2 bales Ulm fustian £30. Robert Taylor: 24 cwt madder, 6 cwt hops £19. John Borne: 10 doz. lbs pack thread, 6 grs thread points, 3 doz. coarse crewel pieces, 1 doz. lbs inkle, 4 doz. thou. pins, 1½ thou. thimbles, 12 thou. awl blades, 3 doz. lbs counters, 1 grs coarse hour glasses £16 10s. John Lambert: 72 cwt flax £48. John Car: 1 half-brl small nails, 4 hd iron plates, 8 doz. small candle plates £9 6s 8d. James Harvie: 17 cwt black latten £11 6s 8d. William Perrie: 90 lbs nutmegs £15. Robert Brook: 6 cwt hops £3. Nicholas Hewet: 13 brls rape oil, 12 pair andirons with 12 tongs 12 fireshovels, 18 cwt ton-flax £34 (2 Sept). William Hewet: 13 brls rape oil £16. Robert Exton: 5 cwt madder, 3 nests empty chests, 40 Turnhout ticks £18 13s 4d. Arthur Hall: 1 ton 'ames' iron, 1 half-brl head nails, 100 doubles, 4 cwt fireshovel plates £13. Roger Knot: 16 cwt battery £32. Thomas Eaton: 15 grs halfpennyware glasses, 3 grs thread-lace, 3 doz. thou. pins, 1 doz. lbs curtain rings, 6 thou. awl blades, 5 doz. lbs inkle, 2 doz. crewel pieces, 1 brl latten £29 1s 8d. Ancelm Becket: 6 cwt flax £6. Thomas Castlin: 2 packs flax £16. Hugh Bradborne: 90 cakes resin £15. Anthony Fytton: 4 brls yellow ochre £2 13s 4d. Richard Billam: 18 Turnhout ticks £14 13s 4d. Roland Erlington: 120 doz. thou. pins £20. Henry Smyth: 63 lbs Spanish silk, 12 doz. thou. pins £65 (3 Sept). Phillip Watkins: 30 lbs satin silk, 80 lbs ferret silk £66 13s 4d. William Sherington: 50 lbs ferret silk, 80 ells sarcenet £34 3s 4d. John Pasfield: 7 cwt iron wire £11 13s 4d. John Spencer: 50 bundles brown paper, 40 lbs thread £2 6s 8d. Francis Wootton: 60 ells sarcenet, 30 yds satin £23 10s. Robert Taylor: 3 pcs stammel £30. William Martin: 192 butts thread, 10 pcs watered camlet £19 3s 4d. Edmund Hugan: 80 half-pcs Genoa fustian £26 13s 4d (4 Sept). John Taylor: 3 bales Ulm fustian £45. Geoffrey Goffe: 250 ells hair and flax tapestry, 8 doz. lince £14 6s 8d. Robert Lence: 6 cwt wrought flax £6. Sir William Chester: 75 cwt madder £50. [f. 254b] Christopher Jewkes: 30 cwt madder £20 (16 Sept).

782. *Pellican* of Haarlem (30) Clayse Jacobson; Haarlem
[f. 241b] Thomas Jenens: 6 lasts barrelled fish, 750 staplefish £47 5s (31 Aug 1568). [f. 246] John Violet: 6 lasts barrelled fish, 750 staplefish £47 5s (3 Sept).

783. *Christopher* of Flushing Garret Cornilison
[f. 241b] John Renolds: 840 lings £28 (31 Aug 1568).

784. *Julyan* of London (90) William Uxley; Narva
[f. 241b] John Brook 'et sociis': 37 half-packs flax, 200 cwt tallow £314 13s 4d (31 Aug 1568). [f. 244b] John Bird: 6 cwt wax £18 (2 Sept).

785. *Willeby* of London (120) Arthur Petts; Narva
[f. 241b] John Broke 'et sociis': 38 packs flax, 1500 calf skins 'in the hair', 40 dicker cow hides, 90 dicker goat skins 'in the hair', 400 cwt tallow £767 6s 8d (31 Aug 1568). William Thomas: 12 cwt unwrought flax £8

(2 Sept). John Brok 'et sociis': 2 cwt wax £6 (3 Sept). [f. 246*b*] John Juget: 8 cwt flax £5 6*s* 8*d* (4 Sept).

786. *Jonas* of Flushing Jacob Stoffles
[f. 242] John Allison: 8 pcs bustian £5 6*s* 8*d* (31 Aug 1568).

787. *John Baptist* of London (60) William Hall; Antwerp
[f. 242] Lawrence Wethers: 1 last soap £8 (1 Sept 1568). John Flower: 15 cwt estrige wool £12 10*s*. John Lambert: 70 cwt unwrought flax £46 13*s* 4*d*. Richard Billingsley: 8 doz. lbs bottom thread, 30 grs harp strings, 20 doz. thou. pins, 4 doz. lbs Bruges thread £9 13*s* 4*d*. William Gifford: 5 cwt flax £3 6*s* 8*d*. William Hobbs: 634 ells hair tapestry, 5½ doz. lince, 1 last rape oil £41 5*s*. William Elkin: 72 yds frizado £18. Edmund Smyth and Robert Bye: 1 bale Ulm fustian, 50 half-pcs Genoa fustian £31 13*s* 4*d*. John Eliets: 6 grs halfpennyware glasses, 16 doz. thread pieces, 10 doz. thou. pins, 8 doz. crewel pieces, 3 doz. lbs crewel, 3 doz. lbs inkle, 25 lbs inkle, 4 doz. lbs counters £18 8*s*. Roger Warfild: 20 cwt soap, 6 brls ochre, 1 cwt candy, 300 lbs matches £24 16*s* 8*d*. William Colles: 14 cwt Castile soap £10 15*s*. Robert Taylor: 60 Turnhout ticks, 21 counterfeit ticks, 6 cwt hops £37. Wolston Dixi: 40 pcs Ghentish cloth £48. John Borne: 10 cwt white plates £6 13*s* 4*d*. Nicholas Hewet: 12 brls soap £8 (2 Sept). William Hewet: 13 brls rape oil, 2 bales Ulm fustian £46 6*s* 8*d*. Robert Exton: 4½ cwt madder, 3 nests empty chests, 5 doz. sword blades £8 6*s* 8*d*. William Ludington: 12 brls rape oil, 3 cwt litmus, 30 lbs sugar candy, 3 cwt almonds, 10 lbs green ginger, 25 lbs verdigris £26 1*s* 8*d*. Henry Bechar: 41 doz. lbs Oudenaarde thread, 10 doz. lbs inkle, 4 doz. thou. needles, 37½ lbs Paris silk, 30 lbs ferret silk, 6 doz. lbs Bruges thread £66 10*s*. Thomas Eaton: 5 grs 'almaine' knives, 15 doz. crewel pieces, 2 thou. thimbles, 120 lbs counters, 12 lbs clavichord wire, 1 grs coarse hat bands, 1 grs thread lace, 2 doz. lbs crewel, 6 thou. pack needles, 3 doz. lbs wrought inkle, 10 thou. awl blades, 5 grs thread points, 10 grs halfpennyware glasses £36 10*s*. Ancelm Becket: 5¾ cwt flax £5 15*s*. Thomas Castlin: 1 pack flax £8. Hugh Bradborne: 100 cakes resin £16 13*s* 4*d*. Anthony Fytton: 3 cwt red lead, 1 cwt sugar candy £7. Harry Bowyer: 5 doz. lince £3 15*s*. Henry Smyth: 37½ lbs Bruges silk, 40 lbs undyed silk, 33 doz. thou. pins £57 3*s* 4*d* (3 Sept). Philip Watkins: 30 lbs satin silk, 80 lbs ferret silk, 40 lbs Bruges silk £90. John Pasfield: 4 cwt kettles, 4 cwt iron wire, 4 pairs latten andirons and 5 pipes of latten for andirons £23 6*s* 8*d*. Thomas Parker: 34 pcs dornick with wool £17. Nicholas Spering: 4½ doz. lbs pack thread, 5 doz. crewel girdles, 120 razors, 12 comb cases, 8 doz. cotton petticoats, 6 doz. writing tables, 1 doz. gold balances, 6 doz. wooden standishes, 28 doz. leathers for cushions, 1½ grs looking glasses, 3 doz. furred stomachers, 1½ doz. pinpillows, 12 lbs wire £32. Francis Wootton: 65 yds taffeta, 50 ells sarcenet £38 6*s* 8*d*. Anthony Warfild: 300 bundles brown paper £10. Thomas Thorp: 2 cwt corn powder £3 6*s* 8*d*. Edmund Hugan: 70 half-pcs Genoa fustian £23 6*s* 8*d* (4 Sept). Geoffrey Goffe: 7 thou. trenchers £1 15*s*. Sir William Chester: 30 cwt madder £20. Robert Kingland: 15 cwt brazil £25 (8 Sept). [f. 245*b*] Christopher Jewkes: 30 cwt madder £20 (16 Sept).

788. *Owl* of Haarlem (30) Florence Jacobson; Haarlem
[f. 242*b*] Thomas Jenens: 6 lasts barrelled fish, 360 lings, 500 staplefish £55 10*s* (1 Sept 1568). [f. 246] John Violet: 2 lasts barrelled fish, 750 staplefish £23 5*s* (3 Sept).

789. *Edward* of London (50) William Cox; Narva
[f. 245*b*] John Broke 'et sociis': 17 cwt tallow, 15 packs flax, 200 calf skins 'in the hair' £276 13*s* 4*d* (3 Sept 1568).

790. *Beniamen* of London (60) John Dryver; Antwerp
[f. 246*b*] Robert Taylor: 6 cwt hops £3 (6 Sept 1568). Edward Jackman: 24 cwt hops £12. William Colles: 12 cwt hops £6. Roger Warfyld: 18 cwt hops £9. Robert Broke: 16 cwt hops £8. John Jackman: 12 cwt hops £6. William Hewet: 6 cwt hops £3. Nicholas Hewet: 11 cwt hops £5 10*s*. William Luddington: 5 cwt almonds £10. George Stockmed: 30 cwt hops, 16 cwt flax £27 13*s* 4*d*. Richard Billam: 5 cwt hops £2 10*s*. Thomas Gardyner: 21 cwt hops, 130 bundles brown paper £14 16*s*. Lucas Lane: 16 cwt hops £8. Robert Stephens: 6 cwt hops £3. William Wale: 6 cwt hops £3. Thomas Longston: 30 cwt mull-madder, 12 cwt estrige wool £13 15*s* (7 Sept). William Cockin: 62 cwt mull-madder, 1120 raw rumney budge skins £69 6*s* 8*d*. John Broke 'et sociis': 45 cwt cordage £30 (9 Sept). [f. 251*b*] Nicholas Savedge: 6 timber mink, 100 beaver bellies, 3 wolverines £19 6*s* 8*d* (11 Sept).

791. *Christopher* of Antwerp (40) Garret Rose; Antwerp
[f. 246*b*] Humphrey Fayrefax: 12 cwt hops £6 (6 Sept 1568). William Colles: 12 cwt hops £6. [f. 247] John Jackman: 100 bundles brown paper £3 6*s* 8*d*.

792. *Spredegle* of Antwerp (26) Gyles Dorne; Antwerp
[f. 247] Roger Warfyld: 2½ cwt gunpowder £4 13*s* 4*d* (6 Sept 1568). John Jackman: 12 cwt hops £6 (7 Sept). Sir William Garrard: 60 reams paper £8. Christopher Vittell: 1 cupboard, 1 walnut table, 60 yds and 3 half-pcs Naples fustian, 8 pcs narrow say, 7 Ghentish carpets £20 10*s*. [f. 250] Thomas Parker: 50 pcs double mockado, 50 papers single mockado £66 13*s* 4*d* (9 Sept).

793. *John* of Flushing (40) John White; Flushing
[f. 247*b*] John White: 180 lings, 240 coal-fish, 100 staplefish, 18 weys bay salt £26 10*s* (7 Sept 1568).

794. *George* of Antwerp (60) John de Bardman;[1] Antwerp
[f. 247*b*] George Stockmed: 32 cwt ton-flax £21 6*s* 8*d* (7 Sept 1568). John Jackman: 100 bundles brown paper £3 6*s* 8*d*. John Killinghewsen: 32 cwt estrige wool £26 13*s* 4*d*. Phillip Jones: 24 cwt madder £16 (9 Sept). [f. 250*b*] Luder van Dorne: 2 packs flax £16 (10 Sept).

    1. Or Bardmaker.

795. *Swallow* of London (60) Richard Poulter; Antwerp
[f. 247*b*] George Stockmed: 42 cwt ton-flax £28 (7 Sept 1568). Thomas

Longston: 60 cwt mull-madder, 10 cwt estrige wool £15 16s 8d. William
Towerson: 100 ells caddis tapestry, 180 ells wool tapestry, 300 ells hair
tapestry, 2 doz. Ghentish carpets £32 6s 8d. John Jackman: 6 cwt hops,
200 lbs ginger, 80 lbs cinnamon £34. Humphrey Fayrfax: 12 cwt hops £6.
Robert Broke: 22 cwt hops £11. Roger Knot: 8 cwt battery £16. James
Harvie: 60 cwt mull-madder £7 10s. Edmund Burton: 4 doz. whip-saws,
6 doz. two-hand-saws, 2 pair latten andirons £11 6s 8d. Joan Bower:
13 pair andirons with tongs and shovels, 20 cwt hops £15. William Hewet:
160 half-pcs Genoa fustian, 3 cwt hops £58 3s 4d. Geoffrey Walkeden:
7 pcs diaper 'tabling', 3 pcs damask towelling, 20 pcs Holland cloth
£44 (8 Sept). Roland Erlington: 32 doz. lbs Bruges thread, 7 doz. lbs
bottom pack thread £22 15s. William Luddington: 1 last rape oil, 7½ cwt
soap, 4½ cwt bay berries, 1½ cwt brimstone £25 1s 6d. John Eliets: 4 doz.
lbs crewel, 40 doz. thou. pins, 6 grs coarse looking glasses, 4 doz. coarse
hour glasses £11 10s. Edward Bright: 4 half-brls head nails, 1 half-brl small
nails, 4 cwt iron plates, 5 cwt shaven latten £24 13s 4d. Thomas Randall:
50 yds taffeta £16 13s 4d. John Pasfyld: 4 doz. small fireshovels, 4 doz.
small tongs, 1 grs small balances £3 13s 4d. John Daniell: 12 cwt hops £6.
Nicholas Spering: 3 doz. cotton petticoats, 4 doz. furred stomachers,
1 grs coarse knives £7. Gervais Simons: 18 cwt hops £9. Robert Exton:
4 cwt unwrought flax £4. Thomas Aldersey: 120 yds velvet £90 (9 Sept).
Roger Warfild: 4 cwt white lead, 5 cwt red lead £6 15s. Anthony Warfild:
2½ cwt white lead, 6 cwt hops £4 17s 6d. Humphrey Fayrfax: 12 hd Flemish
treacle, 100 lbs ginger £23 10s. Anthony Fytton: 5 cwt sugar candy
£16 13s 4d. Thomas Cullimer: 6 pcs Holland cloth £7 3s 4d. Francis
Keightley: 200 yds satin, 60 yds damask £114 (10 Sept). William Hobbs:
832 ells hair tapestry, 3 doz. sealed carpets, 2½ doz. lince, 31 Turnhout
ticks, 18 pcs sealed carpet, 2 lasts grey soap £62 15s. [f. 251b] Robert
Luce: 4 doz. crystal looking glasses £4 (11 Sept).

796. *Ass* of Antwerp (40) Cornilis Henrick; Antwerp
[f. 247b] Thomas Longston: 24 cwt hops £12 (7 Sept 1568). William Cells:
28 cwt hops £14 (9 Sept). Lawrence Wethers: 4 cwt hops £2. [f. 250]
Humphrey Fayrfax: 14 cwt hops, 20 doz. empty barrels £9.

797. *Angell* of Flushing (7) Cornilis Bastianson; Flushing
[f. 247b] John Allyson: 7½ cwt hops £3 15s (7 Sept 1568). [f. 250b] John
Allison: 10½ cwt hops £5 5s (9 Sept).

798. *Fox* of Akersloot (40) Peter Hugan; Akersloot
[f. 247b] Thomas Jenens: 3 lasts fish, 480 lings, 800 staplefish £46 (7 Sept
1568). [f. 250] John Violet: 3 lasts barrelled fish, 1200 staplefish £36
(9 Sept).

799. *Falcon* of Antwerp (30) Vincent Johnson; Antwerp
[f. 248] Hartik van Sprecleson: 1 pack flax £8 (7 Sept 1568). [f. 248b]
William Hewet: 3 bales Ulm fustian £75.

800. *George* of Antwerp Peter Phill
[f. 248] John Picknet: 12 cwt hops £6 (7 Sept 1568).

801. *Pearl* of Dieppe Robert Lovaine
[f. 248] Jacques Fyshet 'et sociis': 10 tuns Gascony wine *net* 9 tuns 27*s* (7 Sept 1568).

802. *Lamb* of Flushing Adrian Johnson
[f. 248*b*] Peter Vegleman: 7 tuns Rochelle wine *net* 6 tuns 18*s*, 6 tuns corrupt wine £18 (7 Sept 1568).

803. *Rosbayard* of Antwerp (36) John de Fysher; Antwerp
[f. 248*b*] John Jackman: 10 cwt hops £5 (8 Sept 1568). Robert Broke: 32 cwt hops £16. [f. 249*b*] William Wale: 10 cwt hops £5.

804. *Angell* of Bergen-op-Zoom Adrian Williamson; Bergen-op-Zoom
[f. 249] William Bower: 2 lasts rape oil £32 (8 Sept 1568). Nicholas Hewet: 22 cwt oakum £4 10*s*. William Hobbs: 16½ cwt flax, 1½ lasts rape oil £40. Robert Exton: 4 cwt flax £4. William Hewet: 12½ cwt unwrought flax £12 10*s*. Ancelm Becket: 17½ cwt flax, 5¾ cwt tow £19 8*s* (10 Sept). [f. 251] George Stockmed: 15 cwt wrought flax, 1 last rape oil £31.

805. *Charitie* of London (100) Thomas Awdley; Russia
[f. 249] John Brook 'et sociis': 170 cwt wax, 750 cwt cordage, 80 lbs raw silk, 100 calf skins 'in the hair', 10 lasts tar, 400 lbs cinnamon, 100 lbs mace, 10 cwt yarn, 3 hd lbs isinglass, sealskins ad valorem £2, 40 wolfskins, 60 wolverines cost £2 a piece, 10 timber minks, 100 ermines, 100 beaver bellies, 5 beaver backs, 20 lbs rhubarb £1 314 (8 Sept 1568).

806. *George* of Antwerp (50) Jacob de Cowper; Antwerp
[f. 249*b*] William Cells: 12 cwt hops £6 (9 Sept 1568). Edward Jackman: 26 cwt hops £13. Lawrence Wethers: 6 cwt hops £3. Humphrey Fayrfax: 20 cwt hops £10. Robert Brook: 20 cwt hops £10. [f. 252] Thomas Aldersey: 340 ells sarcenet £56 13*s* 4*d* (11 Sept).

807. *James* of Antwerp Simon Joyce
[f. 250*b*] Roger Warfyld: 200 bundles brown paper £6 13*s* 4*d* (10 Sept 1568). [f. 251*b*] Thomas Aldersey: 240 ells sarcenet £40 (11 Sept).

808. *Lyon* of Lee (60) John Bonnar; Antwerp
[f. 251] William Bower: 8 cwt hops £4 (10 Sept 1568). Roger Warfyld: 4 cwt fenugreek £2 13*s* 4*d*. George Stockmed: 32 cwt unwrought flax £21 6*s* 8*d* (11 Sept). Thomas Brasye: 186 ells sarcenet £31. Thomas Eaton: 8 doz. lbs Bruges thread, 3 doz. lbs crewel, 15 doz. crewel pieces, 2 doz. thou. needles, 12 lbs clavichord wire, 3 thou. needles £19 16*s* 8*d*. John Lambert: 17 cwt battery £34. Edward Bright: 3 cwt varnish £5. George Sowthack: 4 cwt candy £13 6*s* 8*d*. William Hobbs: 1 last rape oil £16. Roger Knot: 12 cwt battery £24. William Luddington: 10 cwt aniseed £13 6*s* 8*d*. Sir John York: 18 cwt hops £9. Edmund Burton: 10 cwt iron wire, 1 grs files, 5½ grs horse bells, 12 bundles steel £26 10*s*. Richard Billingsley: 36 doz. thou. pins £6 (13 Sept). John Borne: 1 doz. pcs Rennes boultel, 5 grs thread points, 4 grs coarse copper hat bands,

4 doz. lbs counters, 5 grs coarse horse bells, 50 doz. thou. pins, 3 doz. lbs wrought inkle £19 3*s* 4*d*. William Colles: 474 lbs pepper, 45 lbs nuts £47. John Isham: 100 pcs mockado £66 13*s* 4*d*. Thomas Parker: 3 bales Ulm fustian £45. John Fitzwilliams: 80 cwt madder, 40 cwt hops £30. William Hewet: 230 half-pcs Genoa fustian £76 15*s*. John Brook: 132 cwt madder, 30 cwt hops, 850 lbs pepper £173 16*s*. Richard Holliman: 90 half-pcs fustian £30. Thomas Wykyn: 14 cwt woad £8 13*s* 4*d*. Nicholas Spering: 1 grs coarse knives, 2 doz. furred stomachers, 4 doz. gold balances, 6 grs copper bands cost 5*s* the gross £4 3*s* 4*d*. William Meggs: 2 tons rape oil[1] £21 6*s* 8*d* (14 Sept). William Towerson: 50 Turnhout ticks, 60 ells silk tapestry £26 13*s* 4*d*. Thomas Blanck: 16 pcs 1 half-pc. Genoa fustian £11. Richard Clough: 80 lbs ferret silk £33 6*s* 8*d* (15 Sept). Peter Daunser: 15 pcs mockado £10. [f. 254] Thomas Gryme: 6 half-pcs cambric, 1 pc. Holland cloth £7 3*s* 4*d*.

1. Or 16 brls.

809. *Mary Katharine* of London (100) William Thomas of Limehouse; Narva
[f. 251] John Byrd: 6 cwt wax £18 (10 Sept 1568).

810. *Margeret* of Dover (30) Stephen Anderson; Dover [*sic*]
[f. 251] Winholt Brownolf: 40 hand guns £10 (10 Sept 1568).

811. *John* of Antwerp John Joris; Antwerp
[f. 251] George Stockmed: 28 cwt hops £14 (11 Sept 1568). Thomas Gardiner: 23 cwt hops £11 10*s*. George Sowthack: 30 cwt hops £15. John Jackman: 10 cwt hops £5. Humphrey Fayrfax: 6 cwt hops £3. William Wale: 6 cwt hops £3 (13 Sept). [f. 253] Lucas Lane: 4 cwt hops £2.

812. *Cock* of Bruges (60) Jacob Albright; Bruges
[f. 251*b*] John Hall: 25 cwt madder £16 13*s* 4*d* (11 Sept 1568). Richard Renolds: 24 doz. lbs Bruges thread £16 (13 Sept). [f. 252*b*] John Muns: 10 doz. lbs Bruges thread, ½ grs coarse dolls £6 18*s*.

813. *Litle Lyon* of Dieppe (18) William Angell; Dieppe
[f. 252] John Varry: 3 tuns Gascony wine *net* 2 tuns 6*s*, 1 tun corrupt wine £3 (11 Sept 1568). [f. 253] Humphrey Broune: 3 tuns corrupt wine £9 (13 Sept).

814. *Spredegle* of Dordrecht (40) Cort Egle
[f. 252*b*] John Fitzwilliams: 20 cwt unwrought hemp £20 (13 Sept 1568).

815. *Falcon* of Amsterdam (16) Erasmus Canon; Amsterdam
[f. 252*b*] Richard Mouse: 4 lasts barrelled fish, 600 staplefish £33 (13 Sept 1568). George Lubkin: 1500 ells minsters £16 13*s* 4*d* (14 Sept). [f. 253*b*] Thomas Sandford: 2 lasts barrelled fish £12.

816. *Pellican* of Amsterdam William Dirickson
[f. 252*b*] John Rainkin: 20 lasts pitch £40 (13 Sept 1568).

817. *Falcon* of Bergen-op-Zoom Andrew Williamson
[f. 253] William Bower: 5 cwt wrought flax £5 (13 Sept 1568). Robert Scarboro: 12 cwt flax £12. [f. 253*b*] John Boylson: 5 cwt flax £5 (14 Sept).

818. *Pellican* of Amsterdam John Williamson
[f. 253] Henry Weightman: 2 three-quarter packs flax £12 (14 Sept 1568).

819. *Mary Ann* of Maldon (40) John Denis; Rouen
[f. 253] Edward Boyes: 26 grs halfpennyware combs £6 10*s* (14 Sept 1568). John Raines: 8 doz. pcs buckram £12. Richard Pattrick: 30 grs playing cards, 30 grs woolcards, 2 doz. pair playing tables, 10 doz. lbs thread £52 10*s*. Wolston Dixi: 2300 ells canvas £57 10*s*. John Challener: 100 bolts black thread, 180 reams paper £34 (15 Sept). Robert Sadler: 1800 ells canvas £45. Anthony Cage: 1200 ells canvas £30. [f. 254] Hugh Offley: 140 reams paper £18 13*s* 4*d*.

820. *Spredegle* of Amsterdam (40) John Rode; Amsterdam
[f. 253*b*] William Stokes: 30 bundles ton-flax £1 15*s* (14 Sept 1568). Thomas Hecker: 8 brls fish, 480 lings £20. Humphrey Kele: 240 lings, 8 brls fish £12. [f. 254] Richard Mouse: 600 staplefish, 360 lings £21.

821. *Longbow* of Amsterdam Jacob Tyson
[f. 253*b*] Thomas Hecker: 840 lings £28 (14 Sept 1568). Humphrey Kele: 840 lings £28. Thomas Sandford: 2 lasts barrelled fish £12. [f. 254] Richard Mouse: 18 brls fish £9.

822. *Pawlinge* of Amsterdam Jacob Crone
[f. 253*b*] Thomas Sandford: 1 last barrelled fish £6 (14 Sept 1568).

823. *World* of Haarlem Peter English
[f. 254] Adam Couper: 12 pcs Holland cloth £14 8*s* (15 Sept 1568).

824. *Black Dragon* of Amsterdam (30) Lucas Garretson; Amsterdam
[f. 254*b*] John Violet: 4 lasts barrelled fish, 1500 staplefish £46 10*s* (16 Sept 1568). [f. 255*b*] James Dewes: 7 half-pcs[1] linen cloth £4 5*s* (23 Sept).

    1. Alternatively 7½ pcs.

825. *Falcon* of St. Omer (30) Simon de Hortor
[f. 254*b*] John Atkinson: 4500 bunches onions £18 15*s* (18 Sept 1568).

826. *Mary Anne* of Brightlingsea (28) John Chandler; The Bay
[f. 254*b*] John Chandler: 20 weys bay salt £20 (20 Sept 1568).

827. *Grace of God* of London Richard Tye; Rouen
[f. 254*b*] John Newton: 8 grs playing cards, 12 grs combs, 3 reams coarse paper £14 8*s* 4*d* (20 Sept 1568). Matthew Colclough: 1200 ells canvas, 18½ doz. woolcards £39 5*s*. Robert Sadler: 1000 ells canvas, 80 reams paper, 80 reams loose paper £46 6*s* 8*d*. Humphrey Broune: 12 grs playing cards,

25 doz. woolcards, 20 grs halfpennyware combs, 2 grs crewel lace, 6 doz. inkhorns, 80 reams loose paper £41 15s. Anthony Gamage: 900 ells brown canvas £22 10s. Harry Wayght: 20 doz. woolcards £10. Richard Morrys: 1300 ells canvas £32 10s. Thomas Starkey: 4000 ells Tours canvas, 29 cwt prunes £67 16s 8d. Thomas Davy: 1050 ells canvas £26 5s (22 Sept). Hugh Offley: 800 ells canvas, 33 grs playing cards £53. William Playsden: 1500 ells canvas £37 10s. Edmund Ansell: 18 doz. buckrams, 80 yds French dornick £31 (23 Sept). John Challener: 130 reams paper, 8 grs playing cards, 2 grs woollen-lace, 3 grs box combs, 4 sum copper nails, 100 reams coarse cap-paper, 30 reams writing paper £45 8s 4d. Anthony Cage: 400 ells canvas £10. John Hutton: 70 reams paper £9 6s 8d. [f. 255b] Richard Smyth: 130 yds 'tuff' taffeta £21 13s 4d.

828. *Sparrowhake* of Antwerp (50) Mattis Brownyng; Antwerp
[f. 255] Robert Brook: 20 cwt hops £10 (22 Sept 1568). John Smyth: 2 chests Burgundy glass £4 (23 Sept). Garret Dewes: 20 reams unbound books £2. William Bower: 6 cwt hops £3. [f. 255b] John Woodward: 20 pcs Ulm fustian, 60 yds satin, 60 yds damask £71 (24 Sept).

829. *Owl* of Amsterdam (15) John Francis
[f. 256] John Violet: 840 lings, 2½ lasts fish £43 (24 Sept 1568).

830. *Bark Fox* of London (50) Thomas Bolton; Barbary
[f. 256] Matthew Filde: 10 cwt sugar £33 6s 8d (24 Sept 1568).

APPENDICES

I. CHRONOLOGY OF ENTRIES

This table lists chronologically the total daily entries made by merchants, as recorded in the manuscript (E. 190/4/2).

Date	Entries	Date	Entries
30 Sept 1567	14	14 Nov	26
		15	6
1 Oct	17	17	13
2	16	18	43
3	23	19	63
4	25	20	60
6	26	21	27
7	18	22	17
8	19	24	22
9	4	25	31
10	3	26	18
13	5	27	18
14	2	28	18
15	10	29	8
16	10		
17	11	1 Dec	25
20	16	2	21
21	46	3	27
22	43	4	29
23	21	5	21
24	11	6	18
25	6	8	14
27	22	9	12
30	24	10	12
31	16	11	24
		12	15
		13	20
3 Nov	8	15	15
4	5	16	18
5	5	17	24
6	2	18	12
7	12	19	26
8	10	20	12
10	22	22	38
11	6	23	35
12	22	24	15
13	25	29	15

Date	Entries	Date	Entries
30 Dec	6	6 March	19
31	2	8	6
		9	11
2 Jan 1568	4	10	14
3	7	11	16
5	22	12	9
7	10	13	16
8	21	15	27
9	20	16	42
10	8	17	45
12	11	18	27
13	23	19	14
14	8	20	11
15	10	22	7
16	21	23	9
17	26	24	5
19	36	26	19
20	40	27	20
21	25	29	22
22	14	30	4
23	2	31	12
30	3		
		1 April	33
3 Feb	4	2	62
4	10	3	18
5	10	5	6
6	1	6	7
9	23	7	2
10	33	8	5
11	56	9	7
12	48	10	7
13	20	12	1
14	11	14 & 13 [*sic*]	4
16	16	22	25
17	7	23	48
19	4	24	57
20	4	26	64
21	6	27	62
23	8	28	63
24	2	29	20
26	3	30	14
27	6		
28	9	3 May	6
		4	34
1 March	20	5	11
3	29	6	10
4	45	7	12
5	28	10	4

Appendices

Date	Entries		Date	Entries
11 May 1568	10		10 July	6
12	32		12	11
13	6		13	40
14	4		14	36
15	3		15	37
17	30		16	52
18	30		17	24
19	39		19	12
20	20		20	15
21	2		22	8
22	6		23	3
24	2		26	28
25	2		27	23
26	4		28	38
27	8		29	13
29	15		30	14
31	36		31	8
1 June	42		3 Aug	6
2	17		6	2
3	24		7	17
4	5		9	39
5	4		10	39
10	30		11	13
11	26		12	18
12	8		13	5
14	4		14	11
15	5		16	47
16	25		17	72
17	8		18	65
18	9		19	26
19	4		20	31
21	4		21	12
22	18		23	13
23	45		24	10
25	47		26	18
26	39		27	20
28	35		28	5
30	33		30	11
			31	12
1 July	33			
2	29		1 Sept	36
3	20		2	25
5	30		3	20
6	14		4	9
7	23		6	19
8	27		7	28
9	18		8	21

Appendices

Date	Entries	Date	Entries
9 Sept	19	16 Sept	3
10	10	18	1
11	22	20	9
13	21	22	4
14	20	23	9
15	8	24	3

II. DESCRIPTIVE LIST OF COMMODITIES

The list is an alternative to a full index. Although all the commodities in the calendar are listed below, reference is only made to their first entry. The descriptions do not claim to be comprehensive: a few commodities remain unidentified while others are too familiar to require explanation. The following books have been especially useful in supplementing the *Oxford English Dictionary:*

H. R. Schubert, *History of the British iron and steel industry* (1957)
Oskar de Smedt, *De Engelse natie te Antwerpen in de 16ᵉ eeuw* (Antwerp, 1950, 1954)
H. J. Smit, *Bronnen tot de geschiedenis van den handel met Engeland, Schotland en Ierland, 1485–1585.* Rijks Geschiedkundige Publicatiën, 86, 91 ('S-Gravenhage, 1942, 1950)
E. M. Veale, *English fur trade in the later Middle Ages* (Oxford, 1966)
T. S. Willan, *Tudor Book of Rates*

Almonds, 78
Alum, 574
Andirons, iron, 18; latten, 191. *See also* Latten
Aniseed, 18
Apples, 110
Argentum vivum, *see* Quicksilver
Argol, 18. The crude bitartrate of potassium which, when purified, becomes cream of tartar.
Arsenic, 710
Ashes, 480; 'rouse', 660; soap, 437. Wood ashes for making lye, the alkalised water used in cloth manufacture.
Awl blades, 45

'Babies', *see* Dolls
Backs, iron, 234. Probably chimney backs (*q.v.*).
Bags, leather, 710
Baking pans, copper, 258. *See also* Pans
Balances, gold, 808; ounce, 64. *See also* Weights
Balls, 45. *See also* Tennis balls, Washing balls
Bands, copper, 155
Barber's cases, 771
Barley, 365
Barlings, 602. 'Barlings or fir-poles' in the 1611 Book of Rates.
Barrels, empty, 154
Basil leather or skin, 154. Sheepskin tanned in bark.
Baskets, 717; wicker, 410. *See also* Hand baskets
Basnets, latten, 18. Small rounded headpieces with ventail or visor. *See also* Latten

Bastards, 198. A sweet wine; sometimes applied to any kind of sweetened wine.

Bast-ropes, 559

Basts, 563. Any flexible fibrous bark used in rope-making. *See also* Cables, Cordage, Hawsers, Rope

Battery, 18. Articles of metal wrought by hammering, especially kettles, cauldrons, etc.

Bays, bay berries, 46. Fruit of the bay laurel tree.

Beads, glass, 18

Beams, wooden, 178

Beaver backs, 805

Beaver bellies, 790

Bed pans, 18

Beds, 339; Ghentish, 154; sealed, 624; of silk, 653

Bells, 213; dog, 729; hawk, 759; horse, 18; morris, 298

Beryllia, 472. Oxide of berylium or glucinum, otherwise called glucina.

Blankets, 45

'Blues', 539, see 539n

Boards, cutting, 670; paste, 487

Bodkins, 643

Books, unbound, 38

Bottles, earthenware, 334; stone, 346; wicker, 2

Bottoms, brass and copper, 294

Boultel, 154; Beaupreau ('Beapers'), 340; Rennes, 155. A cloth used for bolting or sifting meal or flour.

Bowstaves, 33

'Box combs', 395. The Book of Rates lists 'box pieces for combs', rated by the thou. and 'combs the box' with half a gross the box. *See also* Combs

Boxes, 339; painted, 154; soap, 564

Brazil, 143. A red dye made from the wood of the East Indian tree *Caesalpina Sappan*.

Brimstone, 18

'Brissels', 46. A fabric, associated perhaps with Brussels.

Bristles, 186

Brooches, lead, 458

Brushes, 383; hair, 539; rubbing, 367; weaver's, 156. *See also* Comb brushes

Buckles, latten, 756; paper, 18

Buckram, 47; French, 636. A linen cloth, usually Flemish and blue-dyed.

Budge, rumney, 576. Lambskins, the name being derived from Bougie in North Africa, whence skins were exported to Flanders and Brabant. Rumney (Roumenie) was the name given to lambskins from Lombardy.

Bugle, 572; glass, 580

Bustian, 45. A cotton or cotton and linen cloth.

Buttons, glass, 340; Milan, 296; steel, 435

Cables, 3. *See also* Basts

Calf-forrel, 487. Forrel, a vellum-like parchment for book covers.

Calf skins, 785

Cambric ('Camerick'), 503. A fine white linen cloth from Kamerijk (Cambrai) in Flanders.

Camlet, 45; unwatered, 781; watered, 339. A mixed fabric of uncertain composition but often incorporating silk and probably of high quality. *See also* Grogram camlet

Candle plates, 18; latten, 703

Candlesticks, 146; latten, 213

Candy, 46; brown, 45. Sugar in large crystallised pieces.

Cans, drinking, 740

Canvas, 2; Bar ('barroys' or 'barras'), 18; Castile, 367; 'clincent', 45; cushion, 535; Dutch packing, 45; Newcastle, 46; Normandy, 156; packing, 2; 'spruce', 647; striped, 156; striped with crewel, 405; striped with silk, 389; Tours, 827; Troys, 367; Vitré ('Vetery'), 67; working, 458. Bar canvas was a coarse linen cloth or packing canvas named after the principality of Bar. 'Clincent' may indicate a shiny or burnished canvas (Middle Dutch cleinson, clinsen = cleansed, shiny: English 'clinquant'). *See also* Poldavis

Capers, 46

Cap-paper, 337. *See also* Paper

Cap ribands, 18

Caps, taffeta, 771

Caraway seed, 433

Carpets, 45; Ghentish or sealed, 45; 'turney' (? Tournai or Turnhout), 191; Venice, 46

Carrels, 502. A mixed fabric of silk and linen.

Carving tools, 18

'Catlins', 435. ? catlings, a small surgical knife; or catgut for stringed instruments.

Cauls, 259

Chafing dishes, 2; latten, 389. Vessels which hold burning charcoal or other fuel, for heating purposes.

Chain-lace, crewel, 2. *See also* Crewel

Chains, *see* Dog chains, etc.

Chamber stools, 155. *See also* Close stools

Chamois, 466

'Chaps', 594. ? Chapes or metal pieces attached to buckles, scabbard points, etc.

Checks, check pieces, 154; worsted, 45. Fabric woven with a check or criss-cross pattern.

Cheese, Holland, 110

Chests, 297; Danzig, 632

Chimney backs, 365. Iron plates which protected the back walls of fireplaces. *See also* Backs

Chimney rakes, iron, 178

Chisels, 340

Cinnamon, 45

Citherns, 305. A stringed musical instrument. *See also* Gitterns

Clapholt, clap boards, 28. A small size of split oak, used for barrel-staves and wainscotting.

Close stools, 259. *See also* Chamber stools

Cloth(s), coarse, 628; cradle, 339; dyed, 465. *See* Eeklo, Gelders, Ghentish, Hamburg, Harnesdale, Olonne cloths.

Cloves, 45

Coal-fish, 240. A fish allied to the cod and found in northern seas.

Cochineal, 213

Codsheads, 239

Colombets, 18. An unidentified cloth; perhaps a variation of 'camlet'.

Coloquintida, 466. Or colocynth, the bitter-apple, used as a purgative.

Comb brushes, 45

Comb cases, 435

Combs, 2; halfpenny, 827; horse, 290; paper, 395; pennyware, 64; quarter, 265; wooden, 457. *See also* 'Box combs'

Compasses, 4

Cooper's tools, 46

Copper, *see* Baking pans, Bands, Bottoms, Hangings, Nails, Pans, Wire

Copperas, 155. Iron sulphate, used in dyeing, tanning and making ink.

Cord, 516

Cordage, 28. *See also* Basts

Coriander seed, 45

Cork, 113

Corn powder, 18. Gunpowder that has been granulated. *See also* Gunpowder

Cotton, unspun, 771. *See also* Cyprus cotton

Cotton-lace, 360

Cotton wool, 234

Counters, 45. Pieces of metal or other material, used in counting or keeping accounts.

Creepers, 146. A small iron 'dog', placed in pairs on a hearth between the andirons.

Crewel, 18. A worsted yarn. *See also* Chain-lace, Dornick, Girdles

Crewel lace, 64

Croplings, 3. An inferior kind of stockfish.

Crossbow laths, 462

Cruse, stone, 42. An earthenware pot or jar.

Cucumber seed, 522

Cuit, 198. Wine boiled down to a certain thickness and sweetness.

Cumin, 710. A plant, like fennel, with aromatic seed.

Cupboard, 792

Currants, 757

Curtain rings, 211

Cushion cloths, 335

Cushions, 45

Cyperus, 367. Probably sweet cyperus or gelingale.

Cyprus cotton, 18

Damask, 18; for napkins and towelling, 576

Dates, 45; garbled, 463. Garbled = sifted and cleansed.

Deals, 28; Marienburg ('Meighborro'), 599; spruce, 563

Dials, 234; wooden, 340

Diaper towelling, 237; for napkins and table cloths, 576

Dog chains, 18

Dolls ('Babies'), 491

Dornick, 18; caddis, 367; crewel, 46; French, 236; woollen, 155. Dornick, which takes its name from Doornik in Flanders, was a fine linen cloth. Caddis = crewel.

Doubles, 46; hand, 539; iron, 45. The Book of Rates distinguishes between 'double iron plates', rated by the piece, and double or single plates ('white' or 'black') by the cwt. The distinction is not clear. Iron and other metals were commonly worked into sheets or plates and doubling was a normal method of strengthening them. Grey and white were the two basic types of cast iron. *See also* Plates

Down, 761

Dripping pans, 154

Drugs, 45

Dudgeon, 18. A wood used for the handle of knives, etc.

Ear picks, 463

Eeklo cloth, 157. Eeklo ('Ecclo') was an important centre of linen-weaving.

Eels, 564; dole-, 89; pimper-, 216; shaft-, 239; stub-, 205. The difference between these types of eel is obscure. They may indicate distinctions in age and colouring.

Epithyme, 522. A plant used in medicine.

Ermine, 805

Falcon, 21. Also entered as tercel-gentle ('tassell gentill') = a male falcon.

Fans, 19

Feathers, 21; ostrich, 591

Felts, felt hats, 415

Fenugreek ('Venecreke'), 730. A leguminous plant cultivated for its seeds, which were used both medicinally and to provide a yellow dye.

Figs, 247; Algarve, 207

Figs-dode and -merchant, 113. '-dode' indicates an inferior kind of fig.

Files, 45; goldsmith's, 259

Fireshovel plates, 45

Fireshovels, 18

Fish, 22; green, 597. *See also* Coal-fish, Croplings, Eels, Herrings, Lings, Staplefish, Stockfish, Sturgeon, Titlings

Flaskets, 416

Flasks, gun, 678

Flax, 10; bale, 510; bundle, 477; quartern, 488; ton, 477. Bale, etc. presumably indicate the way the flax was packed.

Flax and hair, 465

Flocks, 501

Foin backs, 67. Foin, the skins of stone marten.

Foin potes, 155. Potes ('pouts') are furs from the paws or *mains* of an
    animal.
Foin tails, 155
Foin wombs, 67
Forrel, *see* Calf-forrel
Fox backs, 67
Fox skins, 624
Fringes, 45; half-silk, 45; silk, 191
Frizado, 154. A fine kind of frieze.
Frying pans, 18
Fustian, 46; Genoa, 154; Milan, 210; Naples, 45; Ulm ('holmes'), 18.
    A cloth of cotton and flax, manufactured principally in Italy and
    south Germany.

Galls, 18. Oak-apples or gall-nuts, used in making ink, tanning, dyeing
    and medicine.
Gelders cloth, 582. Probably a linen cloth.
Ghentish cloth, 18. A linen cloth; Ghent was a main centre of production.
Gimlets, wooden, 643
Ginger, 18; green, 53
Girdles, crewel, 389; velvet, 771
Girdling(s), 64; crewel, 155; worsted, 576
Gitterns, 305. *See also* Citherns
Glass(es), 4; Burgundy, 146; drinking, 155; halfpenny ware, 702; Nor-
    mandy, 64; Rhenish, 20. *See also* Beads, Buttons, Looking glasses,
    Spectacles
Gloves, 572
Glue, 647
Goatskins, 17
Goshawks, 21
Grain berries, 357. The Book of Rates lists grain of Portugal and of
    Seville, the latter in berries. Both were probably forms of the grain-
    like insect kermes or alkermes which produced a scarlet dye.
Grains, *see* Grain berries, Guinea grains
'Greens', 539. Probably green dornick, as listed in the Book of Rates.
Gridirons, 178
Grogram, 155
Grogram camlet, 296
Grogram silk, 62
Guinea grains, 265. Malagueta pepper, obtained from West Africa.
Gum, 296. The Book of Rates lists eight types of gum.
Gum arabic, 191
Gunpowder, 18; serpentine, 341. Serpentine was gunpowder in fine meal,
    as opposed to the corned or granulated kind. *See also* Corn powder
Guns, *see* Hand guns

Haberdashery, 750
Halbert heads, 462
Halberts, 156

Hamburg cloth, 21. A linen cloth.
Hammers, 435
Hand baskets, 242. *See also* Baskets
Hand guns, 810
Hangings, copper, 234
Harnesdale cloth, 18. A linen cloth.
Harp strings, 45
Hat bands, 45
Hatchets, 643
Hats, 340. *See also* Caps, Felts, Straw hats
Hawks, 186
Hawsers, 28. *See also* Basts
Hazebroucks ('Hasbrough'), 18. A linen cloth of Hazebrouck in France.
Heath brushes, 6. 'Heath for brushes' in the Book of Rates.
Hedlack, 381. A linen cloth.
'Hedlands', 18. ? a variant spelling of hinderlands.
Hellebore, white, 367. Plant used medicinally.
Hemp, 18; Cologne, 18
Hemp seed, 232
Herrings, 342
Hides, 761; cow, 785; raw, 590
Hinderlands, 21. A linen cloth.
Holland cloth, 18. A linen, probably woven in Flanders and only bleached in Holland.
Honey, 18
Hooks, 572
Hops, 14
Horns, iron, 643
Horns [writing], 678
Horn-tips, 564
Hose, *see* Silk hose, Stammel hose
Hour glasses, 4

Ink, *see* Printer's ink
Inkhorns, 2
Inkle, 18. A kind of linen tape, or the thread or yarn from which it is made.
Ireos ('Erius'), 154. Root of the Florentine Iris, used in pharmacy.
'Irims' or 'Iruns', 643. Probably iron-ware, but not identified.
Iron, 63; 'ames', 45; faggot, 557; 'Lukes', 466; 'small square', 18; Spanish, 63; spruce, 145. Willan equates 'ames' with Almayne = Germany, but H. R. Schubert, *op. cit.*, 313 more convincingly takes the word to signify the district of Amiens, a centre of iron manufacture in northern France. Faggot indicates iron in rods and bundles; 'Lukes' = Luik *i.e.* Liège; 'small squares' were the smaller of the two sorts of cast iron bars which were normally produced in the sixteenth century, being thinner and lighter than the 'long squares'. *See also* Doubles, Plates; *and* Andirons, Chimney backs, Horns, Pans, Pots, Rakes, Thread, Wire

Ironmongery, 46
Irons, *see* Planing irons
Ironware, 435
Iron-works, 522
Isinglass, 627

Jews' trumps, 490
Joiner's tools, 178

Kerseys, dyed, 156
Kettle bands, 463
Kettles, 702
Knives, 18; 'Almaine', 45; Cologne, 212; German, 541; single, 213.
Almaine = German.

Lace, 45; narrow, 395; passement ('percement'), 45. Passement was a
simple form of lace whereby the threads were passed or interlaced.
Ladles, 178
Lanterns, 4
Lapis calaminaris, 211. Calamine, a zinc ore used medicinally for external
application.
Latten, black, 781; shaven, 156. Latten, a mixed metal either identical
with or closely akin to brass. Black latten was milled brass in
plates or sheets; shaven were thinner sheets. *See also* Andirons,
Basnets, Buckles, Candle plates, Candlesticks, Chafing dishes, Pipes,
Plates, Wire
Lead tablets, 64
Lemons, 533
Lignum vitae, 45. Wood from the guaiacum tree, used in medicine.
Lince, 154. Lince = linsey, a coarse linen cloth.
Linen, 156. *See also* Buckram, Bustian, Cambric, Eeklo, Gelders cloth,
Ghentish cloth, Hamburg cloth, Harnesdale cloth, Hazebroucks,
Hedlack, Hinderlands, Lince, Linsey-wolsey, Middlegood, Minsters,
Olonne cloth, Osnabrücks, Padduck, Soultwich
Lings, 3
Linseed oil, 18. Also called painter's oil.
Linsey-wolsey, 296. A cloth of linen and wool.
Liquorice, 18
Litmus, 18
'Locke persers', 46
Locks, 46; gate, 710; hanging, 211; horse, 710; 'slight', 435. *See also*
Padlocks
Long pepper, 703. Milder than common black pepper, long pepper had
medicinal uses.
Looking glasses, 2; crystal, 45; halfpennyware, 45; pennyware, 730;
steel, 335
Lutes, 305; Antwerp, 703; Cologne, 466; Venice, 53
Lute strings, 45. Or minikins.

Mace, 45; garbled, 710
Madder, 18; Bruges, 763; German, 46. *See also* Mull-madder
Malmsey, 53
Manna, 539. The juice of certain sorts of ash tree, used as a purgative.
Maps, 155
Marking stones, 435
Marmalade, 45
Marten, *see* Foin
Matches, 18
Mattriss cards, 4. Playing cards regarded as defective.
Mazer wood, 617
Middlegood, 3. A linen cloth.
Millstones, 697
Minikins, *see* Lute strings
Mink, 790; untawed, 15
Minsters, 155. A linen cloth originally from Münster.
Mockado, 18. An imitation velvet, of wool and silk.
Molasses, 539. *See also* Treacle
Mull-madder, 45. The most inferior of the four qualities of Dutch madder.
Muscatel, 53

Nails, card, 710; copper, 827; great, 155; head, 18; patten, 178; rose, 290; saddler's, 535; small, 18. *See also* Tacks
Napkins, 285. *See also* Damask, Diaper
Neckerchief bands, 18
Needle cases, 457
Needles, 45. *See also* Pack needles
Nigella, 46. 'Anguilla romayne' or 'nigillum romanum', a plant of which the seeds were used for medicinal purposes.
Nightcaps, quilted, 576; quilted linen, 702
Nutmegs, 38
Nuts, 154

Oakum, 10
Oars, 28
Oats, 140
Ochre, 296
Oil, 154; bay, 298; Seville, 272. *See also* Linseed oil, Rape oil, Train oil
Olives, 242
Olonne cloth ('oulderons'), 213. A linen cloth from Brittany.
Onions, 5
Onion seed, 154
Oranges, 277
Orchil, 365. A red or violet dye obtained from lichens.
Orpiment, 45. Trisulphide of arsenic, used as a pigment.
Osnabrücks ('Ozenbridge'), 3. A linen cloth originally from Osnabrück.

Pack needles, 234
Pack thread, 2; bottom, 462

Padduck, 468. A linen or canvas cloth.

Padlocks, 178. *See also* Locks

Painter's oil, *see* Linseed oil

Panele, 291. Brown unrefined sugar.

Pans, copper, 146; earthenware, 731; iron, 45. *See also* Baking pans, Dripping pans, Frying pans, Warming pans

Paper, 2; brown, 211; printing, 38; writing, 827. *See also* Cap-paper

Paper-pins, 154

Parchment, 45

Parchment skins, 497. *See also* Calf-forrel

Paste boards, *see* Boards

Paving stones, 367

Paving tiles, 365

Penners, 678. Cases or sheaths for pens.

Pens, *see* Writing pens

Pepper, 18. *See also* Long pepper

Petticoats, 46

Piercers, 297

Pincers, 259

Pinpillows, 234; cloth, 710; tin, 384

Pins, 18

Pipes, 339; latten, 298; wooden, 516

Pitch, 13

Planing irons, 710

Plates, black or white, 18; 'funi', 294; furnace, 730; iron, 45; latten, 433. *See also* Doubles, Fireshovel plates

Playing cards, 2. *See also* Mattriss cards

Playing tables, 36

Points, 64; check, 367; half, 212; leather, 435; thread, 18. Cord fastenings for clothes.

Poldavis, 69. A coarse canvas, taking its name from Pouldavid in Brittany.

Potash, 434

Pots, earthenware, 731; galley, 365; iron, 265; stone, 18

Pottingers, 297. Small basins or soup dishes.

Printer's letters, 228

Printing ink, 228

Prunes, 2

Pumice-stone, 522

Pumping stocks, 228

Purse rings, 11

Purses, velvet, 771

Purse wire, 340

Quicksilver, 155. Or argentum vivum.

Quilts, 383

Rackets, 516

Raisins, 78; 'de lixa', 88; Malaga, 112; Marbella, 87

Raisins of the sun, 38. Sun-dried raisins.

Rakes, *see* Chimney rakes
Rape oil, 10. Oil from rape seed, for domestic use.
Rasters, 719. Or Rafter = spar, lath.
Rattles, wicker, 4
Razors, 154
Red lead, 18
Remnants, 62
Resin, 1
Rhubarb, 677
Riband, caddis, 433. *See also* Cap ribands, Thread ribands
Rice, 18
Rings, 4. *See also* Curtain rings, Purse rings
Rods, 50. For basket-making.
Rope(s), tarred, 36; untarred, 761. *See also* Bast-ropes, Cables, Cordage,
        Warps
Rope-yarn, 435
Rosalger, 2. Disulphide of arsenic, used as a pigment.
Roses, 643. Roses for headpieces, *i.e.* rosettes worn on caps or hats.
Ruffs, 18
Rugs, 339; cradle, 212
'Russels', 259.? Linen cloth from Roeselare (West Flanders).
Rye, 772

Sack, 137; sherry, 681; Spanish, 355
Sackcloth, 155; striped, 298. A coarse linen cloth.
Salmon, 217; Scotch, 217
Salmon gills, 342
Salt, great, white and bay, 1. Great salt was coarse grained, white was
        more fine and pure. Bay salt indicates its origin, from Bourgneuf
        bay.
Saltpetre, 19
'Sanderstock', 643. ? Sandarac, which is listed in the Book of Rates as
        sandrake, a resin used in the preparation of spirit varnish.
Sarcenet, 18; Bologna, 647; Florence, 462. A fine silk material.
Satin, 18; Bruges, 522; Genoa, 540
Satin silk, 210
Saws, carpenter's, 781; hand-, 46; tenon-, 211; two-hand-, 46; whip-, 46
Says, 18; gartering, 154; Hondschoote ('Honneskott'), 191. A cloth
        similar to serge.
Scomes, 354. An inferior sort of sugar.
'Sea gills', 406
Sealskins, 805
Seeds, 491; garden, 405
Senna, 46
Shears, 178. 'Sheres for sempsters' in the Book of Rates.
Sheets, packing, 433
Shirt strings, 348
Shuttles, 156; weaver's, 539
Silk, 46; Bruges, 46; ferret ('floret'), 45; Genoa, 540; Paris, 11; 'poll', 296;

raw dyed, 389; sewing, 282; short, 163; Spanish or Seville, 146; thrown, 523; undyed, 466. *See also* Tartarines

Silk cards, 308

Silk hose, 282

Silk nobs, 340

'Sine Alexandrie', 574. Probably some kind of drug: Alexandria (*i.e.* Egypt) was a noted source of pharmaceutical materials.

'Sirrills', 643. Possibly some kind of saw, from the Latin 'serra'.

Skins, Flanders, 211; Spanish or Seville, 242; counterfeit Spanish, 464. *See also* Basil leather, Beaver, Budge, Calf-forrel, Calfskins, Chamois, Ermine, Foin, Fox, Goatskins, Hides, Mink, Parchment, Seal, 'Vents', Wolfskins, Wolverines

Snuffers, 46

Soap, 258; black, 708; Castile, 258; Flemish, 513; grey, 702. *See also* Washing balls

Soap ashes, *see* Ashes

Soap boxes, *see* Boxes

Soultwich, 49. A linen cloth, probably from Salzwedel in Germany.

Spades, 155

Spars, 391

Spectacle cases, 458

Spectacles, 395. *See also* Glasses

Squirts, 272. A tubular piece by which water may be squirted.

Stammel, 18. A woven fabric like linsey-wolsey.

Stammel hose, 653

Standishes, 154; leather, 383. Stands with ink, pens, etc.

Staplefish, 23. Cod or other gadoid fish cured by drying and beating.

Starch, 18

Stavesacre, 574. A plant, the seeds of which were used as an emetic.

Steel, 18; coarse, 643; 'stass', 18. ? 'Stass' (German) = bundle, sheaf.

Stinice, 522. 'Stene' or 'Scinci', small lizards used in medicine.

Stockfish, 49. *See also* Croplings, Titlings

Stomachers, furred, 155

Straw hats, 154

Sturgeon, 145

Succade, 291. Fruit preserved in sugar, either candied or in syrup.

Sugar, 154. *See also* Panele, Scomes

Sugar candy, *see* Candy

Sugar powder, 591

Sumach, 18. Dried and ground leaves, used in tanning and dyeing.

Sword blades, 18

Tablemen, 593. Pieces used in board games.

Tables, 593; walnut, 792. *See also* Playing tables, Writing tables

Tacks, 465

Taffeta, 18; 'caffaes', 465; Florence, 462; Levant, 45; Lucca ('Lukes'), 465; Spanish, 357; Tours, 156. 'Caffaes', perhaps from caffa, a rich silk cloth.

Tallow, 39

Tankards, 381

Tapestry, caddis, 45; hair, 18; silk, 155; wool, 18

Tar, 559

Tartarines, 234. Rich stuff, apparently of silk and originating in the East.

Teazles, 2. The prickly flower-heads of the fuller's teazle, used for raising a nap on the surface of cloth.

Tennis balls, 46. *See also* Balls

Tercel-gentle, *see* Falcon

Tercel-goshawk, *see* Goshawks

Thimbles, 18

Thread, 18; bottom, 18; Bruges, 18; Cologne, 296; 'copper gold', 576; crossbow, 45; 'housewaies', 611; iron, 335; linen, 393; Lyons, 38; Oudenaarde, 18; Paris, 341; piecing, 155; sister's, 433

Thread cards, 710

Thread-lace, 395

Thread riband, 154

Ticks, 365; Brussels, 435; Turnhout, 18. Turnhout ('Tournold' or 'Tourney') was the main centre of the flourishing Kempen tick-weaving industry. Brussels ticks were a relatively new article.

Tiles, *see* Paving tiles

Tinsel, 572

Tin tablets, 642. ? A children's toy.

Titlings, 3. A small size of stockfish.

Tongs, 18

Tooth picks, 771

Tow, 378

Towelling, *see* Damask, Diaper

Train oil, 1. Oil from whales, seal and fish—especially cod.

Treacle, 339; Flemish, 154; Genoa, 154. Flemish treacle was not the syrup called treacle but a medicinal compound, used as a salve.

Trenchers, 45; penny, 678

'Tressel garnet', 643. Garnet, a hinge for doors, etc., or tackle used on ships for hoisting in provisions, etc.: tressel = trestle.

Tripe de velours, 298. An imitation velvet.

'Trosies', 595. Probably trusses or ropes used to hold the yards to the main mast.

Trunks, 178. ? Hollow tubes from which darts or pellets were shot.

Turmeric, 365. The root-stock of an East Indian plant, used both as a dye and in medicine.

Turnsole, 46. A violet-blue or purple colouring matter.

Turpentine, 143

Varnish, 45

Velvet, 18; 'garding', 572; Lucca ('Lukes'), 462. Garding, probably 'garden', indicating a flowered velvet, as in 'garden satin'.

Venice gold, 574

'Vents', 155. A fur or skin, probably 'venter' = the under-belly.

Verdigris, 234

Vermilion, 703. The mineral dye.

Vinegar, 4

Wainscots, 7
Walnuts, 351
Warming pans, 191
Warps, 747. Small ropes.
Washing balls, 463. Toilet soap, sometimes perfumed or medicated.
Wax, 28
Weights, brazen gold, 435; gold, 154; pile, 389; troy, 650. Pile weights,
    usually of brass and fitting one upon another to form a pile. *See also*
    Balances
White lead, 45
Wine, Alicante, 472; Burgundy, 623; Canary, 801; Coniac, 579; corrupt, 80;
    Gascony, 61; Nantes, 621; Oléron, 59; Rhenish, 52; Rochelle, 54; of
    St. Martin, 224; sweet, 53. *See also* Bastards, Cuit, Malmsey, Mus-
    catel, Sack
Wire, clavichord, 18; copper, 598; iron, 229; latten, 18. *See also* Purse wire
Woad, 18; Toulouse, 433
Wolfskins, 805
Wolverineskins, 296
Wood, *see* Barlings, Beams, Boards, Clapholt, Deals, Mazer wood, Oars,
    Rasters, Rods, Spars, Wainscots
Wool, 63; Eastland, 154; estrige, 3; hat, 45; Spanish, 46. Estrige is probably
    a corruption of Estriche and is therefore synonymous with Eastland,
    i.e. the region of Scandinavia and the Baltic.
Woolcards, 2. An instrument of wire, leather and wood, used for combing
    wool prior to spinning.
Woollen edging, 383. For decorating hats.
Woollen-lace, 2
Wormseed, 155. The dried flower-heads of various plants, used medicinally.
Worsted, broad, 18; narrow, 191. *See also* Checks, Girdling, Yarn
Writing pens, 298
Writing tables, 155

Yarn, worsted, 18. *See also* Crewel

III. VALUE OF IMPORTS IN 1559/60 AND 1565/6

The list of imports is made up from two documents, S.P. 12/8, ff. 63–9 and Lans. 8, ff. 75–6. The first is headed 'The particular valew of certayne necessary and vnnecessarye wares brought into the Porte of London in the second year of the Quenes Majestis reigne, the ouerquantyte wherof lamentably spoylith the realme yearly'; the second, which relates to the year commencing Michaelmas 1565, is simply endorsed 'wares brought in to London'. It is a less complete list than the first, with fewer items and others left unvalued. The list below is therefore based on the State Paper. Extra items from the later memorandum and those which are not identical with the earlier are printed in italics. The original spelling has been retained except for the £. *s. d.* symbols which have been modernised.

	1559/60 ad valorem £. s. d.			1565/6	
Allame	7,151	13	4		
Almondes	912	0	0		
Annyseedes	520	6	8		£500
Apples	876	3	4		£260
Ashes vocat Sope ashes	4,665	0	0		£2,600
Babies[1]	178	3	4		
Balles voc Tennys	1,699	0	0		
Bandes for hattes	109	13	4	*Hat bands*	£269
Basketts voc Sports	247	0	0		
Batrye	6,078	15	0		£3,600
Bayeburyes	109	4	0		
Belles	112	18	8	*Bells for hawks, etc.*	£159
Blanketts	368	0	0		
Bokes vnbounde	813	6	8		
Bottells	237	13	4		£52
Bowtell	1,161	16	8		£1,180
Brushes	757	18	8		£365
Buckerams	2,885	3	4		£2,569
				Budge	£1,688
Buttons	108	10	0		
Cabages and turnops	157	16	8		
Canvas	39,072	10	0		£32,124
Canvas for doblett	685	0	0	*Canvas striped*	£600
Cardes	2,837	10	0		£2,800
Carpetts, bankars and cusshion clothes	6,620	0	0	*Carpets*	£887

1. *i.e.* dolls.

	1559/60				1565/6
	£.	s.	d.		
Chambletts	3,627	16	8		£9,268
Chese of Hollande	2,482	13	4		
Chests and coffers	578	0	0		
Cloves	892	0	0		
				Combs	£169
Corrants	2,848	0	0		
Crewell	3,038	0	0		
Damaske	1,269	0	0		£565
Dates	610	0	0		
Diaper and damaske worke	875	0	0	*Diaper*	£475
				Dornick	£500
Eles freshe and salt	1,580	13	4	*Eeles*	£329
Fethers	1,863	0	0		
Figges	5,517	0	0		£2,823
Fyshe voc salt fyshe	7,996	0	0		£1,462
Flaxe	16,852	10	0		£13,217
Fustians	23,349	10	0		£27,254
Gawles	3,611	0	0		
Glasses to drinke in	663	10	0	*Glasses* }	£1,622
Glasses to loke in	667	0	0		
Gloves	2,636	10	0		
Ginger	1,115	0	0		£3,000
Ginger breade	165	0	0		
Gyrdells	998	10	0		
Grenes for womens apernes	3,967	0	0		
Hattes	7,915	10	0		
Hempe	3,288	10	0		£4,308
Herrings white	1,797	0	0	*Herrings*	£2,276
Hoppes	16,925	0	0		£19,100
				Inkhorns	£154
Inkle	8,412	10	0		£1,860
Iron	19,559	10	0		£6,394
				Iron wrought	£519
Knyves	1,558	0	0		£362
Laces for all sortes	775	6	8		
Lemans and oranges	1,756	0	0		
Lynges	3,176	0	0		
Lynnen clothe	61,673	13	4		£86,250
Maces	930	0	0		
Mader	11,135	0	0		£12,133
Marmelade	337	0	0		
Matches	466	13	4		
Meale	1,340	0	0		
Mockados	3,087	10	0		£6,400
Nayles	5,636	0	0		£5,730

	1559/60				1565/6
	£.	s.	d.		
Nedells	471	10	0		
Nutmeggs	677	16	8		£1,300
Nutts	58	0	0		
Onyons	1,489	10	0		£523
				Onyon seede	£770
Otes	2,121	0	0		
Oyle	38,020	13	4		£39,517
Panyles[1]	1,648	0	0		
Paper	3,304	0	0		£3,000
Pepper	11,852	0	0		£27,000
Pynnes	3,297	0	0		£4,274
Pitche and tarr	3,300	0	0		
Poyntes	234	0	0	*Poynts of thread*	£400
Pottes	627	13	4		£316
Proynes	9,405	15	0		£4,500
Raysons	9,135	15	0		£7,325
Rye	2,728	0	0		
Roddes for basketts	129	13	4	*Rods*	£258
Ropes and cables	2,303	10	0	*Ropes*	£2,759
Sables and other furres	3,793	0	0	*Skins of sables, etc.*	£800
Sackclothe	717	15	0	*Sackcloth of thread*	£1,600
Salmon	1,387	0	0		
Salte	2,943	0	0		£3,325
Sarcenett	1,903	0	0		£9,934
Satten	3,436	0	0		£3,264
				Saws	£259
Sayes	3,630	0	0		
Silke	7,130	0	0	*Sowing silk*	£8,004
Sinamon	2,333	0	0		
Sipers	780	0	0		£1,627
Skynnes	4,838	0	0		
Sope	9,725	15	0		£4,422
				Spanish skins and	
				shameys	£3,691
Stile[2]	2,920	0	0		£5,007
Stockefishe	2,605	0	0		
Sugar	18,237	0	0		£18,000
Taffeta	1,632	16	8		£3,452
Tappistrye	5,405	16	8		£5,588
Threde	13,671	13	4		£15,745
Tykes for bedds	5,939	0	0		£4,955
Velvett	8,614	0	0		£1,292
				Vinegar	£1,000
Wheat	9,285	0	0		
Wyar	1,375	0	0		£2,197

1. Panele.
2. *i.e.* steel.

	1559/60			*1565/6*
	£.	s.	d.	
Wyne ⎧Gascoyne ⎨Frenche ⎩Rochelle	36,210	0	0	*Wynes* £48,634
Wyne voc malvesay and muskadell	4,905	0	0	
Wyne Reynish	4,340	0	0	
Wyne Sacke	21,742	0	0	
Wyne bastarde	1,252	10	0	
Woade	33,431	0	0	
Woolle voc ⎧estrige wolle ⎨cotton wolle ⎩Spanish wolle	5,683	0	0	*Woll for hatts* £7,469
				Wormsede £192
Wursteds	17,314	0	0	£18,374
				Yarne £627
Summa totalis of the particuler valewes afore wrytten	643,319	18	0	
Summa of the residewe inwarde for this year	49,480	16	6	

Note: the list for 1565/6 includes several commodities not in the earlier document but without assigning values to them. These are: 'banketing bred, bricks, caroweys, calls of lynen, flowers of feathers, molasses, musterd seade, quayles, racketts, rattells, ruiffs, sleves of gold and silk'.

IV. DOCUMENTS AND NOTES RELATING TO THE PORT OF LONDON

1. THE SURVEY OF 1559. E. 159/34, rot. 222.
Note: the survey was authorised by letters patent under the exchequer seal, dated 14 June 1559 and addressed to the lord treasurer, his under-treasurer Sir Richard Sackville and the chancellor, Sir Walter Mildmay. The three, or two of them, were required to survey the creeks, wharfs and quays of the port and recommend which should be used for handling cargoes, in accordance with the statute 1 Eliz. I, c. 11.[1] Their survey and recommendations were recorded in the following schedule or certificate.

The certificate of vs William marques of Winchester lorde treasourer of England Richard Sackevile knight vnderthreasourer of the quenes highnes courte of theschequier at Westminster and Walter Myldemay knight chauncellor of the same courte appoynted and auctorised by the quenes highnes letters patents hereunto annexed for the lymytacon assigninge and appoyntinge of all kayes and wharfes and places apper-teyninge and belonginge to the porte of London for the charginge and landinge discharginge vnlodinge and laynge on lande there of wares and merchaundizes accordinge to an Acte of Parliament made and enacted in the Parliament begonne at Westminster the xxiij^ty day of January in the first yere of the raigne of our soueraigne lady Elizabeth by the grace of God of England France and Ireland Quene defendour of the faithe etc., and there proroged vntil the xxv^th day of the same moneth and then and there holden kept and contynued vntill the dissolucon of the same beinge the eight day of May in the said first yere of our said soueraigne lady the quenes majesties reigne. Be it remembred that we the commys-sioners aforesaid accordinge to the quenes majesties commyssion to vs directed dated the xiiij^th day of June in the yere of her graces reigne above written have the xxiiij^th day of August in the firste yere of our said soueraigne lady the quene searched surveyed and vywed by all the wayes and meanes we can all the open places kayes and wharfes and other ladinge and discharginge places for the chardge and dischardge of merchandizes within the porte of London and in all creeks to the same apperteyninge. And vpon deliberate advise by metes and boundes have by thauctorite of the said statute and commyssion aforesaid appointed assigned and limyted the places here vnder written to be open ladinge and discharginge places of wares and merchaundizes accordinge as they be hereafter seuerally lymytted and assigned and all other places of ladinge and dischardginge of wares and merchaundizes heretofore accustomed within the said porte and all creekes and places to the same porte belong-inge vtterly to be abolyshed and debarred by force of the said statute and

1. See above p. x.

other the premysses. First we have appoynted limitted and assigned by force of the premysses these kayes or places next folowinge that is to say the quenes majesties twoo kayes in London lyenge together at the Custome House there the one called the Newe Wolle Kay otherwise called the Custome House Key conteyninge by estymacon est and west in length fourescore and eleven footes. And from the water of Thames southe and northe in breadeth fourtie and three footes. The other of the quenes kayes is called the Olde Wooll Kay and conteyneth est and west in length one hundreth and seven footes and a half and from the water of Thames south and north in breadeth fortie and eight footes and a half. One other key in London aforesaid called Galley Kay next the Tower of London conteyninge est and west in length one hundreth and fyftene footes and from the water of Thames south and north in breadeth fiftie and one footes. One other kay in London aforesaid called Andrewe Morys Kay conteyninge est and west in length threscore footes and from the water of Thames north and south in breadeth fiftie and one footes and a half. One other Kay in London aforesaid called Ambrose Thurstanes Kay conteyninge est and west in length thirtie and twoo footes and from the water of Thames south and north in breadeth twoo and twenty footes. One other kay in London aforesaid called Raffs Kay conteyninge est and west in length fourescore footes and from the water of Thames north and south in breadeth xxxviij footes. One other kay in London aforesaid called Cocks Kay in the tenure of William Lothbury conteyninge est and west in leingth thre and fiftie footes and from the water of Thames south and north xxxiiij footes eight ynches. One other Kay in London aforesaid called Gybsons Kaye conteyninge est and west in length liij footes and from the water of Thames south and north in breadeth lx footes. One other kay in London aforesaid called Haddocks Kay conteyninge est and west in breadeth fiftie and fyve footes and in length from the Ryver of Thames vnto the strete beinge south and north clxxvij footes. One other kay in London aforesaid called Dyce Kaye conteyning in length from the water syde to the strete south and north clx footes and in breadeth est and west liiij footes. One other kay in London aforesaid called Beare Kay conteyninge est and west by the Thames syde in breadeth xxxij footes and in length from the Thames south and north lxij footes. One other kay in London aforesaid called Somers Kaye conteyninge est and west in length lxxiiij footes and from the water of Thames south and north xxx footes. One other kay or wharffe in London called Botolphe Wharffe conteyninge est and west in length lxxviij footes and from the water of Thames south and north fiftie and twoo footes. One other kay in London called Sabbys Kay conteyninge south and north in length lxxviij footes and est and west in breadeth xxxv footes. One other kay in London called Younges Kaye conteyninge north and south in length twoo hundreth and tenne footes and est and west in breadeth xlvj footes. One other kay in London called Crowne Kay conteyninge est and west in length fiftie and foure footes and from the water of Thames south and north xxxvij footes. One other kay in London aforesaid called Smartes Kaye adioyninge to Byllingesgate conteyninge est and west in breadeth xix footes and from the water of Thames south and north cx footes. And one other wharfe or kay called

Freshe Wharfe conteyninge north and south xxxj footes and est and west
xlij footes. And one other kay or wharfe called Gaunts Key liynge betwixt
the said kayes or wharfs called Cocks Kay and Freshe Wharff conteyninge
xxxvj footes euery wey fouer square to be open places for ladinge chardg-
inge or shippinge landinge dischardginge and vnladinge of all manner of
wares and merchaundizes both inwardes and outwardes within the porte
of London. Item we have appoyncted and lymyted by vertue of the
premisses one open place called Byllingesgate in London aforesaid
conteyninge one the west side from the water of Thames south and north
in length clx footes and at thend of the same est and west xl footes and more
est and west all the length of the same clx footes it conteyneth fouretene
footes in breadeth to be an open place appoyncted for the landinge or
bringinge in of any fyshe corne salt stones victualls and fruicts (grocery
wares except) and to be a place of carienge furth of the same or the like
and for noe other merchaundizes. Item we have further appoyncted
assigned and lymyted by vertue of the premysses one place in London
aforesaid commonly called the Three Cranes in the Vintre conteyninge
from Dunghill Lane on the est towards the west in length cclxj footes and
from the water of Thames south and north in breadeth lviij footes to be
an open place for the landinge or dischardginge of all maner of wynes and
oyles. And also we have appoincted the same Three Cranes one kay in
the tenure and occupacon of Thomas Johnson beinge in the parishe of
great Alhallowes in Temmestrete in London conteyninge fourtie footes
est and west that is to say from Cosyn lane one the west to the Styllyard
on the est and from the water of Thames northwarde twenty footes.
And one wharffe or kay called Busshers wharfe beinge above London
Bridge in the parish of St. Magnes conteyninge est and west in lengthe
lxxij footes that is to say from the Stockefysshemongers hall one the west
vnto Churcheyarde Alley on the east and south and north in breadeth
xlviij footes to be open places for the landinge or dischardginge and
layenge on lande of any the goodes hereafter ensuynge that is to say
pytche tarre flaxe iron waynescotts clapbordes deles ores rasters ashes
to make sope osmonds eles cabells halsers hemp stones chests playenge
tables and all manner of fyshe and hoppes and to be open places for the
shippinge and ladinge of any wollen clothes of the price of sixe poundes
or vnder the cloth and conyskynnes and for no other merchaundizes.
Item we have further appoincted assigned and lymyted bv vertue of the
premisses that the Bridgehouse in Southwarke shalbe an open place for
the landinge dischardginge or layenge on lande of any kinde of corne
bought and provided or to be bought and provided for the provision of the
victuallinge of the citie of London and for no other merchaundizes.
Item we have further ordred and appoincted by vertue of the premisses
that all sea coles otherwise called Newe Castell coles prouided or to be
provided to be caried to the parties of beyonde the seas shall and may be
shipped in any place within the porte of London. So that the same coles
from tyme to tyme be shipped and laden in the presence of the searcher
to and for the quenes highnes her heires and successors within the said
porte of London or in the presence of one of his servaunts sworn to serve
in that office. Item we have appoynted assigned and lymyted that all

manner of beare shipped and to be shipped over the seas by way of merchaundize from any parte of the porte of London shalbe firste entred in the quenes majesties custome bookes in the Custome House within the said porte and then to be shipped or put in any vessell or vessells at any staires or wharffs within the Citie of London Southwarke or St. Katherins in the day tyme in the presence of the quenes majesties searcher of and within the said porte for the tyme beinge or one of his servaunt or servaunts sworne to serve in the said office and that done to be caried over the seas at the pleasure of the owner thereof. Item we have appoynted essigned and lymyted by these presents that all manner of deales bordes clapbordes wainscotts sparres rasters owers corn roddes to make basketts heath to make brushes bricks and salte which shalbe brought vnto any parte of the porte of London shall and may be dischardged and layed on lande in the day tyme at any place within the saide porte of London in the presence of one of the wayters sworne belonginge to the quene Custom Howse of and for the saide porte for the tyme beinge anythinge before remembred to the contrary notwithstandinge. And we have further appoynted assigned and lymyted by vertue of the premysses that the stayers and wharfe or kaye at the house in the Citie of London called the Styllard otherwise Guihalda Theutonicorum shalbe an open place for landinge or shippinge layenge on lande and dischardginge of all manner of wares and merchaundizes apperteyninge and belonginge to any merchaunts of the hanse havinge the said house called the Styllard and free of the same. And that the said merchaunts nor any of them nor any other person or persons for them shall not shippe or put to the water from the said stayers wharfe or kaye any merchaundizes but in the presence of the searcher for the quenes majestie her heires and successors within the porte aforesaid or one of his servaunts nor shall not take vp or discharge or lay on lande any merchaundizes at the same stayers wharfe or kaye but only in the presence of one of the wayters to the said Custome House appeteyninge or belonginge and not to be vsed as a place for the ladinge or dischardginge of any merchaundizes apperteyninge to any other person or persons but only suche as be free of the said house. This order for the Stilliard to endure duringe the pleasure of the quenes majestie her heires and successors and no longer. Item for the better aunsweringe of the revenues of the quenes majesties customs and subsydyes in the porte aforesaid the said commyssyoners have ordred and further appoynted that from and after the feast of Easter next comynge there shall no straunger nor straungers borne whether be or they be or shalbe made denyzen or not aswell inhabyte or be comorante in at or vpon any of the said wharffes or kayes or any parte of theym (the Stillyarde excepte). And that euery tenaunte or keper of euery of the said kayes wharfes and stayers shall from tyme to tyme be bounden in suche some or somes of money to the quenes highnes vse her heires and successors as by the lorde treasourer of England or other officers of the quenes majesties courte of theschequor for the tyme beinge shalbe thought good and convenient vpon condicon that there shalbe no goodes whereof custome or subsidy is or shalbe due layd on lande at their kayes wharfes or stayers or shipped or put from thence vpon the water to be caried ouer the seas by way of merchaundize before the said goodes be entred in the quenes custome bookes in the said porte. And also to be laden in the presence of the said searcher or one of his servaunts for the tyme beinge and dischardged and laide on lande in the presence of one of the said wayters for the tyme beinge. And other articles to be put in the said condicon as to the said treasurer and officers hereafter from tyme to tyme shall seeme good mete and convenient as the case shall require. And that all creeks wharfes kayes ladinge and dischardginge places in Gravesend Wolwyche Barkinge Grenewych Depford Blackewall Lymehouse Ratclyff Wappinge Saynt Katheryns Tower Hill Redderethe Southwerke London Bridge and euery of them. And all and singuler kayes wharfes and other places within the Citie of London and the suburbes of the same citie or ells where within the said porte of London (the seuerall kayes wharfes stayers and places before lymyted and appoynted only except) shalbe from hensfourth no more vsed as ladinge or dischardginge places for merchaundizes but be vtterly debarred and abolyshed from the same for ever by force of the said statute and other the premysses. In wytnes whereof we the commyssioners aforesaid to thies presents have put to our seales the xxviij[th] day of August in the yere aforesaid.

2. THE LEGAL QUAYS. E. 178/7075.
Note: the following document was drawn up in 1584 when the extent of the 'legal' port of London was re-examined.[1]

Porte of London	The names of all the kays and wharffs in the Porte of London vsed for landinge of wares and merchandizes before the makinge of the statute in anno primo that doth appoynt landinge and ladinge places together with a declaracon with what kyndes of wares they were most occupyed before that tyme begynnynge att the kaye next the Tower and namyng them in order as they lye towards the Three Cranes in the Vyntrew.
Gallye Kaye	was greatly occupied with all kynde of merchandizes bothe inward and outward.
Olde Wollkaye	was used only for shippinge of wolle and felts and when the Staplers had ended there shippinge then cost men occupyed it for woode and other cost wares.
Custom Howse Kaye	well occupied with all kyndes of merchandizes both inward and outwarde.
Greenberys Kaye	well occupied with wares inward and outward for Fraunce and with cost mens goodes.
Crowne Kaye	occupied but with cost men.
Beare Kaye	with Portingall commodities by reason the merchants of that contree did lye and had ther ware howses there and with some cost men.
Thrustans Kaye	well occupied with all kynde of merchaundizes inward and outward.
Sabbes Kaye	with pitche tar and sope ashes and such like.

1. See above p. x.

Gibsons Kaye	with lead and tynne and other cost wares.
Yongs Kaye	with wares belonginge to merchants of Portingale by reason they did lye there and was vsed for shippinge of straungers of clothes.
Raffs Kaye	with all kynde of merchandizes inward and outwarde.
Dyse Kaye	altogether with cost wares.
Old Thrustons Kaye	with goodes of certan Flemyngs lyeinge there and with cost wares.
Smarts Kaye	altogether with fyshe.
Sommers Kaye	wholly inhabited with Flemyngs and vsed for there merchandizes.
Buttolphe Wharff	with straungers goodes that ley and had ware howses there and with wynes and by cost men.
Cocks Kaye	Altogether for straungers goodes who had merchandizes and lodgings.
Gaunts Kaye	for landinge of barrell fyshe and suche like havinge no crane.
Freshe Wharff	for fyshe and eele shippers.
The Stillyard	for all theire owne merchandizes only.
Three Cranes	for wynes and waynscotts onely.

3. NOTES ON THE LEGAL QUAYS.

The quays are listed in the order as they lay west of Tower Dock.

GALLEY QUAY. Owned by the Marowe family from the fifteenth century at least until 1538,[1] it was acquired by alderman Sir Ralph Warren and on his death in 1553 by his son Richard, who was leasing it out in 1582 for £80 a year. It then had a crane and a jibbet.[2] The quay did not extend right up to Tower Dock: there were several quays to the west which may have been too small to be authorised as legal quays in 1559. Later, however, they were merged into Brewers and Chesters Quays, which were authorised lading and landing places when the port was surveyed in 1667 after the Great Fire.[3]

OLD WOOL QUAY. One of the oldest quays in London (dating back at least to the thirteenth century) it took its name from the wool-fleets which used to land there. The crown bought it in 1556 for £400 from the coopers' company which had acquired it four years earlier from a member, John Charley, who was trustee of the estate of Nicholas Gibson, the owner on his death in 1540.[4] The crown's tenant in 1582 was John Porter who paid £22 a year rental.

CUSTOM HOUSE QUAY. Also called New Wool Quay, it was purchased by the crown in 1558 from the heir of Phillip Linne of Bassingbourn for

1. L[ondon] C[ounty] C[ouncil] *Survey of London*, xv (1934), 44–9.
2. Lans. 35, ff. 127–8: a document of 1582 headed 'The names of all such keys as be appoynted by statue for ladeinge and unlading of goods'. It provides valuable information about ownership etc. at that time. Unless otherwise stated these notes on the quays are based on this manuscript.
3. The survey is printed by Strype in his edition of Stow's *Survey*, bk. v (1720), 281–4.
4. L.C.C. *Survey*, xv, 35.

£600.[1] The rental in 1582 was £40 a year. The quay then had two jibbets. Subsequently it returned to private ownership, as did the Old Wool Quay.[2]

GREENBERRIES QUAY. Known also as the Andrew Morrice Quay, it was acquired by the fishmongers' company in 1518 as part of the bequest of Sir Thomas Kneseworth's estate. It was then named after the owner but had been given the name Greenberries, presumably from a tenant, by 1550.[3] The lessee in 1582 was John Porter, who was also tenant of the fishmongers' adjacent Crown Quay. By 1666 the two quays had been merged into one, named after Porter: as such it was known until the company disposed of the property to the crown in the eighteenth century.[4] In Porter's time the rent was £24; the quay then had 'a good crane'.

CROWN QUAY. Also acquired by the fishmongers, with Greenberries Quay, in 1518; and also leased to John Porter in 1582. Porter sub-let for £40 a year. The quay, used only for coastal traffic in corn and wood in 1559, had acquired a jibbet by 1582 and was used 'for merchaundize'.

BEAR QUAY. The property of the heirs of Sir William Roche (d. 1549), it had a jibbet in 1582 but was considered 'very unfitt for merchaundize'. The deputy searcher had his office on this quay.

THRUSTANS QUAY. Or Ambrose Thurstons Quay, it was owned in 1582 by William Page who leased it for £50 a year. It had one jibbet. By the time of the Great Fire it had apparently lost its separate identity.[5]

SABBES QUAY. The property of Widow Bulley in 1582 with a rental of £50. It had a jibbet but was described as being 'very vnfitt to be vsed for marchaundize'.

GIBSONS QUAY. Formerly called Asselynes Wharf after John Asselyne, who owned it in 1366, it was purchased by Sir Christopher Draper a few years before the survey of 1559.[6] The quay, with one jibbet, was let in 1582 for £50 a year to William Wiggens. It was subsequently known by his name.

YONGS QUAY. Worth £52 a year in rent, the quay was owned in 1582 by Richard Warren, heir of Sir Ralph Warren (d. 1553). It had a jibbet.

RAFFS QUAY. The property in 1582 of a Mr. Hearsdon who received £100 a year in rent. The quay had a crane and jibbet.

DYSE QUAY. Owned by James Bacon who inherited from his father, alderman James Bacon, in 1573. The alderman had bought it for £900 from Robert Brittein, who presumably acquired the property from William Breton, the owner in 1559.[7] The quay, described in 1582 as being

1. The Lansdowne document states that Linne himself had sold the quay; but it was still in his possession when he died the previous year. PCC 22 Wrastley.
2. Sir Anthony Cope owned both at the time of the Great Fire. T. F. Reddaway, 'The London Custom House, 1666–1740', *London Topographical Record*, xxi (1958), 4–5.
3. *I.p.m. London*, iii, 319–23; *Calendar of Patent Rolls 1549–51*, 392.
4. W. Herbert, *History of the worshipful Company of fishmongers* (1837), 102–3.
5. It is not mentioned in the 1667 survey; nor does John Leake include it in his map or *Exact Surveigh* of 1666. Probably it had been merged into Bear Quay which then had a frontage of 62 ft. 4 ins. In 1559 Bear and Thrustons Quays were each 32 ft. long.
6. *Calendar of plea and memoranda rolls 1458–82*, ed. P. E. Jones (1961), 45; C. L. Kingsford, 'A London merchant's house and its owners, 1360–1641', *Archaeologia*, 74 (1923–4), 144.
7. PCC 28 Peter; *I.p.m. London*, ii, 70–1.

'open without protection', was used almost entirely by coasters. The tenant was alderman William Webb.

OLD THRUSTONS QUAY. Also called Haddocks Quay, it was owned in 1582 by alderman Webb who leased out part of the property with Dyse Quay for £40.

SMARTS QUAY. This quay ran along the east side of Billingsgate. When surveyed in 1559 it was in private hands,[1] but by 1582 it had apparently become the property of the city chamber. It was then described as being 'very vnfitt for merchandize'.

BILLINGSGATE. A 'common key or place'[2] Billingsgate was described by Stow as 'a large Watergate, Port or Harbrough for shippes and boats, commonly arriuing there with fish, . . . Orenges, Onions and other fruits and rootes, wheat, Rie and grain of diuers sortes . . .'.[3] The landing places for these cargoes were on the west-side and at the head of the harbour.[4]

SOMMERS QUAY. Adjoining Billingsgate on the west-side, it was also owned in 1582 by the city chamber. It had a jibbet.

BUTTOLPHE WHARF. Owned by the city chamber and leased to the Russia company.[5] It had a crane.

COCKS QUAY. The owner in 1573 was Sir Anthony Cooke of Gidea Hall, Essex, who leased it to Lawrence Cockson, haberdasher. The rental in 1582 was £70 a year. The quay then had a jibbet. The Cookes subsequently sold the property to Robert and Edward Thurston.[6]

GAUNTS QUAY. About the time of the 1559 survey Gaunts Quay was owned by John Cheyne of Amersham, Buckinghamshire. In 1562 Vincent Ancotts, a fishmonger of London, acquired the quay from Cheyne as part of a property exchange.[7] The quay was small and ill-equipped.

FRESH WHARF. The last of the legal quays east of London Bridge In 1582 Sir Roger Manwood was owner; his will in 1597 also mentions the wharf.[8] The rental was £100. The wharf had a jibbet.

BUSSHERS WHARF. This wharf or quay was probably one of two wharves which were part of a property owned in 1559 by Thomas Carter. His tenant was a Christopher Bussher.[9] There are no further references to the wharf, but Stow does mention two which were in the same area— Drinkwater and Fish wharves.[10]

1. *Calendar of wills in the husting*, ed. R. R. Sharpe (1890), 673–4. The owner in 1559 was Thomas Nicholson who bequeathed it, after a life interest to his wife, to the cordwainers' company. Since the company owned it at the time of the Great Fire, it may be that the 1582 account is confusing the city chamber with the cordwainers. *Fire Court*, ed. P. E. Jones, i (1966), 193.
2. So described in the 1667 survey.
3. Stow, *Survey*, i, 206.
4. Leake's *Exact Surveigh* names this west-side 'Billingsgate Key'.
5. By 1573. T. S. Willan, *Early history of the Russia Company* (Manchester, 1956), 29, 135.
6. Guildhall MSS. 14007, 14008.
7. *ibid.* 14006.
8. William Boys, *Collections for an history of Sandwich*, i (Canterbury, 1792), 260.
9. *I.p.m. London*, i, 174–6; ii, 20.
10. Stow, *Survey*, i, 215.

THE STEELYARD. Containing the Hansards' Guildhall and wharf. An Elizabethan plan of the Steelyard shows stairs and a crane.[1]

THOMAS JOHNSONS QUAY. Like Busshers Wharf there is no mention of Johnsons Quay after 1559. It must have been virtually an extension of the Steelyard.

THREE CRANES WHARF. The largest lading and landing place in the port. Its exact location is obscure since Dunghill lane, its eastern boundary according to the 1559 survey, is difficult to identify. A Dunghill wharf or stairs lay near to Anchor lane,[2] but this could not be the lane of the survey unless it is assumed that the surveyors had confused east for west. Otherwise the land must have been east of Three Cranes lane, which is shown on contemporary maps (*e.g.* the 'Agas' map and Wyngaerde's 'view') as separating one of the cranes from the other two.

BRIDGEHOUSE, Southwark. The only authorised landing place on the south bank, the Bridgehouse stood close to St. Olave's Church on the Thamesside. In Tudor times it had important connexions with the grain trade, providing granaries for storage, ovens for baking as well as landing places.[3]

1. S.P. 46/36 no. 21.
2. H. A. Harben, *Dictionary of London* (1918), 178, 207.
3. D. J. Johnson, *Southwark and the City* (1969), 125.

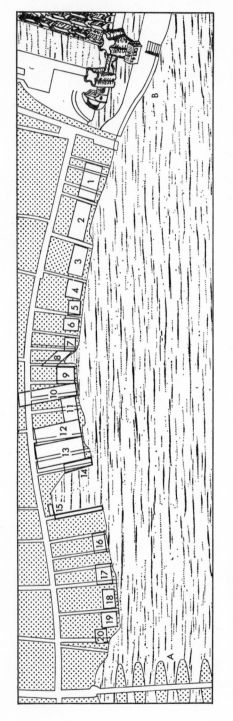

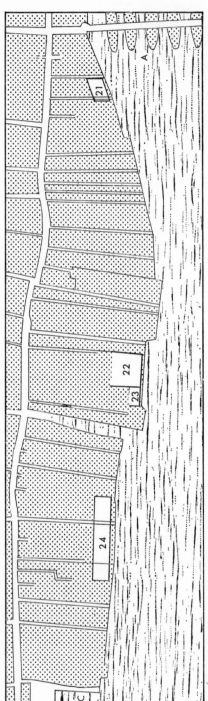

PLAN OF THE ELIZABETHAN PORT OF LONDON

The map facing this page shows the approximate location and size of the legal quays on the north bank of the Thames as they were surveyed and established at the beginning of Elizabeth's reign. The scale and outline of the river front are taken from Wenceslaus Hollar's engraving of John Leake's *Exact Surveigh* of 1666 (1667). Evidence for the location and size of the quays will be found in Appendix IV. The survey and limitation of the port are discussed in the Introduction.

Scale: One inch to 300 feet

Key:

A	London Bridge	12	Dyse Quay
B	Tower Dock	13	Old Thrustons Quay
C	Queenhithe	14	Smarts Quay
1	Galley Quay	15	Billingsgate Quays
2	Old Wool Quay	16	Sommers Quay
3	Custom House Quay	17	Buttolphe Wharf
4	Greenberries Quay	18	Cocks Quay
5	Crown Quay	19	Gaunts Quay
6	Bear Quay	20	Fresh Wharf
7	Thrustans Quay	21	Busshers Wharf
8	Sabbes Quay	22	The Steelyard
9	Gibsons Quay	23	Thomas Johnsons Quay
10	Yongs Quay	24	Three Cranes Wharf
11	Raffs Quay		

INDEX

References are to serial numbers unless otherwise indicated. Entries have been grouped under the following heads:

For further explanation, see Notes on Editorial Method (p. xxiii).

MASTERS

Aborro, Stephen (London), 39
Adrian, Giles (Flushing), 209
Adrianson, 750
  Cornilis (Bergen-op-Zoom), 189, 445, 568, 731
  Cornilis (Haarlem), 317
  William (Amsterdam), 528
Alardson, Allertson,
  Alard (Amsterdam), 32, 105, 302, 483, 549
  D., 673
  Simon (Amsterdam), 27, 90, 391, 513, 652
Alben, Cornilis (Bruges), 628
Albright, 308
  Cornilis (Bruges), 163, 393, 626, 763
  Govert (Bergen-op-Zoom), 547
  Jacob (Bruges), 491, 606, 717, 812
  Lucas (Bruges), 548
Alden, John (Harwich), 645
Alverman,
  Henrik (Hamburg), 232, 501, 615
  Peter (Hamburg), 186, 500
Anderson, Stephen (Dover), 148, 614, 810
Andros, Thomas (Lee), 62, 416, 556
Angle, Eyngell,
  Christian (Dordrecht), 675
  Corst (Dordrecht), 442
  Gillam *or* William (Dieppe), 687, 813
Antewurs, Gomer (Flushing), 608
Antonison, Anthony (Flushing), 55, 406, 509
Apleton, Richard (Ipswich), 282 *bis*
Auger, John (Saucats), 642
Awdley, Thomas (London), 805

Backhouse, John (Ipswich), 354
Baker, Thomas (Aldeburgh), 79
Balle, Lorance (Amsterdam), 24
Bame, Leonard (Flushing), 384
Barber, Mark (Newcastle), 454
Bardmaker, Bardman, *see* Bare
Bare,
  John de, *also* Bardmaker, Bardman (Antwerp), 464, 794
  Otto (Hamburg), 185

Barret, Thomas (Lee), 120, 424
Bart, Garet (Amsterdam), 160
Bassyn, John (St. Malo), 464
Bastianson, Cornilis (Flushing), 366, 797
Bauwins, Bowin, Francis (Bruges), 47, 237, 349, 444
Bayed, John ('Marvers'), 86
Bayly, Baylyf, Walter (Newcastle), 271, 557
Beam, John (York), 605
Bebell, Bepell, Richard (London), 77, 331
Becker, Christian (Hamburg), 3
Benet,
  Elles (Dartmouth), 257
  John (London), 204, 551
Bepell, *see* Bebell
Beversham,
  Robert (Aldeburgh), 537 *bis*
  Thomas (Aldeburgh), 9 *bis*, 224 *ter*, 534
Body, Michel (Cherbourg), 80
Bolton, Thomas (London), 830
Bondman, Harman (Hamburg), 21, 381, 734
Boner, Bonner,
  John (Lee), 18, 365, 808
  John (London), 143
  John, the younger (Lee), 63, 388
Bothe, Jacob (Amsterdam), 373
Bowart, Hans (Hamburg), 28
Bowenson, Garret (Dordrecht), 746
Bowin, *see* Bauwins
Boyse, Thomas (Lee), 539
Bred, Joachim (Königsberg), 559 *bis*
Brendjam, John (Saltash), 328
Broune,
  Matthew (Antwerp), 307
  Richard (Brightlingsea), 123
Brounge, Brownyng, Matthew *or* Mattis (Antwerp), 320, 502, 828
Browmantyne, Richard (Dieppe), 623
Brownyng, *see* Brounge
Bullart, Nicholas (St. Omer), 223
Burrell, Burwell,
  John (London), 112, 659
  Robert (London), 81, 443

171

MERCHANTS

James, grocer, 248
John, native, 332
Richard, 354, 576; mercer, 38, 62, 95, 155, 234, 285, 334, 357, 360, 383, 435, 463, 466, 530, 531, 539, 540, 639, 677; merchant taylor, 210, 259, 296, 367, 462, 465, 522, 530, 539, 540, 574
Hillson, Robert, 557, 567; mercer, 28, 69, 510, 563, 586, 587, 600, 616, 617, 632, 648, 722, 728
Hinchinson, John, native, 277
Hobbs, William, 462, 547, 643, 647; draper, 10, 45, 154, 156, 189, 210, 212, 259, 260, 262, 339, 365, 378, 389, 433, 435, 522, 523, 568, 574, 576, 624, 702, 703, 710, 729, 730, 738, 781, 787, 795, 804, 808
Hobson, William, 650; haberdasher, 395, 456, 457, 514, 516, 535, 556, 653, 678, 686, 750, 759, 767
Hodchet, Richard, mayor of Newcastle, 4
Hodson, Christopher, haberdasher, 558
Holand, John, salter, 271
Holanside, John, 281; fishmonger, 242
Holiday, Leonard, merchant taylor, 154, 340
Holingworth,
Leonard, draper, 591
Reynold, 245, 354, 681; draper, 95, 198, 245, 679, 689
Hollyman, Richard, mercer, 191, 296, 298, 808
Holmes, James, native, 598
Holt, Dirick van, Hanse, 434
Honnyngborne, Peter, armourer, 702, 704, 729, 730
Hooker, Thomas, fishmonger, 229
Hope, Matthew, 595; Hanse, 3, 21, 184, 185, 232, 434, 500, 501, 567, 734
Hopkins, Richard, 591; fishmonger, 354
Hopworth, John, native, 677
House, Thomas, 763; embroiderer, 299, 349, 393, 405, 444, 474, 491, 504, 607, 674; leatherseller, 548; draper, 760, 767; native, 628
How, Robert, salter, 95, 137, 245, 354, 443, 592, 679; grocer, 591
Howle, Richard, salter, 297
Howlet, Richard, grocer, 15, 19
Hoy, Edward, fishmonger, 278
Hugin, Huggan, Edmund, 647; mercer, 18, 244, 273, 522, 523, 592, 684, 685, 781, 787
Hungat,
Henry, mercer, 45, 191, 212, 229, 260, 367, 435, 685
Robert, 341; mercer, 298, 335, 339, 462, 722
Hunwick, John, of Colchester, 108
Hutton, John, haberdasher, 465, 540, 827

Isham, John, 462; mercer, 18, 45, 46, 339, 340, 341, 367, 388, 433, 435, 463, 465, 466, 522, 523, 539, 540, 574, 630, 643, 647, 808; native, 191
Ireland, John, salter, 664
Ivie, Thomas, native, 512

Jackman,
Edward, 330, 456, 457, 458, 462, 465, 540; alderman, 14, 18, 19, 45, 46, 78, 154, 244, 245, 291, 352, 354, 365, 415, 475, 558, 574, 591, 594, 659, 684, 790; grocer, 155, 539, 689, 806
John, 14, 15, 461, 467, 469, 470, 471, 625, 792, 794, 795; grocer, 19, 45, 154, 339, 359, 368, 465, 473, 476, 492, 530, 539, 540, 607, 702, 703, 704, 710, 730, 781, 790, 791, 794, 803, 811; salter, 18
Jackson, John, grocer, 78
James,
Roger, brewer, 235
William, 69; joiner, 13, 28, 145, 563, 567, 583, 616, 648, 699, 728, 741, 754, 772, 774; armourer, 586, 587; native, 632
Jaques, Robert, merchant taylor, 769
Jenens,
George, 374; fishmonger, 35, 109, 149, 240, 342, 343, 344, 364, 366
Thomas, fishmonger, 206, 343, 344, 582, 597, 602, 612, 654, 655, 666, 711, 712, 713, 723, 732, 782, 788, 798
William, 600; joiner, 617
Jenyngs, John, clothworker, 750
Jerard, Remand, of Bordeaux, 65
Jerrard, André, of Oléron, 59
Jervaies, Arthur, 249, 252, 253, 265
Jewkes, Christopher, 488; mercer, 182, 187, 191, 212, 213, 229, 234, 258, 260, 262, 298, 310 *bis*, 335, 367, 378, 540, 781, 787
John, Baptist de, of Venice, 53, 757
Johnson,
Anthony, clothworker, 176
John, haberdasher, 45; native, 667, 668
Martin, native, 313
Jones, Joanes, Phillip, 158; grocer, 463, 794
Joris, Randolph, native, 328
Jugart, John, pilot, 785

Keel, Keil, Kele,
Henry, 239
Humphrey, 545, 562, 566, 658, 670, 820, 821; fishmonger, 54, 209, 217, 219, 267, 709, 725, 735, 736; native, 217, 218, 231, 720
Keeling, William, clothworker, 244
Keightley, Kightley,
Francis, leatherseller, 45, 46, 462, 522, 540, 574, 795

Temple, Robert, draper, 428
Tench, William, draper, 45, 191, 523
Thirling, Reynold, 297, 312; Hanse, 33, 147, 212, 324, 327, 368, 531 *bis*, 649, 733
Thomas,
John, merchant taylor, 272; mercer, 368; draper, 584
William, mercer, 679, 683; native, 785
Thompson, John, of Newcastle, 265
Thorp, Thomas, 18; grocer, 15, 45, 462, 464, 475, 523, 574, 576, 634, 703, 704, 710, 729, 762, 787
Throgmorton, Anthony, mercer, 282
Thwates, William, fishmonger, 37, 771
Tooke, Francis, mercer, 361, 389, 569, 710, 729
Tornull, Paul, Hanse, 21
Towerson, Thowerson,
Thomas, skinner, 212
William, skinner, 18, 155, 156, 296, 298, 335, 340, 365, 367, 388, 389, 433, 435, 462, 463, 466, 522, 539, 574, 576, 647, 703, 710, 729, 730, 771, 795, 808
Toy, Humphrey, stationer, 359, 528, 541
Trapham, Robert, merchant taylor, 703, 729
Travers, John, merchant taylor, 465
Tuck, Francis, mercer, 702, 703
Turnbull, Thomas, 515; fishmonger, 88, 245, 250, 352, 354, 443, 681; mercer, 679
Turvil, Robert, 540; mercer, 18, 155, 296
Twerdico, Stephen, of Russia, 39, 40
Tymbreman, Maurice, Hanse, 28
Tyrill, Lewis, of Dieppe, 581

Vaghen, William, 552; draper, 36, 282, 683
Valutella, Acerbo, of Lucca, 578
Valyam, John, of Middleburg, 651
Vanart, Charles, of St. Malo, 355
Van de Lam, Jasper, 713n
Varry, John, denizen, 623, 676, 764, 813
Vazey, Francis, 576
Vegelman, Peter, of Bruges, 669, 802
Venables, Richard, merchant taylor, 95, 246, 684
Vezie, Randolph, grocer, 389
Violet,
Henry, fishmonger, 343, 345, 350
John, 394, 656; fishmonger, 23, 27, 57, 90, 103, 151, 159, 160, 199, 397, 549, 560, 575, 612, 655, 666, 708, 711, 712, 713, 724, 770, 782, 788, 798, 824, 829
Richard, fishmonger, 182, 188
Vittell, Christopher, leatherseller, 792

Waight, Waite, Wayt,
Francis, 522
Henry *or* Harry, 620, 764; grocer, 38, 64,

108 *bis*, 418, 422, 516, 535, 555, 556, 614, 619, 635, 678, 717, 756, 767, 827
Wale, William, grocer, 790, 803, 811
Walkeden,
Geoffrey, 234; skinner, 576, 710, 795
Godfrey, skinner, 389, 433
Robert, 339, 365; skinner, 703, 730
Walker, Thomas, 272, 358, 360, 392; leatherseller, 191, 246, 296, 337, 534
Wall, Peter van der, alien, 398, 696
Wallis, Henry, fishmonger, 88, 352
Walton,
Dunstan, mercer, 36, 69, 510, 563, 567, 583, 586, 646, 716, 728, 743, 754; native, 616
Henry, clothworker, 352
Wanton, John, 154, 647; grocer, 2, 45, 46, 62, 210, 236, 265, 339, 380, 384, 389, 414, 465, 514, 643, 702, 703
Ward, James, native, 507
Warfilde, Warfyld,
Anthony, 18, 191, 234, 402; grocer, 154, 155, 212, 229, 259, 260, 262, 296, 297, 298, 335, 340, 365, 388, 462, 463, 464, 465, 466, 469, 470, 540, 729, 787, 795
Roger, 18 *bis*, 539, 540; grocer, 18, 45 *bis*, 154, 155, 212, 258, 262, 294, 296, 298, 339, 340, 341, 365, 367, 388, 389, 433, 462, 465, 466, 522, 523, 574, 607, 643, 669, 703, 710, 722, 730 *bis*, 781, 787, 790, 792, 795, 807, 808
Warner, Nicholas, skinner, 2, 435, 729
Warren, Francis, 154, 191, 296; merchant taylor, 212, 465, 522, 523; mercer, 389; native, 294, 367
Watkins, Phillip, merchant taylor, 433, 463, 466, 781, 787
Watson, John, 684, 743; goldsmith, 254, 257, 282, 330, 679; mercer, 728; merchant, 354, 357, 384
Watts, William, 197; native, 145
Weightman, Henry, 489, of Hamburg, 818
Wellfcrast, Thomas, native, 520
Wells, John, haberdasher, 339, 340, 341
Wethers, Withers, Wythers, Lawrence, 522, 523; salter, 45, 156, 189, 574, 729, 787, 796, 806
White,
John, draper, 62, 64, 305, 336, 402, 409, 461, 572, 653; haberdasher, 212, 340, 341, 365, 523
Sir John, alderman, 49, 689
Steven, haberdasher, 234, 260, 463
Whitelock, Whitlok,
Humphrey, merchant taylor, 45, 367, 574
Richard, 122; cooper, 75, 135, 289, 419
Wight, Francis, grocer, 17, 246, 308, 606
Wignall, *see* Wydnall
Wilford,
Christopher, merchant taylor, 84

SHIPS

LONDON RECORD SOCIETY

The London Record Society was founded in December 1964 to publish transcripts, abstracts and lists of the primary sources for the history of London, and generally to stimulate interest in archives relating to London. Membership is open to any individual or institution, the annual subscription is £3·15, which entitles a member to receive one copy of each volume published during the year and to attend and vote at meetings of the Society. Prospective members should apply to the Hon. Secretary, Mr Brian Burch, c/o Leicester University Library, University Road, Leicester.

The following volumes have already been published:

1. *London possessory assizes: a calendar*, edited by Helena M. Chew (1965)
2. *London inhabitants within the Walls, 1695*, with an introduction by D. V. Glass (1966)
3. *London Consistory Court wills, 1492–1547*, edited by Ida Darlington (1967)
4. *Scriveners' Company Common Paper, 1357–1628, with a continuation to 1678*, edited by Francis W. Steer (1968)
5. *London Radicalism, 1830–1843: a selection from the papers of Francis Place*, edited by D. J. Rowe (1970)
6. *The London Eyre of 1244*, edited by Helena M. Chew and Martin Weinbaum (1970)
7. *The Cartulary of Holy Trinity Aldgate*, edited by Gerald A. J. Hodgett (1971)

Price: to members £3·15 each, and to non-members £4·50 each.

The following Occasional Publication is also available:
London and Middlesex Published Records, compiled by J. M. Sims (1970)
Price: free to members, and to non-members £1.

A leaflet describing some of the volumes in preparation may be obtained from the Hon. Secretary.